Latino Politics in America

THE SPECTRUM SERIES

Race and Ethnicity in National and Global Politics

Series Editors: Paula D. McClain and Joseph Stewart Jr.

The sociopolitical dynamics of race and ethnicity are apparent everywhere. In the United States, racial politics underlie everything from representation to affirmative action to welfare policymaking. Early in the twenty-first century, Anglos in America will become only a plurality, as Latino and Asian American populations continue to grow. Issues of racial/ethnic conflict and cooperation are prominent across the globe. Diversity, identity, and cultural plurality are watchwords of empowerment as well as of injustice.

This series offers textbook supplements, readers, and core texts addressing various aspects of race and ethnicity in politics, broadly defined. Meant to be useful in a wide range of courses in all kinds of academic programs, these books will be multidisciplinary as well as multiracial/ethnic in their appeal.

Titles in the Series

American Indian Politics and the American Political System, Third Edition, by David E. Wilkins and Heidi Kiiwetinepinesiik Stark

Asian American Politics: Law, Participation, and Policy, edited by Don T. Nakanishi and James L. Lai

Media & Minorities, by Stephanie Greco Larson

Muted Voices: Latinos and the 2000 Elections, edited by Rodolfo O. de la Garza and Louis DeSipio. Introduction by Robert Y. Shapiro

The Navajo Political Experience, by David E. Wilkins

LATINO POLITICS IN AMERICA

Community, Culture, and Interests

SECOND EDITION

John A. García

ROWMAN & LITTLEFIELD PUBLISHERS, INC.
Lanham • Boulder • New York • Toronto • Plymouth, UK

Published by Rowman & Littlefield Publishers, Inc.
A wholly owned subsidary of The Rowman & Littlefield Publishing Group, Inc.
4501 Forbes Boulevard, Suite 200, Lanham, Maryland 20706
http://www.rowmanlittlefield.com

Estover Road, Plymouth PL6 7PY, United Kingdom

British Library Cataloguing in Publication Information Available

Library of Congress Cataloging-in-Publication Data

García, John A.
    Latino politics in America : community, culture, and interests / John A. García. — 2nd ed.
        p.   cm. — (The spectrum series : race and ethnicity in national and global politics)
    Includes bibliographical references and index.
    ISBN 978-1-4422-0772-1 (cloth : alk. paper) — ISBN 978-1-4422-0773-8 (pbk. : alk. paper) —
ISBN 978-1-4422-0774-5 (electronic)
    1. Hispanic Americans—Politics and government. 2. Political participation—United States.
3. Hispanic Americans—Social conditions. 4. Hispanic Americans—Ethnic identity.
5. Community life—United States. I. Title.
    E184.S75G367 2012
    305.868'72073—dc23
                                                                                    2011023136

∞™ The paper used in this publication meets the minimum requirements of American National
Standard for Information Sciences—Permanence of Paper for Printed Library Materials, ANSI/
NISO Z39.48-1992.

Printed in the United States of America

Contents

List of Figures, Tables, and Boxes   vii

Acknowledgments   xi

Acronyms   xiii

1   AN INTRODUCTION TO LATINO POLITICS   1

2   COMMUNITY BUILDING IN LATINO AMERICA   13

3   CULTURE AND DEMOGRAPHICS   25

4   LATINO SUBGROUPS IN THE UNITED STATES   45

5   THE POLITICS OF INTEREST AND CULTURE   63

6   LATINO POLITICAL PARTICIPATION   77

7   LATINOS IN THE ELECTORAL ARENA   97

8   LATINO ORGANIZATIONS AND LEADERSHIP   123

9   IMMIGRATION AND LATINO IMMIGRANTS   141

10   EDUCATION AND VOTING RIGHTS   163

11   BUILDING POLITICAL ALLIANCES   183

12   THE LATINO COMMUNITY: BEYOND RECOGNITION POLITICS   209

Notes   225

Glossary   233

References   239

Index   257

Figures, Tables, and Boxes

Figures

3.1 Population size of Latinos, 2000 to 2006   26

3.2 Historical view of Hispanic population in the United States, 1970 to 2050   27

3.3 Examination of Hispanic population growth as percentage of total U.S. population, 1970 to 2050   28

3.4 Percentage Hispanic and their contributions to annual components of change, 2000 to 2006   28

3.5 Percentage change in population by region for Latinos, 2000 to 2006   29

3.6 Distribution of U.S. population by nativity status and Hispanic and total population, 2006   35

3.7 Levels of educational attainment for the total population and Hispanics by gender, 2006   37

3.8 Median age among Hispanics by gender, 2006   38

3.9 Occupational distribution among employed Hispanic males, 2006   39

3.10 Occupational distribution among employed Hispanic females, 2006   39

3.11 Median earnings among Hispanics and the total population by gender, 2006   41

Tables

3.1 Number, Percentage, and Percentage Distribution of U.S. Population by Nativity and Race/Ethnicity with Hispanic Subgroups, 2007   30

3.2 Population Five Years and Older Who Spoke a Language Other Than English at Home by Language Group and English-Speaking Ability, 2007   32

3.3 Hispanic Population by Nativity and Type, 2007   36

6.1   Reported Civic Participation among Latinos in the National Survey
       of Latinos, 2004   81

6.2   Reported Volunteer Activity among Latinos in the National Survey of
       Latinos, 2004   82

6.3   Manner of Addressing Issues or Problems by National-Origin
       Category among Latino Respondents to the Latino National Survey   83

6.4   Actions Taken to Help a Party or Candidate Win an Election by
       Racial and Ethnic Group in the National Political Ethnic Survey   85

6.5   Contacting Officials by Generation and Citizenship among
       Respondents to the Latino National Survey   86

6.6   Interest in Politics and Public Affairs by National Origin among
       Respondents to the Latino National Survey   87

6.7   Summary of Participatory Scores for Respondents to the
       Participation in America Study   88

6.8   Latino Parents Who Meet with Their Child's Teacher in the Latino
       National Survey   89

6.9   PTA Meeting Attendance by Generation and Citizenship   91

6.10   Assessment of Parents' Interactions with School Officials among
       Latino National Survey Respondents by Educational Attainment   92

7.1   Reported Registration by Race, Gender, and Age: U.S. Presidential and
       Congressional Elections, 1992 to 2008   102

7.2   Reported Voting by Race, Gender, and Age: U.S. Presidential and
       Congressional Elections, 1992 to 2008   103

7.3   Reported Reasons for Not Voting among Those Who Reported
       Registering but Not Voting by Race, Gender, and Age: U.S.
       Presidential and Congressional Elections, 1992 to 2008   106

9.1   Legal Permanent Resident Flow by State of Residence, Fiscal Years
       2007 to 2009   147

9.2   Persons Naturalized by Region and Country of Birth, Fiscal Years
       2007 to 2009   153

11.1   Distribution of Ethnic and Pan-ethnic Identities among Latino
       National Survey Respondents   185

11.2   Pan-ethnic Identities among Respondents to the Latino National
       Survey   185

11.3   Strength of Latino/Hispanic Identity by Generation and Citizenship 187

11.4   Race/Ethnicity of Friendship Network by Generation and Citizenship 188

11.5   Race/Ethnicity of Coworkers by Generation and Citizenship   189

11.6   Reason for Unfair Treatment by Generation and Citizenship   193

11.7   Levels of Commonality among Latino National Survey Respondents
       Regarding Socioeconomic and Political Domains   194

11.8   Measures of Linked-Fate Questions among Latino National Survey
       Respondents   195

11.9   Latinos and African Americans Doing Well by Generation and
        Citizenship   197

11.10 Extent of Commonality among Latinos Regarding Jobs, Education,
        and Income Attainment with African Americans and Whites   202

11.11 Extent of Commonality among Latinos Regarding Their Political
        Situation with African Americans and Whites   202

11.12 Competition with African Americans in Getting Jobs by Generation
        and Citizenship   203

11.13 Competition with African Americans Having Access to Education and
        Quality Schools by Generation and Citizenship   205

12.1   Hispanic Eligible Voters by Nativity, 2000 to 2007   214

Boxes

4.1   The Changing Faces of Latino America   46

4.2   Other Latinos: Salvadorans and Guatemalans   51

4.3   The Colombian Community   57

5.1   Another Focus Group Vignette, 2006   66

6.1   Today We March, Tomorrow We Vote   80

7.1   A Latino's Cultural and Political Realities   100

7.2   Hispanics in the U.S. Congress, 1877 to 2010   114

7.3   Hispanics Who Have Served As Cabinet Secretaries   115

7.4   Latinos and the 2010 Midterm Elections   116

8.1   Latino Organizations   125

8.2   Latino Politics at the Grass Roots   135

8.3   Newer Latino Organizations Come Forward   136

8.4   Social Movements, Latinos, Immigration, and Organizational
       Elements   137

9.1   Immigration Policies and Developments from 2005 to the Present   148

11.1 The *Washington Post* Latino Survey   191

11.2 Another Look at the *Washington Post* Survey   198

11.3 Racial/Ethnic Coalitions in Los Angeles?   201

11.4 Vieques and Coalitional Partners   206

Acknowledgments

PREPARING A SECOND EDITION OF A BOOK that tackles a very dynamic set of communities, as well as a new millennium in which strong political currents and changes are occurring, presents a real challenge. Writing a second edition would suggest making modest updates and adding a few sentences to distinguish this work from the previous "product." While this edition took less time to prepare than the original version, the thought, reflection, and reevaluation involved in its creation consumed a lot of my attention. What we refer to as Latino politics and Latino studies has grown exponentially, theoretically, and empirically since the original 2003 publication of *Latino Politics in America*. Just as this edition reinforces a long-standing theme of continued and substantial population growth, the field of Latino politics and Latino studies has been maturing and expanding its visibility and impact.

By maturing, I mean moving beyond the testing of prevalent models and theories about politics to extensions of theories and models, as well as developing newer ways of understanding politics (both from the perspectives of individual and structural factors and also at the intersection of different levels of our political system). This broader scope and insightful understanding of Latino communities can affect the existing understanding about the American political system and prevailing myths. For example, many Latinos are blending into the American fabric while maintaining both a sense of self and their customs and traditions. While some observers and commentators have portrayed this as antithetical to the American ethos and culture, the Latino community has moved the discourse to include what it means to be an American and the distinctive manifestations of being Latino as part of the American fabric. This pattern raises questions as to the real bedrock of being American in terms of beliefs, values, and attachments. The growth of the Latino community and its impact on American life have created tensions and a mixed public-opinion climate, as well engaged the rest of America in clarifying and defining itself in the twenty-first century.

The other aspect of maturity centers on the social scientists and other contributors to the knowledge base about Latinos and their political worlds. As one of the senior citizens of this field, I see a newer generation of people advancing the field and disseminating their results and interpretations in a wider array of publication outlets (both academic and popular). In addition, this recent cohort of scholars has formed a dense social network in which members share, interact, and engage each other's works and ideas. I would add a gentle reminder: there is rarely anything totally new under the sun, so the connection to earlier works and ideas provides both an intellectual and ideological foundation and important elements of that evolving knowledge base.

My reference to these fields expanding their visibility and impact refers to practitioners' moving from a growing presence to active participants in both public and intellectual discourses about the American political system and how Latinos are effecting contemporary change and visions. The energy emanating from these contributors has been grounded in the pursuit of justice, equity, and effective civic and political engagement for Latino communities and the nation as a whole, combined with rigor and standards of excellence in the projects engaged in. With the "busy," often hostile and negative voices focusing on the Latino community, welcome analytical and strategic advocacy on behalf of Latinos' experiences and conditions is also evident in the work of contemporary scholars of Latino politics. As I revised this book, the contemporary works, especially those published since the turn of the millennium, helped me present, analyze, and discuss the developments occurring in the American political system, as well as further the understanding of the Latino community. This is reflected both in the test and the expanded references section. I would encourage readers to explore in greater depth the articles and books listed in the references.

In a more traditional sense, any acknowledgments section cites individuals who had a bearing on the task of preparing a publication. My exchanges at professional meetings and conferences with the scholars of Latino politics whose works I have utilized helped me to crystallize important themes and emphases. Sylvia Manzano (Texas A&M), Gabriel Sanchez (University of New Mexico), Michael Jones-Correa (Cornell University), Gary Segura (Stanford University), Rodney Hero (University of California, Berkeley), Valerie Martinez-Ebers (University of North Texas), Ricardo Rodríquez (Notre Dame University), and several graduate students (Marcela García-Castañon, Vanessa Cruz, and Ngoc Phan) were all valuable resources to me. Moving more closely to family, I wish to acknowledge my wife, Nancy Ellsworth García, who was introduced to the tedium of preparing a second edition. She waded through all of the existing and new references to insure proper inclusion and edited the new sections. Much of the collection of materials for the second edition occurred during my last years at the University of Arizona (School of Government and Public Policy), which was a good institutional base to develop my career and accomplishments. More recently, during my time at the Inter-university Consortium for Political and Social Research and the Institute for Social Research (University of Michigan), I was able to complete this revision with their support.

Also, since the first edition of this book, I became a grandfather twice over to Jackson Dylan and Ella Sophia, who serve as living and loving reminders of a future full of promise and hope. Of course, my mother, Dora G. García, at the age of ninety-three remains bright, inquisitive, and so supportive. She is living evidence of the benefits of coming from a good gene pool. Finally, Rowman & Littlefield's commitment to publishing a second edition has been encouraging and keeps a focus on Latino politics, adding to the number of textbooks now available.

Acronyms

ATEDPA	Antiterrorism and Effective Death Penalty Act
CANC	Cuban American National Council
CANF	Cuban American National Foundation
CBDG	Community Block Development Grant
CCD	Committee for Cuban Democracy
CHC	Congressional Hispanic Caucus
CHCI	Congressional Hispanic Caucus Institute
COPS	Community Organized for Public Services
CSO	Community Services Organization
DANR	Dominican American National Roundtable
DHS	Department of Homeland Security
HACR	Hispanic Association for Corporate Responsibility
HERE	Hotel Employees and Restaurant Employees International Union
HNBA	Hispanic National Bar Association
IAF	Industrial Areas Foundation
ICE	Immigrations and Customs Enforcement
IIRIRA	Illegal Immigration Reform and Immigrant Responsibility Act
INA	McCarran-Walter Act
INS	Immigration and Naturalization Service
IRCA	Immigration Reform and Control Act
LADO	Latin American Defense Organization
LCLAA	Labor Council for Latin American Advancement
LNPS	Latino National Political Survey
LNS	Latino National Survey
LULAC	League of United Latin American Citizens
LUPA	Latinos United for Political Rights
MALDEF	Mexican American Legal Defense and Education Fund
MWVREP	Midwest Voter Registration and Education Project
NAACP	National Association for the Advancement of Colored People
NABE	National Association of Bilingual Educators
NAHD	National Association of Hispanic Dentists

NAHJ	National Association of Hispanic Journalists
NALEO	National Association of Latino Elected and Appointed Officials
NCLB	No Child Left Behind Act
NCLR	National Council of La Raza
NHCC	National Hispanic Corporate Council
NPES	National Political Ethnic Survey
NSBA	National Survey of Black Americans
OLAW	Organization of Los Angeles Workers
OMB	Office of Management and Budget
PRA	permanent resident alien
PRLDEF	Puerto Rican Legal Defense and Education Fund
PRWORA	Personal Responsibility and Work Opportunity Reconciliation Act
SEIU	Service Employees International Union
SHPE	Society of Hispanic Professional Engineers
SIG	special interest group
SSI	Supplementary Security Income
SVREP	Southwest Voter Registration and Education Project
UNITE	Union of Needletrades, Industrial and Textile Employees
USHCC	U.S. Hispanic Chamber of Commerce
VAP	voting age population
VEP	voting eligible population
VRA	Voting Rights Act

CHAPTER 1

An Introduction to Latino Politics

Emprendimos una peregrinación y nos pre-guntamos ¿Donde estan nuestras raices, los hilos de la historia y las experiencias en estas tierras las conocidas tanto como las nuevas? Al hacer el reconocimiento, perc-ibimos perspectivas de todas las direcciones y siempre miramos hacia el futuro con esperanza y dignidad.

Undertaking a pilgrimage to find our community, we ask ourselves, Where are our roots, those strands of history and experiences in lands both known and new? As we search, our reconnaissance takes in views from many sources, and we are always looking to the future with hope and dignity.

"EL CENSOS 2010: Esta en Nuestras Manos" ("Census 2010: It's in Our Hands")—the Spanish-language version of the 2010 U.S. census—was one of more than forty versions in which the decennial census campaigns reached out to a more diversified United States. The information collected produced population tabulations with counts and detailed descriptions of all persons, including Hispanics. How are people classified, and what are the consequences and implications of the classification? What is reported, when are data released, how accurate is the information, and how will it be used are all important questions for Latino communities and their organizations. These questions raised in the first edition of this book in 2003 apply just as much with the current decennial census. During the previous decade, Latinos have been pronounced as America's largest minority group. This "proclamation" has engendered both greater national presence and greater expectations within this community for influence and empowerment.

The Spanish-origin question included in the decennial census first appeared in the 1970 census as an ethnic self-identifier. The information elicited by the Spanish-origin question serves as the basis for voting and civil rights legislation and implementation, as well as a variety of service-delivery programs. Recently the Office of Management and Budget (OMB) revised how racial and ethnic data were collected.[1] After lengthy public input and feedback from federal statistical agencies, the OMB revised the race question format for Census 2000. A person had the option of marking more than one racial category (white, black, Asian, Pacific Islander, Native American/Alaska Native, and other). In addition, the OMB separated Asians from native Hawaiians and Pacific

1

Islanders to create five racial categories. The ability to mark more than one option enables persons of multiracial background to self-identify from all of the various appropriate racial categories.

For multiple responses, a resulting issue lies with the method in which the population tabulation method(s) are conducted and reported. In previous censuses, each person fell into only one racial category. For Census 2000, the tabulation was more complicated as persons could indicate multiple responses. For example, indigenous populations from Mexico and Central and South America were included in the American Indian/Alaska Native category. Yet, this racial category generally represents legally recognized tribes in the United States rather than indicating whether the respondent is of indigenous origin, regardless of national origin. What happens to the individual who marks herself as African American and white and checks off Spanish origin on the ethnic-origin question? How is this person counted and in how many different ways? The classification method selected has a direct bearing on civil and voting rights and program-participation monitoring, as well as on how the government determines who Hispanics/Latinos are. To further complicate the classification issue, plans are under consideration, for the future, to tabulate multiple responses on the Spanish-origin question and potentially merge the Spanish-origin and race questions into one item. For example, an individual marks that he is of Spanish and non-Hispanic origin (i.e., of mixed Hispanic origin). How is that person counted?

At the same time, a count has much greater political significance beyond the numbers of Latinos living in the United States. My brief and not so simple description of current governmental policy decisions and classification schemes is based on the concepts of race and ethnic origin. While significant media attention has highlighted the continual growth of the Spanish-origin population, it is not always clear whom we are discussing or why persons whose ancestry is tied to Chile are associated with others whose ancestry is connected to Hondurans. Public Law 85-983 established the "Spanish origin" designation for purposes of federal data collection, combining persons from twenty-two countries of origin into a single category.

Under the broad scope of Latino politics, this book addresses the dialectics of diversity and similarity among persons and communities of Spanish origin. In many ways, Latinos and their politics reflect a community that is being influenced by Latino elites and organizations, "mass" intergroup interactions,[2] the mass media, and governmental policies and agencies. Regardless of the derivation of the Latino/Hispanic concept, the idea of a group of peoples tied together by language, cultural values and practices, similar histories in the United States, and public policies is clearly visible on the American landscape, and its political ramifications are very dynamic.

Critical to this discussion of Latinos and the American political system is an examination of both the basis and construction of identity and the salience of group identification. This central dimension affecting Latinos residing in the United States informs the nature and basis for community among a collection of persons from twenty-plus national-origin groups. Most Latinos think of themselves in terms of their own national-origin group (Honduran, Cuban, Argentine, etc.), and this subgroup identification is an important component of the core definition of community (F. C. García 1997). At the same time, a sense of **pan-ethnicity**,[3] or seeing oneself not only in national-origin terms but also as part of a broader community, has been a more recent development. The "Hispanic" or "Latino" label has been serving as an important product in the formation of a Latino community. Yet it is the meaning beyond the use of the label that establishes a sense of working community and means of identifying common concerns, interests, and situations.

The concept of **ethnicity** (and, to a lesser degree, race) represents social boundaries in which group identity exists, is created, and is redefined. The **social construct of race** usually refers to a group of persons who define themselves as distinct due to perceived common physical characteristics (Cornell and Hartman 1998). This group is socially defined based on physical characteristics and fated by biological factors. Historical precedents and policies—such as the one-drop rule that operated in the South—construct a racial category. A common practice in the South categorized any person with any African lineage (as little as one drop) as Negro or African American. As a result, Jim Crow laws in the region defined participation in social life based on one's race. In this case, the state defined as being of black racial identity anyone with one-thirty-second Negro ancestry, or one drop of "Negro" blood (Payne 1998).

The work of Omni and Winant (1994) further extends the development of race as a social product of human actions and decisions. The concept can be changed over time by members of the racial group and/or through "external" social actions. Identity can be comprehensive in forming the basis for a nearly complete social organization and lifestyle, or, minimally, it is symbolic and periodically emotive. For example, honoring of one's group could be manifested in annual parades and celebration of one's ancestry, culture, and music. In most cases, membership in a racial group has direct consequences. In the case of Latinos, members can be categorized into racial as well as ethnic groups and targeted for specific policies or governmental actions.

Ethnic groups deal with group attachments connected to descent. In reality, direct "blood" ties to ancestry are less important, with belief in a descent being more critical. This reinforces the socially constructed basis of ethnicity. The "strands" that cultivate this belief in common descent can include physical attributes, cultural practices, and a shared historical experience (Cornell and Hartman 1998, 16–17). What makes ethnicity distinctive is that this shared affinity serves as the basis for community formation.

The work of R. A. Schermerhorn (1970) reinforces this view of ethnicity by defining it as a "collectivity within the larger society having a real or putative common ancestry, memories of a shared historical past, and a cultural focus on one or more symbolic elements defined as the epitome of their peoplehood." Consistent with these definitions is the presence of self-consciousness among members of an ethnic group. Ethnicity lies within the core of one's identity. At the same time, the self-identification that a person "takes on" may be influenced by external factors such as public policies that provide punitive costs or possible benefits for ethnic group membership. Thus, ethnicity operates among persons who identify with others of their descent and are also influenced by individuals outside their group's boundaries.

Race and ethnicity differ in the greater pervasive burden and consequences for those carrying the racial designation. Movement across racial boundaries is more restricted by social traditions and customs than that across ethnic categories. For ethnic individuals, the demarcation by the larger society may also be externally imposed; yet, affiliation with the group is usually asserted by members of the ethnic group. Race becomes a way in which defining and assigning differential status is associated with power, control, inferiority, and majority-minority-group status.

As we began with a reference to the decennial census, my distinction between race and ethnicity may be clearer for academics and less so for others. For example, in the 2000 census over 13 million Americans checked the "some other race" option, and Latinos/Hispanics constituted more than 95 percent of this category. So Latinos are checking off the ethnic question as well as indicating a different "racial option" than the established OMB designations. Do you interpret this response as many Latinos signifying that Latinos are a race? Or are Latinos using the notions of race and ethnicity as interchangeable? Or are Latinos trying to state that we are a distinctive group in the racial/ethnic scheme of America? For the most part, there is evidence that all three scenarios resonate with segments of the Latino community.

Ethnicity also shares an external group designation. But it includes an element of self-concept and identification that is also associated when members of an ethnic group start to define their ethnic category. They fill in their own content and meaning, casting their own histories and experiences and determining what it means to be "an ethnic." This process can be described as the social construction of ethnicity from within. In many ways, this book is an examination of the social construction of Latinos in the United States as a viable community and how that manifests itself politically. Clearly, race and ethnicity overlap concerning a sense of group identity and the nature of **power relations** that position a group's members in the larger society.

While we may think of **ethnic identity** as primarily a matter of individual choice or circumstances, the development of such identities can be influenced by sources external to the ethnic community, such as political institutions (the courts, political parties, etc.) and agencies (Equal Employment Opportunity Commission, Civil Rights Commission, Department of Justice, etc.) that designate policies (voting rights, civil rights protection, entitlements, etc.) in terms of specific group categories (minorities, African Americans, Hispanics, etc.). For example, the **Voting Rights Act of 1965** focused initially on institutional exclusionary voting practices directed toward African Americans in the South. The prohibitions against literacy tests, grandfather clauses,[4] limited voting registration location(s), and so on, were policy interventions intended to open up the electoral process. The Voting Rights Act amendments later incorporated the concept of linguistic minorities and implemented bi- or multilingual voting materials and assistance.

Legislation, official governmental data gathering, and mass media characterizations of Hispanics/Latinos serve as ways to simplify their world by reducing a large and potentially diverse collection of persons to a simpler grouping. One of the issues confronting many Latino subcommunities is the extent to which Latino subgroups (Guatemalans, people of Mexican-origin, Argentineans, etc.) are connected to one another and whether an inclusive appeal to work on common causes will be effective. The use of the labels "Hispanic" and "Latino" gives to the broader society a much simpler picture of who persons of "Spanish origin" are and what they are about. Rather than examining and assessing each national-origin group in terms of "its own political needs and status," such labeling converts them from a diverse and complex mix of groups into a simplified and more manageable package of a new "ethnic group." This helps policy makers deal with their political world and the new demands made on it.

One result of a new formulation of group status, often referred to as pan-ethnicity, is the creation of concrete benefits to which organizations and members of this new group category can now respond. For example, bilingual educational programs are based on the existence of students who have limited English proficiency, as well as the perception that bilingualism is primarily a Latino issue. Consequently, a pan-ethnic grouping, with a much larger population base, can emphasize its need and use its sizable constituency to maintain and expand bilingual education programs. An in-depth understanding of Latinos and community building would integrate the role of public policies and social institutions (mass media, governmental agencies, decision-making bodies, etc.) into Latino subgroups' activities and developments, as well as the links that tie several Latino subgroups in collaborative efforts.

Another critical factor for community building is the general climate and the broader public's mood toward and awareness about Latinos. Public concerns about cultural and linguistic balkanization, immigration swells, multilingualism, and the like portray Latinos as problematic. These issues carry an underlying theme in which segments of non-Latino communities see many Latinos as unwilling to Americanize and assimilate. Such concerns highlight their presence and increase the possible costs of being Latino.

For example, the 1997 welfare reform legislation barred "permanent resident aliens" from participating in Social Security's Supplementary Security Income (SSI) and other federal entitlement programs. Congress did not choose to differentiate between undocumented immigrants and permanent resident aliens. Similarly, initiatives in California regarding immigrant access to social services and discontinuing bilingual education programs have targeted Latinos. This has put many persons of Spanish origin on the defensive and even sent them into survival mode. Latino civic engagement has increased in the form of protest activities, higher voter-registration and -turnout levels, and greater political interest (Sierra et al. 2000). Throughout this book, I emphasize the need to understand identity, its constructions and dynamic character, as well as its sources, in order to interpret and analyze Latino politics.

Latino politics are found in many social contexts (F. C. García 1997; Bonilla and Morales 1998), including in institutions like schools and federal and local decision-making arenas, as well as in referenda and initiatives, public policies, public opinion, and political representation at all levels. Yet scholars focusing on the Latino community have not thoroughly researched many of these dimensions of politics. For example, researchers have only recently begun to examine Latino community organizations and their political involvement with urban redevelopment, local school issues, and environmental "racism" (Pardo 1998; Pulído 1996). More research findings exist for the Mexican-origin population as opposed to Central and South Americans and other Caribbean groups. Only in the past five to ten years have researchers begun to examine the political domains and actions of Latinos in their own communities. At the same time, a limited number of national databases and subsequent analysis have become more readily available for discussion of Latinos and their politics.

An examination of Latinos and the political sphere needs to start with an assessment of power relations among Latinos, Latino subgroups, and established power holders and institutions. This examination includes both historical and contemporary power relations and how Latinos have survived, adapted, and succeeded in power-exchange terms. That is, have Latinos or Latino subgroups (Mexican Americans, Cubans, Puerto Ricans, Panamanians, etc.) successfully accessed political and economic institutions or placed key issues or concerns on the policy-making agenda?

Power relations focus on political resources, agenda setting, organizational development, leadership and **mobilization**, authority, influence, and legitimacy. Inquiring into governmental policies (at the federal, state, and local levels) that have influenced Latino communities can lead to a greater understanding of the extent and use of power by them. In some respects, governmental initiatives and actions that classify persons by group terms or identities (i.e., race, ethnicity, and social class) can serve as indicators of political presence. Part of the political-empowerment process entails recognition of the group, even in symbolic ways.

Whether or not the political system is organized to be responsive to Latino communities, political institutions through their practices and/or benign neglect clearly indicate the power basis that Latinos must develop effective strategies to contend with. The 1980s were designated the "decade of the Hispanic." Projections of extraordinary population growth, with Latinos becoming the nation's largest minority group by 2003, heightened an expectation of Latinos basking in the "political sun." At the same time, through the 1980s, Latinos' socioeconomic status (household income, families living below the poverty line, single-parent-headed households, and percentage of adults with a high school diploma, etc.) continued to lag even farther behind that of whites. Recognition and responsiveness from governmental institutions was much slower than the rapid Latino growth rate. To a significant degree, Latinos were evolving in the U.S. political system from being a relatively obscure or invisible group into one that political institutions had some degree of political awareness about and familiarity with, especially at the national level.

In addition to the contextual elements that contribute to the basis and content of Latino politics, other important factors include sociodemographic status, such as occupational locations in the labor market, economic status, residential and regional concentrations, access to social institutions (their own or societal), and legal prohibitions (restricted immigrant rights and participation, reduced impact on **redistricting**, etc.). The sociodemographic map identifies the resource bases for Latinos as well as possible policy issues and concerns. Given the youthfulness of the overall Latino population and the significant proportion of Latinos who are foreign-born, issues such as educational quality, persistence in staying and completing their education, immigration reform, and increased militarization of the border are all likely policy extensions of Latinos' sociodemographic profile. In addition, the relatively lower percentage of high school and college graduates among Latinos, as well as their concentration in service-sector industries, has implications for political mobilization and resources. Lower levels of educational attainment, lower job status, and lesser income levels reduce the conventional type of personal resources that individuals can convert for political purposes.

Political participation and mobilization (Verba, Scholzman, and Brady 1995; Rosenstone and Hansen 1993) are closely connected to an individual's socioeconomic status, positive political predispositions (or attitudes), and available time to engage in political activities. Chapter 3 develops a sociodemographic "map" of Latinos to assist in the construction of the extent of their political resources and the range of issues that will compose our discussion.

This book focuses on the creation, maintenance, and redefinition of community and the role that external stereotypes and perceptions about Latinos and/or Latino subgroups play in framing Latino politics. Culture and its expression within the Latino communities through the mass and Spanish-language media, traditions and practices, and Spanish-language maintenance define and sustain a sense of community. In addition, individual membership in and attachment to the Latino community is reinforced through social networks, living in Latino residential areas, experiences with discrimination, and shared experience in the workplace. These "arenas" are at the core of creating bridges for a Latino community at the grassroots level.

Ethnicity and identity reflect self-choice in how an individual places himself within a group affiliation. Latinos who continue to use Spanish, maintain ethnically "dense" social contacts with fellow Latinos, and participate in cultural events and practices are living their Latino-ness. The whole spectrum of being Latino or Cubano or Dominicano lies in the daily routine. How one communicates, the composition and content of one's interactions, lifestyle preferences, and behaviors, and the extent of affinity toward persons of similar ancestry contribute to the definition of who one is and its relevance to one's life.

Immersion as a Latino—or, more likely, a Cuban, Puerto Rican, or member of another Latino subgroup—is related to social contexts and the involvement of activists and organizations that link the daily experiences of Latinos with directed social and political actions. Numerical growth helps Latino communities assert their identity and command necessary resources. Awareness of the key distinctions between citizens (native-born and naturalized), permanent resident aliens, undocumented persons, and political refugees is critical to understanding the range of similarities and diversities within this dynamic community. Similarly, class differentiation among Latinos serves to create close-knit communities or, perhaps, accentuate class bifurcation.

There is literature that deals with class bifurcation in the African American community and its impact on mobilization, organizational growth and development, and maintaining consensus on public policies (West 1994; Dawson 1994). The connectedness, or lack of it, between the African American underclass and the upwardly mobile and successful middle class can create different policy agendas and alliances that may not include each other. The existence or extent of class bifurcation, defined for Latinos as potential cleavages between the foreign- and native-born, has not been researched adequately. Cultural maintenance and practices are critical for group identity and community building.

At the same time, our theme of similarity and diversity suggests that the Latino community does not require unanimity or complete consensus in order for its members to engage as a political community. Like many political coalitions, Latino politics entails common bonds, experiences, conditions, and interests that can bridge Latino subgroups for collective action on various occasions. These introductory comments and ideas serve as an overview for an examination of Latino politics. The rest of my commentary in this introduction delineates specific dimensions of community building and politics for the more than 49 million Latinos in the United States.

The basis for a Latino community will be shared interests, with culture serving as the vital connection. It is important to establish definitions of ethnicity, identity, and community, as well as to analyze how political institutions, processes, policies, and political actors help shape the nature and substance of Latino politics. An "inside and outside" set of processes and actions is at play. Latino activists, organizations (local and national), political parties, and national "events" (such as **English-only initiatives**, Proposition 209, fatalities along the border, and other political events that have occurred) weave a set of contributing factors that can bring people together for common purposes. One of the real challenges for me lies in achieving sufficient breadth and depth in covering the many different Latino subgroups. In many cases, only a sparse literature is available.

Chapter 3 provides a demographic profile of Latinos in the United States incorporating the characteristics of shared interests, social status, cultural "indicators," geographic concentrations, and institutions within the Latino subcommunities. The demographic profiles are then linked to community building and agenda setting. The themes of diversity and similarity are interwoven throughout this book. We will explore two particular bases for community: a **community of interests** and a **community of common or similar cultures** (García and Pedraza-Bailey 1990). A community of common cultures exists when individuals are linked closely by their participation in a common system of meaning with concomitant patterns of customary interactions of culture. Shared cultural practices, celebrations, and traditions serve to bridge Latino subgroup boundaries and potentially provide common bases and resources for effective mobilization.

Other writers (Espiritu 1992; Hayes-Bautista 1980) refer to these dynamics as elements of a pan-ethnicity in which several national-origin groups coalesce under a broader identity and community reference. A community of interests represents the conditions, statuses, and experiences that Latinos share with members of other Latino subgroups. Except for Puerto Ricans, a significant proportion of each Latino subgroup consists of foreign-born persons and immigrants. The current national climate is filled with serious concerns about immigration policies and perceived negative consequences of continued immigration. Latinos are seen as the dominant source of immigrants. Therefore, immigration impacts many Latino communities and can serve as a contributing factor in developing a broader community of interests.

Chapter 4 attempts to provide a substantive understanding of the many Latino subcommunities and includes focused discussions of the subgroups and their historical and power relations in the United States. In addition, I present an overview of how communities may exist in relative isolation from other Latino communities or be linked in various ways to other Latino subgroups. An interesting aspect of intergroup dynamics is discernible in the Census 2010 findings. Not only have Latinos increased in numbers during the past decade, but their migration patterns have become more regionally diverse, extending into areas less traditionally identified as Latino. For example, increases among Mexican-origin individuals exceeding 80 percent in southern states such as Arkansas, Georgia, North Carolina, and Tennessee represent major gains in rural and urban communities. This migration of Mexican-origin persons to the Northeast and the South is substantial in terms of population and political activities.

Similarly, Central Americans (especially "refugees") since the mid-1980s have migrated in significant numbers to traditional areas of Latino concentrations with established Mexican, Cuban, or Puerto Rican enclaves. One result has been a reconfiguration of Latino issues, a more diverse organizational milieu, and intergroup competition. An analysis of Latino politics must address the dynamic nature of the composition of the Latino community and its evolving political networks. Analyzing power relations and particular public policies is one way to explore the nature and character of Latino subcommunity politics and their connections to "broader collective Latino politics."

Ethnicity, group identity, and pan-ethnicity involve the social construction of identity, which occurs within the respective groups and is influenced externally. The contributing factors of culture, daily experiences, social contexts, and public policies are introduced to assess the extent and "permanence" of Latino subcommunities and the broader Latino national community. Pan-ethnicity is explored in terms of both its political utility for Latinos and the interplay of mass and elite "forces" involved in this social construction. Authors like Peter Skerry (1993) have suggested that many Latino leaders perpetuate a sense of ethnicity or "Latino-ness" to maintain their power bases. In this vein, the social construction of ethnicity and resulting community is an artificial one, or at best one contrived for the benefit of a limited number of activists. On the other hand, our basis for community indicates that Latino identity and affiliation must include dimensions of self-choice and conscious acceptance of belonging to a community defined as Latino or a specific Latino subgroup. Again, the basis for community will be related to the viability of pan-ethnicity.

Latino political participation is discussed in a number of chapters that break down the contributing factors of participation into individual, organizational, social, attitudinal, and **structural factors** for Latino subgroup members. I attempt to differentiate the crucial factors of foreign-born and native-born, gender, class, and regional location in analyzing political participation and incorporate the dimensions of time, money, and skills (Verba, Scholzman, and Brady 1995). The participation chapters will then move to the many modes of participation: voting, electoral activities, organizational involvement, protest, individualized contact, and office holding. I will use the extant research on specific Latino subgroups to portray the variations and similarities that exist across the Latino community.

The next aspect of Latino politics is the area of political mobilization. When Latinos are asked to get politically involved, whether by organizational leaders, neighbors, or the like, who gets involved, and who does not? Political involvement is not solely a function of an individual's decision. Persons can be asked, approached, and enticed to get involved. This is a simple way to define political mobilization as the "outside" forces that influence individual political involvement. Characterizing mobilization in this manner also serves as a mechanism for introducing organizations and leadership into the Latino politics equation. Using specific Latino-focused organizations, I illustrate the range and scope of organizational goals, arenas of involvement, membership and resource bases, and political impact in a variety of policy areas. We examine the extent of Latinos' involvement in organizations and how Latino organizations are involved with the Latino community and its needs.

I then address Latinos' leadership styles, communication skills, and linkages with the "masses." Leadership is studied in terms of the goal articulation conveyed to Latinos and its coherency, which can influence specific political activities. Some have suggested that Latino political empowerment would be greatly enhanced if there were one or even two national Latino leaders who had followings in all of the Latino subcommunities. Others have argued that the core of Latino interests and needs resides in local communities, where leadership activities and development are more critical. A singular leader or two or three would be a difficult challenge for any community of this size and diversity to overcome.

The role of Latino leadership serves to crystallize issues, strategies, and "targets." The issue of gender bias, which is inherent in the discussion of leadership, is examined.

Viable national leaders are more likely to be males, whereas leaders at the grass roots are often women. Characterizing leadership in this manner serves to introduce the concept of vertical and horizontal leadership. Again, specific examples are adduced to illustrate the issues and impact associated with leaders.

Although great attention has been focused on the national and state levels, Latino politics at the local level is an active arena. It has been suggested that the intensity and soul of Latino politics deal with local struggles (location decisions regarding toxic waste sites, delivery of services, educational equity and quality, residential gentrification, etc.). A number of locally focused community organizations have arisen over the past two decades in several Latino subcommunities. Organizing principles, efforts, strategies, and outcomes are important dimensions of Latino politics. They are often overlooked and underanalyzed. I attempt to characterize and analyze Latino local politics in the context of Latino empowerment and political development.

An understanding of Latino politics involves a focus on the political dynamics occurring within the Latino communities, as well as external forces and actions in the larger society. In this context, legislative initiatives and policies like the Civil Rights and Voting Rights acts have played an important role in generating electoral representation, equal opportunities, and fuller civic participation. In the latter chapters of this book, I examine the origin of voting and civil rights legislation and policies that have impacted Latinos. Other legislative changes (Titles VI, VII, and IX of the Higher Education Act, the Equal Employment Opportunity Act, etc.), lobbying efforts, and major court decisions will be analyzed as part of the political assessment of Latinos and the political system. Organizations like the Mexican American Legal Defense and Education Fund and Puerto Rican Legal Defense and Education Fund are key groups considered in this section.

This discussion of Latinos focuses on specific public policy areas to maintain consistency with our theme of community, which includes shared interests, culture, and conditions that help shape the critical issue areas for Latinos. The politics of culture is connected with language, cultural distinctiveness, English-only initiatives, and other xenophobic movements directed toward Latinos. First-generation immigrants and international migration bring immigration policies, border enforcement, immigrant and noncitizen rights and political integration, and avenues for participation into our discussion of Latino politics. To some extent, the immigration question is a test of political loyalty, with Latinos being placed on the defensive.

Equality-of-opportunity issues deal with educational quality and resources, labor market participation (i.e., access to jobs and opportunities for advancement, preparation for employment with job mobility, protection from discrimination, and equal and competitive pay), economic participation and income mobility, access to higher education, and social service participation. Within this context, the debate over and impact of affirmative action are pertinent. To some extent, foreign policy concerns (Cuba and the Castro regime, the economic embargo of Cuba, Puerto Rican statehood/independence, the North American Free Trade Act, U.S. economic investments in Latin America, drug interdiction, etc.) are aspects of the public policy discussions with particular relevance to Latinos. Integral to this section is attention to an understanding of the American policy-making process. Understanding agenda setting, monitoring policy implementation, and reviewing policy consequences form an integral part of analyzing specific policy areas.

Finally, this analysis points to the future of Latino politics and revisits the concepts of community, shared interests, culture and organizations, and identity construction, as well as external factors and actions in the political system. The last two chapters look at coalition formation, within the Latino communities and other minority communities. A discussion of trends for the next millennium closes out our discourse. Where will the Latino community be in the next twenty years, and will its identity be thinner and more externally assigned rather than thicker and more assertive? Given the changing demography of the Latino community (growing numbers of Latinos from Central America and the Caribbean, greater geographic dispersion and intermixing of Latino subcommunities, etc.), will the agenda and its leadership structure also undergo some changes? I develop four possible scenarios based on different directions of community building and their political manifestations.

Conclusion

In this introduction I have tried to lay out important concepts with which to describe and analyze Latino politics. The challenge is to discuss the politics of Latino subcommunities without necessarily assuming that Latino politics (in the pan-ethnic sense) is the pervasive mode. That is, I define politics at the national-origin community level (Cuban, Salvadoran, Mexican-origin, etc.) for both national and local arenas. At the same time, there exists a Latino political force that, at times, is more like one group than a collection of multiple independent Latino subgroups. An important question in regard to identifying Latinos in American society is the extent to which they impact political arenas and agendas as a pan-ethnic community rather than a loose consortium of semi-independent interests. The task has begun, and the chapters that follow try to analyze Latino politics with the vitality and personality that constitute the Latino peoples.

Discussion Questions

1. What defines a Latino? Do Latinos comprise an ethnic group, a racial group, or some other differently characterized social grouping?
2. How well does the concept of ethnicity fit the Latino community in the United States?
3. This book tries to establish a sense of community among Latinos. How well does the framework of communities of common culture and interests help in understanding Latinos?
4. We introduce the concept of pan-ethnicity and suggest its utility for understanding Latino politics. Discuss this concept and how applicable it is to contemporary American politics.

CHAPTER 2

Community Building in Latino America

Píntame un cuadro donde se representan imagenes de nuestra comunidad. El/la artista pinta de acuerdo su propio punto de vista. Todas las perspectivas, la abundancia de rostros y figuras forman el carácter de lo que significa ser parte de una comunidad que es evolucíon.

Paint me a picture in which images of our community are represented. The artist paints according to his or her own point of view. With so many perspectives, a multitude of faces and personalities make up the character of our changing community.

OUR EXAMINATION OF LATINO POLITICS in the United States can be seen as the dynamic formulation of community with all the diversities and similarities among its members. Discussion of politics can center on the substance of power, influence, resources, and interest articulation. Thus, Latino politics represents an aggregation of persons whose origins and/or ancestry can be connected to over twenty countries in Latin America and on the Iberian Peninsula. What brings this grouping together can include Spanish language; similar cultural values, practices, and histories; and targeted public policies (Gómez-Quiñones 1990; Stavans 1996; Fox 1997). Underlying this perspective is the assumption that persons with a common ancestry and culture will come together to achieve common objectives and address common concerns.

In this chapter, I develop some political and cultural bases for Latino politics, as well as the resultant directions this political community can take. Prior to the 1980s, Latinos were characterized as specific national-origin groups in certain regions of the United States. The Chicanos/Mexican Americans in the Southwest trace their ancestry to the sixteenth century, as do newly arrived Mexicanos from Mexico's central plateau. Puerto Ricans live in the Northeast, especially in the New York metropolitan area. There was a significant post–World War II out-migration from "La Isla" to the industrial centers of the Rust Belt as well as to the agricultural sectors in the Northeast and the South. After Fidel Castro came to power in 1959, several waves of Cuban political refugees and exiles descended on the southern United States. Even though

Cuban refugees participated in refugee-placement programs that included resettlement throughout the United States, most preferred to reside in Florida. Subsequent waves of Cuban refugees in the 1980s and 1990s augmented an entrepreneurial and better-educated community in Miami-Dade County.

Mexicans, Puerto Ricans, and Cubans, comprising the three largest Latino communities, are more established within and visible to the larger American public. At the same time, the post-1970s saw a major influx of Latinos from Central America and, to a lesser extent, South America. The liberation struggles in El Salvador, Nicaragua, and Guatemala, together with high birthrates, political instability, and inadequate economic growth and opportunity, have fueled out-migration of Central Americans into almost every region of the United States. For the most part, Central Americans have been designated as economic migrants rather than political refugees. Public policy distinctions (which I discuss further in chapter 9) between economic and political migrants reflect national foreign policy commitments rather than individuals' conditions or situations.

Even though I started out in this book by placing many persons of Latin American ancestral origin under the rubric of "Latino" or "Hispanic,"[1] doing so implies some degree of group membership and affinity. Consequently, we will consider the nature of community within and across the Latino subcommunities as incorporating affinity and identification. Our discussion of a Latino community also assesses the strength and character with which communities are built and maintained. The word "community" refers here to the connections between persons that formulate a sense of place, being, and membership in a larger whole. The origins of Hispanics or Latinos can be traced to various strands of U.S. history and events. For example, federal legislation in the mid-1970s initiated by Congressman Edward Roybal required all federal agencies to maintain records and designations of persons of Spanish origin, generally defined as individuals from Spanish-speaking countries and the Iberian Peninsula. One challenge of implementing this policy entailed determining a uniform "standard" for identifying persons of Spanish origin. The range of standards included Spanish surname, ancestry, birthplace, foreign-born parentage, self-identification, and language used when growing up.

The 1970 census also reflected the different methods for identifying persons of Spanish origin. On both the short and long census forms,[2] ancestry and self-identification determined Hispanicity. That is, an individual who deemed herself a person of Spanish origin would self-identify as such. No prescribed criteria such as Spanish-language use or foreign-born status directed one to declare Spanish origin. The self-identifier introduced in the 1970 census has been the consistent Hispanic "marker" ever since. Technically, it is referred as the **ethnicity** item or Spanish-origin identifier. Thus, it might be helpful to distinguish between race and ethnicity.

Many scholarly and popular literatures have discussed race in terms of phenotype, skin color, biology, social structure, and ancestry. Public policies like the one-drop rule have reinforced the concept of race as more directly connected to skin color and a defined racial categorization. On the other hand, ethnicity is commonly associated with ancestry or national origin. To be an ethnic is to be, for example, Irish American, Italian American, or Cuban American, with ties to cultural practices and traditions. Although I do not discuss the conceptual and theoretical underpinnings of race and ethnicity, the social and historical context of these terms is an important dimension of politics, power, and influence in American society. For our purposes, we will operate on the notion that ethnicity and race are interrelated concepts that establish group boundaries, behaviors, and inter- and intragroup relations.

Following the census distinction between race and ethnicity, a Spanish-origin person can be of any race.[3] While the American understanding of race is strongly related to skin color and serves as an external influence on group identification, ethnicity is viewed more as one's national origin and ancestry and is influenced greatly by assimilation and acculturation processes. Therefore, an important factor contributing to the configuration of "Hispanic" or "Latino" as an umbrella term was the formulation of public policy establishing the collection and operationalization protocol to categorize Spanish-origin persons.

The mass media are another important factor contributing to the development of the umbrella term *Latino/Hispanic*. The mass media response to the changing demography of the United States evolved from reporting on specific national-origin Latino subgroups (Puerto Ricans, Mexicans, Dominicans, etc.) to using the more **pan-ethnic** label of "Hispanic." Toward the end of the 1970s, the media began reporting and discussing both established and recently arrived Latinos; many major newsmagazines and newspapers started referring to the 1980s as the decade of the Hispanic. Sound bites like "Hispanics' day in the sun," "fastest-growing minority," and "soon to be the largest minority group" became typical characterizations of this aggregation of persons from twenty-two Spanish-speaking countries.

Ironically, descriptors such as "an awakening sleeping giant," "the invisible minority," and "bronze/brown power" were used in the early 1960s to depict Mexican Americans in the Southwest. One parallel theme for both periods was potentiality and promise. The focus on significant population growth and its continuation in the future projected Latinos as a "new" political and economic force in American society. Mass media centers in the eastern part of the United States conducted exploration and fact-finding projects on the relatively unknown Hispanics. There was utility in the media's assigning one label and identity to varied national-origin group members. Such clustering of the many national-origin groups into one ethnic status[4] simplified discussions of public policy and news regarding Latinos. This illustrates how factors outside the Latino community play an important role in shaping understanding and characterization of it. Clearly, some subgroup differentiation does take place, but even then the "Hispanic/Latino" descriptor is used.

Thus, persons of Spanish origin came to be seen as having similar cultural traditions and a common language. The discovery of Latino people by the mass media heightened public awareness of them and led to the ascription of general characteristics, such as Spanish speaking, largely immigrant, religious, committed to family, and having traditional values. The accuracy and relevance of these images actually depend on how Latinos see themselves. Nevertheless, the configuration of persons of Spanish origin was greatly impacted by the discovery and portrayal of Hispanics by the media, especially during the "decade of the Hispanic."

A third factor in the development of an umbrella term is based in the so-called Latino community itself. The combination of the swelling growth rates among Latino subgroups and the creation of "situational ethnicity" by Latino activists served as key elements in the promotion of a Latino community. There was a significant influx of Latinos into the United States beginning in the mid-1970s, and the fastest-growing elements within the Latino community were persons from Central and South America and the Spanish-speaking Caribbean. Movement by Central American and Caribbean Latinos was initially followed by their migration to the Northeast and Midwest and then to states like California and Texas and to the South. Chapter 3 provides more specific demographic profiles of these developments. One result of greater Latino migration throughout the United States was a more diverse mix of Latino subgroups, a pattern that held strongly for the established Mexican American, Puerto Rican, and Cuban communities, which began to have contact with individuals from Central and South America. Such a confluence of persons with linkages to the Spanish language, Spanish colonial histories, and U.S. hegemony assists with possible cultural and political connections.

While each group was growing faster than the national average, its respective size and regional concentration was limited on a national scale. Mexican Americans were seen as a regional minority primarily concentrated in the Southwest and oriented toward regional issues. Puerto Ricans were a New York metropolitan phenomenon, coping with a declining manufacturing economy and living on the mean streets of "El Barrio." Cubans, on the other hand, were seen as focused on ethnic enclaves and entrepreneurship and promoting anticommunist policies in Congress. These oversimplifications summarize dominant perceptions of the situational and policy domains of the three larger subgroups. The development of pan-ethnic grouping and identity becomes a means to expand group size, scope, and national visibility. Thus, the outgrowth of "Hispanicity" or "Latino-ness" represents a strategic decision among activists to enlarge the community and, potentially, its political capital and resource base.

The changing internal Latino demography and the strategic development of an expanding Latino population base are not mutually exclusive evolutions. Some writers on Latino politics have characterized the political actions of Latino activists as perpetuating ethnicity or pan-ethnicity in order to ensure a political base and a following. Thus, these leaders may not reflect the assimilation and upward mobility that many Latinos are achieving. This perspective goes to the very heart of community and community building. The realities of daily living among Latino subgroup members include contact and awareness of not only fellow national-origin members but also other Latinos in their community and elsewhere.

The four factors that I have identified in Latino development in the United States are intended to provide consistent themes and concepts that will carry the discussion throughout this book. The themes include (1) diversity within and between Latino subgroups; (2) common linkages across the subgroups historically, culturally, linguistically, and politically; (3) the internal dynamics among Latinos defining, refining, and strategically developing their communities; and (4) the role of external forces, such as public policies (Voting Rights and Civil Rights acts, affirmative action initiatives, etc.) and public opinion and movements (antibilingual, anti–affirmative action, and **English-only initiatives**, restrictive and punitive immigration measures, etc.) that activate the Latino communities. Thus, Latino politics result from the interaction of initiatives undertaken by persons and organizations across the various Latino subcommunities, as well as the social and political structures, practices, and attitudes of the larger U.S. political community. I began this chapter by introducing the concept of community and its current and historical operationalization within the broader Latino communities. In the next section, I provide greater clarity and direction.

Is There a Latino Community and What Does That Mean?

The delineation of Latinos or Hispanics has centered on notions of a group of people linked by a common language, interrelated cultural traditions and values, and similar experiences in the United States. Since the 1990s, social scientists have added that a common experience with discrimination and relegation to minority status in most facets of American life have accented a sense of group identification. Measures of socioeconomic and political disparities are often used to enjoin ethnic status with unequal opportunities and rights.

Each Latino subgroup has a unique history in the United States, experience of contact with and migration to this country, social class distribution, and legal status: that of political refugee, legal permanent resident alien, or undocumented migrant. Two bases of community I will present are associated with the concepts of commonalty of culture and commonalty of interests (García and Pedraza-Bailey 1990; Cornell and Hartman 1998). **Communities of common or similar cultures** endure when persons are tied together naturally by their involvement in a common system of purpose with accompanying patterns of traditional interactions and behaviors rooted in a common heritage (Cornell 1985). This common heritage or tradition includes national ancestry, language, religion and religious customs, observance of holidays and festivals, and familial networks. For the Mexican-origin population, Keefe and Padilla (1989) explore Chicano ethnicity and identify several dimensions of culture. When familial interactions are primary and serve as conduits of cultural transmission, the "products" are customs, folklore, linguistic loyalty, ethnic loyalty, and group identity. Thus, a person can be enveloped by a sense of ethnicity, usually within a national-origin context (Mexican American, Salvadoran, Dominican, etc.). However, this sense of ethnicity may not automatically lead to community actions.

The idea of a **community of interests** revolves around persons who are united by a common set of economic and political interests. This connection may be due in part to group members' concentration in certain industries and occupational sectors and in residential enclaves (Denton and Massey 1988; Croucher 1997); it may also be due to their common experience of political disenfranchisement (T. Smith 1990; J. A. García 1986a) and differential treatment based on ancestry, phenotype, immigrant status, language, and various other cultural traits and practices. Clearly, there is an intersection of cultural status and interests. The result of perceived and accepted common interests may lead to the development of a new or reinforced identity. For example, the "official usage" of pan-ethnic terms such as *Hispanic* may reorient a person to incorporate that label and strategically use that identity to maximize political effect. A Mexican American activist in Arizona might oppose a referendum effort to remove bilingual education programs because such programs do not ensure educational excellence and equity for all Hispanic children. The Latino subcommunity is the reality experienced by Mexican-origin children; yet, the broader identifier "Hispanic" is used to contextualize the issue nationally as well as locally.

The concept of a community of interests works to examine and construct new boundaries of group affiliation; it also aids analysis of comparable conditions among other social groups and of structural relations between the group and social and political institutions. A central element within these analytical insights is the role played by discriminatory practices and prejudicial attitudes on the part of the larger society and manifested in public policies.

For example, the Immigration and Naturalization Service may conduct sweeps only or primarily in Latino residential neighborhoods. If only individuals who appear Latino are detained to show proof of legal status, then that policy action has a disparate impact on Latino communities. This dimension, discrimination, is certainly attached to being recognized as a minority. In 2010, the state of Arizona passed a law enabling local and state law enforcement officers to detain persons until they provide proof of legal status. (I discuss this particular issue and resulting litigation battles in chapter 9.) For our purposes, minority status is a relational concept in which minority-group members have limited access, opportunity, power, and influence. The issues of empowerment, representation, equity, power, access, and participation become a major part of defining a community and its interests.

The dimension of commonalty—community linkages, bonds, affinities, interactions, and individual affiliations—is important in our discussion of Latino community. This collectivity is a nexus of various associations, but this does not require uniformity or complete consensus among all of the Latino subcommunities. The theme of diversity and similarity emphasizes that conformity and unanimity are not realistic expectations for community membership and operations. While the analogy is not perfect, variations in character, lifestyle, personality, and so on, can be found within most families and can challenge the maintenance of a family entity, but the family structure still remains.

If Latino subcommunities can share commonalties of culture and interest, each can work interactively with the other. That is, cultural cues and symbols can encourage persons of Spanish origin to work toward specific goals and objectives. At the same time, cultural maintenance and practices can serve as the political content of a Latino political agenda. For example, the use of—or at least exposure to—Spanish language while growing up serves as a common cultural experience. It also serves as a point of political conflict in respect to English as the official language of the United States, structuring and maintaining bilingual educational programs, and loyalty to and assimilation with American society. The persistence of Latino culture fuels the politics of culture. In our broadest sense, commonalty of culture and interests can be seen as perceptions and experiences among Latinos that reflect positive affinities and substantial interactions and awareness of Latinos in the various subcommunities.

In the past twenty years, a growing body of literature has developed the concept of pan-ethnicity (Espiritu 1992; Hayes-Bautista and Chapa 1987; Cornell and Hartman 1998). The work by Padilla (1986) explores this concept in the context of the Latino population in Chicago. Padilla espouses the idea of Latino consciousness, which includes both an ideological and a pragmatic sense of group identity. The ideological aspect conceives of the interrelatedness among persons of Spanish origin in terms of their communal cultural values and routines in addition to political, economic, and social conditions and consequences. The latter connection ties in structural biases and policies that disadvantage persons who are Mexican, Guatemalan, Colombian, and so on. Thus, there is a cost to being Latino, in terms of opportunities, equity, access, and rights, that transcends any specific Latino subgroup.

The pragmatic dimension of Padilla's Latino consciousness contemplates the potential benefits of expanding community beyond national-origin boundaries. In this way, a group is significantly enlarged. I have already referred to the demographic explosion within the Latino subcommunities. Rather than 1 million Cubans in the United States, we can talk about 45 million Latinos. The larger population base and greater national geographic dispersion serve to enhance greater political effectiveness and visibility. At the same time, larger numbers do not necessarily translate into guaranteed political power. In some ways, the pragmatic nature of creating a Latino community is a strategic move to expand the potential political resource base by accenting both commonalties of culture and interests.

I use the concepts of commonalty of interests and culture as two foundational bases for the creation and maintenance of the Latino community. I explicitly view these clusters as both perceptions and experiences that can produce positive affinities and meaningful interactions between activists in the various Latino subcommunities. I present two significant challenges: converting the conceptual discussion into explicit operational indicators of these community links and gaining access to data and other measures to explore community building. I have chosen to use some demographic information to move beyond the conceptualization of community.

Referring to the results of the **Latino National Survey** (LNS) (Fraga et al. 2006a), I examine cultural factors and socioeconomic status among Latinos living in the United States during 2005 and 2006. The LNS affords me the opportunity to examine more Latino subgroups than the earlier **Latino National Political Survey** (LNPS). In this way, my examination of the extent of a broad community among Latinos has significant political ramifications for the future of Latino political influence and impact in the larger political system.

Spanish Language Use among Latinos

Spanish language has consistently been identified as one of the cultural glues for Latinos, an identification supported by the LNS. While several items tapped Spanish language, we chose to use the language of the interview that the Latinos employed in the survey, which is a more direct measure of language use than self-reporting (Padilla 1974). Among the 8,634 respondents, 61.9 percent conducted their interview in Spanish. While Spanish is still prevalent among the Latino communities, some variations exist among the various Latino subgroups. More than 66 percent of the Cubans answered the survey in Spanish, while 39.7 and 61.6 percent of Puerto Rican and Mexican-origin respondents, respectively, conducted their interviews in Spanish. On the other hand, Dominicans (79.1 percent), Salvadorans (81.8 percent), and Guatemalans (81.9 percent) demonstrated much higher rates for conducting Spanish-language interviews. Obviously, there was an overlap between language of the interview and birthplace (whether in the United States or abroad). Over the course of our analysis, the distinctions of language use, nativity, and generational status in the United States are key elements in assessing the cross-cutting connections among Latinos.

Age Structure and Latinos

Another way to illustrate some differences of language use among Latinos is age. If we look at Latinos under twenty-five, for this age group, only 49.4 percent of respondents completed the survey in Spanish, as opposed to 58.9 percent of Latinos over the age of fifty-five. Thus, the issue of connectedness among Latinos is only partially demonstrated by the language respondents used in the LNS. Other aspects related to language—use, awareness, loyalty, and exposure—also contribute to the language domain of Latinos. For example, the growth of Spanish-language media—especially on television (Telemundo, Galávision, and Univision)—confirms the existence of Spanish-language markets and mass media transmission of culture and Spanish language. The number one radio station in the Los Angeles metropolitan area is KLVE, whose programming includes Latin pop, urban hip-hop, and traditional music.

Educational Attainment Levels

Another demographic dimension common to Latino group members is educational attainment. The extent of education achieved provides valuable political resources as well as potential areas of common interest. In the LNS, we find some differences based on nativity among the Latino respondents. For example, slightly less than 3 percent of the Latino foreign-born had no education, while only 0.66 percent of the native-born had no education. On the other hand, for those who had less than eight years of schooling, the difference was more marked (23.8 percent versus 3 percent). Finally, if we look at the other end of the educational spectrum (i.e., those with college degrees), there are nearly twice as many native-born graduates (19.2 percent versus 10.3 percent). Again, the factors of age, language use, and nativity proved to be key determinants of educational attainment for all Latinos. I explore subgroup differences as I develop the notion of a community of interests and common or similar cultures. For example, the nature of Cuban migration and selective class out-migration reinforced exodus of the professional and educated classes from Cuba (Portes and Rumbaut 1990; Pedraza-Bailey 1985). The Mexican-origin respondents have the greater concentration of persons at the lower end of the educational range (i.e., 31.4 percent with six years of schooling or less), as well an overrepresentation of foreign-born persons in the lower educational categories.

Household Income among Latinos

Another dimension of similarity is economic resources and household income. Again, if we differentiate income levels by nativity, native-born Latinos consistently have higher levels of household income. More than two-fifths (41.7 percent) of the foreign-born households earn less than $25,000 per year, compared to 17.4 percent of the native-born households. At the other end of the income spectrum (households with $65,000), five times as many native-born households (23.1 percent versus 4.7 percent, respectively) fall into this upper-income bracket. This brief use of the LNS serves to illustrate an economic divide based upon nativity status; yet, examination of occupational location and employment status does not exhibit as significant differences. Nevertheless, the maintenance of a community centers on the connections that exist and operate among a large and diverse Latino base.

Religious Affiliation and Religiosity

Commonalties of culture and interests include the religious dimension. The popular view of the religious affiliation for most Latinos is that Catholicism dominates across all of the subgroups. If we look at the religious affiliation of LNS respondents, we find general support for this characterization. Fully 71.3 percent of all Latinos are Catholics with some subgroup variations. Puerto Rican Catholics are closer to 60 percent; Mexican-origin respondents, 75.4 percent; Salvadorans, 57.5 percent; Cubans, 66 percent; and Dominicans, 72.2 percent. On the other hand, 13 percent of Latinos are affiliated with Protestant denominations, with the balance (8.8 percent) practicing some other religion or having no affiliation. The centrality of Catholicism is a major aspect of Latino communities.

Another view of religion, its significance, and its commonalty is provided by a follow-up question to LNS respondents regarding frequency of religious attendance. The Latinos were asked to indicate how often they attended church (from every week, to once or twice a month, to almost never).[6] Slightly more than half answered at least once every week; yet, there were noticeable differences between Catholics and non-Catholics. Of the Latino Protestants, over three-fourths attended church weekly compared to 55 percent for Catholics. In addition, the LNS included an item that asked Latinos how much religion served as a significant guide for their daily lives. Again, there were some differences between Latino Catholics and Protestants. Over three-fifths of Latino Catholics responded that religion provided a great deal of guidance, whereas four-fifths of their Protestant counterparts responded as such. The pervasiveness of religion in the Latino community can serve as another basis for connectedness to help establish one kind of commonalty—religion. But Latinos are not monolithic, and religiosity is somewhat stronger among Latino Protestants. The critical point is that there is warrant for considering religion a cultural connector for Latinos.

The Pan-ethnic Dimension and the "Latino-Hispanic" Label

Pan-ethnicity, as discussed so far, refers to the process of group formation due to common conditions and bases for community. The other critical component lies with the situational nature of pan-ethnicity. That is, individuals can consciously choose a group identity that serves a specific utility—political, for our purposes. Since Latinos can be viewed as aggregating over twenty national-origin groups, I would posit that there need not be a "natural" clustering based on that connection, as practical and strategic purposes are served by using a pan-ethnic identity. Works by Padilla (1986), Espiritu (1996, 1997), Nagel (1996), and Cornell and Hartman (1998) have helped develop the concept of pan-ethnicity.

Group consciousness and social identity constitute significant building blocks for this concept. Group consciousness refers to the cognitive elements of group attachment; a person incorporates group identity(ies) as part of his social identity, along with evaluative assessments about the group's relative position in society. This identity represents an attachment and affinity to social groupings. For our purposes, persons of Mexican, Dominican, and Colombian origin, for example, can include a sense of pan-ethnic group attachment and affiliation in addition to their own national origin or ancestry. In addition, many other social identities (parental roles, work groups, etc.) can constitute a person's social identity constellation. While the literature on social identity and group consciousness focuses on the individual dynamics of identity, clearly the social context can establish or reinforce the basis for group affiliation and affinity. For students of American politics, a long-standing phenomenon is the transformation of ancestral groups into minority groups. Minority status is associated with differential treatment and power, being an identifiable group, and group awareness. For Latinos, language, customs, phenotype (to some extent), and social networks help promote that identifiability. At the same time, stereotypes and prejudicial attitudes toward Latinos, as well as unfair treatment, can serve to perpetuate identifiability.

The "Latinization" of the United States (Fox 1997; Cuello 1996; Benitez 2007) over the last three decades has been accompanied by the transformation of immigrant and indigenous groups into minority groups (Wilson 1977). Miami is now recognized as a Latino city in which Cubans have important political and economic influence. Los Angeles, with its sizable Mexican-origin and growing Central American communities, rivals cities in Latin America in terms of population concentrations. One out of every five persons in Chicago is Latino, with a mix of Mexican, Puerto Rican, and Central American origins. New York has not only a large Puerto Rican population but also fast-growing Dominican, Colombian, and Peruvian communities. Three national Spanish-language television networks broadcast daily throughout the United States and Latin America. In sections of many U.S. cities, most residents speak English infrequently, and streets are lined with Latino-based and -oriented businesses. As Cuello (1996) points out, this nation has undergone dramatic and cultural changes in a very Latino sort of way.

For our purposes, the Latinization of the United States has a direct impact on the U.S. political system and processes. I have begun to define this connection in terms of building community among these diverse and similarly based subcommunities. In this section, the focus on pan-ethnicity reflects the cognitive and psychological dimensions of group identity and consciousness. Such group identity represents an affinity with and sense of attachment to a broader social category than national origin alone. Obviously, other social groupings can serve as the basis for other group identities. In the earlier edition of this book, relying on the LNPS, evidence of group identity is concentrated within national group boundaries (García et al. 1994); each person is attached to a Mexicano, Cubano, or other Latino subgroup country.

Building on the concept of group consciousness (Verba and Nie 1972; Miller et al. 1981; J. A. García 1982), we focus on two key dimensions: an evaluation of one's group status politically in American society and a collective orientation toward social and political action. For Latinos, individuals with a group consciousness have a positive affinity for being Latino; they assess their group as experiencing lower levels of socioeconomic and political status, and they are inclined to participate in some collective activity to change the situation. My reference to pan-ethnicity falls within the general discussion of group identification. That is, instead of a Guatemalan thinking of himself in exclusively national-origin terms,[7] he could include Latino (a broader group aggregation) as well. Works by Padilla (1986), Espiritu (1992), Nagel (1996), Hayes-Bautista and Chapa (1987), and Nelson and Tienda (1985) have used, to varying degrees, the concepts of group identity and group consciousness to construct pan-ethnicity.

By exploring the extent of "Latino-ness" or "Hispanicity" in the context of community building or bridging the twenty-plus Latino national-origin groups, we can establish the basis for a political community. In addition, we are examining the relevance and impact of such community formation on the larger political system. The latter point encompasses the identification of issues and public policy preferences, organizational and leadership development, political **mobilization**, electoral politics and representation, and policy implementation. While much attention has been directed toward the phenomenal population growth of Latinos over the past several decades, our perspective does not revolve around growth per se. Population size and geographic location and concentration can serve as a resource base, but converting numbers of persons into an effective political base requires additional elements.

As is consistent with the internal and external dynamics affecting Latino community building, the process of constructing or developing a Latino identity and affinity can stem from situations and conditions within the Latino subcommunities as well as general societal developments. For example, work by Padilla (1986) in Chicago highlights the conscious efforts by leadership in the various Latino communities (Mexican, Puerto Rican, Cuban, etc.) to promote a pan-ethnic identity. The use and social meaning of the word "Latino" to reflect a community of Spanish-speaking and culturally and politically similar groups was evident in the early 1970s.

One of the focus groups conducted as part of the Latino National Survey in 2005 was held in Chicago. A central area of exploration was identity and labeling. A group of fifteen to twenty Latinos (of varied national origins and ages) participated in a discussion of how each saw him- or herself. For the most part, each person included being Latino as part of his or her social identity. In fact, without any cues from the focus facilitator, the use of "Latino" and/or "Hispanic" was very commonplace in most everyone's conversation. In addition, participants' characterization of what use of those terms meant reflected a sense of community among all persons of Latino background. For our purposes, self-description as Latino or Hispanic indicates the integral role of that identity without its being the only identity a person internalizes.

An earlier example from the LNPS Chicago focus groups is the set of responses from one young adult Latina. Her parents were of "mixed" Latino background—one was Puerto Rican and the other Mexican. She had married an Italian and lived in a South Side Polish Catholic neighborhood. Her parents were divorced. She described a series of situations in which her four-year-old daughter was already attuned to her sense of identity. When visiting her grandmother, the granddaughter referred to her Mexican-ness, and when visiting her grandfather, she accented her Puerto Rican identity. At the same time, while living in her South Side neighborhood, the young girl placed greater emphasis on her father's Italian ancestry. In school, the young girl was more likely to refer to her European or white ethnic background. When traveling on the bus from the far South Side to the Loop (downtown commercial area), she was quick to identify herself as a minority or person of color. Finally, with her mother and her uncle (mother's brother), she referred to herself as a Latina.

Conclusion

This real-life illustration is intended to present a clearer picture of the identity process and how situations help influence it. Persons can assume multiple identities without feeling divided loyalties or confusion. It also illustrates how within-group socialization and external cues influence the identification process. For our purposes, the development of a sense of being Latino can be a "product" of shared cultural values and practices (language, origins, traditions, etc.), intergroup interactions, and societal constructs (positive, but usually negative) of persons of Spanish origin. As we examine the development and existence of community among persons of Latino origin in the

United States, our primary purpose is to explore the linkages of community to the political realms of agenda setting, political mobilization, political resource development, and public policy outcomes and implementation.

Discussion Questions

1. Communities of interests and common or similar cultures have been identified as building blocks for Latino communities. Given a significant foreign-born segment, how much do such persons' experiences connect with those of their native-born counterparts?
2. It is common for the media, individuals, and public officials to use the terms *Latino* and *Hispanic*. What is in a label? That is, how are these terms used, and what difference does it make to use one descriptor or the other?
3. A good part of this chapter examines socioeconomic characteristics among Latinos as a basis for identifying common interests. How else might you approach this connection, and what indicators would you use?
4. Latinos include persons from many different countries of origin and live in different parts of the United States. How do these aspects affect the development of Latino common interests?

CHAPTER 3

Culture and Demographics

¿Somos parte de la amplia comunidad de latinos o principalmente parte de una comunidad específica y bien definida? Los valores, el idioma, las tradiciones y estilos de vivir son aspectos del carácter de cada uno de nosotros. ¿Las dimensiones de las culturas comunes y las circunstancias diarias son nuestra realidad o dudamos eso?

Are we part of an extended Latino community or primarily a part of a specific, well-defined community? Values, language, traditions, and lifestyles are aspects of the character of each one of us. Are these dimensions of our common cultures and our daily circumstances part of our reality, or do we doubt that?

THIS CHAPTER INTRODUCES ANOTHER WAY to amplify the bases for community among Latinos. Clearly, there is a greater awareness among the larger public about the presence of Latinos. Continued releases by the U.S. Census Bureau regarding racial and Spanish-origin population counts have emphasized the sustained levels of growth for Latinos. The major themes have been continuing high population growth and the broader geographic presence of Latinos throughout the United States. The visible "impressions" about Latinos' significant population growth (to which immigration is a major contributor) and their cultural persistence (manifested mostly through Spanish-language use) have reinvigorated public interest in these communities. Who are Latinos? How many are there? Where do they live, and what are they like? Our basic theme of community building is grounded on the understanding that even though Latinos are ancestrally linked to a variety of countries, they have historic and cultural ties as well as common circumstances and conditions living in the United States. The labels "Latino" and "Hispanic" have been used to identify persons of Spanish origin. In some cases, these persons can point to long-established communities in the United States dating to the seventeenth century. Other Latinos are more recent residents of the United States, while still others have been here for some intermediate length of time. Latinos are among both the oldest groups in America and the most recent newcomers.

Pan-ethnic group affinity is not automatic; nor is it always positive. Individuals are more likely to have stronger affinities with their country of origin than with a larger, "socially constructed" grouping or cluster called "Latino/Hispanic." The term *social construct* refers to any occurrence or phenomenon invented or constructed by a society. This group of people could get together and formulate the idea of something like a different sense of **ethnicity**. When we say that something is socially constructed, we are focusing on its dependence on contingent variables of our social selves rather than any inherent quality that it possesses in itself. Thus, our notion of a Latino—what this term does and does not include and what it means to us—does not exist out there in the world but only in and through the social institutions and leadership that give it meaning within a culture. Typically, assumptions about reality, knowledge, and learning form the basis for social constructs.

The notion of a socially constructed group is usually contrasted with the idea of primordial or fundamental characteristics that attach individuals to a group, such as language, ancestry or bloodline, phenotypical traits, and other aspects of culture and tradition. I have tried to make clear that an essential part of Latino politics is bridging national-origin boundaries and developing an additional sense of being connected to other persons and communities of Spanish-origin ancestry and background. Thus, we are exploring the expanded boundaries of social identity that incorporate a sense of group consciousness and connectedness that goes beyond national boundaries. This is accomplished through conscious efforts, policies, and consciousness raising by leaders and social institutions to create this additional social category. In this chapter, I provide a brief demographic profile of the Spanish-origin communities to help identify some important features of these populations and essential background information contributing to a sense of being Latino in America.

By 2010, the Hispanic or Latino population numbered over 48.4 million persons. This represented approximately 12.5 percent of the total U.S. population (see figure 3.1). Our theme of significant population growth can be seen over a longer period. In the 1970 census, the Spanish-origin population (Hernandez, Estrada, and Alvirez 1973) was 9.6 million and constituted some 4.7 percent of the U.S. population. Subsequent growth was most evident between the 1990 and 2000 decennial censuses, when the Latino population increased by over 57 percent to reach 35.3 million persons (the total U.S. population increased by 11.5 percent). The 1990 census revealed the same

FIGURE 3.1. Population size of Latinos, 2000 to 2006.

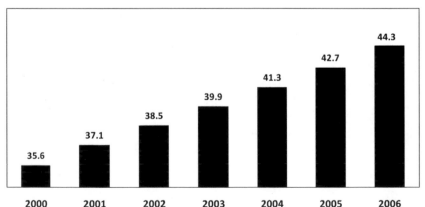

Source: Adapted from a presentation created by the Ethnicity and Ancestry Branch Population Division, U.S. Census Bureau.

pattern as Latinos had increased by 53 percent (compared to 9.8 percent for the overall population) to number 22.4 million (see figure 3.2). In the first decade of the new millennium, Latino growth continues to outpace that of the general non-Hispanic population (32.9 percent versus 4.7 percent). The growth trajectory predicted that Hispanics would become the largest minority group by 2005; yet, Census 2000 indicated that mark was reached by 2001.

Our theme of the continued significant growth rate among Latinos is reflected further by population projections well into the mid-twenty-first century. As indicated in figures 3.2 and 3.3, Latinos are projected to exceed 100 million and comprise nearly one-fourth of the total U.S. population in 2050. According to the 2050 projection, a base population of 12.5 million (in 2000) will have doubled in the span of forty years. Figure 3.4 indicates the annual components of population change from 2000 to 2006. This substantial growth rate is attributed to the three primary factors associated with most population increases: (1) significant portions of the female population in the fertility age range, (2) higher birthrates than the general population, and (3) international migration. The spike in international migration evidenced in the mid-1990s remains significant as 52.4 percent of the contribution of Latino growth is attributed to net international migration (see figure 3.4). With a younger population and greater percentage of Latinas in the fertility age range, births as a contributor of growth will be higher in the future.

A more recent trend is the wider geographic distribution of Latinos across more states. Figure 3.5 illustrates the percentage change in population by region for the general population and Latinos. While the overall rate of change for Latinos was 24.3 percent, two regions exceeding that level were the Midwest and the South. The southern region

FIGURE 3.2. Historical view of Hispanic population in the United States, 1970 to 2050.

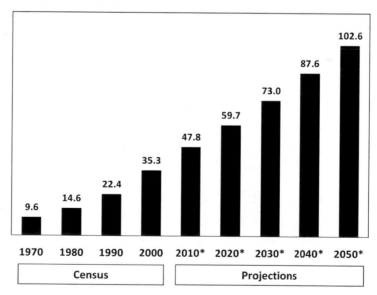

Source: Adapted from a presentation created by the Ethnicity and Ancestry Branch Population Division, U.S. Census Bureau.

FIGURE 3.3. Examination of Hispanic population growth as percentage of total U.S. population, 1970 to 2050.

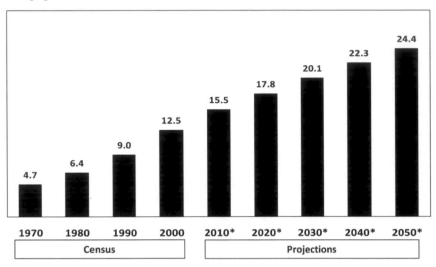

*Projected Population as of July 1

Source: Adapted from a presentation created by the Ethnicity and Ancestry Branch Population Division, U.S. Census Bureau.

especially experienced marked gains of Latinos in Georgia, North Carolina, Arkansas, and South Carolina. In the Midwest, rural counties saw Latinos, especially immigrants, moving to these destinations. One of the resultant effects has been major adjustments with residential populations that are quite unfamiliar with Latinos, including immigrants.

FIGURE 3.4. Percentage Hispanic and their contributions to annual components of change, 2000 to 2006.

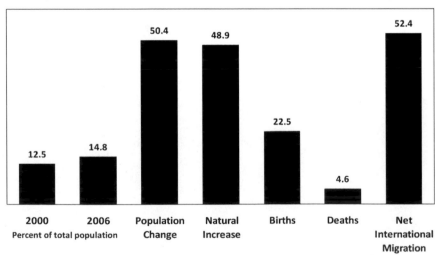

Source: Adapted from a presentation created by the Ethnicity and Ancestry Branch Population Division, U.S. Census Bureau.

FIGURE 3.5. Percentage change in population by region for Latinos, 2000 to 2006.

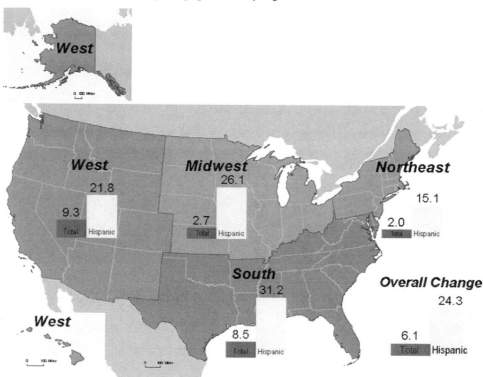

Source: Adapted from a presentation created by the Ethnicity and Ancestry Branch Population Division, U.S. Census Bureau.

In addition, we need to examine the makeup of the Latino community by looking at the major subgroups' composition. The Mexican-origin community has been historically the largest subgroup, composing almost 60 percent of all Latinos. Persons of Mexican origin, Mexican Americans, or Chicanos have had even higher growth rates than the overall Latino rate (92.9 percent from 1970 to 1980 and 54.4 percent from 1980 to 1990). This pattern continued into the 1990s with both higher birthrates and immigration contributing to these gains (64.3 percent in 2007) (see table 3.1). The second-largest component of the Latino communities is the Puerto Rican, or Boricua, population, numbering 4.1 million persons. The next largest group is the Cubans, or Cubanos, who represent 3.5 percent of all Latinos. Beyond these three largest Latino subgroups, greater specificity has been more difficult to achieve.

Demographically, the rest of the Latino community is consolidated into three general categories: Central Americans, including persons from El Salvador, Guatemala, Panama, and Nicaragua; people from Spanish-speaking South American countries such as Colombia, Peru, Venezuela, and Argentina; and people from the other Spanish-speaking areas of the Caribbean, particularly the Dominican Republic. These segments have represented the faster-growing elements since the 1990s. They include more immigrants and refugees[1] (fewer native-born persons) and are settling in both longer-established Latino communities and newer destinations in the South, Midwest, and New England. Part of their settlement pattern includes certain eastern suburban com-

TABLE 3.1. Number, Percentage, and Percentage Distribution of U.S. Population by Nativity and Race/Ethnicity with Hispanic Subgroups, 2007

Race/Ethnicity and Subgroup	Total Population	Percentage Native	Foreign-born		
			Number	Percentage	Percentage Distribution
Total[a]	301,621,200	86.1	41,820,700	13.9	100.0
White	198,594,500	95.4	9,097,000	4.6	21.8
Black	36,624,900	91.8	3,002,900	8.2	7.2
Hispanic	45,378,600	56.4	19,806,300	43.7	47.4
Mexican	29,189,300	59.5	11,812,300	40.5	28.3
Puerto Rican	4,114,700	64.8	1,448,300	35.2	3.5
Cuban	1,608,800	37.5	1,004,900	62.5	2.4
Dominican	1,198,800	37.9	744,000	62.1	1.8
Salvadoran	1,473,500	33.3	983,400	66.7	2.4
Other Central American	2,059,100	31.2	1,417,000	68.8	3.4
South American	2,500,800	28.9	1,779,000	71.1	4.3
Other Hispanic or Latino	3,233,500	80.9	617,300	19.1	1.5
Two or more races	4,785,900	92.6	356,000	7.4	0.9

Source: U.S. Department of Commerce, Census Bureau, American Community Survey, 2007.
Note: Population estimates may differ from those in other tables due to time of year of estimation. Race categories exclude persons of Hispanic ethnicity. Detail may not sum to totals because of rounding.
[a]Total includes other race/ethnicity categories not separately shown.

munities, such as Long Island, New York. The influx of Latinos into areas of previously low concentration became quite significant during the 1990s. For example, Central Americans have become the largest Latino element in Washington, DC; Dominican and Colombian populations are rivaling the Puerto Ricans in New York City; Puerto Ricans and Central Americans are the fasting-growing Latino subgroups in Florida. It has been estimated that both the Salvadoran and Dominican communities will exceed the size of the Cuban community by 2011. Salvadoran Americans are now the fourth-largest Latino group in the United States, according to 2010 census figures. Those whose roots extend to El Salvador, one of the smallest and densest countries in the Western Hemisphere, now number more than 1.6 million in the United States, and about 35 percent reside in California. The latest tally means that Salvadoran Americans have surpassed Dominican Americans in number and are swiftly gaining on Cuban Americans (O'Brien 2011).

Even though the distribution of Latinos by state has broadened, the established states of settlement have remained. That is, the top ten states for Latinos (California, Texas, New York, Florida, Illinois, Arizona, New Jersey, New Mexico, Colorado, and Washington) represent almost 88 percent of the total Latino population. California and Texas are home to almost half of all Latinos—nearly 22 million. Other states with significant Latino populations include New York, Florida, Illinois, New Mexico, and Arizona. Latinos reside in large, populous states, with substantial electoral votes and industrial and expanding service economies. The numbers of Latinos for these primary state residences have exceeded critical mass.[2] That is, Latino populations are the largest minority group in twenty-seven states, and in an increasing number of states, they comprise more than 5 percent of the state's population. This development illustrates that a Latino political presence has been established, and political **mobilization** is a critical element for further political development.

In 1998 then Texas governor George W. Bush incorporated a targeted effort to seek Hispanic support through public policies such as bilingual education reform and funding and opposition to anti-immigrant and **English-only initiatives.** On the other hand, between 1994 and 1998, former California governor Pete Wilson supported several statewide propositions (e.g., against immigration, affirmative action, and bilingual education) that resulted in increased Latino **political participation** and declining support for the Republican Party. Since 2003, the rise in anti-immigrant state initiatives (e.g., **Arizona Senate Bill 1070**) has had a partisan effect. For the most part, these initiatives have been proposed and passed by Republican elected officials with substantial Latino protests. In chapter 6 on political engagement, we discuss this and related developments in light of the significant Latino immigrant segment.

In addition, the population growth of Latinos within the various states has been appreciable. For example, while Latinos represent one-third of the state population of California, their 29.1 percent increase has occurred since 1990. Similarly, in states like Texas and Florida, the Latino population has increased since 1990 by more than 30 percent. Resultant gains in political representation (i.e., additional congressional seats via reapportionment) are quite evident in these top ten states. The decennial census for 2010 has resulted in additional congressional seats for Arizona, Nevada, Texas, and Florida, which are among the top ten states for Hispanics. Even in states that may lose some congressional seats (New York, New Jersey, Massachusetts, etc.), Latinos can position themselves to compete actively for the redrawn congressional districts or to serve as a critical voting bloc. We will examine the electoral activities and outcomes in chapter 7.

In the run-up to the 2012 national elections, Latino concentration in California, Texas, Florida, New York, Illinois, and other large electoral college states would see them playing a more pivotal role in congressional and statewide campaigns (i.e., over 220 electoral college votes). The results presented in the tables in this chapter reinforce and amplify the theme of substantial population growth for Latinos over the past three decades. The U.S. Census Bureau population projections for the United States until 2050 corroborate a continued higher growth rate for Latinos than the general population, and Latinos will constitute over one-fifth of the U.S. population.

Culture, Latinos, and Demographics

So far, this demographic profile has centered on the size and national-origin makeup of the Latino communities in the United States. We have also suggested that an important element of the **community of common cultures** would include language and foreign-born origin. The common perception is that the Spanish language unifies Latinos. In 1990, about 14 percent of the U.S. population spoke a language other than English at home; in 2007, the percentage was 19.7 percent. Spanish was the most common non-English language, spoken by over 62.3 percent of all non-English speakers. This represents over 34 million persons. For all Latinos, nearly 79.4 percent reported

TABLE 3.2. Population Five Years and Older Who Spoke a Language Other Than English at Home by Language Group and English-Speaking Ability, 2007

Characteristic	Number or Percentage	English-Speaking Ability			
		Very Well	Well	Not Well	Not at All
NUMBER					
Population five years and older	280,950,438	(X)	(X)	(X)	(X)
Spoke only English at home	225,505,953	(X)	(X)	(X)	(X)
Spoke a language other than English at home	55,444,485	30,975,474	10,962,722	9,011,298	4,494,991
Spoke a language other than English at home	55,444,485	30,975,474	10,962,722	9,011,298	4,494,991
Spanish or Spanish Creole	34,547,077	18,179,530	6,322,170	6,344,110	3,701,267
Other Indo-European languages	10,320,730	6,936,808	2,018,148	1,072,025	293,749
Asian and Pacific Island languages	8,316,426	4,274,794	2,176,180	1,412,264	453,188
Other languages	2,260,252	1,584,342	446,224	182,899	46,787
PERCENTAGE					
Population five years and older	100.0	(X)	(X)	(X)	(X)
Spoke only English at home	80.3	(X)	(X)	(X)	(X)
Spoke a language other than English at home	19.7	55.9	19.8	16.3	8.1
Spoke a language other than English at home	100.0	55.9	19.8	16.3	8.1
Spanish or Spanish Creole	62.3	52.6	18.3	18.4	10.7
Other Indo-European languages	18.6	67.2	19.6	10.4	2.8
Asian and Pacific Island languages	15.0	51.4	26.2	17.0	5.4
Other languages	4.1	70.1	19.7	8.1	2.1

MARGIN OF ERROR[a]

NUMBER

Population five years and older	+/– 17,610	(X)	(X)	(X)	(X)
Spoke only English at home	+/– 109,811	(X)	(X)	(X)	(X)
Spoke a language other than English at home	+/– 106,562	+/– 91,882	+/– 63,961	+/– 62,294	+/– 52,259
Spoke a language other than English at home	+/– 106,562	+/– 91,882	+/– 63,961	+/– 62,294	+/– 52,259
Spanish or Spanish Creole	+/– 75,004	+/– 73,911	+/– 54,178	+/– 46,667	+/– 49,121
Other Indo-European languages	+/– 68,048	+/– 54,386	+/– 27,604	+/– 19,313	+/– 12,666
Asian and Pacific Island languages	+/– 45,036	+/– 32,514	+/– 24,871	+/– 25,587	+/– 14,138
Other languages	+/– 43,582	+/– 33,444	+/– 14,425	+/– 9,743	+/– 5,102

PERCENTAGE

Population five years and older	(X)	(X)	(X)	(X)	(X)
Spoke only English at home	+/– 0.0	(X)	(X)	(X)	(X)
Spoke a language other than English at home	+/– 0.0	+/– 0.1	+/– 0.1	+/– 0.1	+/– 0.1
Spoke a language other than English at home	+/– 0.0	+/– 0.1	+/– 0.1	+/– 0.1	+/– 0.1
Spanish or Spanish Creole	+/– 0.1	+/– 0.2	+/– 0.1	+/– 0.1	+/– 0.1
Other Indo-European languages	+/– 0.1	+/– 0.3	+/– 0.2	+/– 0.2	+/– 0.1
Asian and Pacific Island languages	+/– 0.1	+/– 0.3	+/– 0.3	+/– 0.3	+/– 0.2
Other languages	+/– 0.1	+/– 0.7	+/– 0.5	+/– 0.4	+/– 0.2

Source: U.S. Census Bureau, American Community Survey, 2007.

Note: An "(X)" means that the estimate is not applicable or not available.

[a]This number added to or subtracted from the estimate yields the 90 percent confidence interval. For more information on the American Community Survey, see www.census.gov/acs/www.

speaking Spanish at home while growing up. In contrast to the percentage of Spanish-speaking Latinos, the second-largest non-English language group was Chinese (5.7 percent). About half of Latinos indicate that they speak English well[3] (see table 3.2).

The data in table 3.2 provide another way to look at Spanish-language use among Latinos. Again, data from the 2007 American Community Study series asked follow-up questions of respondents who indicated they spoke a language other than English. These individuals were questioned about their self-reported English-speaking proficiency. As already mentioned, among all Latinos, slightly more than half speak English very well. Yet, variations surface when the language dimension is examined in terms of Latino subgroups. The Mexican-origin population mirrors the overall percentage of Latino Spanish use. On the other hand, higher percentages of Central Americans and Dominicans do not speak English very well (65.5 and 63.7 percent, respectively). Almost 55 percent of Cubans do not speak English well, while Puerto Ricans have the lowest percentage of persons not speaking English very well.

Speaking Spanish is still a fairly universal experience for most Latinos. The ability to speak Spanish (to whatever degree) and understand or speak English well suggests a bilingual language environment rather than a predominantly non-English-speaking, isolated population. Thus, English-only and loyalty issues continue to occupy the political landscape. Latinos can be seen more as a bilingual group, with a significant first-generation (or foreign-born) segment, than as holding onto their mother tongue exclusively. The role of Spanish-language use, the extent of language loyalty, and the degree to which the public arena reinforces or discourages bilingualism are aspects of Spanish-language persistence for Latinos. In addition, the growth of Spanish-speaking media, particularly networks like Univision and Telemundo, and Spanish-language radio helps meet the service needs of Latinos. Spanish-language media also provide a vehicle for Spanish-language maintenance and acquisition among primarily younger and native-born Latinos. The role and impact of Spanish-language media will be discussed in chapter 7, especially in relation to campaigns and elections.

Latino communities are composed significantly of persons born in Spanish-origin countries. Thus, nativity, or the significant presence of foreign-born persons, perpetuates Spanish-language use, customs, and traditions. Since the 1970s, more Latinos have immigrated into the United States than members of any other group. The composition of U.S. immigration changed dramatically in the latter half of the twentieth century as Latin American and Asian immigrants came to dominate the migration stream. Almost two-fifths of all Latinos residing in the United States are foreign-born. While the percentage of American permanent resident aliens overall is slightly greater than 10 percent,[4] the overall percentage for Latinos is 40 percent (6.1 percent for non-Hispanics). At the same time, the proportion of immigrants for Cubans is the highest of any group.

The number of foreign-born Latinos varies across the different subgroups. Over 60 percent (60.8 percent) of Cubans are foreign-born, as are 77.5 percent of Central Americans and 69.5 percent of South Americans. The Cuban community's foreign-born members have refugee status with access to specific governmental assistance programs, while the rest of Latinos are viewed as economic migrants (there have been initiatives by Salvadorans and Guatemalans to obtain refugee status). Overall, the percentage of foreign-born Latinos is 40 percent compared to foreign-born non-Hispanics at 12.5 percent. Finally, the distinction of Puerto Ricans born in the United

States or on the island is associated with their citizenship status. Puerto Rico is a commonwealth, and Puerto Ricans are U.S. citizens. At the same time, perspectives and experiences among Puerto Ricans may be affected by their place of birth.

Language and nativity (country of birth) are critical cultural dimensions that help define the Latino community of common cultures. The coexistence of native-born and "immigrant" Latinos in the same or proximate neighborhoods, sharing familial social networks, common work environments, and business interactions, provides a regular basis for cultural exchanges and experiences. These interactions can reinforce cultural expressions and values or, perhaps, create cultural tensions over assimilation, acculturation, or even cultural authenticity. Cultural dynamics would be less likely to exist without the persistence of Spanish-language use and the steady influx of immigrants. In addition, the sizable percentage of foreign-born members in Latino communities helps bring forth the extended and complex set of issues and policies related to immigration rights, legal standing, and access to services.

A clear political connection for Latino communities with a significant foreign-born segment is either the extent or the lack of naturalization. Citizenship status links directly with electoral participation, which tends to offset the rapid growth rate that Latinos have experienced. That is, while Latino population growth is very high, the youthfulness and significant noncitizen segment of the Latino community undercuts its corresponding electoral base (see figure 3.6). A legal permanent resident alien can pursue U.S. citizenship after five years' residence. Naturalization requires demonstrating good moral character, knowledge of U.S. government and history, respect for the law, and competence in the English language, as well as completion of a personal interview process and payment of the naturalization filing fees.

There are almost 28 million foreign-born persons in the United States, of whom 41 percent are Hispanics. Of all foreign-born persons in this country, 35.1 percent are naturalized, whereas only 21.6 percent of Hispanics have become citizens (the rate is

FIGURE 3.6. Distribution of U.S. population by nativity status and Hispanic and total population, 2006.

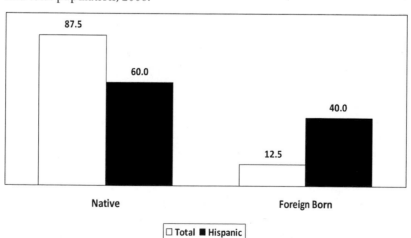

Source: Adapted from a presentation created by the Ethnicity and Ancestry Branch Population Division, U.S. Census Bureau.

45.8 percent for non-Hispanics). Examining those rates by specific Latino subgroups reveals some variation. According to the National Association of Latino Elected and Appointed Officials (NALEO) Educational Fund analysis, 461,317 Latino permanent residents became U.S. citizens in Fiscal Year (FY) 2008. From FY 2007 to FY 2008, Latino naturalizations increased by 95 percent compared to a 58 percent increase for all naturalizations. Mexico was the leading country of birth for persons naturalizing in 2008 (231,815), representing 22 percent of all new citizens. The other Latino subgroups that experienced significant increases in naturalization in FY 2008 were Cubans (160 percent), Salvadorans (109 percent), Nicaraguans (120 percent), and Guatema-

TABLE 3.3. Hispanic Population by Nativity and Type, 2007

Hispanic Type	Total		Native		Foreign-born	
	Number	Percentage	Number	Percentage	Number	Percentage
Total	45,427	100.0	27,361	100.0	18,067	100.0
Caribbean	6,940	15.3	5,181	18.9	1,758	9.7
Cuban	1,611	3.5	628	2.3	983	5.4
Dominican	1,208	2.7	482	1.8	726	4.0
Puerto Rican	4,120	9.1	4,071	14.9	49	0.3
Central American	32,706	72.0	18,713	68.4	13,993	77.5
Costa Rican	118	0.3	47	0.2	70	0.4
Guatemalan	872	1.9	265	1.0	607	3.4
Honduran	533	1.2	153	0.6	380	2.1
Mexican	29,167	64.2	17,538	64.1	11,629	64.4
Nicaraguan	302	0.7	100	0.4	202	1.1
Panamanian	135	0.3	65	0.2	69	0.4
Salvadoran	1,474	3.2	506	1.9	968	5.4
Other Central American	106	0.2	39	0.1	67	0.4
South American	2,499	5.5	761	2.8	1,738	9.6
Argentinean	194	0.4	60	0.2	134	0.7
Bolivian	83	0.2	29	0.1	54	0.3
Chilean	107	0.2	37	0.1	69	0.4
Colombian	799	1.8	243	0.9	555	3.1
Ecuadorian	533	1.2	172	0.6	361	2.0
Peruvian	462	1.0	125	0.5	336	1.9
Uruguayan	50	0.1	13	—	38	0.2
Venezuelan	178	0.4	49	0.2	129	0.7
Other South American	93	0.2	33	0.1	60	0.3
All other Hispanic[a]	3,283	7.2	2,705	9.9	577	3.2

Source: U.S. Census Bureau, 2007 American Community Survey.
Notes: Dash (—) represents zero or rounds to zero. Numbers are in thousands. Data are based on a sample. For information on confidentiality protection, sampling error, nonsampling error, and definitions, see www.census.gov/acs/www.
[a]This category includes all other general Hispanic-origin responses such as "Hispanic," "Spanish," or "Latino."

lans (109 percent). The naturalization percentage for Central and South Americans has been increasing since the turn of the new millennium. Even with these gains, millions of eligible Latinos still have not applied for citizenship, and the increased financial costs have been identified as an impediment. Again, we discuss the foreign-born segment in chapters 4, 5, and 9. The consequences of lower numbers of foreign-born Latino citizens are connected to elections, job opportunities, immigration petitions,[5] and scholarship opportunities (see table 3.3). This demographic sketch serves to establish the size and extent of the group of foreign-born Latinos. Its implications will be analyzed in chapters 7 and 9.

Communities of Interests

Language and immigrant status are two markers of culture and linkage to one's country of origin. In sociological terms, Latinos' social networks can be very dense ethnically with interactions that incorporate Spanish language, cultural practices, and familial contacts with recent arrivals. At the same time, common conditions and situations contribute to a sense of community. Matters like differential treatment, societal stereotypes, and similar socioeconomic status, for example, can serve to connect elements of the Latino community. One such area lies with educational attainment and Latinos. Lower levels of educational attainment, living in poorer school districts, lack of available bilingual programs, and attending "lower-quality" schools are more common experiences among a major segment of the Latino community. Figure 3.7 provides some recent information on the levels of schooling for Latinos and non-Latinos. For the general adult population over twenty-five years of age, over 25 percent graduated from college, and over 80 percent graduated from high school. In comparison, only 11 percent of Latino males and 13 percent of Latinas are college

FIGURE 3.7. Levels of educational attainment for the total population and Hispanics by gender, 2006 (population twenty-five years and older).

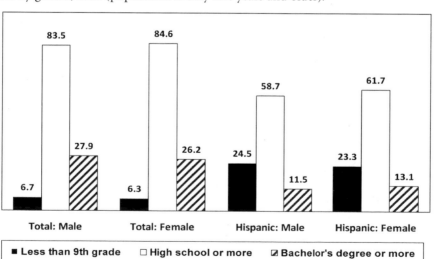

Source: Adapted from a presentation created by the Ethnicity and Ancestry Branch Population Division, U.S. Census Bureau.

FIGURE 3.8. Median age among Hispanics by gender, 2006.

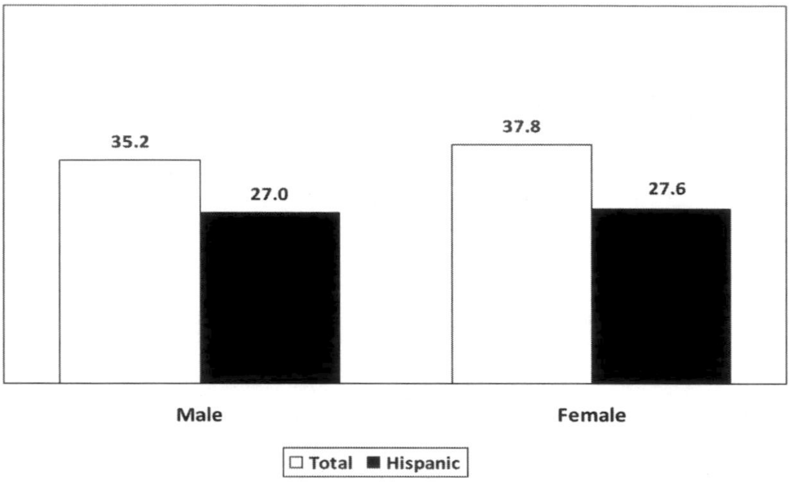

Source: Adapted from a presentation created by the Ethnicity and Ancestry Branch Population Division, U.S. Census Bureau.

graduates, and less than 60 percent are high school graduates. There are indications that younger cohorts of Latinos are completing more schooling than older ones; yet, the gap between non-Latinos and Latinos is widening. In terms of subgroup educational attainment, some differences are present. The Mexican-origin segment fares less well, as 47 percent are high school graduates, whereas 64 percent of Cubans graduated from high school.

Another important consideration is the differential in the educational attainment between U.S.-born and foreign-born Latinos (70 percent versus 42 percent are high school graduates, respectively). Again we see how immigrant status influences socio-economic status and highlights certain institutions and policy areas. In addition to Latino subgroup status, the age structure for each group is relevant. For example, the Mexican-origin segment and Puerto Ricans have young populations, while the Cubans are older than the median age for non-Latinos (see figure 3.8). Therefore, the presence of Latino children in our school systems comes primarily from the former two Latino subgroups. The gamut of relevant educational issues includes bilingual education, quality of educational facilities and programs, access for immigrant children, school retention rates and discipline policies (Meier and Stewart 1991; San Miguel 1987), and participation in school decision making. A discussion in chapters 8 and 9 of public policy will relate these issues to the Latino community.

Another aspect of socioeconomic life for Latinos lies in the labor market. Labor force participation rates, especially for Latino males, have been higher than those for the general population. In addition, Latinos are more concentrated in blue-collar jobs and in the service, manufacturing, and construction industries. Thus, if more Latinos tend to be occupationally "stratified" and located in particular industry sectors, then issues, problems, and union or organizational connections serve as common bases for mobilization and action. Figures 3.9 and 3.10 present occupational information for Latinos and non-Latinos by gender and the total population for comparison. One significant feature lies in the differential unemployment rate between the two. Latino

FIGURE 3.9. Occupational distribution among employed Hispanic males, 2006 (population sixteen years and older).

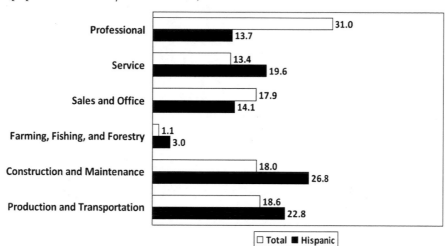

Source: Adapted from a presentation created by the Ethnicity and Ancestry Branch Population Division, U.S. Census Bureau.

unemployment for males and females is 50 to 100 percent greater than for their non-Latino counterparts.

Two general occupational clusters (professional, administrative and sales, and service versus skilled and production and transportation) illustrate a common foundation among Latinos. Whereas non-Latino males are evenly divided between the professional/administrative and skilled/semiskilled occupations, the distribution among Latino males is more skewed toward the service and skilled/unskilled jobs (27 and 73

FIGURE 3.10. Occupational distribution among employed Hispanic females, 2006 (population sixteen years and older).

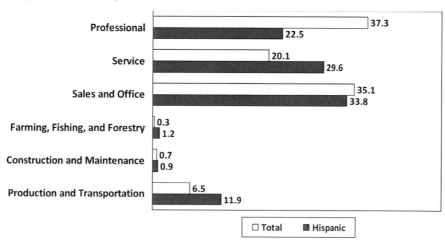

Source: Adapted from a presentation created by the Ethnicity and Ancestry Branch Population Division, U.S. Census Bureau.

percent). In a similar pattern for Latinas, the disparity exists but is not as extreme (74 and 26 percent for non-Latina females versus 56 and 46 percent for Latinas). Latinas are more commonly found in the sales and office sectors as well as in production and transportation.

There are measurable differences between most of the Latino subgroups and the Cubans. While Cubans are still below the non-Latino males in percentage employed in professional/administrative work (44 percent versus 50 percent), the other Latino subgroups range from a low of 23 to 37 percent. A similar pattern exists for Cubanas in comparison to other Latinas. Finally, the occupational location of Latinos is also influenced by nativity, as U.S.-born Latinos fare better occupationally. As labor force participation rates continue to increase, especially for Latinas, all Latinos in the labor market will play a greater role in the composition of the workforce, contribute more to the Social Security system, and have more human resource labor force mobility[6] (Morales and Bonilla 1993). Thus, issues like job mobility, job training and educational preparation, labor market discrimination, and entrepreneurship become salient issues for Latino communities. This dimension of communities of interests will appear in the discussion of public policy and Latinos in chapters 9 and 10.

This introductory discussion of the foundations of the Latino community next examines the Latino family, presenting information on family income status, Latino families living below the poverty line, and family type. A substantial literature, both social scientific and literary, portrays the central value of family life for Latinos as a source of social and financial support as well as cultural reinforcement. Values such as respecting elders, maintaining extended families, supporting familial social and cultural rituals, and the centrality of family for identity and well-being have been identified as core for Latinos. In a way, this demographic information has dimensions of both culture and common situations (i.e., interest).

Data on the number of Latino families relative to all families in the United States for 2007 show that Latinos represent over 13 percent of the total U.S. population, constituting 10.5 million families. An important factor is the larger size of Latino families. Also, two-fifths of Latino households include children younger than eighteen. Another relevant aspect of Latino families is the percentage of individuals born outside the United States (60.8 percent). Again, there is a substantial difference based upon nativity, given the percentage of foreign-born Latinos in the Latino population.

If we check the income status by gender of Latinos in comparison to non-Latinos, then economic disparities are quite evident (see figure 3.11). More than twice as many Latino families have incomes under $10,000 as non-Latino families (16 percent versus 7 percent). In the case of Puerto Rican families, the rate is three and a half times greater for family income under $10,000. For families earning $25,000 or more, two-thirds fewer Latino families fall into this category than non-Latino families. The percentage of Latino households without health insurance is 30.7 percent. The household income difference for Latinos and non-Latinos creates a significant disparity such that lack of resources has implications in terms of socioeconomic mobility, political engagement, and organizational activities.

Another indication of the economic disparities between non-Latinos and Latinos is the percentage of families living below the poverty level. Among all family types (two parents, female headed, etc.), three times as many Latino families live below the

FIGURE 3.11. Median earnings among Hispanics and the total population by gender, 2006 (for employed, full-time, year-round workers sixteen and older in 2006 inflation-adjusted dollars).

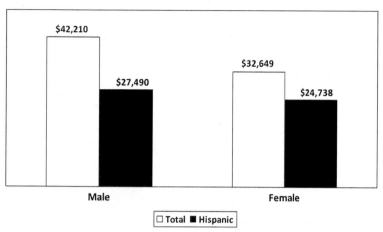

Source: Adapted from a presentation created by the Ethnicity and Ancestry Branch Population Division, U.S. Census Bureau.

poverty level as non-Latino families. The poverty rate among Latinos is 23.2 percent, up from 21.5 percent in 2007. Almost two-fifths of all Latina-headed families live below the poverty level. The rate is considerably higher for Puerto Rican female-headed households (64 percent). The interrelated factors of a youthful age structure (especially for Mexican-origin and Puerto Rican populations), residential locations in central cities, and declining urban economies contribute to the situations of many Latino families. With the centrality of family as a positive value for many Latinos, the economic condition of a substantial segment of Latino families warrants concern and attention. Thus, the linkage of family economic status as a common interest is quite likely.

A complementary demographic presentation is a profile of Latino families. Data information on family type and family size confirms a greater number of members in Latino than in non-Latino households. In 1997 both Mexican-origin and Cubans "couple" families had a similar percentage as non-Latino "couple" families (72.2 percent, 76.9 percent, and 77.2 percent, respectively). On the other hand, female-headed households are much more prevalent among Mexican-origin, Puerto Rican, and "other Hispanic" demographics. The more telling information lies with the size of families. Latinos are three-fifths less likely to fall into the category of two-person families.

On the other hand, Latino households are 2.2 times more likely to include five or more persons. Mexican-origin households are 2.6 times more likely to have five or more members. Central and South American families exhibit a similar larger-family tendency among the other Latino subgroups. Larger family, lower levels of family income, and corresponding higher rates of family poverty place Latino families at risk in terms of quality of life (e.g., housing conditions, educational isolation,[7] limited employment opportunities, economic segregation, and vulnerability to violent crime), which suggests both common ground and limited political resources to mobilize for effective change.

Conclusion: Communities of
Interests and Common Cultures

In this chapter, I have developed some demographic indicators supporting the concepts of the community of common or similar cultures and the **community of interests**. If Latinos of various national origins share some commonalties central to life's experiences and situations, then these commonalties can serve as bases for common and collective actions. The following chapters examine and discuss developments within the Latino community in a variety of political arenas and activities. In the community of culture segment, the dimensions of Spanish language and nativity (or the extent of foreign-born status) constitute a significant constellation of cultural connections. Spanish-language persistence, reinforced to a large degree by continuous Latino migration, establishes and expands Latino enclaves, maintains "ethnically and culturally" dense social networks, contributes to a sustained Latino presence and visibility in the United States, and creates demands for business and media services.[8] The net effect is that culture is dynamic and extends beyond the traditional boundaries of Latino national-origin communities. One other aspect of a visible maintenance of "Latino culture" is that segments of the "host" society raise concerns about integration, incorporation, assimilation, loyalty, and a general notion of whether Latinos belong.

A community of interests consists of similar socioeconomic conditions and statuses. I have presented information on occupational status, educational attainment, and family type among different Latino groups. There are more similarities, or clusters of traits, among Latino subgroups than there are substantially differential statuses. The one somewhat less similar group is the Cuban population. Nevertheless, the basis for a pan-ethnic community is evident and open to greater community-building efforts.

I am not suggesting that either or both sets of similarities of culture and interests will automatically result in political empowerment or influence. Rather, if some forms of community are present, then the accompanying factors of active and effective organizations and leadership can serve as a conversion component for political capital. In addition, situational conditions—such as negative activities and legislation targeting Latinos or even positive appeals to Latino communities by businesses, political parties, and the like—can assist in the dynamic formation of communities of interests and common cultures. The basis and direction of community building across Latino subgroups does serve as the crux of the analysis and discussion of Latino politics in this volume. The next chapter focuses on the psychological dimension of identity and the dynamics of political mobilization relevant to Latinos.

Discussion Questions

1. A pan-ethnicity is viewed as a socially constructed category or identity. As a result, there is debate as to whether the Latino/Hispanic identity has real meaning and concrete applications in an individual's daily life. Discuss whether this identity is "real" for persons of Latino origin and their daily lives.
2. At least twenty-two national-origin subgroups can be placed under the Latino group umbrella. Some of these groups are linked to other Latino national-origin groups, while others seem not to have that much in common. Discuss

how a person's national-origin background and experiences impact a sense of pan-ethnicity in the United States.

3. A major segment of the Latino community, demographically and culturally, comprises the foreign-born immigrants. Discuss the uniqueness within this subcommunity and its impact on the Latino native-born population.

4. This chapter focuses on culture and demographics. How much does being farther removed from the immigration experience (i.e., multigenerational status in the United States) affect the cultural dimensions of a Latino community?

CHAPTER 4

Latino Subgroups in the United States

*Los latinos somos de muchas naciona-
lidades distintas. Pero, dime que nombre
prefiere, y yo puedo calibrar nuestra afini-
dad como una familia más grande. Pues,
quizás no pueda. El proceso de extenderse
más allá de familia, de patria, depende en
las experiencias que compartimos y como
nos entendermos y nuestras interacciónes.
Pero, primero necesito definir a cual grupo
pertenezco.*

Latinos are of many distinct nationalities. But tell me which name you prefer,
and I can gauge our relationship in the
larger family. Well, perhaps I cannot.
The process of extending one's identity
beyond family and country depends on
the experiences that we share, how we
understand one another, and our interactions. But, first, I need to decide to which
group I belong.

UNDERSTANDING LATINOS and their political involvement can be
accomplished by examining the formation of a community and intergroup
linkages. Even though Latinos have been grouped together by the mass
media and governmental policies, the extensiveness of community across the Latino
subgroups has tended to be more hidden. Social surveys on the national (**Latino National Political Survey**, CBS News, CNN–All Politics Polls, etc.) and regional (Florida
International University, Texas A&M University, UCLA) levels have portrayed many
Latinos as more familiar and interactive within their own national-origin group than
with other Latinos. This characterization prevailed until a sustained set of systematic
surveys of Latinos after 2000 (Pew Hispanic Survey, **Latino National Survey**, Bendixon & Associates surveys, etc). The pattern of subgroups' regional concentration
(80 percent of the Mexican-origin population in the Southwest; 60 percent of Cubans
in Dade County, Florida; 80 percent of Puerto Ricans in the Northeast) has changed.
New destinations in the South and the Midwest and increased international migration since the 1990s have produced greater geographic dispersion among Latinos. But
the opportunity to interact across Latino groups is not limited by geography alone;
it is also related to family, historical, and homeland connections, as well as common
experiences.

BOX 4.1. The Changing Faces of Latino America

The historically Mexican face of the Texas Latino community has changed in the past decade. Lori Rodríquez (2001) of the *Houston Chronicle* puts real faces to stories about this diverse mix. She describes the Chanax family (from Guatemala), which since the 1990s has migrated to Texas. The seven nephews of Don Esteban worked, started families, and settled in Houston. He speaks minimal English, but one daughter speaks with a "Latin lilt," and his son Giovanni, a college-bound marine veteran, speaks English with a Texas accent. They represent a non-Mexican influx into Houston, whose proportion of the state's Latinos has more than doubled since 2000 (from 10.3 to 24 percent). The proportion of Mexican-origin immigrants shrank from 80 to 73 percent in Harris County. Similarly in Brazoria County (part of the Houston metropolitan area), the proportion of non-Mexican population grew from less than 10 percent to 23 percent, with similar jumps in the other counties in the metro area. Whereas Mexican Americans have accounted for around 90 percent of all Latinos in Texas, the abrupt shift to other Latinos now residing in the state is quite striking. The same patterns are evident in Austin (12.7 to 23.3 percent), El Paso (4.7 to 16.7 percent), Dallas (12 to 17 percent), and San Antonio (8 to 30 percent).

In Houston, Guatemalan immigrants have secured employment in one of the city's largest supermarkets, Randall's, now estimated to employ over a thousand Guatemalans. Other indicators of an ethnic mix are found in the Randall's bakery, which offers coronas, roscas, and other traditional Guatemalan breads next to bolillos, pan de huevo, and other Mexican pastries. Nestor Rodríquez (University of Houston), who has examined migration to the Houston area, notes the significant migration from Central and South America with a "sprinkling" of Puerto Ricans and Cubans. While this is documented in Houston and other parts of Texas, similar additions of other Latinos to traditional concentrations of Mexicans, Puerto Ricans, or Cubans are evident in Florida, New York, California, and other regions with established Latino communities.

This chapter provides some characterization of Latin subgroups, followed by demographic profiles in the next chapter. The short synopsis of several Latino subgroups will highlight their settlement and historical development in the United States. There is a wealth of historical and interpretative accounts of Latino subgroup experiences over an extended period of their history in the United States. This brief introduction might encourage you to explore in greater depth the diverse set of national-origin Latino groups. The greater influx of Latino immigrants since the 1990s has led to a significant increase in the Latino population, which is an additional factor in affecting these dynamic communities in the process of being shaped. These brief sketches will hopefully give a fuller picture of the many subcommunities that make up what we call Latinos or Hispanics.

Mexican-Origin Communities:
Growing throughout the United States

Historically, the Mexican-origin population has been the largest and oldest of the Latino subgroups. Consistently representing more than three-fifths of the total Latino population, they predate the English settlements in the eastern section of the United States. Spanish expeditions to what is now the American Southwest began in the early sixteenth century. Mission settlements lined much of the region, particularly in the current states of California, New Mexico, Arizona, and Texas. The presence of Spaniards, Mexicans, and mestizos (i.e., descendants of Spanish and Indian or indigenous cultures) is also reflected in the names of many southwestern states (e.g., Nevada, Montana, Colorado, Nuevo Mexico) and numerous cities and towns. At the same time, Mexican-origin people include recent migrants (both legal permanent resident aliens and undocumented persons). These migratory patterns to the agricultural regions and industrial sections of the United States were established in the latter 1800s and early 1900s. Now, the service sectors of the American economy serve as destination areas for more recently arrived Mexicanos.

For much of the period since the Treaty of Guadalupe in 1848 to the present, Mexicanos have been concentrated in the five southwestern states. Then, heavy manufacturing in steel, auto, and railroads largely influenced the noticeable migratory stream to the Midwest. In the second decade of the new millennium, the presence of Mexican people is also evident throughout other regions of the country (the Northwest, Northeast, and South). For example, meat-processing plants, textile manufacturers, and service industries in states like Arkansas, Florida, and North Carolina have become destinations for Mexican immigrants. Similar patterns are still developing in the other regions mentioned. Obviously, Mexico's physical proximity and its economic dependence on the American economy serve as major contributors to the flow of goods and people across the border. Similarly, U.S. immigration policy has provided impetus for alternately freer and more restricted movement across the border (the current immigration developments will be discussed in chapter 9). Finally, Mexico's proximity and continuous migration have also served to maintain cultural contact and economic exchanges with family, relatives, and other social networks.[1]

In this brief accounting of the Mexican-origin population, the themes of long-standing residence and continuous international migration coexist as the context for Mexican American/Chicano political life and issues. The demographics of this group, as well as its cultural maintenance (largely in terms of social affinity and identification, bilingualism, and familialism), contribute to the people's experiences in the United States and their political integration. Regions of the Southwest (southern Texas, northern New Mexico, and Southern California) provide examples of power and economic relations for Mexican Americans. The preponderance of Mexicanos in South Texas (El Valle del Rio Grande) serves as evidence that population size alone does not automatically translate to political and economic power and influence.

Mexicanos have served as a labor force and flexible labor pool for the agricultural economy without controlling property or the means of production. It was once as if two separate societies existed—the owners and the others—with worker status and **ethnicity** being the dividing line (Montejano 1987). The 1960s saw the advent of

Chicano power and major efforts by Mexican Americans to achieve political control. The rise of a third-party movement (La Raza Unida) in primarily rural South Texas saw a number of city councils, school boards, and county offices secured by Chicano candidates. Although short-lived, this "electoral takeover" set the foundation for subsequent political efforts and organizational development. Middle-class organizational efforts among workers and targeted educational reforms assisted ensuing political advances and **mobilization** (Shockley 1974; Foley 1988). The following chapters, especially chapters 6 through 8, focus on political resource development (socioeconomic and psychological predispositions and political attitudes), organizational expansion in resources, strategies, and skills, and leadership development, which are primary components of Latino political involvement.

The Hispano experience in New Mexico differs from that of rural South Texas, where economic and political subjugation had been a long-standing reality (Montejano 1987). The Hispanos included a propertied and business class before the Mexican-American War of 1848. Even though the advent of territorial government and resulting statehood saw Hispanos' economic and political power diminish, they maintained political leverage. Ironically, contemporary New Mexico has experienced significant interregional migration of non-Latinos into the state, particularly in the north. Hispanos, with two-fifths of the state's population, continue to serve as "players," yet engage in continuous political struggles to maintain their political position. The 2000 elections in New Mexico saw the statewide election of Hispanos as attorney general, secretary of state, state treasurer, and state auditor. In 2002, Bill Richardson, a Latino, was elected governor.

Southern California represents the legacy of the Californios (Pitt 1966) but even more so the rise of extensive Mexican migration to this state. After World War II, noticeable numbers of Mexican Americans migrated from Texas to California in search of better opportunities and less discrimination. After the 1960s California became the major destination state for international migration, especially from Mexico. The combination of push-pull factors (lack of job opportunities in Mexico, peso devaluations, proximity to the U.S. border, economic pull of jobs, and an established Mexican-origin community) contributed significantly to the growing Mexican-origin population. The expansive California economy (in the service sectors, traditional agriculture, high-tech manufacturing operations, etc.) made it the major port of entry for immigrants. The translation to appreciable political and economic influence did not become evident until the 1990s.

During the previous decade, **redistricting**, activism by Mexican American organizations (Mexican American Legal Defense and Education Fund, Southwest Voter and Education Project), and anti-immigrant and nativism movements set the stage for increased Mexican American political group awareness and activity. In the mid-1990s, state initiatives such as **Propositions 187**, 209, and 237 stimulated Mexican Americans and their organizations to mobilize and register to vote. One result of this increased activism has been rising numbers of elected officials at the state and federal levels (e.g., Lieutenant Governor Cruz Bustamante, Speaker of the Assembly Montearroyos, Congresspersons Loretta Sanchez and Edward Roybal). For over four decades, the Mexican-origin community was portrayed as "the sleeping giant," "an awakening minority," and "a group whose time for a place in the sun has arrived." As we began the new millennium, these projections had become concrete.

The Mexican-origin population has grown from a territorial minority (de la Garza, Kruszewski, and Arciniega 1973) to become a national presence with expanding political involvement. Mexican American organizations have been able to diversify their goals and objectives as well as their constituency base, incorporating other Latino subgroups into their membership as well as focusing on a broader range of issues and policies. For example, the National Council of La Raza (NCLR) was called the Southwest Council of La Raza in the late 1960s. Its primary goals were economic development, social services, and advocacy on behalf of Mexican Americans. Since its inception, the organization has taken a national orientation with its headquarters in Washington, DC. Its constituency base includes all Latinos, with membership and board members representing most segments of the diverse Latino community. It has developed a film production company, supplies venture capital for small businesses, provides resource development for community-based organizations, and engages in applied research, policy analysis, and advocacy. NCLR illustrates the evolution of Mexican American organizations in the latter half of the twentieth century. Subsequently, NCLR took on the role of advocacy for all Latinos with a national base.

The wider dispersion of Mexican Americans throughout the United States has broadened their contact with other Latino subgroups and expanded their identity beyond purely national origin. For example, the concept and label use of "Latino" in Chicago is widespread among Latinos of Mexican, Puerto Rican, Cuban, Salvadoran, and Central and South American ancestry. While conducting field research with several Latino community-based organizations in the early 1970s, I encountered a consciously constructed Latino identity. The activist elements instilled a sense of identifying as Latinos to help broaden the population base of the emerging Latino community. Almost twenty years later, when the Latino National Political Survey was conducting focus groups in Chicago, the presence of a Latino identity was evident. Focus participants had integrated a sense of national-origin awareness and identity, as well as broader group identification as Latinos. Again, fifteen years later (spring 2005), as part of the Latino National Survey research group, we conducted focus groups in over ten communities. Be it to Spanish speakers, English monolinguals, immigrants, or native-born citizens, those referring to persons of Spanish origin consistently used the "Latino" and "Hispanic" labels. For Mexican Americans, broadening intergroup contacts and incorporating a **pan-ethnic**[2] identity serve as building blocks for a Latino community.

The long-standing Mexican American community has established social networks, traditions, and cultural practices that contribute to the definition and maintenance of community. In addition, the evolution of Mexican American organizations (e.g., mutual aid societies, labor movements, cultural organizations, civil rights and professional groups, and advocacy/litigation organizations) represents a substantial history of organizational activities and definable agendas. In general the core of that agenda has focused on civil rights, access to and participation in the economic and political arenas, educational quality, and greater political empowerment.

The community's leadership has expanded from grassroots and labor leaders to include others with corporate skills and a national reach. The continuous migration of Mexicanos adds to the population growth and their geographic dispersion. At the same time, enjoining themselves with other Latino subgroups needs to occur at both the elite and grassroots levels. This broadening of community can affect the scope of the public policy agenda as well as meet the need to integrate more recent immigrants into the body politic. With the Mexican-origin community being the largest subgroup, it has the role of helping to coalesce all of the Latino subgroups.

Puerto Ricans: Manhattan or La Isla Borinquen (Puerto Rico)?

A popular notion about Puerto Ricans has to do with the significant number of island transplants, who migrated largely after World War II to the New York metropolitan area. But the current population of slightly over 4 million has a longer history in the United States. In the late nineteenth century, some Puerto Ricans migrated to the Northeast, attracted to agricultural labor and cigar making. With the Spanish-American War, Puerto Rico became a U.S. possession. The Jones Act of 1917 established Puerto Ricans as U.S. citizens and allowed them a congressional "observer" without a vote. In 1947 the act was amended to enable Puerto Ricans to elect their governor and other officials, except members of the Supreme Court.

Puerto Rico's status has been a long-standing concern. As a commonwealth, it enjoys a degree of autonomy while participating in entitlement programs and citizenship benefits. The independence movement in Puerto Rico reached an apex on July 25, 1952, with a push for the island to become a free associated state. Alternatives to commonwealth status include free associated state status, statehood, and independence. There have been several plebiscites in 1967, 1993, and 1998 (HR 856, United States–Puerto Rico Political Status Act). In each case, maintaining the status quo, commonwealth status, has received the greater number of votes. The statehood option has been the second most preferred, with independence running a distant third. There are some variations among supporters for these options as the more conservative Puerto Ricans favor statehood, and liberals favor independence. The status of Puerto Rico remains an issue among many Puerto Ricans on the U.S. mainland. Intertwined in these debates are themes associated with autonomy, trade options, cultural maintenance, identity, and the costs and benefits of each option.

For Puerto Ricans living on the mainland, a number of dimensions relate to the political-status question. The first is an interest in being directly involved in the discussion and vote. With the framing of House Bill 866, one of the points of contention was whether Puerto Ricans living on the mainland would be allowed to vote in the plebiscite. The close cultural and familial contact and affinity between Puerto Ricans living in the United States and Puerto Rico stirred both interest and support from Puerto Rican organizations to ensure mainland participation in the plebiscite. Second, cultural and group identity among Boricuas in the United States interprets the political-status question as activating issues of cultural identity, economic opportunity, and pride, which are important in both locations. The terms *Boricua* and *Newyorican* refer to Puerto Rican populations in the United States. Third, the question of political status can serve as a focal point for the political status of Puerto Ricans in the United States. For example, numerous Puerto Rican leaders advocate for the inclusion of the population of Puerto Rico into the total count of Latinos in the United States (an additional 3.9 million). Empowerment, active political engagement, cultural maintenance, and targeted policy advocacy from their own perspective (Jennings and Rivera 1984; Jennings 1994; J. Cruz 1998) motivate the Puerto Rican community.

BOX 4.2. Other Latinos: Salvadorans and Guatemalans

While Latinos continue to be described as the fastest-growing minority, this characterization is most appropriate for the Central American communities. The two largest segments come from El Salvador and Guatemala. Salvadorans now represent the fourth-largest Latino subgroup (1.6 million), slightly larger than the Dominicans. They are a heavily foreign-born group (64.7 percent), with 58.4 percent having arrived in the United States since 1990. Political unrest and U.S. intervention in the region served as a major impetus to emigrate. Geographically, a majority of Salvadorans are found in California (40 percent) and Texas (14 percent), with the rest scattered throughout the United States. As a largely "immigrant" group, Salvadorans place the highest priority on issues of social and economic well-being, securing asylum as political refugees, and U.S. immigration policies in general.

Guatemalans are now the sixth-largest Latino subgroup (986,000), and 69.4 percent are foreign-born or among the first generation born in the United States. Similarly to Salvadorans, 70 percent of Guatemalans have arrived in the United States since 1990. California (33.9 percent) and the southern region (32.4 percent) are the major areas of settlement. The Coalition of Guatemalan Immigrants in the United States (CONGUATE) advocates for Guatemalan interests (i.e., political and economic rights and opportunities). CONGUATE represents some twenty-five organizations in Los Angeles, Chicago, New York, Houston, and Washington, DC. Guatemalans' policy agenda reflects their interests in the United States and their home country. Matters of educational opportunity and health access (over 40 percent are without health insurance) and maintaining an active role in Guatemalan politics (Guatemala approved expatriate voting in national elections) serve as good examples. In addition, Guatemalans have initiated over a million petitions for political asylum, with some receiving temporary asylum status, granting work authorization and no deportation. Most Central Americans experience the same challenges as other Latinos, such as adapting to life in the United States, navigating the opportunity structures they encounter and the obstacles they face, as well as maintaining continued ties to their home country.

The historical concentration of Puerto Ricans in the Northeast has changed since 1995. While 55.6 percent of Puerto Ricans live in the Northeast, 27.2 percent live in the South (with Florida having 17.8 percent of all Puerto Ricans). Other Puerto Rican communities are located in Holyoke, Hartford, Chicago, Miami, Bridgeport, and Los Angeles. The status and conditions of Puerto Rican communities can be compared with those of many of the other Latino subgroups. With a median group age of twenty-nine years, the younger Puerto Rican population faces problems with inadequate housing, lesser educational resources, and higher rates of unemployment, single-headed households, poverty, and residential segregation. Their long-standing location in the New York metropolitan area highlights these problems. The elimination of low-skill central city manufacturing jobs, economic globalization, and relocation have contributed to higher rates of joblessness, social welfare participation, inferior schools, and limited and substandard housing (Kasarda 1985, 1989).

Work by Denton and Massey (1988) on residential segregation highlights the formation and perpetuation of subcultural practices and social networks that have impeded the incorporation of Puerto Ricans into mainstream economic and social life. Torres-Saillant and Hernández (1998) and Moore and Pinderhughes (1993) suggest that the distinctive Puerto Rican island culture and language, along with targeted labor recruitment by certain industries (e.g., agriculture and manufacturing) and racial discrimination, have contributed to economic disparities and barriers in the housing market.

Clara Rodríquez (1998, 2000) discusses the American basis of race and how it constitutes a different racial order from that found in Puerto Rico. Whereas Rodríquez characterizes race in America as white and other (primarily black), Puerto Rico has a multiplicity of "racial categories" or distinctions: black, indigo, trigueno, negro, moreno, and white or Spanish. Thus, the U.S. schema, which categorizes persons as white, black, possibly white, not white, and not black, leaves Puerto Ricans outside the racial order. Rodríquez contends that race, ethnicity, and culture are interconnected in the Puerto Rican experience and inconsistent with the American view of race. For Puerto Ricans, the phenotypical variations form an integrated system. Yet, America and its institutions may differentiate between Puerto Ricans by different racial categories when they identify themselves in cultural terms with race as a subset. The introduction of race and ethnicity also brings forth discriminatory theories that can bar Latinos from equal opportunities and access to many realms of life in the United States.

Overall, issues confronting Puerto Rican communities center on housing costs and access, urban relocation due to gentrification and urban renewal, educational quality and curriculum (including the dropout problem, language and bilingual education, and participation in higher education), unemployment, female-headed households, poverty and children living in poverty, and crime and public safety. Especially since the 1960s, Puerto Rican organizations have targeted community improvement, adaptation, and empowerment goals. For example, from the origins of the Puerto Rican Forum came ASPIRA and the Puerto Rican Community Development Program (Fitzgerald 1971). The leadership of Antonia Pantoja was instrumental in the development of all three organizations.

Organizations like the Puerto Rican Merchants Association and the Puerto Rican Civil Service Employees Association address the economic dimensions of life in the United States. The theme of continued connection with the Commonwealth of Puerto Rico is further reinforced by the presence of its office in New York City to assist Puerto Ricans with referrals. In the 1980s the commonwealth office also participated in a voter-registration campaign in the city. Finally, organizations like the Puerto Rican Legal Defense and Education Fund and the Institute for Puerto Rican Policy deal directly with issues of political empowerment and policy advocacy. Limited studies on Puerto Rican political behavior indicate lower rates of **political participation**, especially in the electoral process (Nelson 1979; Falcón and Santiago 1993), on the mainland as opposed to by those living on the island.

Nelson's (1979) analysis of Puerto Rican political involvement saw assimilation as aiding greater degrees of political activity. Only in the case of voting did the "more assimilated" Puerto Ricans participate at higher levels. Nelson found a negative association between participatory attitudes and assimilation. Although Puerto Ricans have a lower voting rate, they are oriented toward signing petitions, protesting, and joining community organizations.

The Puerto Rican communities have broadened their geographical presence and are actively engaged in local politics and policies, especially in central Florida (Orlando). The social and economic issues mentioned in the demographic profile constitute much of the political agenda for Puerto Ricans. Continued close ties with Puerto Rico and well-established neighborhoods on the mainland have served to maintain a strong sense of cultural identity, Spanish-language use, and pride (J. Cruz 1998; C. Rodríquez 1998; Jennings 1994; Jennings and Rivera 1984). Again, culture, ancestral ties, limited socioeconomic mobility, and discrimination compose a significant portion of Puerto Rican experience and are the foundation for community empowerment. Immigration has been characterized as a lesser concern for Puerto Ricans because of their status as U.S. citizens. In 2010, Ohio turned down Puerto Rican birth certificates as acceptable documents for a U.S. driver's license, arguing the greater possibility of fraud. Puerto Rican leaders, however, see this policy change as part of the anti-Latino/ anti-immigrant climate embroiling many state and local policies.

Cubanos: Still an Exile Community?

Cubans in the United States are usually described as living primarily in southern Florida, hostile toward the Fidel/Raul Castro regime, ardent anticommunists, listeners to *el son y boleros* (forms of Cuban music and rhythms), and active politically. While the broader public knowledge about Cubans usually begins with the political demise of Fulgencio Batísta in 1957, Cubans in the United States have an earlier presence. Historically, Cubans have lived in Florida since the 1850s along the Gulf of Mexico. Major numbers, largely involved in the cigar industry, populated the Key West area. Trade, labor, and commerce connected Cuban workers and entrepreneurs during the expansion of cigar production for much of the latter part of the nineteenth century. The Spanish-American War and subsequent U.S. control of Cuba established both political and economic ties. American investments, export partnerships, and extended foreign relations almost made Cuba a U.S. satellite.

In a more contemporary context, the rise of Fidel Castro and his communist regime helped create an exile community for many Cubans. Accounts since the late 1950s have referred to Cuban migration as the "golden exile," the flight of Cuban elites and professionals from the Castro regime. These exiles were primarily white, well-educated professionals and entrepreneurs, and urban residents. Between 1963 and 1972, 296,000 Cubans resettled into twenty-four hundred communities. Because they immigrated as political refugees, American policy provided assistance in the following areas: job training, English instruction, college loans, free certification for health professionals, housing subsidies, food stamps and food surpluses, and citizen exemption from certain jobs. Between 1961 and 1971, federal allocations for Cuban refugee assistance equaled $739 million. In addition, federal funds went to Dade County schools ($120 million) to assist with refugee children and youth. When federal immigration law changed in 1965, the Cuban Adjustment Act of 1966 exempted Cubans from the newly imposed 120,000-immigrant ceiling for persons from Western Hemisphere countries. Cubans share a similar immigrant segment to that characteristic of other Latino subgroups.

The status of political refugee and the corresponding federal legislation differentiate Cubanos from other Latinos. The contrast lies in the program and financial assistance received to facilitate adjustment to life in the United States and in their political motivation to leave Cuba, which conveys a strong commitment to political issues and concerns. Anti-Castroism and anticommunism are central elements of many Cubans' politics and activities. Organizations like the Cuban American National Foundation (CANF) (previously led by Jorge Mas Canosa) and movements such as Brigade 2506, Alpha 66, and Omega 7 focus their activities on efforts to wrest control of Cuba from the Castro regime. Military efforts, economic sanctions and embargoes, and Radio-TV Martí show why Cubans have been referred to as an exile community. For the most part, exile communities address their concerns to the political regime in control and seek policies in their "new" home to affect regime-change pressures.

Cuban migration underwent significant socioeconomic, racial, and political changes with the Mariel boatlifts. Unlike their pre-1980 counterparts, these refugees were more likely to be single adults, service and semiskilled workers, "social misfits," rural people, and less-educated individuals. Racially, this wave of Cubans included more Afro-Cubans instead of the predominantly white, elite refugees of earlier years. Politically, Cuban refugees had enjoyed a receptive climate as exiles leaving a communist regime and producing economic and social successes in America (e.g., bringing major entrepreneurial ventures, educational advances, stable and supportive family structures, economic revitalization of urban centers). Yet, the nature and timing of the Mariel flotilla was interpreted as Fidel Castro's "dumping" of social misfits and criminals, and a growing anti-immigrant hostility began to develop in the United States. The unsuccessful efforts of Haitian émigrés to gain a favorable entry status, with their boatlifts being turned back, angered African Americans and heightened the sense of intergroup conflict in South Florida. For example, the Dade County Commission passed an **English-only** ordinance despite the positive contributions that the Cuban community had made to the revitalization of the South Florida economy.

The politics of an exile community has focused on containing Castro's Cuba in the short term and on policies that would achieve the "demise" of Fidel Castro and his communist regime, assist with continued family reunification in the United States, and provide long-term resettlement assistance. For example, the CANF lobbied the Bill Clinton administration to support the Cuban Democracy Act, which tightened trade embargoes with tougher sanctions for firms involved with Cuba and established Radio-TV Martí. Radio Martí, situated in South Florida, conducts news and informational broadcasts targeted at Cuba, much like the Radio Free Europe model for communist Eastern European countries. Yet, by the late 1990s, Cuba and its leadership comprised only one of a broader range of domestic agenda issues. Some have described this development as a transition from the politics of exile to American ethnic politics. Limitations on travel and remittances by Cubans to family members in Cuba have been viewed as too restrictive and as failing to inflict political instability on the Castro regime as intended. Since 2000, there have been more directed policies to limit travel and remittances while allowing for trade of agricultural and medical products. In 2009, a poll conducted by Bendixon & Associates indicated that 67 percent of Cuban Americans wanted the restrictions removed (an 18 percent increase from the second George W. Bush administration). There are indications of some impatience with the old policies. The Barack Obama administration is easing such restrictions, and legislation was passed to enable Cubans to receive Social Security checks in Cuba.

Interestingly, second-generation Cubans display some political attitudes that differ from those of their parents. This generation, representing 37 percent of the Cuban population, consists of individuals who have lived all their lives in U.S. society (Hill and Moreno 1996). They express lower levels of trust in the U.S. government, show greater diversity in partisan preference (less Republican domination), identify less with the Cuban community, and favor decreased governmental spending (Moreno and Warren 1992; Hill and Moreno 1996). In addition, second-generation Cubans are more likely than their parents to use a pan-ethnic identity (i.e., Latino or Hispanic) by a percentage of 27.7 to 5.8 percent. This generation speaks Spanish less frequently, and whereas 58.9 percent of their parents perceive no discrimination, 23.5 percent of the second generation responded that they do. There are other indications of a more moderate orientation toward Castro's Cuba. Organizations like Cambio Cubano and the Committee for Cuban Democracy (CCD) describe themselves as moderate and support a willingness to negotiate with the Castro regime. Eloy Gutierrez-Menoyo's return to Cuba (Elliston 1995) was marked by the government's show of tolerance and respect. Marcelino Miyares of CCD advocates dialogue, reconciliation, and respect for Cuban sovereignty. At the same time, a desire for democratization is a central element among moderate Cuban Americans. The election of Alex Perales as Dade County executive mayor marks the rise of second-generation Cubans to elective office.

Another central feature of Cubanos is their entrepreneurship. The numbers of Cuban entrepreneurs and the growth of firm receipts and new firms far surpass figures for any other Latino subgroup or other minority. It has been suggested that this changing exile community's elite background and geographic concentration in southern Florida contributed significantly to the development of ethnic enclaves and enterprises (Portes and Mozo 1985; Portes and Stepnick 1993). Personal resources and attitudinal dimensions such as motivations tied to family ambitions, entrepreneurial role models, and family norms for independent business formation influenced the rise of the Cuban business class (Petersen 1995). In addition, a large Spanish-speaking social network provided consumer demand and access to a Cuban labor force. Loans were available, if necessary, and when resources were lacking, a rise in partnerships occurred. The opportunity structure, market conditions, resource mobilization, and access to ownership propelled the Cuban community to experience a faster rate of upward economic mobility than any other Latino group. At the same time, their entrepreneurial successes helped revitalize the southern Florida economy and served as a major U.S. gateway to Latin American trade.

The Cuban community maintains its share of exile fervor in this new millennium while expanding its focus to include domestic issues (economic development, civil rights, immigration policy, etc.). Cuban leadership was instrumental in the passage of the Cuban Liberty and Solidarity Act,[3] which includes expropriations after 1959. At the same time, the exit polls in the 1996 presidential elections indicated more support for Bill Clinton than during his previous presidential race. Similarly, in 2008, Barack Obama garnered almost half of the Cuban votes in Florida. The Cuban community exhibits the character of a resource-affluent group, with active leadership and a focused agenda emphasizing U.S. relations with Cuba. It is generally well organized, geographically concentrated, culturally immersed, and politically active. Within our theme of examining the various Latino subgroups as dynamic communities, the Cuban community exhibits common ground with other Latinos (e.g., social welfare policies, civil rights, language and immigration, economic mobility), as well as distinct policy perspectives and priorities regarding economic sanctions and isolationist policies for Cuba, lower levels of support for affirmative action, lower perceptions of discrimination toward Latinos, greater support for political refugee status, and arguments for "pro-democratization" initiatives. Its political activeness and economic resources continued in the first decade of the twenty-first century, while it has been surpassed by Dominicans and Salvadorans as the third-largest Latino subgroup.

Central and South Americans: America's Other Hispanics

Public awareness of Latinos/Hispanics is usually limited to some knowledge of Mexican Americans, Cubans, or Puerto Ricans, Yet, a breakdown of the various Latino subgroups shows that the "other Hispanic" category is increasing at the highest rate. Under the rubric of Central and South Americans, we have grouped Latinos from Central and South American countries as the "other Latinos." The Central American countries include Guatemala, Honduras, Nicaragua, Panama, El Salvador, and Costa Rica. The South American countries include all of the Spanish-speaking countries of that continent. Brazil is sometimes excluded from this cluster and sometimes included. Among all Latinos, this grouping has the highest proportion of foreign-born persons and constitutes those more recently entering the United States. We should note that labor migration among Central and South Americans occurred in the late 1800s and early 1900s. Industries such as cigar and munitions factories, sugar cane and other agricultural product processing, and shipyards, for example, were venues for earlier labor market relations between Central and South Americans and the United States (Figueroa 1996). More significant migration has occurred since the mid-1970s and continues at a high rate. Whereas the three largest Latino subgroups tend to concentrate in certain regions of the United States, Central and South Americans are more widely distributed.

Among South Americans, Ecuadorians (60 percent), Colombians, and Peruvians are more concentrated in the New York metropolitan area. While the residential patterns of Central and South Americans are distributed in many parts of the United States, their geographic locations have a close proximity with the communities in which established concentrations of Mexican Americans, Puerto Ricans, and Cubans are found. For example, the Peruvians in 2010 numbered 509,000 with 69.8 percent being foreign-born. Almost two-thirds of Peruvians have arrived in the United States since 1990. Three-fifths of Peruvians live in four states (Florida, 20 percent; California, 16.6 percent; New York and New Jersey, 12.5 percent each). The Association of Peruvian Institutions in the United States and Canada (AIPEUC) helps to maintain ties to the homeland while seeking better opportunities for expatriates in the United States. Education and health care are the two highest priorities. The homeland ties were reflected by the passage of a dual citizenship provision in 1993. In July 2010, Keiko Fujimori campaigned in New Jersey for the Peruvian presidential elections as Peruvian expatriates are the fourth-largest source of revenue for Peruvian political

BOX 4.3. The Colombian Community

Semana highlighted an example of the growth and involvement of the Colombian community. In early May 2001, Colombian Americans held their first Convention of Colombian Organizations in the United States in Atlanta, Georgia. The *Semana* story emphasized that a half million "legal" Colombians reside in the United States (primarily in Miami and New York), representing a 60 percent increase since 1990. The story also mentioned that an estimated 1.5 million undocumented Colombians could be living in the United States. In addition, estimated remittances of $2.5 billion annually are sent to Colombia. Concerns about political clout and representation constituted much of the convention discussions.

For the Colombian community, issues of health-care coverage and improving educational opportunities for their children have affected the formation of political and social clubs. Geographically, Colombians are found in the Northeast (New York, 22 percent; New Jersey, 14 percent) and Florida (31 percent), with Texas and California newer areas of growth. Many Colombians' belief that they will eventually return to their homeland makes them a center of attention for Colombian political parties and presidential candidates. It is not uncommon for Colombian presidential candidates to visit Colombians in New York City and elsewhere to secure votes and campaign contributions. Now, Colombians living abroad are able to elect a senator to represent their interests in Bogotá, solidifying their link with their homeland. This brief example demonstrates the growth of "other Latino" communities, their efforts to engage the American political system and the challenges they face, and their active involvement in transnational politics.

parties. Continued and active ties with their homeland represent the growing interest in understanding transnational politics among Latinos.

Many of you will remember Daisy Cuevas not by name but by her exchange with First Lady Michelle Obama in May 2010. As a seven-year-old student in a Washington, DC, elementary school, Daisy Cuevas asked Mrs. Obama about her mother's future in America without having her papers. While it caught the First Lady off guard, Daisy's query encompassed a wide range of issues embedded in the policy area of immigration: undocumented status, mixed legal status within households, separated families located in the United States and the home country, visa overstays, and so forth. When surveyed about salient issues and concepts by the Peruvian Ministry, respondents listed the top three issues as immigration (38.9 percent), jobs (25.2 percent), and discrimination (12.5 percent).

The relatively broad geographic distribution of Central and South Americans throughout the United States and their close proximity to the three larger Latino subgroups demonstrates a pattern of maintaining their own community identity but extending the range of interactions with other Latino groups. The Latinization of a national community can be assisted by the presence of diverse Latino subgroups living in the same residential areas. The nature and extent of intergroup contact will establish a positive, supportive relationship or, at times, a competitive, conflictual one. As a fast-growing segment of Latinos, Central and South Americans are establishing their presence and impact in the United States, as well as altering the mix and chemistry of Latinos and their primary interests.

While relatively little research literature has been generated about Central and South Americans, one important dimension is the extent of foreign-born and immigrant standing that characterizes these communities. Overall, Latinos constituted almost half of the foreign-born population in the United States in 1996 (Hansen and Faber 1997). The foreign-born percentage among Central and South Americans exceeds three-fifths of their residential population. Political instability and revolutions in El Salvador, Guatemala, Honduras, and Nicaragua forced many Central Americans out of their homes into neighboring Mexico and the United States. Gaining entry to the United States as political refugees and the U.S. role in military and covert operations and foreign policy in that region are major concerns for Central Americans.

The difficulty of achieving political refugee status for Central Americans has had a direct bearing on undocumented migration since the 1990s. One of the accompanying results of many Central Americans' plight was the advent of the "sanctuary movement" in which religious organizations and other groups established an underground network to help them enter the United States. In addition, these organizational efforts focused on obtaining official political refugee status for Central Americans. Providing proof of clear danger of persecution and personal harm upon returning home due to political beliefs and activities has been difficult. Individuals caught in the cross fire between government and rebel forces were considered victims of a civil war or political instability rather than political dissidents.

Immigration policy and rights are central issues for Central Americans. Besides the question of political refugee status, specific areas of concern include equal protection, actions of the Immigration and Naturalization Service, access to entitlement programs, and discriminatory practices in the labor market and housing. The actions of organizations like the Task Force for New Americans, the Latino Coalition for Racial Justice, and Sanctuary for Salvadorans (Jordan 1995) represent efforts to protect and advocate on behalf of Central American immigrants and their families. The Central American communities are still in the early stages of developing resources, stable organizational structures, and maturing leadership. In 1996, over 2.9 million Central Americans resided predominantly in nine states. Since 2009, federal policies that require a formal "judicial process" for persons apprehended as illegal entrants have heightened critical responses to extant immigration policies. We will explore this policy area in greater detail in chapter 9.

Global economic forces of devaluation, high inflation rates, significant market fluctuations for goods and materials, and political instability have driven immigration factors for South Americans. Significant contributing countries have been Colombia, Venezuela, Peru, and Ecuador. With settlement patterns primarily in the Northeast, California, and Florida, South Americans' organizational agenda entails adjustment issues (labor market information and opportunities, the educational system, housing availability and affordability, immigrant treatment and rights) as well as maintaining cultural practices and traditions.

The growth of these communities has created some competition with other Latino subgroups. For example, growing numbers of Colombians and Ecuadorians in New York City have generated demands for greater involvement and participation in

Latino politics and leadership. These demands include more attention to immigration and rights, political recognition, and greater allocation of governmental resources for South Americans. There have been greater levels of political involvement by these Latino subgroups around local issues and an expanding national network centering on immigration legislation and proposals. For example, the 1997 Immigration Reform Act, which significantly curtailed access by permanent resident aliens to federal entitlement programs, was a major focal point for Central and South American communities.

Any discussion of Central and South Americans as part of the Latino aggregation tends to be speculative rather than informed through systematic research and study. These subgroups form both the "youngest"[5] and the fastest-growing element of the Latino community. Their American "character and demeanor" is still in the process of taking a more definitive form. U.S.-born and/or educated Central and South Americans are exerting an effect on their organizational development and goals and defining their public policy concerns. Their residential location in areas proximate to the existing major Latino subgroups can both broaden the scope of what is Latino and heighten intergroup competitiveness. Their increasing demands entail greater focus on immigration and immigrant rights, access to social programs, and inclusion in the Latino leadership. At the same time, there are some indicators of cooperative ventures among Puerto Ricans, Dominicans, and Colombians. Overall, the expanding presence of Central and South Americans in the Latino landscape defines the changing parameters of evolving Latino politics.

Los Dominicanos

The Dominican population in the United States has been experiencing continuous growth, particularly since the mid-1960s. This predominantly immigrant community is slightly over 60 percent foreign-born. In 2008, its population numbered almost 1.2 million, with primary residences in the New York metropolitan area. Other areas of concentration include New Jersey (11 percent), Florida (less than 3 percent), and Massachusetts (less than 1.5 percent) (Waldinger 1989; Torres-Saillant and Hernández 1998). The Washington Heights area on the Upper West Side of Manhattan represents the largest concentration of Dominicans (41.1 percent). It has been the site of many organizations (Centro Cívico Cultural Dominicano, Alianza Dominicana, Asociación Communal de Dominicanos Progresistas, etc.) and police-community conflicts. As a consequence of their population growth, Dominicans (along with Salvadorans) are rivaling the Cuban community as the third-largest Latino subgroup.

The notable migration of Dominicans has been most evident since 1966. During the twelve-year regime of President Joaquín Balaguer (1966–1978),[6] family planning policies and economic forces stimulated the migration of Dominicanos to the United States and Puerto Rico. Economic policy, high unemployment, external debt crisis, high international interest rates, and the deterioration of commodity prices motivated them to go to the urban areas of the East Coast. Even though the Dominican Republic altered its economic policy to establish free trade zones, expand tourism, and export nontraditional products, the economic push factors remained strong. Dominican migrants are primarily persons from rural areas who are less educated, unskilled, and of lower socioeconomic status. Disproportionate numbers of women, as well as persons between the ages of twenty-five and forty-four, are in the migration stream.

The initial waves of Dominican migration to the New York metropolitan area occurred during the economic restructuring from a manufacturing to a service economy. Many Dominican workers were employed as operatives in manufacturing or in wholesale segments of the service and manufacturing sectors. The demographic profile of Dominicans in New York reflects slightly lower rates of labor participation (60.7 percent versus 67.9 percent for Latinos and 68.3 percent for all workers) (Torres-Saillant and Hernández 1998). Their **human capital** resources (or lack of them) contribute to their depreciated socioeconomic status. For example, the Dominican poverty rate is 45.7 percent, compared to 37.2 percent for all Latinos or 23.8 percent citywide. In addition, the percentage of Dominican female-headed households exceeds that for other Latinos (49.7 percent versus 44.1 percent) as well as the citywide rate (25.6 percent).

The rise of organizations has accompanied the growth of the Dominican community, especially in the Northeast. Initially, many organizations reflected the cultural and immigrant-related adjustments of newcomers to the United States. Their focus centered on immigration, the educational system, and employment and social counseling (Sassen-Koob 1985; Guarnizo 1994). Groups like the Centro Cívico Cultural Dominicano, Asociación Dominicanas, and Club de San Juan Pablo Duarte represent efforts of voluntary organizations to facilitate the transition to life in a new country. Some of these organizations date back to the early 1960s, with a movement toward advocacy and political empowerment taking shape in the late 1980s. For example, the Asociación Communal de Dominicanos Progresistas incorporated activities dealing with employment, empowerment, financial support, and advocacy for more responsive social institutions. In addition, gender-specific organizations (Collectivo de Mujeres Provincianas) have emerged that advocate for services and opportunities for women. Similarly, there are increasing numbers of professional or work-related organizations for travel agents, accountants, and so on. The Dominican American National Roundtable (DANR) serves as a forum for planning, action, and analysis of the Dominican community's status and position in American society. Political and economic rights, educational quality and relevant programs, and immigration policies remain primary concerns. Dominican organizations have ties with other Latino organizations (i.e., LULAC, NCLR, NALEO, ASPIRA, etc.).

Until recently, Dominicans have been portrayed as almost invisible politically. Given the community's high foreign-born percentage, they rank ninth in naturalization rates. Since 2008, the DANR has focused attention on aggressive voter registration and promotion of naturalization. Currently Dominicans represent 13 percent of Latino voters and 3.5 percent of all New York City voters (Falcón and Santiago 1993; Pew Hispanic Center 2009). To some extent, anti-immigrant sentiment and policies have activated greater political interest and activity among Dominicans. For example, immigration-reform legislation potentially eliminated participation in some entitlement programs by permanent resident aliens. Even though much of policymakers' attention has been directed toward the southwestern U.S. border and Mexican and Central American immigrants, the broader sweep of "restrictive" immigration reforms has had a direct impact on most Latino immigrants. Issues like immigrant rights, policy backlash that targets the foreign-born, crime and drugs, and representation are part of the political agenda for Dominicans.

Dominicans, like many other Latino subgroups, are confronting issues of cultural and political identity and political orientation focused on the United States. Recent gains in electoral representation at the city and state levels serve as indicators of political development in the Dominican community. Yet, there is support for a state of mind in which individuals remain engaged with their native country, while becoming acclimated to the norms and activities of U.S. society. Some researchers have referred to this as "political duality." A person has dual loyalties and interests in both the home and "host" countries. Political duality became an option for Dominicans in 1996 as the Dominican Republic provided for dual citizenship. The impact of this policy reflects the development of both a domestic policy agenda as well as homeland engagement in U.S. foreign policy (Portes, Escobar, and Radford 2007).

The advent of Dominican studies at City University of New York and continued organizational growth and activity should advance Dominicans' political development as a community in the United States. Greater activity and involvement will open more interactions within the New York metropolitan area with other Latino subgroups. The growth of the Dominican and Colombian communities in the Northeast is already reconfiguring the larger Latino community in this region. For example, there is some indication of competitiveness between Dominicans and Puerto Ricans for political visibility, advantage, and systemic attention from the major institutions. The future of Latino political activity lies not only with community formation across national-origin boundaries but also with the bases for independent and interdependent agendas and strategies[7] across all Latino subgroups.

Conclusion: Latino America— Rich in Diversity and Commonalties

This brief portrait of the histories and experiences of the different Latino subgroups in the United States is intended to provide insights into the nature and content of these subgroups. The demographic profiles in the next chapter furnish a picture of the size, socioeconomic status, and residential location of each group. These portrayals take into consideration the themes of common interests and common cultures. The factors of language, Spanish influences on cultural practices, institutions, religion, and the like cut across all the Latino subgroups. At the same time, unique experiences and variations occurred in the Dominican Republic versus Cuba versus Peru, and so on. The immigrant strand prevalent among the Latino subgroups helps define much of the Latino experience in relation to continued ties with one's home country, adjustment to most phases of life in the United States, and focus on cultural maintenance.

The socioeconomic status of many Latino subgroups (education levels, labor market participation, income levels, family structures, household size, etc.) is quite similar and presents opportunities for cooperative ventures. The overlap of residential location in areas with significant concentrations of Puerto Ricans, Cubans, and Mexican-origin persons affords opportunities for different kinds of interactions, particularly for Central and South Americans. These interactions can be beneficial, conflictual, or very infrequent. Yet, common cultural orientations and customs and situational conditions that warrant action can stimulate the bases for contact and interactions. The next chapter focuses on the sociodemographic underpinnings of community for Latinos. The nature and existence of common cultural and socioeconomic situations have a fundamental linkage to political resources and involvement.

Discussion Questions

1. The Mexican-origin community continues to be the largest Latino subgroup as it comprises more than three-fifths of all Latinos. What are the implications of being so much larger than the other subgroups in terms of leadership, agenda, and intergroup relations?

2. Until the mid-1990s, in thinking about Latinos in the United States, the big three (i.e., the Mexican-origin, Puerto Rican, and Cuban subgroups) dominated the Latino community. Presently Dominicans and Salvadorans will be the third- and fourth-largest Latino subgroups. What changes have occurred within the Latino community with the significant increases among Central and South Americans?

3. While the foreign-born segment in the Cuban subgroup remains the majority, how has the increase in the native-born segment affected the nature of the Cuban community's political agenda and partisan politics?

4. Even though the location of specific national-origin Latino subgroups is geographically concentrated, there is evidence of greater Latino residential diversity. What are the implications of more contact among different Latino subgroups in building a pan-ethnic community?

CHAPTER 5

The Politics of Interest and Culture

Nuestro pueblo, la comunidad, nuestra gente, todos son expresiónes de haber entendido que somos una familia con una voz fuerte y unida. Sin embargo, igual que muchas comunidades, nuestras vidas son diferentes con relación a la comunidad, la cultura, la política y la familia. El gran desafío para la comunidad latina es de utilizar esos elementos de nuestra cultura y experiencias para tener verdadero poder político.

Our towns, our community, our people—all are expressions of having understood that we are a family with a strong, united voice. Nevertheless, like many communities, our lives vary in relationship to the community, the culture, the politics, and the family. The great challenge for the Latino community is to use these common elements of our culture and experiences in order to obtain real political power.

SO FAR IN THIS BOOK, discussions of Latinos have explored community and many of the contributing factors that develop a sense of commonality and group affiliation. Using the concepts of **community of common or similar cultures** and **community of interests**, I have tried to identify and describe aspects of the various Latino subgroups that serve to build a larger community. Implicit in this discussion is the idea that the construction of a Latino community is the result of external forces (**structural factors**, social movements, and public attitudes) and activities within the Latino community and organizational efforts to connect across subgroup boundaries. In this chapter I add another dimension to the community-building process: the sense of belonging to a group or community with psychological and emotive connections.

Latinos can share common cultural traditions and practices, as well as similar situations in the workplace, education, and the like. Yet, identification with and emotive attachment to a community builds and maintains an organic community and can work on behalf of its known interests. Since Latinos come from a number of national-origin ancestries, my discussion uses the concept of **pan-ethnicity**: a sociopolitical collectivity made up of people of several different national origins (Espiritu 1992). In identifying with others of different national origins, individuals undergo a shift in their level of identification from smaller boundaries to broader affiliations. These individuals augment, but do not necessarily replace, their national-origin identity by including a broader identity of Latino/Hispanic.

Various works by Espiritu (1992), Nagel (1996), and Cornell and Hartman (1998) have explored the world of pan-ethnicity, which transcends the long-standing group status of **ethnicity** and race. In the United States, Latino/Hispanic identity has been developing for almost three decades. The introduction of a self-identified Spanish-origin item in the 1980 census (E. Fernández 1985) was an early attempt to cluster persons from Spanish-speaking countries of the Western Hemisphere and the Iberian Peninsula as a major ethnic group. Almost at the same time, legislation initiated by Mexican American congresspersons (i.e., Congressman Edward Roybal, D-CA) sought to have federal agencies collect and report statistical information on Spanish origin.

The national media had "discovered" the rapidly growing Latino population and produced major news and feature stories during the late 1970s and the 1980s. The 1980s were designated the "decade of the Hispanic" by many national news media. In the U.S. context, ethnicity took on a different character, since groups were not limited to persons of particular national origins or ancestries. Pan-ethnicity for Latino persons also affected American Indians and Asians. The American mosaic was dramatically changing, and minority standing incorporated the notion of "pan-ethnicity."

For the most part, ethnicity was thought of in terms of national and ancestral origin: Italian, Polish, Irish, and Mexican Americans were American ethnic groups. Before the 1970s, the Latino world primarily comprised three groups—people of Mexican origin, Puerto Ricans, and Cubans—as well as much smaller numbers of other Latino subgroups. Each had its own history, organizations, leadership, and internal ethnic networks. Ethnicity included an emotive element in which persons maintained affinity to and affiliation with others from their country of origin or ancestry. Cornell (1988) describes ethnicity as a web of sentiments, beliefs, worldviews, and practices that individuals hold in common. A sense of ethnicity guaranteed group solidarity as a natural companion. Culture, traditions, and language served as the glue for this attachment.

Internal group definitions and experiences did not solely define the nature and origin of ethnicity, as structural conditions and treatment also create and reinforce ethnic groups. Legislative policies that categorize individuals by groups and define them by national origin, ancestry, race, and so on, control both benefits and enforcement in the areas of civil rights and increasing access to educational opportunities, labor markets (job training, language classes, etc.), and health services. Yet, this type of policy categorization has other costs, including stigmatization and victimization, in addition to creating benefits for group membership. How political and economic institutions treat and interact with persons from different ethnic groups can help impose and define ethnicity. In this sense, ethnicity has dimensions of voluntary status as well as imposed group affiliation.

An example of this in the case of Latinos is Mexican Americans' experience since the 1960s and the development of the pan-ethnic term *Hispanic*. As already indicated, the term became widely used after the 1970s. Critics like Gómez (1992) suggest that the term was a product of Madison Avenue public relations firms, Capitol Hill press corps, major media outlets, and governmental bureaucrats. This analysis sees the rise in marketing efforts (Mattel's Hispanic Barbie, Coors's Decade of the Hispanic, etc.) as reinforcing the evolution toward identifying Mexican Americans and other Latinos as

Hispanics. This helped to blur distinctions across the various Latino subgroups. Consequently, both print and visual media and governmental reporting promoted usage of the term, which has now exploded throughout the country. "Hispanic" has become the primary descriptor both for specific Latino national-origin groups like Mexican Americans or Chicanos and for all clusters of groups of Spanish origin.

So the term *Hispanic* has been the product of external forces trying to simplify and homogenize a diverse aggregation of Latino subgroups. A data-gathering agency, the U.S. Census Bureau, is credited with institutionalizing the label "Hispanic" by including it in the 1980 census. Yet Edward Fernandez of the Census Bureau's Ethnic and Spanish Division (Del Olmo 1998) indicates that the impetus for the Spanish-origin category came from Mexican American policy groups that were trying to respond to undercounts of Mexican Americans and other Latinos. The adoption of this broader term was one way to ensure a fuller portrayal of Latinos, as well as nationalization or pan-ethnic labeling of all the various Latino subgroups.

For the Mexican American community, there had been a long evolution of labels to differentiate this population, from "Mexicanos" to "Spanish Americans" to "Latino Americans" to "Mexican Americans" and "Chicanos" (Acuña 1988; Gómez-Quiñones 1990). Distinguishing in-group and out-group contexts was an important factor in the derivation and use of specific labels. There were in-group preferences for specific labels, which varied by class, region, and generational distance from Mexico (J. A. García 1982). Different segments of the Mexican-origin community used labels like "pocho," "Mexicano," "Raza," "Chicano," "Manito," and "mestizo," among others. The various ethnic labels usually reflected class, national origin, nativity, racial identification, cultural traditions, and language use (J. A. García et al. 1994; Patterson 1975). In addition, during the 1960s, labels also indicated political orientations and ideologies. For example, the Chicano label (Hirsch and Gutierrez 1973, 1974; Gómez-Quiñones 1990) incorporated a more radical political ideology and approaches for social change and justice. In a contemporary sense, the endorsement of "Hispanic" by some Mexican American political elites recognizes a modern form of **ethnic identity**.

For our purposes, ethnic identity is dynamic and multidimensional and has both symbolic and instrumental functions. While Mexican-origin political activists used "Mexican American" and "Chicano" during the 1960s and 1970s, the use of labels has been broadened and altered. Mexican Americans, like other individuals, have multiple changing ethnic and social identities. Broader inclusiveness and multiple layers of affinity and loyalty reflect the contemporary nature of identity. Thus, a Mexican American can have multiple identities that connect her with local situational factors and the larger social context, which can trigger a variety of specific identities. For example, a Mexican-origin woman may identify herself as a minority, a Hispanic, a Mexican American, a person of Mexican ancestry, a Spanish speaker, and as bicultural. Each identity can serve to extend a person in a variety of networks and frames of reference. Modern ethnicity, including among Latinos, results from a dynamic, fluid, and contextual process (Barvosa 2008).

"Hispanic" can define who is not Hispanic as much as who is. Padilla (1986) outlines the Latinization of groups in Chicago in which a pan-ethnic label ("Latino," in this case) expanded the size of the local community and forged an added identity for greater political **mobilization**. The dynamics related to ethnicity, national origin, and race are constantly changing. The advent of pan-ethnicity and the broadening of its

BOX 5.1. Another Focus Group Vignette, 2006

I was fortunate to be part of the team of principal investigators of the Latino National Survey (LNS) in 2005 and 2006. We conducted eighteen focus group sessions in large urban areas as well as rural communities in the Midwest and the South. Participants included recent immigrants, noncitizens, and second-generation and beyond Latinos, as well as a range of ages and near even distribution by gender. This chapter has directed particular attention toward a sense of being part of a pan-ethnic community of persons of "Spanish origin." One interesting outcome of the numerous focus groups was an almost universal use of the terms *Latino* and *Hispanic*. Whether participants were newly arrived to the United States, long-term residents, or native-born, they seemed to incorporate the use of these terms naturally to talk about themselves, friends, neighbors, and coworkers. Contributing to this sense of pan-ethnicity was the composition of their social networks, which included persons from other Latino subgroups, other racial and ethnic groups, and both immigrants and native-born persons. Key connectors were social networks that began with their family members, circle of friends, and coworkers. Our focus group respondents also demonstrated a greater sense of ease and comfort with other Latinos as opposed to non-Latinos around certain activities (i.e., tamaleadas, dancing venues and genres, cultural events). There was clear evidence that the 2006 LNS focus group participants lived in a much more interactive world in which knowledge and experiences about America were widespread, regardless of geographic location; yet, their Latino world was an integral part of their daily lives.

scope beyond national origin has redefined group parameters, but it remains a loose coupling that does not precisely explain what determines who is a Hispanic at all times and in all situations. The Latino pan-ethnic community has developed into a perceived and actual interest group that shares cultural traditions, situations, and practices. At the same time, the involvement of Latino elites and activists affects the evolution and development of an identifiable Latino community.

Latino Political Elites and Activists

Political elites and activists translate and interpret political and social necessities and realities. They frame critical meanings and contexts for the Latino community to advance political agendas and enhance their empowerment. Thus, Latino leaders inform, educate, and motivate members of the Latino community to relate their own circumstances, as well as opportunities and obstacles, regarding governmental institutions, policies, and actions. The Latino community is further defined and identified, increasing its involvement with American political life. The use of the terms *Hispanic* and *Latino* broadens the size of these subcommunities and creates greater visibility in national arenas like Congress, the national media, and federal agencies. Many leaders of national Mexican American organizations participated in discussions focusing on clarifying some common denominators for this loose aggregation of Latino national-origin subgroups.

The 1980 census incorporated the ethnic term *Spanish origin*, which applies to persons in over twenty Spanish-origin countries, and this category is deemed as the ethnicity question in the census. As a result, this ethnic category has expanded the size and geographic base of the Latino community vis-à-vis non-Hispanic political elites and has won support at the grassroots level. This new ethnic group has national force as a significantly larger and more geographically dispersed group than a single Latino subgroup like Mexican Americans. A Latino/Hispanic community can be shaped by Latino political elites who project both potential and actual power and influence. In addition, it can create more opportunities for political mobilization, broaden the scope of awareness for group affinity and membership, and expand the resource base for Latino interests. All of these factors represent central elements of Latino community building.

Some key components for a Latino community include some degree of group identification, affinity, and attachment among persons of Spanish origin with other persons of Spanish origin. Consensus, solidarity, and cohesion are objectives of community building, but they are not absolutely essential to it. Elements of community (group identity and affinity, common interests and circumstances) provide pragmatic opportunities to engage in collective efforts. The presence and perception of a national community serves as political capital for Latino leaders. It becomes the primary responsibility of leadership to capitalize on the various strands of Latino community life to direct its members toward specific actions and connections with regard to the policies in the public and private sectors.

Communities of common cultures and interests and the resulting networks established across the Latino subcommunities serve as connections from which communication, interactions, and collaborative opportunities are created. Consensus, coherency of interests and actions, and unity are all components of community in which variation will exist at any given point. The Latino community is evolving and developing on the foundation of common culture and situations. Latino organizations and leadership have made direct efforts that recognize these connections and build on them. Dialogue about the development of pan-ethnicity is an example of the community-building process among Latinos.

The Latino community's political capital is enhanced with the appearance of coherency and unity. This is an important resource because, on many occasions, political leaders, officials, and institutions (Congress, state legislatures, etc.) place the onus on Latino leaders to present their issues, positions, demands, and so on, as one voice. The absence of consensus is thus viewed externally as undermining the legitimacy of organizations and their leadership. The development of Latino pan-ethnicity (and community) provides a broad set of group parameters in which ambiguity and loose boundaries (regarding the inclusiveness and total cohesiveness of Latinos) do not necessarily undermine the effort. This highlights the strategic nature of pan-ethnicity and its flexibility and fluidity.

Such an umbrella descriptor for a wider range of Latino subgroups takes on a more pragmatic and broader issue orientation. It also promotes the formation of intergroup political coalitions among Latino subgroups not limited to purely national-origin and regionally driven groups and issues. Consequently, the use of "Latino" and "Hispanic" shifts the emphasis of community-based activities from primarily local to state- and national-level electoral and policy advocacy.

A larger Latino configuration, which has been influenced internally by the Latino subcommunities and externally by political institutions and officials and the national media, is a realistic characterization of Latino development in the early twenty-first century. Regardless of the origin of "Hispanic" or "Latino," the role of Latino leaders is to define the labels' meaning and relevance. The movement to redefine the boundaries of communities complements strategies of Latino political elites to promote and add specific meaning to pan-ethnic terms. Three specific developments have contributed to the movement toward a broader definition of ethnicity for Latino subgroups: (1) the transition to modern ethnicity that further interconnects race, ethnicity, culture, class, and gender[1] into broader categorizations; (2) the contextual nature of ethnic labels and identity; and (3) the coexistence of multiple identities (Barvosa 1999, 2008), with salient ones influenced by utility and context.

Our theme of community building includes pan-ethnic group awareness and identification. I am not suggesting that pan-ethnic identity takes the form of "primordial" affinity and attachment. It becomes an acquired identity whose meaning and relevance are contextually defined and interpreted. It delineates loosely defined parameters of group membership and interests. Such broad characterizations may be more effective in identifying non-Hispanics than providing clear, concise identifications of Hispanics.

Puerto Rican, Cuban, and Central and South American political elites have followed a similar evolution and development. The broader distinction of the Latino umbrella has enabled different Latino subgroups to advance their issues and concerns in both local and national arenas. For example, the Salvadoran and Guatemalan communities have focused significant efforts on obtaining political refugee status in order to facilitate the legal status of many Salvadoran and Guatemalan immigrants. In addition to enabling pursuit of policy changes within their own organizations, the broader inclusion of Central Americans with other Latinos, especially immigrants, helps expand the constituency base, political visibility, and potential clout to affect immigration reform and policy adjustments. The Central American segment represents the most recent influx of Latino subgroups and the fastest-growing Latino segment. The utility of this group's adopting the Latino identity and its members' labeling themselves as such fuels the well-established image of a fast-growing population.

Community building among Latino subgroups does not preclude the persistence of Latino subgroup organizations or targeted efforts for their respective community needs and interests. The recognition that an individual has multiple identities has a parallel politically. Thus, political involvement on behalf of Latinos may be salient at times, while on other occasions Latino subgroup interests (Dominican, Cuban, etc.) may be more prominent. This differentiation is also relevant in terms of the political arenas in which Latinos' political actions take place. This exploration of community among individuals and Latino subgroups reveals a network of connectors in which some degree of affinity and attachment occurs. It manifests itself politically with enough frequency to sustain a sense of community and, perhaps more importantly, to deepen a sense of community.

Latino Identity: Two Vignettes

The utility of Latino identity and its promotion by Latino activists and leaders is illustrated through two incidents that took place in Chicago some sixteen years apart. The first involved cross-communication between two local Latino community organizations, and the latter was a focus group discussion of identity.

In 1971 and 1972, I engaged in fieldwork with several progressive neighborhood-based community organizations—the Brown Berets, Latin American Defense Organization (LADO), Young Patriots, Black Panthers, and Young Lords, among others—that were involved in free health clinics (J. A. García 1977). All of these organizations were very politicized and viewed community control and radical reform as central to their mission. During this time, the city of Chicago was determined to close the clinics by requiring physician ownership. Each clinic was independent, and there was very little contact and communication between the different organizations. Ironically, as they faced similar problems, there was potential for cooperative and coalitional efforts. The Brown Beret clinic (Benito Juarez) and the LADO clinic (Pedro Albizu Campos) had arranged a joint meeting to discuss possible cooperative activities to deal with pressure coming from the Richard J. Daley political machine.

The meeting was held in the Brown Beret neighborhood (Pilsen), with many members of each organization attending. The youthful Brown Beret membership had a militaristic style of dress and demeanor. At the meeting, they marched in formation into the room with their leaders at the head of the line. LADO was based in West Town in an area with a mix of Latino subgroups—primarily of Puerto Rican and Mexican origin. Its organizational membership was a combination of families, young persons, and seniors. Its members were diverse in terms of age and family status and entered the meeting in a less structured way.

The Brown Berets perceived the LADO organization as primarily a Puerto Rican group and less tied to the U.S. mainland. The Brown Berets saw themselves as cultural nationalists concerned about liberation politics. As a result, the meeting highlighted national origin, cultural nationalism, and cultural differences rather than similarities of ideology, organizational goals, and culture. The meeting became tense, and little progress was made in finding common ground and proposing joint initiatives. Some of the LADO members, lacking child care, had to bring their young children. The divisiveness of the two organizations centered on their respective national origins and perceived cultural differences.

At one point, a Brown Beret leader pointed to a couple in LADO—the male was Puerto Rican and the female, Mexican American. Their three-year-old daughter was also present. He reminded the parents that their daughter would one day have to decide whether she was Puerto Rican or Mexican American/Chicana. The LADO parents, without consulting each other or hesitating, simultaneously responded, "She does not have to decide that; she is a *Latina!*"

Some sixteen years later, I was a co–principal investigator for the **Latino National Political Survey** (the first probability sampling of Cuban, Mexican-origin, and Puerto Rican adults living in the contiguous United States). As part of the preparation of the survey instrument, a series of ten focus groups in five cities was conducted in 1988. Chicago was the site of two focus groups. One of the primary topics of discussion was how individuals see themselves and the topic of social identity. A group of fifteen to twenty Latinos (bilingual or primarily English speakers) agreed to talk for a couple of hours. As the conversation on identity progressed, many of the participants comfortably identified themselves as Latino/a. Over the previous fifteen to twenty years, Latino activists had made concerted efforts to promote Latino identification. At the same time, each participant assumed several other identities, such as Puerto Rican, Salvadoran, Mexican(o), immigrant, and so on.

The group included a brother and sister with one Puerto Rican parent and one of Mexican origin. The sister was married to a man of Italian ancestry living on the South Side of Chicago in a primarily white ethnic neighborhood. The Latina had a daughter who attended a parochial school in the neighborhood. A discussion followed in which the Latina described a series of identities and situations for her daughter. When visiting her grandmother, the daughter emphasized and identified herself as a Mexican American. While visiting her grandfather (the grandparents were divorced), she was a Puerto Rican. At home, the daughter's identity was Latina. At school, the daughter took the ethnicity of her father. Finally, the mother described trips they took together on the Chicago Transit Authority bus. On their bus route toward the Loop (the central retail and business section of the city), the daughter was aware of her minority status and identity. Many of the other bus passengers were African Americans, and the daughter recognized the broader concept of people of color. It was clear from the focus group setting that these people were cognizant of their multiple identities and how different situations trigger a different identity and label. An individual's multiplicity of identities can be transferred and learned by children. The socialization process has been researched in terms of the development of identities (gender, racial, ethnic, etc.) and how early that process begins (Bernal and Martinelli 1993; Barvosa 2008). In box 5.1, I recount how pan-ethnicity manifested itself in focus groups associated with the **Latino National Survey** in 2005.

Latino Community Building and Mobilization: The Critical Political Link

Community building among Latino subgroups is directly connected to common interests, circumstances, experiences, cultural traditions and values (in this case for Latinos), personal networks, and affinities. Consequently, a Latino community and its subgroups participate in various political arenas to pursue their interests and goals. The examination of Latinos and their politics does not assume that political dynamics occur only because some basis for community exists. Another essential element is the mobilization of individuals and group members to act collectively. Mobilization is the process by which political candidates and parties, activists, and groups try to induce other people to participate. Effective mobilization occurs when efforts by these individuals or groups increase the likelihood of involvement by others (Tilly 1978; Rosenstone and Hansen 1993).

Political participation in the United States declined through much of the latter half of the twentieth century. In the electoral arena, fewer persons voted in national, state, and local elections. One of the ironies is that registration systems and access to the registration process have been made easier (motor voter legislation, deputy registrars, mail-in registration, same-day registration, etc.). Yet, the 2000 election showed that problems still exist, especially for minority populations. Outdated voting machines, inaccurate voting lists, challenges to voting status, and intimidation were among the problems identified by the 2001 U.S. Civil Rights Commission study in Florida. Political scientists have examined the decline of political involvement since the beginning of the discipline. Since the late 1990s, such factors as declining social and political trust, heightened cynicism, and the decline of community and social networks have been identified as some of the primary contributors (Putnam 2000; Nie, Junn, and Stehlik-Barry 1996).

Political participation can be viewed as individually driven. It is up to each person to determine how, when, and why to get politically involved. Participation is mostly episodic, and only a small proportion of the citizenry maintains a continual practice of involvement. For our purposes, participation involves the process of influencing the distribution of social goods and values (Rosenstone and Hansen 1993). Participants may be public or private actors in the political arena using direct or indirect means to influence. We know that on an individual basis, the critical factors for involvement are resources, time, opportunities, beliefs, values, ideology, and participatory political attitudes. Participation is also affected by contact with organizations, leaders, and political parties that strategically choose to activate specific individuals or groups. Therefore, a person's participation is due to choices she makes and the available incentives to participate. Overall, the pull factors than can motivate a Latino to participate are the nature of political life (interest, impact, excitement, etc.), important social networks for which politics is a key element, contact with political actors and activists, available time, issues, and group identification.

A Latino who becomes involved in the political process faces both opportunity costs and resource requirements, which include time, skills (communicative, organizational, etc.), money, knowledge, self-confidence, and efficacy (Rosenstone and Hansen 1993; Verba, Scholzman, and Brady 1995). The acquisition of education (usually in terms of schooling) translates into greater accumulation of pertinent knowledge and familiarity with political processes and institutions. In addition, more schooling is associated with the development of political skills (letter writing, oral presentations, research and informational access, etc.). Individuals with a strong sense of personal and political efficacy are more likely to be self-confident and competent in political arenas. Time, resources, and positive predispositions constitute the key ingredients for an active citizenry.

While costs and resources tend to differentiate individuals who choose to and do participate in politics, there are benefits and rewards for political involvement. Researchers (Verba, Scholzman, and Brady 1995; Wolfinger and Rosenstone 1980; Rosenstone and Hansen 1993) have categorized the political benefits as material, solidarity, and purposive. Material benefits are tangible rewards that are converted to a monetary benefit like a job or a tax break. Solidarity rewards are intangibles such as status, deference, and friendship (Rosenstone and Hansen 1993). Finally, purposive benefits are inherent rewards that a person derives from participation in and of itself. Even within this schema, the reward system can extend beyond personal rewards. Political involvement can result in the attainment of collective rewards that have diffuse group benefits.

For example, the extension of the **Voting Rights Act** with bilingual provisions for election information and assistance could have both individual and collective benefits for Latinos. Clearly, the community has a direct stake in the well-being and advancement of Latinos in terms of political involvement and outcomes. As more Latinos vote and make use of bilingual materials and assistance, the community gains a potentially louder voice. Latinos who do not need bilingual election services can be supportive of such policies for both overall community benefits and the symbolic value of addressing the Latino community. Community is defined in terms of essential elements and interests, so preferences are articulated with specific political outcomes in mind. Latinos who identify with Latino organizations (locally and nationally) and with Latino leaders and advocates can develop a strong psychological attachment and become more likely to engage in a variety of political arenas.

A significant amount of research on Latinos and Latino subgroups portrays a relatively politically inactive population. The general political-participation research literature (Verba, Scholzman, and Brady 1995) suggests why some persons do not participate. One segment does not participate because its members are unable to do so. For the most part, such persons are not old enough or are noncitizens. Age and citizenship are requirements for the major kinds of participation. Nevertheless, many young people and noncitizens engage in political activities such as electoral campaigns, community-based organizations, and discussions of community issues with coworkers and neighbors. In discussing the policy area of immigration in chapter 9, I will direct attention to the substantial number of marches and protests by largely immigrants (including those of undocumented status) and the intersection of individuals' motivations to express themselves politically and organizational involvement in channeling their efforts.

Another segment consists of persons who are not interested in participation because of either nonparticipatory attitudes or inadequate resources. For example, Latinos who are cynical about or alienated from politics, its institutions, and its processes are less inclined to get involved, especially in the more conventional modes of political involvement (voting, partisan activities, campaigning). A view of politics as highly complicated or incomprehensible (J. A. García 1989; Michelson 2006) can distance an individual from things political. Political distrust, inefficacy, and lack of political interest can serve as disincentives for political involvement. The final category for nonparticipants includes those who lack contact with others who might ask them to get involved in a particular situation, activity, or issue. A survey by the *Los Angeles Times* (1994b) reported that during the 1994 California election period, no political party or organization soliciting Latino support or involvement had contacted over four-fifths of the sampled Latino electorate. Subsequent research on Latino political mobilization (Leighley and Vedlitz 1999; Barreto, Segura, and Woods 2004; Rodrígues and Segura 2007) supports this view of the general "neglect of political parties and campaigns to invest less in the Latino community. At the same time, when attention is directed toward Latinos, especially by co-ethnics and use of both English and Spanish language media, then greater interest and engagement occurs" (DeSipio and Uhlaner 2007). Again, in chapter 6 on Latino political participation, I will illustrate the key factors and agents of mobilization.

So far this discussion has focused on the distinction between individually motivated involvement and the role of mobilization. In very concrete ways, mobilization deals with the social temperament of political life. The identification and use of social networks, activating key influencers in those networks, and the knowledge of persons' concerns make political involvement more personal and translatable to individuals' personal situations and everyday world. A person who is connected to a political issue or candidate is generally more likely to respond favorably and get drawn into political affairs.

Since 1990, there have been many national debates, actions, policies, and public perceptions about immigration, especially undocumented migration. This policy area holds the attention of both the public and policy makers. Obviously the immigrant community is well aware of the policies and circumstances related to immigration, labor and housing markets, law enforcement, educational access, and adjustment to life in the United States. The California State initiative **Proposition 187** directly targeted access to education and health services among undocumented and permanent resident aliens. The mobilization that took place within the Latino community regarding Proposition 187 involved local neighborhood organizations as well as national civil rights groups. The result was raised awareness and increased voter registration for the upcoming elections, as well as public rallies and protests around the proposition. More Latinos ran for elective office in California, and their numbers increased in state and local government, accentuating the rising level of political expression and involvement among Latinos.

Since 2005, Arizona **Senate Bill (SB) 1070** represented the latest wave of state-initiated legislation in the immigration policy area. In the late spring of 2010, the Arizona State Legislature passed SB 1070, which gave new powers to state and local police to detain and arrest suspected undocumented immigrants. This legislation produced greater polarization between proponents of more restrictive immigration policies and those advocating more "humane" and "immigrant-friendly" reforms. In addition, SB 1070 represented more active efforts by state and local governments to take action due to increased impatience and frustration with the federal government. SB 1070 raised the issues of Latino profiling and scapegoating of Latinos specifically. Public protests, organizational responses, and litigation have followed, but other state legislatures have followed suit, enacting similar legislation. The immigration-reform area is a good example of how mobilization efforts by leaders, activists, and Latino-based organizations induced Latinos to get involved through a number of different venues and forms of political interest.

Political mobilization includes both direct and indirect forms of inducement and persuasion. The direct form lies in opportunities to participate, such as signing petitions, posting campaign signs, registering to vote, or attending rallies. By creating participatory venues, the mobilizers subsidize political information and the personal costs of involvement. Mobilization usually does not take the form of a blanket call for involvement but is more strategic in nature. **Targeted mobilization** involves identifying persons who, when contacted, are more likely to respond to the calls for involvement. The targeting has to be done efficiently, as resources are always limited. So the people most likely to be contacted are those who are knowledgeable about politics and issues, those positioned in established networks, those whose actions are effective, and those likely to respond (Rosenstone and Hansen 1993). For the general population these persons are more likely to be employed, belong to organizations, be affluent, have higher levels of educational attainment, and be partisan. For the Latino community, these persons will likely be opinion leaders in their neighborhoods or at work, possess political knowledge, and be positively disposed to involvement.

We know that individuals with higher socioeconomic status (education, income, and occupational status) are more likely to participate politically than those at the lower end. Higher socioeconomic status affords a person greater skills, resources, and opportunities for participation. In the case of Latinos, the current socioeconomic distribution of community members is located at the lower end of these class indicators than for the non-Latino population. Consequently, enhanced issue awareness and greater salience, coupled with a sense of group identity, become an additional cueing element for targeted mobilization. Considerable research (J. A. García 1997; de la Garza et al. 1994; Michelson 2005) has documented relatively lower levels of political involvement among Latinos, while at the same time income and occupational status are not as strong determinants for political participation as they are for other groups (J. A. García 1995).

More recent research (Hardy-Fanta 1993; Pardo 1998; Saito 1998; Barreto et al. 2005) has found political activism and interest among Latinos to be quite evident at the local and neighborhood levels. For example, state and local government initiatives to locate a prison facility and waste management site in the East Los Angeles section of the county activated strong concerns among Latino residents, especially mothers and other women in the area. As a result, the Mothers of East Los Angeles was formed to oppose these two projects (Pardo 1998). Eventually they were successful, but in the process of organizing and strategizing around these issues, the mothers and other involved Latinos developed a better understanding of the political process and empowered themselves. Community struggles against unfavorable governmental proposals and actions enabled leadership development and heightened interest in a wide range of community issues. Success in achieving objectives provided greater incentive to pursue other issues of importance and interest with like energy and commitment. Similar events occurred in other communities with Latino populations, such as Miami (Portes and Stepnick 1993), New York City (Falcón 1993), and other major metropolitan areas (Jennings 1992, 1994; J. Cruz 1998).

The timing dimension of mobilization is critical for efficient and effective campaigns. Persons who are contacted need to be ready to follow leaders and have an interest in the issue. The directed activity needs to have a consequential effect (eventually) on the problem or issue. Also, the action must be timed to occur when a decision is impending and the outcome is hanging in the balance. The timing should not compete with other concerns that may diminish a response and commitment to act. For example, in its earlier organizational development, the Southwest Voter Registration and Education Project (SVREP) began extensive voter-registration campaigns. Cities and neighborhoods were selected, and a local organizing committee conducted the campaign. Registration campaigns were held during years in which elections were several months away or when no elections were held. In the latter case, there were lower returns (i.e., sustained interests and actual voting) among the recently registered Latino voters.

Newly registered persons did not vote, or they let their registration lapse. Subsequently SVREP timed its registration campaigns to coincide with election years and to take place closer to primary and general elections. In addition, volunteers talked to prospective registrants about local problems and concerns. These exchanges served to increase awareness about linkages between community problems and the political system. If not having a voice in government or nonresponsiveness were concerns, then registering to vote became a real tie to political participation and change. Finally, Latino political mobilization is directed toward legislative arenas, which are overtly political and visible, rather than bureaucratic ones.

Conclusion

This chapter's discussion has centered on the bases for community among Latinos with an important ingredient of group identity and the resulting linkages with political involvement. There is a clear link between individual motivation, resources to participate, and mobilization efforts by organizations and activists to assist in that process. The individual component provides insight about the motivations and capacities that a person develops as well as his cumulative experiences in different political arenas. Political participation in America is voluntary, which contributes to overall participatory rates, as politics must contend with work, family, social interests, and other daily activities and concerns. For Latinos, limited resources, language barriers, a historic lack of political engagement in the United States, and lack of contact with recruitment networks have all contributed to lower levels of political involvement.

The remaining chapters examine the individual and mobilization aspects of Latino participation in a variety of different venues (voting, campaigning, organizational involvement, partisan activities, school-related activities, letter writing, etc.). For the most part, our knowledge about participation levels for specific Latino subgroups (primarily Mexican Americans, Cubans, and Puerto Ricans) is limited, while the more recent research tends to group all Latinos together. In addition, the data are pertinent only to particular participatory modes (primarily voting and election returns). Only in the last ten years have information, studies, and accounts of the political participation of the "other Latinos" become available. I use the extant research information to characterize a participation "map" for these politically emerging communities. In addition to characterizing Latino participation, I present the essential factors that influence those who become involved and in which arenas. Latinos cite a lack of time or interest, a perceived lack of relevance, and a lack of understanding of politics (Verba, Scholzman, and Brady 1995) as the major reasons for their political inactivity. However, our discussion of externalities also suggests that public policies, public opinion and the social climate, and organizational activities can hinder as well as facilitate political activeness.

This discussion would not be complete without considering the mobilization dynamics in which individual political behavior and attitudes intersect with the targeted actions of organizations and activists. With the development of a stronger Latino community, how do Latino-based organizations and Latino leaders and activists motivate and influence fellow Latinos to get more involved in the American political process? Does organizational affiliation and engagement, whether the group is specifically political or not, provide interest, knowledge, and networks from which to mobilize? Does greater attention to and visibility of Latinos on the American landscape become an extra incentive to be more political? How does issue salience serve to activate Latinos and/or give mobilizers the substance to encourage and reduce the costs of Latino participation? Finally, the nature and form of political engagement are always affected by the context in which Latinos reside. This statement affirms the cliché that "pace matters."

Discussion Questions

1. How people label themselves usually indicates an identity to which they have a strong attachment. What interpretations can be made about persons who label themselves as Latino or Hispanic?
2. Even when a person identifies him- or herself with a specific label, other identities may also be important. Discuss the concepts of multiple and situational identity and how they relate to the development of a Latino community?

3. There has been discussion that Latino and/or Hispanic is a socially constructed category promoted by Latino elites to develop a base from which they can operate and benefit. Discuss the "realness" of being Latino or Hispanic in "everyday life" for many Latinos and their political engagement.

4. The linkage of mobilization and political participation has been illustrated through discussions of California's Proposition 187 and Arizona's SB 1070. Can you think of any other incidences that demonstrated the mobilization–politics link?

CHAPTER 6

Latino Political Participation

<table>
<tr>
<td>

Y ¿que tal tu vida cívica? ¿Aprendiste de tus padres? ¿Qué talentos desarrollaste para trabajar en la comunidad? Si se te pide que trabajes en la comunidad ¿cómo vas a responder?

</td>
<td>

And how is your civic life? Did you learn from your parents? What talents have you developed to serve our community better? If someone asks you to join in the effort with other members of our community, how will you respond?

</td>
</tr>
</table>

SINCE THE MEMORABLE 2008 ELECTION of Barack Obama, Latinos have received some attention from the political parties and the national media. The previous presidential cycle clearly marked Latinos as an important segment of the American electorate. I will discuss the 2008 presidential election in chapter 7. The 2010 midterm elections, however, raised concerns about the continued upswing of Latino **political participation** and Democratic Party support. Latino Decisions, a series of interviews conducted by the University of Washington's Center for the Study of Race and Ethnicity prior to the 2010 elections, found the salience of immigration and the economy affecting Latino voters' interest and level of enthusiastic support for the Democratic Party. A preliminary interpretation would suggest a strong connection between partisan support and policy responsiveness.

The midterm elections provide a means of examining Latino political participation at the end of the first decade of the new millennium. In the twenty-first century, will the rising trajectory of Latino political involvement be reconfigured? Will it backtrack to earlier low levels of collective involvement? Or will it surge to have an even greater impact and visibility on the American political landscape? For Latinos, the objective of converting a growing adult population into a more politically oriented and immersed population remains a central target. This chapter examines current patterns of Latino political participation, the critical contributing factors, and areas in which there is a need for systematic information.

American political culture envisions political participation as a fundamental right obliging each person to play a role in political processes and institutions. Having access, pursuing political interests, knowing the rules of the game,[1] developing effective political resources, having responsive representatives, and influencing the policy-making process are central dimensions of political participation.

Political participation can be described as the involvement of an individual or group in the central objective of influencing the policy-making process and the substance of policies themselves. This entails accumulating and utilizing resources, developing positive participatory orientations, and recruiting others to get involved. Political resources include time, money, and communication and organizational skills. Resources equip a person to engage in the political arena with knowledge, available time, and the pertinent skills to articulate their objectives and effect change. Participatory orientations develop political attitudes conducive to participation, political and personal efficacy, political trust and interest, and a sense of group consciousness. The third side of the participation triangle is recruitment. A person may initiate his or her own actions as a result of being encouraged by persons or organizations to get involved in a particular way. In other words, a person may become active because he or she was asked to do so.

Early socialization also plays a critical role in the development of an individual's participatory future. Family discussion of things political and exposure to political events such as rallies and campaigns can make a lasting imprint on a young person. Similarly, early preadult experiences such as involvement in extracurricular activities, participation in religious organizations, and having politically active parents make a strong impression on children and help to teach them about civic and political life. Such background characteristics as gender, race, and **ethnicity** also play an important role in early socialization. For instance, familial expectations that girls will be less involved—or not involved at all—can affect a woman's political participation. Being subjected to discriminatory treatment can cause a person to become politically involved to combat such treatment in the future (de la Garza and Vaughn 1984; Umana-Taylor and Fina 2010). The cycle of life experiences and early socialization establishes the foundation from which an individual chooses to get involved or not. However, early socialization does not completely predetermine any individual's participatory life. One final note about the role of political socialization: among Latino immigrants, the children (both the U.S.-born and those who migrated to the United States at an early age) may be socializers of their parents (García-Castañon 2010; V. Cruz 2010).

The literature on political participation (Verba and Nie 1972; Verba, Scholzman, and Brady 1995; Milbrath and Hoel 1977; Rosenstone and Hansen 1993) identifies who participates, as well as when, where, and how. According to Verba, Scholzman, and Brady (1995), participation involves (1) resources, (2) psychological orientation, and (3) recruitment. Resources include the accumulation of time, money, and skills. Time refers to having both opportunities to participate and the time available to do so. Money provides a valuable resource for engaging in political activities and being identified in networks. Skills include the ability and confidence to engage in political activities. Education plays a major role in skill acquisition. Educational attainment provides greater political knowledge and information, as well as communication skills (writing, public speaking, organization of thoughts and ideas, etc.). Higher educational attainment generally positions a person in higher job and income levels. In addition, positive participatory orientations like personal and political efficacy, political trust, and sense of civic duty are associated with greater educational attainment. Finally, higher levels of education are generally associated with organizational affiliation and involvement.

All of these ingredients for political participation center on an individual's abilities and acquired skills,[2] position in a job setting, and resource base from which to engage in political matters. As already noted in the demographic profiles, Latinos as a group do not as often possess the necessary time, money, and skills. A discussion of participation must include recruitment and **mobilization**: persons get politically involved when they are asked to be active. Political mobilization entails efforts by political parties, organizations, candidates, and leaders to persuade individuals to participate. Mobilization efforts can be direct, contacting and encouraging persons for specific actions and responses, or indirect, using social networks to communicate the message. The primary networks are based in the workplace or the neighborhood.

So far I have identified political participation as originating in the individual or in targeted efforts by third parties to persuade persons to get involved in a specific activity or issue. The results of **targeted mobilization** include creating opportunities to participate and subsidizing the costs of both gathering political information and conducting political activism. The latter point refers to providing materials, rides to the polls, individuals to assist, and the like so that the targeted individual does not have to expend as much time and energy as he would if he were participating alone. Thus, the act of mobilizing entails identifying people to contact and persuade and the most efficient manner to reach them. In the identification process, mobilizers have a good sense that the persons contacted will likely respond to the call for action. Research by Rosenstone and Hansen (1993) indicates that the persons most likely to be targeted are employed, belong to and serve as leaders in organizations, are more educated, have higher income levels, and have some partisan (political party) history.

Mobilization efforts tend to be more successful if the contact is made between persons who know each other. Personal connections establish a more receptive setting for the message and request. It is also important that once contacted, the person will be effective and well positioned to solicit the help of others in his or her networks. Timing is the other essential ingredient. When you ask someone to participate, the issue (e.g., a city ordinance) or event (e.g., hearing or election date) is usually very near. Thus, the outcome is hanging in the balance, and identifiable consequences will affect the targeted individual.

Political participation centers on obtaining volunteers when other circumstances, situations, opportunities, and distractions compete for people's involvement. Most Americans' political participation is very limited and sporadic. Participation involves time, resources, opportunities, knowledge and interest, and the motivation to engage in a wide range of possible political activities. Nonparticipants are individuals who cannot participate, do not want to, or have not been asked to get involved. Persons who cannot participate are excluded by restrictions like age requirements, noncitizen or felon status, language barriers, and the like. Persons who do not want to participate are usually not interested, deem other things more important, do not have enough time, find politics too complicated or boring, or feel distrustful of and cynical about politics. The last category of nonparticipants is never asked by anyone or any organization to get politically involved because the mobilizers do not perceive such individuals as likely participants or as positioned in useful networks. The size of the nonparticipant group varies by the type of political activities available.

How and where do Americans participate politically? The most common form of political participation centers on elections. The United States holds the greatest number

BOX 6.1. Today We March, Tomorrow We Vote

In the spring of 2006, millions of persons took to the streets in virtually every major city and many others throughout the United States to protest the Sensenbrenner immigration bill[1] and advocate for a more "humane," comprehensive immigration policy. A substantial proportion of the participants and organizers were immigrants (mostly Latino) of both documented and undocumented status. It was estimated that over 3 million people in 130 cities participated in pro-immigrant marches (Cano 2008). This note serves to highlight some major patterns of mobilization regarding Latino immigrants who had been considered either apolitical or politically uniformed and uninterested in American politics (García and Sanchez 2004; García and de la Garza 1985). Traditional forms of mobilization formed part of efforts to organize and direct participants toward collective action (i.e., developing strategy, accessing resources through unions and other sources). In many regards the object of the protest marches was to put a public and personal face on the objects of punitive and restrictive policies, including the scapegoating of immigrants for many societal ills (e.g., unfair job competition, drains on social and health programs, lost taxes, increased criminal activity), and to develop policy discussions and initiatives that are both more comprehensive in scope (away from the emphasis on border enforcement and criminalization) and responsive to immigrant and Latino interests and concerns.

From a mobilization perspective, the less expected techniques included utilizing modern technology and the mass media to publicize and stir up support for this cause. More specifically, Spanish-language media (especially radio and radio personalities), websites (e.g., www.march25coalition.org), text messaging, and social networking sites (e.g., Facebook) played a role by providing the necessary information for participation as well as the "rules of engagement" and the rationale for the protest marches (Reyes 2006). The size of these marches and degree of organizational effectiveness challenge perceptions of immigrants as apolitical and politically unsophisticated. Chapter 9 on immigration policy provides more discussion and analysis about the Latino immigrant sector and its political engagement.

of elections each year. As a result, political participation is seen as election dominated, and voter registration and turnout become the primary indicators. In addition to voting, political campaigns involve making campaign contributions, doing volunteer work, posting campaign signs or wearing campaign buttons, and attending rallies.

The ultimate form of participation is seeking political office, but a very small fraction of persons actually obtain it. At the same time, political participation extends beyond the electoral arena in both individual and collective ways. Persons can make direct contact with public and/or bureaucratic officials regarding an individual problem or on behalf of their neighborhood or group. The other dimensions of political participation include belonging to organized groups, which can be explicitly political or nonpolitical. Involvement with an organization as a member, financial contributor, or leader gives one access to information and knowledge, policy preferences, organizational skills, and experience with collective efforts.[3] Other forms of political participation include protest activities, talking about politics or trying to persuade another individual to support a given candidate or proposition, and partisan activities. The opportunities for political participation are substantial, and many persons choose to become politically engaged.

While active political participation is an integral part of a viable democracy, and laws, practices, and traditions try to reinforce an individual's regular political engagement, the actual practice of participation is very uneven. I will try to construct a systematic picture of Latino political participation and examine why the current picture exists. This portrait will have some blank spots because social scientists, marketers, and journalists have only recently chronicled Latinos in the political system.

Latino Political Participation

Early works on Latino political participation (Tirado 1970; García and Arce 1988) focus almost exclusively on Mexican-origin people. From 1970 to 2000, systematic examination of Mexican American and other Latino political behavior has been restricted to specific communities or limited forms of political participation (e.g., voting or organizational activities) (Briegal 1970; Márquez 1985; Allsup 1982; J. A. García 1986a, 1998; Chapa 1995). General conclusions regarding Latino political participation may be summarized as follows: (1) overall rates of participation are lower than those for the general population; (2) there is evidence of accepting participatory orientations, but participation does not necessarily follow; (3) rates of organizational involvement and activities are lower; (4) rates of voter registration and turnout are lower; (5) a significant proportion of the Latino subcommunities comprises foreign-born noncitizens; and (6) there is a feeling of distance from and disinterest in the political world (J. A. García 1997; Falcón 1992; Moreno and Warren 1992; García and Sanchez 2004).

The three primary sources for my portrayal of Latino political participation include the Participation in America II study by Sidney Verba, Kay Scholzman, and Henry Brady (1995), the Latino National Survey (Fraga et al. 2006), and the Pew

TABLE 6.1. Reported Civic Participation among Latinos in the National Survey of Latinos, 2004

Forms of Civic Participation	Percentage of Latinos Who Said They Had . . .		
	Registered Latinos	Nonregistered Citizens	Noncitizens
Attended public meeting or demonstration	26	10	14
Contacted an elected official	22	7	4
Contributed money to a candidate	16	2	2
Attended a political party meeting	16	5	3
Worked as a volunteer or for pay for a candidate	7	3	2
Percentage who said they had done any of the above activities	45	21	18

Source: Pew Hispanic Center/Kaiser Family Foundation, National Survey of Latinos: Politics and Civic Engagement, July 2004 (conducted in April–June 2004).

Hispanic Research Center surveys. I begin by examining reported civic participation among Latinos in Pew's 2004 National Survey of Latinos across a range of political activities. Ironically, the increased numbers of social surveys since 2000 have concentrated more of their attention on voting and vote choices.

Table 6.1 includes five forms of civic participation that Latinos can engage in, excluding voting. The highest percentage of Latino participants is among the registered voters in all five of the different activities. The largest response category is having attended a public meeting or demonstration. Contacting a public official is the second most frequent activity, followed closely by contributing money to a campaign and attending a political party meeting (16 percent each). Among registered Latino voters, almost half (45 percent) had done at least one of these activities. In comparison, the nonregistered Latino citizens and Latino noncitizens had significantly lower rates of civic participation across all of the six activities. These two groupings are relatively similar to the registered Latino voters only in the area of attending a public meeting or demonstration. Interestingly, the significant noncitizen segment within the Latino community was viewed both electorally and in other realms of political participation as apolitical, uninterested, and/or uninformed.

In domains outside the electoral arena, Latino political participation is lower as well. Individual, direct contact with public officials is a preferred way of expressing political viewpoints and concerns. Latinos are much less likely to contact officials, and real differences exist between registered and nonregistered Latinos (22 and 7 percent, respectively). Our focus on civic engagement looks at individuals' involvement in various sectors of public life. Table 6.2 draws on the same 2004 Pew Hispanic survey to examine organizational activities. With the same clustering, we find that registered Latinos have higher levels of organizational involvement than the other groupings. At the same time, the differences are not as great as in table 6.1. This is more evidence regarding membership in a church or religious group. For church- and school-related activities, noncitizens are the second highest group in terms of levels of engagement. Historically, education has been the most salient policy concern among Latinos, and the immigrant segment, with its youthfulness and larger families, may contribute to higher levels of involvement in the schools (42 percent for registered Latinos, 27 percent for nonregistered Latinos, and 29 percent for noncitizens). In addition, membership in a group representing a particular

TABLE 6.2. Reported Volunteer Activity among Latinos in the National Survey of Latinos, 2004

Volunteer Activity	Percentage of Latinos Who Said That in the Past Year, They Had Volunteered Their Time to . . .		
	Registered Latinos	Nonregistered Latinos	Noncitizens
Church or religious groups	42	27	29
School or tutoring program	34	14	23
Neighborhood, business or community group	31	17	13
Organization representing their particular nationality, ethnic, or racial group	16	9	10
Percentage who said they had done any of the above activities	63	43	44

TABLE 6.3. Manner of Addressing Issues or Problems by National-Origin Category among Latino Respondents to the Latino National Survey

Response		Cuba	Dominican Republic	El Salvador	Mexico	Puerto Rico	Other Central America	Other South America	Other	Missing	Total
Do nothing	Freq.	81	57	83	1,087	134	76	63	14	18	1,612
	Row%	5.03	3.55	5.12	67.40	8.31	4.72	3.88	0.86	1.12	100.00
	Col%	28.24	20.61	23.43	20.87	22.49	25.50	18.65	18.06	24.90	21.49
Get together informally	Freq.	103	106	104	1,394	190	73	118	23	21	2,631
	Row%	3.90	4.01	3.94	71.99	7.23	2.76	4.50	0.86	0.82	100.00
	Col%	35.66	37.93	29.45	36.38	31.92	24.35	35.27	29.36	29.60	35.06
Use existing organizations	Freq.	83	74	138	1,693	204	115	118	30	30	2,484
	Row%	3.36	2.99	5.57	68.13	8.19	4.63	4.74	1.20	1.20	100.00
	Col%	29.00	26.70	39.28	32.51	34.15	38.49	35.11	38.91	41.03	33.11
Both	Freq.	20	41	28	533	68	35	37	10	3	775
	Row%	2.63	5.30	3.56	68.71	8.79	4.49	4.75	1.35	0.42	100.00
	Col%	7.10	14.77	7.84	10.23	11.44	11.66	10.97	13.67	4.48	10.33
Total	Freq.	287	278	352	5206	596	299	336	77	73	7,502
	Row%	3.83	3.71	4.69	69.39	7.94	3.98	4.47	1.02	0.97	100.00
	Col%	100.00	100.00	100.00	100.00	100.00	100.00	100.00	100.00	100.00	100.00

Table Tests of Independence:
National origin: (24 d.f.) 61.0102 (P = 0.0062).

Question wording: "When an issue or problem needs to be addressed, would you work through existing groups or organizations to bring people together, would you get together informally, or would you do nothing to deal with this matter?"

ethnic or racial group finds less of a drop-off between registered Latinos and the other two groupings (16 percent registered Latinos, 9 percent for nonregistered Latinos, and 10 percent for noncitizens). While there is a noticeable difference in the extent of organizational engagement between registered Latinos and the other segments of the Latino community, there is some indication that this gap is narrowing. If that is the case, theories of civic and political engagement would suggest that greater civic engagement has positive effects on increasing political engagement.

Another vantage point from which to look at Latino political participation is to characterize politics as a problem-solving activity. That is, when an individual or group recognizes and identifies a problematic situation, do public entities or institutions become the means of seeking a resolution? The **Latino National Survey** (LNS) (Fraga et al. 2006) asked, "When an issue or problem needs to be addressed, would you work through existing groups or organizations to bring people together, would you get together informally, or would you do nothing to deal with the matter?" Table 6.3 produces the responses based on the national origin of the Latino respondents. A noticeable percentage (18 to 28 percent) would do nothing. On the other hand, over three-fifths would either work collectively in a formal organization or on an ad hoc basis. Interestingly, the Latinos who fall into the "other Hispanic" category have the highest percentage (over 70 percent) of individuals who would pursue collective action. For some Latinos (5 to 14 percent across national-origin groups), pursuing formal and informal collective action is not an either/or option.

The LNS was conducted between November 2005 and August 2006. During the spring of 2006, immigrant protest marches took place in both large cities and smaller communities. Box 6.1 presents some major aspects of this movement, especially among the immigrant communities. These participatory modes and activity levels are a function of individual resources and motivation, as well as mobilization efforts by groups. Most of the contemporary surveys of Latinos do not provide a comparative basis for levels of civic and political engagement across racial and ethnic lines. Yet, for the most part, Latinos still lag behind Anglos and African Americans in these areas.

The category of informal community activity usually involves being immersed in neighborhood issues, school-related matters, or other locally based activities. Overall, the level of Latino informal activity is comparable to that for Anglos and African Americans, especially for Latino citizens. The overall mean number of activities involved still reveals the lower levels of involvement for Latinos. Clearly an understanding of Latino political participation needs to go beyond an overall summary of activities to explore specific political arenas. The electoral arena has been well examined, and Latinos are making noticeable progress. A newer development in Latino political engagement and mobilization is the role of Spanish-language media, the use of the Internet and social-networking venues, and service-sector labor unions' efforts.

Table 6.4 introduces some comparative data across the major racial and ethnic groups. Using the 2004 National Political Ethnic Survey (NPES), we present some comparisons regarding electorally related activities. The primary goal of the NPES was to gather comparative data about individuals' political attitudes, beliefs, aspirations, and behaviors at the beginning of the twenty-first century. Exploring the nature of political involvement and participation among individuals from different racial and ethnic groups, the survey included questions about voting preferences, party affiliation, organizational membership, immigration, racial consciousness, acculturation,

TABLE 6.4. Actions Taken to Help a Party or Candidate Win an Election by Racial and Ethnic Group in the National Political Ethnic Survey

Range of Election-Related Activities a Person Has Done by Percentage Answering Yes

Racial Group Members	Worked for a Political Party or Campaigned for a Candidate?	Talked to People to Persuade Them to Support a Candidate	Gone to Political Meetings, Rallies, etc., in Support of a Candidate	Given or Helped Raise Money for a Candidate	Helped Campaign for a Racial-Minority Candidate?
Whites	27.2	55.0	31.0	26.5	7.7
African Americans	24.4	44.9	19.0	18.0	12.4
Latinos	12.4	39.9	13.0	8.6	5.9
Asian Americans	11.8	50.0	13.1	14.1	6.6
Caribbean Blacks	17.1	46.9	18.6	14.9	10.7

Source: J. Jackson et al. 2004.

and views on government policies. A total of 3,339 telephone interviews were conducted throughout the United States. The sample consisted of 756 African Americans, 919 non-Hispanic whites, 404 Caribbean blacks, 757 Hispanic Americans, and 503 Asian Americans.

The political activities asked about involved things an individual might do to assist a political candidate in his or her campaign. More specifically, the question was, "Next, I would like to find out about some of the things people do to help a party or candidate win an election." As you can see, there are variations across the racial and ethnic groups. Consistently, more white respondents answered affirmatively than members of any other group. African Americans have the second highest percentages for these activities. We have indicated that surveys over the past forty years have shown that Latinos have lower rates of participatory activities (especially in the electoral arena) than whites and African Americans. For Latinos, talking to others about supporting a candidate is the highest response category, followed by going to rallies. Latinos donate the least money to campaigns. Interestingly, half of the Asian American respondents have talked to others about supporting a candidate. Finally, the percentage of respondents who have worked for a minority candidate is relatively low across all minorities.

So far we have examined Latino participation by differentiating Latino citizens and registered voters from non-Latino citizens and by national origin. Table 6.5 introduces the generational dimension, another critical component of Latino political behavior. As more than half of Latino adults are foreign-born, factors such as assimila-

TABLE 6.5. Contacting Officials by Generation and Citizenship among Respondents to the Latino National Survey

| Response | Freq. | First Generation | | | Second+ Generation Citizen | Grand Total |
		Noncitizen	Citizen	Total for First Generation		
Yes	Freq.	657	750	1,407	1,122	2,529
	Row%	46.70	53.30	55.64	44.36	100.00
	Col%	17.21	38.36	24.37	41.48	29.83
No	Freq.	3,161	1,205	4,366	1,583	5,949
	Row%	72.40	27.60	73.39	26.61	100.00
	Col%	82.79	61.64	75.63	58.52	70.17
Total	Freq.	3,818	1,955	5,773	2,705	8,478
	Row%	66.14	33.86	68.09	31.91	100.00
	Col%	100.00	100.00	100.00	100.00	100.00

Table Tests of Independence:
First and second+ generations: Chi-square (2 d.f.) 257.376 (P = 0.000).
Citizen/noncitizen (first generation only): Chi-square (2 d.f.) 461.307 (P = 0.000).

Source: Fraga et al. 2006.
Note: Island-born Puerto Ricans are coded as first generation.
Question wording: "Have you ever tried to get government officials to pay attention to something that concerned you, either by calling, writing a letter, or going to a meeting?"

TABLE 6.6. Interest in Politics and Public Affairs by National Origin among Respondents to the Latino National Survey

Response		Cuba	Dominican Republic	E. Salvador	Mexico	Puerto Rico	Other Central America	Other South America	Other	Missing	Total
Not interested	Freq.	81	92	169	1,778	182	143	105	7	23	2,579
	Row%	3.13	3.55	6.56	68.92	7.05	5.54	4.06	0.28	0.91	100.00
	Col%	25.12	30.61	43.88	30.75	28.31	44.56	29.03	9.07	28.76	31.19
Somewhat interested	Freq.	124	139	153	2,997	309	130	169	41	35	4,097
	Row%	3.03	3.39	3.72	73.15	7.54	3.17	4.13	1.01	0.85	100.00
	Col%	38.58	46.44	39.53	51.84	48.13	40.51	46.85	52.79	43.13	49.53
Very interested	Freq.	117	69	64	1,006	151	48	87	30	23	1,595
	Row%	7.32	4.31	4.01	63.11	9.49	3.00	5.46	1.87	1.43	100.00
	Col%	36.30	22.95	16.59	17.41	23.56	14.93	24.12	38.13	28.12	19.28
Total	Freq.	321	299	386	5,781	642	321	361	78	81	8,271
	Row%	3.89	3.62	4.67	69.90	7.76	3.88	4.36	0.95	0.98	100.00
	Col%	100.00	100.00	100.00	100.00	100.00	100.00	100.00	100.00	100.00	100.00

Table Tests of Independence:
National origin: (16 d.f.) 179.7615 (P = 0.0000).

Source: Fraga et al. 2006.
Question wording: "How interested are you in politics and public affairs? Would you say you are interested, somewhat interested, or not at all interested?"

tion, acculturation, and longer exposure to American society would suggest an upward participatory slope across generations (Segura and Santoro 2004). We examined the extent of contact with elected officials for the first and second generation and beyond. In addition, we differentiated the foreign-born into noncitizens and naturalized citizens. Second-generation and beyond Latinos are two and a half times more likely to contact a public official than noncitizens. Naturalized citizens almost mirror the level of contact of second-generation and beyond individuals. These differentials can be the result of lesser familiarity among the foreign-born, a lower sense of the efficacy of and less trust in agents of U.S. political institutions, a hostile climate directed toward immigrants, or a weaker political orientation than that of their native-born counterparts. At the same time, we are highlighting an activity in which many persons do not engage. The distinction of generation has become an important area of research on Latinos (J. A. García 2009), which can further define the political map of Latino political participation.

An examination of Latino political and civic engagement demonstrates that having a participatory set of attitudes or orientations serves to enhance involvement. Persons who are more interested in and informed about politics, political actors, and public policies tend to be more politically engaged. Table 6.6 presents degrees of interest in politics and public affairs among Latinos in the LNS. Another means of understanding the Latino community is to break it down into national-origin subgroups. The large sample size of the LNS enables me to present the responses of five specific subgroups and to separate Central from South Americans. The question was, "How interested are you in politics and public affairs? Would you say you are interested, somewhat interested, or not at all interested?"

Among our Latino subgroups, the Central American respondents evidenced higher percentages of disinterest in politics. At the same, more than one-fourth of the other Latinos also indicated disinterest. On the other end of the interest spectrum, the Cubans fell into the highest percentage of political interest, with Puerto Ricans coming second. The modal response lies in the middle ground (or "somewhat interested"), as two-fifths to half of the Latino respondents fell into this category. Given our previous discussion of the role of mobilization and generational differences among Latinos, the relatively low to moderate levels of political interest might represent a higher percentage of first-generation Central and South Americans who are less familiar with and

TABLE 6.7. Summary of Participatory Scores for Respondents to the Participation in America Study

Indicator of Participatory Measures	Political Engagement Scores	Political Interest Scores	Political Efficacy Scores	Political Information
All respondents	19.1	5.8	9.2	4.6
Anglo males	20.4	6.0	9.6	5.3
Anglo females	18.8	5.8	9.1	4.5
African American males	18.5	6.0	8.8	4.0
African American females	16.9	5.5	8.6	3.2
Latino males	17.8	5.3	9.1	3.8
Latinas	14.8	4.6	8.0	2.5

Source: Verba, Scholzman, and Brady 1995, 349, figure 12.4.

exposed to American political institutions and actors. Those Latinos having some interest in politics represent opportune "targets" for organized interests and leaders to "connect" their concerns and awareness to concrete political actions and issues. The general literature on levels of political interest indicates that higher socioeconomic status and greater educational attainment, personal and political efficacy, and economic resources are major contributors (Verba, Scholzman, and Brady 1995).

Our earlier discussion of political participation introduced the concepts of political engagement, interest, efficacy, and relevant information. Persons who are psychologically oriented toward participation and its relevance to their lives are more likely to be politically involved. Knowledge, interest, and personal and political efficacy all contribute to active involvement. Table 6.7 summarizes participatory scores for all respondents, males and females.[4] Interestingly, the disparities by racial/ethnic group and/or gender vary by the different indicators. For example, in the political engagement dimension, the range of scores is 20.4 for Anglo males to 14.8 for Latinas. Latinos fall at the lower end of this dimension. Similarly, summary scores of political interest reflect a drop among African American females and Latino/as. On the other hand, political efficacy is viewed as an important set of political attitudes to encourage involvement. The score range is relatively narrow, with Latinas at 8.0 (at the lower end) and Anglo males at 9.6 (at the higher end). Finally, noticeable differences are evident with political information scores. Again Latinos and African American females have the lower scores. Our brief view of participatory measures indicates the negative impact of participatory levels affected by both gender and ethnicity (i.e., being Latino and female).

In order to provide a full picture of Latinos' participatory profile, I draw on the LNS (Fraga et al. 2006). Given the now steady wave of polls that either focus on Latinos specifically or include significant numbers of Latino respondents, much more attention has been directed toward the electoral arena (i.e., voter turnout and registration,

TABLE 6.8. Latino Parents Who Meet with Their Child's Teacher in the Latino National Survey

Response		Male	Female	Total
Yes	Freq.	706	1,203	1,909
	Row%	36.98	63.02	100.00
	Col%	85.84	93.13	90.30
No	Freq.	116	89	205
	Row%	56.78	43.22	100.00
	Col%	14.16	6.87	9.70
Total	Freq.	822	1,292	2,114
	Row%	38.90	61.10	100.00
	Col%	100.00	100.00	100.00

Table Tests of Independence:
Gender: One way/chi-square (1 d.f.) 40.6412 (P = 0.000).

Source: Fraga et al. 2006.
Question wording: "Here is a list of things that some parents have done and others have not regarding their children's school. Have you met with your child's teacher?"

partisanship, electoral activities) than other political domains and nonelectoral activities. Chapter 7 discusses in greater detail the electoral activities of Latinos. We glean from the LNS an area of particular concerns for Latinos: the educational sector. From the early social science surveys to the contemporary ones, education has ranked consistently as the leading policy concern. Among Latinos, parents support educational attainment to enhance their children's future and hold high educational aspirations (Martinez-Ebers et al. 2000). As a result, we will explore some contact points for Latino parents in the educational system.

The LNS included a battery of questions asking Latino parents whom they had contact with in the schools. Table 6.8 presents the responses to the following question: "Here is a list of things that some parents have done and others have not regarding their children's school. Have you met with your child's teacher?" The responses are broken down by the gender of the parent. Overall, 90.3 percent of Latino parents have met with their children's teacher. This is truer for Latinas (63 percent) than for their Latino counterparts (37 percent). Nevertheless, the very high level of contact at the "ground floor" of the school system does challenge some common notions about the relative values that Latinos give educational attainment and quality. For the most part, a major explanation for the lower levels of educational attainment for Latino students had been attributed to a Latino "value system" that does not value education and in which parents remain less involved in the school matters of their children. The LNS included a similar battery dealing with contact with the school principal and attending school board meetings, attending PTA meetings, and meeting with their child's teacher.

We explore the educational arena further by examining the extent of PTA meeting attendance by generation and citizenship status. Table 6.9 shows that the extent of Latino attendance at PTA meetings is also high, although not at the level of contact with teachers. In fact, first-generation or foreign-born parents are more likely to attend than second-generation and beyond parents. Naturalized and nonnaturalized Latinos show no difference in this regard. Obviously the wording of the question does not allow us to determine how many meetings a parent attended. An examination of marital status and children in the household shows that foreign-born Latinos are more likely to be married with school-age children. In addition, the LNS battery included an item that asked the Latino parents if they had volunteered at their child's school. For this activity, an overall majority (52.9 percent) responded affirmatively. Second-generation and beyond parents had the highest incidence of volunteering (66.7 percent), followed by naturalized citizens (56.7 percent); the noncitizen parents were at 47.8 percent. Again, a reasonable interpretation is the demonstrated salience of education among Latino parents and behavioral manifestations of their interests. Given this general reporting of parental involvement in education and some variations based upon gender and generational status, some attention to explain such differences and possible patterns would rest upon explicatory sources from the Latino respondents, as well as institutional conditions and situations (i.e., access, language capacities to deal with non-English-speaking parents and students).

We continue our examination of Latino engagement in the educational arena by assessing parents' interactions with school officials (table 6.10). In this examination, we differentiate the Latino respondents by level of educational attainment. The question asks, "When you have had contact with school officials, would you say your experience has been very good, somewhat good, not too good, or not good at all?" A relatively

TABLE 6.9. PTA Meeting Attendance by Generation and Citizenship

Response	Freq.	First Generation			Second+ Generation Citizen	Grand Total
		Noncitizen	Citizen	Total for First Generation		
Yes	Freq.	784	419	1,203	364	1,567
	Row%	65.17	34.83	76.77	23.23	100.00
	Col%	77.32	78.17	77.61	64.08	73.98
No	Freq.	224	115	339	203	542
	Row%	66.08	33.92	62.55	37.45	100.00
	Col%	22.09	21.46	21.87	35.74	25.59
Don't know	Freq.	5	1	6	1	7
	Row%	83.33	16.67	85.71	14.29	100.00
	Col%	0.49	0.19	0.39	0.18	0.33
Refused to answer	Freq.	1	1	2	0	2
	Row%	50.00	50.00	100.00	0.00	100.00
	Col%	0.10	0.19	0.13	0.00	0.09
Total	Freq.	1,014	536	1,550	568	2,118
	Row%	65.42	34.58	73.18	26.82	100.00
	Col%	100.00	100.00	100.00	100.00	100.00

Table Tests of Independence:
First and second+ generations: (3 d.f.) 110.364 (P = 0.000).
Citizen/noncitizen (first generation only): (3 d.f.) 26.954 (P = 0.006).

Source: Fraga et al. 2006.
Note: Island-born Puerto Ricans are coded as first generation.
Question wording: "Attend a PTA meeting?"

small percentage had had no contact with school officials (6.2 percent). On the other hand, those parents who rate the interaction with school officials as very good differ little by the educational level attained (57.8 percent for college graduates versus 53.62 percent for parents with no high school). Noticeable differences occur across educational levels in the middle categories. Those with less favorable interactions tended to be Latino parents with less than a high school degree and to a lesser extent high school graduates. More parents with no high school gave a positive assessment (somewhat good). So, there is an association with parents having attained a higher educational level and more positive interactions with school officials. At the same time, the vast majority (60.5 percent) of Latino parents have less than a high school education. Given our earlier tables outlining the extent of parental contact, it is important to determine the nature of Latino parents' expectations of schools and their aspirations for their children. In addition, given the widespread parental engagement (across educational, nativity, and gender lines), the educational arena serves as one of not just civic but political engagement. It would be interesting to examine how parental engagement may lead into broader domains of political engagement.

TABLE 6.10. Assessment of Parents' Interactions with School Officials among Latino National Survey Respondents by Educational Attainment

Response	Freq.	No High School	High School Graduate	College Graduate	Total
Have Had No Contact	Freq.	66	9	6	81
	Row%	82.04	10.89	7.07	100.00
	Col%	8.33	2.17	4.99	6.21
Not Good	Freq.	17	9	1	27
	Row%	61.51	35.01	3.48	100.00
	Col%	2.10	2.35	0.83	2.07
Not Too Good	Freq.	29	23	10	62
	Row%	46.87	36.46	16.67	100.00
	Col%	3.70	5.65	9.13	4.75
Somewhat Good	Freq.	254	146	31	431
	Row%	58.99	33.83	7.18	100.00
	Col%	32.25	36.34	27.24	33.03
Very Good	Freq.	423	215	66	704
	Row%	60.13	30.53	9.34	100.00
	Col%	53.62	53.49	57.81	53.95
Total	Freq.	789	402	114	1,305
	Row%	60.49	30.79	8.71	100.00
	Col%	100.00	100.00	100.00	100.00

Table Tests of Independence:
Education: Oneway/chi2 (8 d.f.) 36.6573 (P = 0.000).

Source: Fraga et al. 2006.
Question wording: "When you have had contact with school officials, would you say your experience has been very good, somewhat good, not too good, or not good at all?"

One of the ongoing debates regarding Latino involvement and interests is taking place in the educational policy arena. Some studies (Meier and Stewart 1991) cite low socioeconomic status, immigrant background, and cultural barriers to explain low Latino involvement. Other studies (Carter and Segura 1979; San Miguel 1987) see levels of aspirations and commitment to children's educational attainment, significant percentages of Latinos in the school-age ranges, and a base of immigrants who seek to improve their children's future as indicators of Latino support and interest in education. Yet, recent research by Meier and Leal (forthcoming) has indicated how increased representation of Latinos as elected school board officials, administrators, and teachers has a positive effect on Latino involvement in the schools and higher levels of perceived responsiveness. The concomitant arena of education and political outcomes and activities is now being pursued more systematically. Its local nature suggests that there are implications at the state and national levels. Policy making at these levels has direct consequences for educational resources, programs, and quality.

Our discussion of Latino political participation portrays a population that has been less active than its non-Latino counterparts but has, in the last decade, demonstrated higher levels of civic and political engagement. Results from the LNS, Pew Hispanic surveys, and public opinion surveys have documented gains in voter registrants, improving turnout rates, and increased targeting for political mobilization efforts. Our earlier discussion of community emphasized the coexistence of commonality and diversity. That is, commonalities of culture and interests connect the various Latino subgroups, while at the same time each has unique experiences and situations.

Contributors to Latino Political Participation

This discussion of political participation has outlined essential factors that affect a person's propensity toward and level of political activity. Political participation centers on individuals or groups that try to influence the policy-making process. In the political arena, political resources are critical for active involvement. The primary contributing factors are time, money, communication and organizational skills, and participatory orientations. For the most part, Latinos have been characterized as less politically involved than other segments of the American body politic.

Contemporary research results reinforce that assessment; yet, it is not universally the case. Clearly the demographic profile of Latinos reveals a mixture of liabilities and potentials. Liabilities include a youthful population, a significant foreign-born subcommunity, relatively lower levels of educational attainment, a greater proportion of non-English or limited-English speakers, lower rates of organizational affiliation and involvement, lower income levels and higher rates of poverty, and low rates of naturalization. The assets include a rapidly growing population that will also increase its proportion of the adult population, population concentrations in populous states and metropolitan areas, the rise of organizational capacities and experienced leadership, effective mobilization strategies, and slowly improving socioeconomic status.

The liabilities identified have a direct effect on the extent of political resources that come with being youthful, having a lower socioeconomic status, and having a significant immigrant segment. The youthfulness of Latinos tends to be negatively associated with high rates of political participation. Younger persons are less oriented to organizational and community involvement and less interested in politics. At the same time, more research is being directed toward the political socialization process among young Latinos (both native- and foreign-born) and their impact on the political socialization of foreign-born parents. The participation of Latino youths in immigrant protest marches indicates that mobilization efforts can have success with this segment.

Their relatively lower levels of education and income afford Latinos fewer opportunities and resources of time, knowledge, information, and money to get involved. The significant proportion of foreign-born Latinos presents a number of potential liabilities. For one, the legal status of "resident alien"[6] places limitations on electoral involvement because permanent resident aliens cannot register or vote. Naturalization requirements, as well as continued connections to their mother country, keep naturalization rates lower for Latino immigrants than the overall average for all immigrants. In addition, some research (J. A. García 1981a; DeSipio and de la Garza 1998) indicates that levels of political integration and political involvement and knowledge are lower for immigrant populations. Similarly, they have lower rates of organizational affiliation and participation. Again, recent work on transnationalism and its political "effects" (Segura 2007; Portes, Escobar, and Arana 2008; J. A. García 2011) on political and civic engagement indicate a complementary effect of being transnationally engaged and investing more in U.S. civic life. Obviously, we must move away from popular notions of "the myth dream of return" (Jones-Correa 2009) and the lack of political knowledge and sophistication of immigrants (Renshon 2009) to develop a deeper and more complex examination of the "political world of the Latino foreign-born."

The assets related to this Latino profile are manifold. The Latino community's continued high growth creates a substantial political base from which to mobilize and exercise political influence. In addition, the concentration of Latinos in nine states (over 90 percent of all Latinos are found in states like California, Texas, New York, and Florida)[7] puts them in highly urban areas and more populous states. Recently Latinos began to transform this population potential into political activity in California with gains in the state legislature and municipalities. Several ballot propositions (**Proposition 187**, 211, and 209)[8] heightened Latino interest and involvement in elections. In 2009, the passage of **Arizona Senate Bill 1070** empowered state and local enforcement personnel to question the legal status of individuals in the process of conducting their law enforcement functions. Latinos were the main (if not exclusive) targets of this legislation. In addition, Arizona had passed numerous other laws that targeted undocumented immigrants and affected the larger Latino community. A substantial number of local ordinances and state laws were passed throughout the United States as well. As a result, Latinos have responded by mobilizing locally and across the nation to protect their rights and seek greater policy responsiveness from political institutions and parties. The mobilization processes and its political effects are becoming more evident in the Latino community. This is in part because an ever-evolving, higher level of political development and external factors (i.e., negative governmental actions, hostile public opinions, polarizing viewpoints, scapegoating) have served to heighten Latinos' political interest, awareness, and motivation to engage in collective political behaviors.

Conclusion

This chapter has laid out the basis for political participation in America and how the Latino community conforms or does not conform to those patterns. For the past thirty-five years, Latino political participation has been characterized as limited or marginal. At the same time, the social science knowledge base about Latinos has existed for only forty years, and the primary focus has been the Mexican-origin community. Only since the mid-1990s has research into Latino political participation been conducted and published. We know little more about the patterns of involvement for the other Latino subgroups, primarily Puerto Ricans and Cubans. Social science knowledge about Central and South Americans is slowly becoming available.

Part of the nature of trying to understand Latinos and their politics is the dynamic and changing situations and developments that are ongoing. The next chapter examines the electoral arena to explore Latino political participation further, looking at past and present voter-registration and -turnout patterns, partisan candidate choices, partisan affiliation and ideology, and the development and role of Latino organizations.

At the same time, the election of Latinos to office is a function of political interests, organizational density, political base, leadership, and opportunity structures.

This presents a challenging analytical question. Does the political assertiveness of Latinos to ensure equal status and representation produce a more positive orientation toward governmental responsiveness? Or do individual efforts by Latinos to seek and win elected office increase the Latino community's perception of governmental non-responsiveness? What level of support do Latinos have for coethnic candidates and officeholders? Obviously these factors are very much interrelated, and understanding their relationship is critical to understanding what Latino politics involves. Finally, our discussion of political participation has expanded to include and understand more systematically the foreign-born segments of the Latino community.

Discussion Questions

1. Socialization effects, especially for children, have been found to be critical in shaping political attitudes, behaviors, and knowledge. For Latinos, a major segment of the population is foreign-born. What are the socialization effects on this segment of the Latino community?
2. In general, the overall levels of political participation for Latinos are lower than for non-Latinos. Discuss the factors involved and why Latinos do not participate in American politics.
3. While more attention is given to the electoral arena, nonelectoral political engagement is an important mode of participation. Explore ways Latinos engage in nonvoting behaviors and why they choose to do so.
4. Targeted mobilization can be quite effective in awakening Latinos to political engagement and directing them to specific kinds of actions. What are the key ingredients for effective political mobilization?

CHAPTER 7

Latinos in the Electoral Arena

Su voto es su voz. Ya conozco este llamado desde mucho antes del comienzo de este siglo. Las decisiones, los candidatos, los temas, los derechos, las campañas y hasta adquirir más atención. ¿Y qué hago? ¿Con quién consulto, y sobre que? Ya basta. Me tengo que mover tengo que actuar.

Your vote is your voice. I know that call from long before the beginning of this century. Decisions, candidates, issues, rights, and campaigns—they all require attention. And what do I do? With whom do I consult and about what? Enough! I have to get going and act.

THE PRECEDING EXAMINATION of political participation among Latinos noted two major themes: (1) there has been a pattern of generally lower rates of political participation (although it has improved significantly since 2004) among Latinos in most arenas[1] of political involvement; and (2) the early evidence was driven largely by research into the Mexican-origin populations of the Southwest. Since 2000, the Pew Hispanic Center, university research centers, and the **Latino National Survey** (LNS) have provided more detailed and expansive profiles and sets of interrelationships to help us understand Latino political and civic engagement. In the case of the LNS (both the initial survey and the New England supplement), the richness of a large and diverse group of national-origin respondents does provide information on the full array of Latino subgroups, especially Central and South Americans. In addition, more systematic information has been collected about Latino political participation, its antecedent influences, and the **mobilization** process.

In addition to social science research results, governmental reports, polls, and media accounts have portrayed Latinos in the electoral arena (candidates, campaigns, fund-raising, issues, partisanship, and elections), which usually receives the main focus of attention when individuals think or talk about politics. Popular notions of political involvement tend to describe Latinos as less active in the electoral arena than other groups in the United States. Lower voter-registration and voter-turnout rates characterize their less-than-active role. A major contributing factor to this historic pattern lies with the significant segment of the Latino population that is foreign-born and not naturalized. In addition, data cited in chapter 6 indicate that Latinos participate less in campaigns and tend to donate less money to them. Overall, the discussion of Latinos in the electoral arena has concentrated on their potential to play a significant role in electoral outcomes rather than determining who gets elected. This chapter examines the electoral participation of Latinos, focusing on emerging patterns that deviate from general notions of limited Latino electoral participation.

Setting the Electoral Scenario

A major interest regarding Latinos and elections lies in their electoral impact in national elections, especially during competitive presidential races. The 2008 presidential election was a historic marker in American politics, bringing the first African American (Barack Obama) to the U.S. presidency. There were other noteworthy developments in 2008: greater use of social media to contact and activate segments of voters, greater use of Spanish-language media to reach Latino voters, greater investment and mobilization by service labor unions targeting Latin voters, and Latinos representing the fastest-growing segment of the electorate.

Thus, this discussion of Latino electoral participation focuses on the national level. How have Latinos been important in overall electoral situations? Are there certain conditions or circumstances in which their role is pivotal in national outcomes? Another important aspect of Latinos and elections is the extent of bloc voting among Latinos for candidates and political parties. Effective Latino bloc voting has been seen as motivating Latinos to vote in unison for the same candidates and political party to provide one or the other with a winning margin. The further aspect of an effective Latino voting strategy is converting the community's large population base into a sizable registered and voting electorate. The potential political, economical, and cultural significance of continued population growth among Latinos hinges on conversion into a stronger voting force. This remains a high priority for Latino organizations and leadership. Finally, the salience and coherence of identifiable policies and issues motivate Latinos to vote as well as become important constituencies for political parties and candidates. We will focus on this constellation of critical factors as we examine in greater detail the patterns and dynamics of Latino electoral participation. Yet, the universe of Latino political participation does not revolve exclusively around national elections and voting. An old axiom about politics is that all politics are local. In many respects, the proximity of local concerns and issues has initiated significant mobilization of Latino communities with carryover effects for other local, state, and national issues and movements. To some degree, the governmental level has jurisdiction over which issues will receive the Latino response.

Latinos As a Critical Determinant of Election Outcomes

Historically, discussion of Latinos and presidential elections focused on close outcomes and which factors, voters, or both influenced the results. To some degree, with such close voting totals in many states, different voting blocs (e.g., the religious Right, labor, Latinos, African Americans) would indicate that their votes made the difference. A League of United Latin American Citizens (LULAC) white paper outlined a scenario in which the concentration of Latinos in Illinois, Texas, California, and New York could affect the outcome of the 1960 election. The basic premise revolved around Latino bloc voting, moderate turnout levels, and Democratic candidates as the primary benefactors of the Latino vote. If the election was close, then the states with significant numbers of electoral college votes would determine the final outcome. States with a large number of electoral votes and high Latino concentrations were key ingredients in the LULAC white paper. The Kennedy-Nixon race produced one of the closest votes in American presidential history. Analysis of the Texas returns indicated that the Latino vote (primarily Mexican American) was a critical factor in John F. Kennedy's victory. Since that white paper, the "critical swing vote" thesis has been a major theme in discussions of Latino electoral participation at the national level.

Latinos number over 45 million persons and constitute about 14 percent of the U.S. population. The U.S. Census Bureau population estimate division projects Latino growth will continue such that by 2050, Latinos will comprise one-fourth of the nation's population. The image of the community as largely immigrant is only partially true. While international migration from Latin America was significant during the 1980s and 1990s, the larger growth segment is among the native-born, especially the segment under eighteen years old. Since 2000, native-born Latinos have outnumbered their foreign-born counterparts.

With our focus on the American electoral arena, is there conversion of population counts into actual numbers of registrants and voters? Where are the growth sectors of the Latino community? Are immigrants naturalizing? What about second-generation Latinos? Rates of naturalization for Latino immigrants have been increasing since the late 1990s (due in part to a more hostile anti-immigrant climate and policy initiatives, as well as promotion by Latino advocacy to encourage naturalization). The overall Latino electoral base is increasing at a faster rate than for any other group. These gains are due in part to significant increases among the youthful segment turning eighteen. For example, between 2000 and 2007, there was a 21.1 percent gain among naturalized Latinos and a 21.1 percent increase among second-generation Latinos. This trajectory is slowly closing the long-standing gap in voter turnout relative to other racial/ethnic groups, although the registration and turnout gap as compared to white and African American voters remains significant (about 10 to 18 percentage points lower).

Another consideration in assessing Latinos' political capital is their concentration in certain states. In a political sense, states in which Latinos reside represent a sizable proportion of the electorate (i.e., large numbers of electoral votes). For example, they constitute 19 percent of the population in California, 15 percent in Texas, 11 percent in Florida, 10 percent in Illinois, and 8 percent in New York. Residence in these key electoral college states enhances their value to candidates and political parties.

An evident theme for the future development of Latino capital lies with conversion of political resources (i.e., growing adult populations and organizational development) into more concrete political gains (i.e., increases in voter registration, turnout levels, active campaign involvement, etc.). Such progress occurs when rates of voter registration and turnout improve from election to election. Some trends include the following: Every year 425,000 Latinos turn eighteen, but they have significantly lower voter turnout and registration than their other younger counterparts. There has been a 55.8 percent growth rate among Latino voter registrations (2000–2004). One in seven Latinos is a voter (this is expected to be one in five by 2012), yet 1.7 million of 3 million Latino youths are not registered. For the youth segment, an effective method of voter

BOX 7.1. A Latino's Cultural and Political Realities

A Salvadoran living in Washington, DC, might be employed as a computer engineer with very good English-language proficiency and a non-Latina spouse. At the same time, he might belong to a Salvadoran social club and live in the Mount Pleasant neighborhood; most of his friends would be Salvadorans or Guatemalans. Thus, acculturation entails maintaining degrees and aspects of cultural values and practices during the acquisition of "American" customs and practices. The acculturation scenario leads to a pluralist model of American politics. That is, Latinos are an organized interest group for whom ethnicity and identity provide a primary basis for membership, resources, and issues. Whichever route is taken, the road to participation involves major adjustments and critical strategies in order for the Latino community to be effective in the American political system. This explanation focuses on how the individual adjusts to life in American society and makes a variety of choices. The role and impact of culture and language are central elements from this perspective, as is an understanding of how they operate in the American political system. Structural analysis offers another basis for examining and explaining levels of political participation for Latinos.

registration is through DMV registration. The liabilities of inattention by political parties and leadership also have an effect on political activity and motivation. Political learning, exposure, mobilization, and activation fall more on the Latino community to channel its resources and energies to convert its political potential.

The dramatic show of immigrants and supporters during the immigration-reform protest marches in 2006 and 2007 marked an unprecedented mobilization of a previously invisible group. In addition, immigrant workers have fueled the revitalization of the American labor movement (especially in the service sector). This development has had an impact in shaping federal policy directions and served as a political catalyst for the broader Latino community. The rate of naturalization for Latino immigrants has been characterized as lower than for immigrants from other parts of the world. Yet, since 2007, 1.4 million Latinos have filed naturalization applications with the **Department of Homeland Security**. Naturalized citizens now comprise one-fourth of the Latino electorate. Naturalized citizens register and vote at a rate about 8 to 10 percent higher than their native-born counterparts, and naturalization rates among Latino subgroups have risen dramatically since 2001.

Yet, of the 9 million immigrants eligible to naturalize, 4.95 million are Latinos. Rising costs and fewer English-language and naturalization classes have deterred some Latino immigrants from becoming citizens. Currently, there is an eighteen-month wait period, so the foreign-born segment has faced a real challenge in moving through the citizenship pipeline. Research indicates that the hostile external climate and punitive policies directed toward Latinos have resulted in an important motivation to become more politically engaged. There is clear evidence of a greater number of organizational initiatives and support for the foreign-born segment, and heightened unity has had a direct effect on higher rates of naturalization.

In general, connecting this growing Latino voting base with greater mobilization efforts will result in enhanced political import. The 2008 election period evidenced progress for Latinos. The rate of Latino electoral growth is three times higher than that of Anglos and four times that of African Americans. From 2000 to 2004, the number of registered Latinos increased by 23.4 percent (Anglos, 7.5 percent; African Americans, 5.8 percent). Between 1990 and 2000, the increase in Latino voters was 105 percent, versus 23 percent for Anglos and 60 percent for African Americans. Now, targeted community-based registration drives are demonstrating effectiveness among the predominantly Spanish-speaking population. Finally, Latinos are receiving greater attention from political parties and Latino advocacy groups to increase the electoral base.

Proponents of a truly active Latino electorate will point to the rise of Latino elected officials at the federal, state, and local levels. In California alone, Latinos now occupy 762 elective offices, 20 percent of assembly and senate positions, and six seats on the state's congressional delegation (Verdin 2000). The year 2000 was declared the year of the Latino voter as Latinos had become 8 percent of the national electorate (a 60 percent increase from 1996) and were openly courted by the major political parties and presidential candidates (Milbank 2000). Newspapers such as the *Dallas Morning News* and news services such as the Associated Press and CNN identified the Latino community as a critical voting bloc, a deciding factor, and the "soccer moms of 2000." In addition, changes in voter registration and turnout, as well as increased naturalization among foreign-born Latinos, indicated a more active Latino electorate.

Latino Voting Patterns and Subgroup Variations

The effect of collapsing the various Latino subgroups into one general group can overstate the case and misdirect researchers, policy makers, and journalists into thinking of Latinos as primarily a singular, unified group. Their voting patterns are not uniform, and we know little about the electoral patterns of many of the Latino subgroups. Our knowledge base of Latino electoral participation is rooted primarily in studies of the Mexican-origin community. As a consequence of dealing with the Latino communities as primarily one large group, the distinctiveness and specific history of each subgroup is muted. Nevertheless, one theme of this book is the extent of community and connectedness across the various Latino subgroups. Thus, my reporting of Latino voting patterns reflects their aggregate totals, with the exception of data derived from the **Latino National Political Survey.**

Latino Voter Registration and Turnout: Patterns and Explanations

To register to vote in American elections, people must meet the age and citizenship requirements. The Latino youth segment will produce more voter-eligible registrants, and additional mobilization efforts would aid their conversion into active voters. Recent gains in the naturalization rates among Latino immigrants will be affected by a variety of factors: motivation and practical knowledge to pursue naturalization; the sociopolitical climate (both hostile, punitive, and structurally encouraging); the role of

Latino organizations in facilitating the naturalization decision and process; and connections made between civic and political engagement and Latinos' collective interests. In the latter case, we are talking about a politicization process wherein Latino immigrants become more politically engaged and assess the value of becoming electorally eligible. As we will see in chapters 9 and 10, external factors such as anti-immigrant attitudes and referenda directed toward limiting Latino and immigrant access and participation have played a major role in motivating Latinos to become electorally involved, as well as to engage in other forms of political expression. Next we will consider in greater detail the factors that influence permanent resident aliens (i.e., individuals who have sought and been approved for legal residence by the Immigration and Naturalization Service) to pursue or not pursue citizenship.

The **Voting Rights Act of 1965** and its subsequent extensions include a provision that mandates the reporting of registration and voting data for presidential and congressional elections by race, Hispanic origin, and gender. These figures represent *national* registration and voting rates, although they do not differentiate among the different Latino subgroups.

Table 7.1 provides a longitudinal record of registration of Americans to vote in presidential elections since 1992. Overall, the percentage of voter registrants during this period has been relatively stable. The gender gap for male and female registration has disappeared over the past twenty years, and in 2011 women have higher registration rates. The differential between Hispanics and non-Hispanics remains significant. A comparison of Hispanic registration with that of Anglo registrants reveals a consistent fifteen-point difference. Historically (i.e., going back to the period from 1960 through the 1990s) the gap was closer to a twenty-five-point difference.

TABLE 7.1. Reported Registration by Race, Gender, and Age: U.S. Presidential and Congressional Elections, 1992 to 2008

	1992	1996	2000	2004	2006	2008
Total voting age (in thousands)[a]	185,684	193,651	202,609	215,694	220,603	225,499
Overall registered (%)	68.2	65.9	69.5	72.1	67.6	71.0
Race (%):						
White	70.1	67.7	71.6	73.6	69.5	72.0
African American	63.9	63.5	67.5	68.7	60.9	69.7
Hispanic origin[b]	35.0	35.7	57.3	57.9	53.7	59.4
Gender (%):						
Male	66.9	64.6	68.0	70.5	66.0	69.1
Female	69.3	67.3	70.9	73.6	69.0	72.8
Age group (%):						
18–24	52.5	48.8	50.7	57.6	46.3	58.5
25–44	64.8	61.9	63.3	69.3	63.8	68.2
45–54	75.3	73.5	75.4	79.1	72.1	73.5
55+	78.0	77.0	78.4	79.1	77.1	77.0

Source: Current Population Reports Series P-20, nos. 440, 466, 542, 556, 557, 562.
[a]This refers to the civilian noninstitutional population.
[b]Hispanics may be of any race.

It is important in examining voter-registration figures to determine how the base population is calculated. For example, voting age population (VAP) takes eighteen as the age baseline; from this, one can determine the registration rate based on all persons who are eighteen and older (VAP = population 18+). For Latinos, this would produce a lower percentage due to a higher percentage of foreign-born adults. The alternative base is the voting eligible population (VEP), which takes into consideration both age and citizenship status. If we remove noneligible Latinos (i.e., noncitizens), the gap is closed by half. Similarly, if we compare the percentage vote based on the registered voters only, then the gap between Latinos and non-Latino whites is 10 to 12 percent. From 2000 to 2008, the percentage of Latino registered voters ranged from 57.3 to 59.4 percent. The earlier registration figures (i.e., 1992 and 1996) reflect a VAP baseline (thus a lower percentage) for those election years. Nevertheless, the registration gap is closing, although slowly.

Table 7.2 shows that American voter turnout was variable over this period (ranging from 47.8 to 63.8 percent). The 1996 election marked the lowest presidential turnout in the latter part of the twentieth century. That decline in voter turnout cuts across all racial and Hispanic-origin groups and all age groupings. The figures for Latino voters are significantly lower than for any other grouping (from fifteen to twenty points lower). Turnout figures are also low for the eighteen- to twenty-four-year-old group, which can compound the challenges for the Latino community to be more competitive electorally.

Again, the low percentage of Latinos voting is partially attributed to the inclusion of all Latino adults, including noncitizens, except in the 2000 Current Population Re-

TABLE 7.2. Reported Voting by Race, Gender, and Age: U.S. Presidential and Congressional Elections, 1992 to 2008

	1992	1996	2000	2004	2006	2008
Total voting age (in thousands)[a]	185,684	193,651	202,609	215,694	220,073	225,499
Overall voting (%)	61.3	54.2	59.5	63.8	47.8	63.6
Race (%):						
White	63.6	56.0	61.8	65.4	49.7	64.4
African American	54.0	50.6	56.8	60.0	41.0	64.7
Hispanic origin[b]	28.9	26.7	45.1	47.2	32.3	49.9
Gender (%):						
Male	60.2	52.8	58.1	62.1	46.9	61.5
Female	62.3	55.5	60.7	65.4	48.6	65.7
Age group (%):						
18–24	42.8	32.4	36.1	46.7	22.1	48.5
25–44	58.3	49.2	56.1	60.1	54.8	60.0
45–54	70.0[c]	64.4[c]	56.1	68.7	53.8	67.4
55+	70.1[c]	67.0[c]	67.3	71.8	62.5	70.8

Source: Current Population Reports Series P-20, nos. 466, 504, 542, 556, 557, 562.
[a]This refers to the civilian noninstitutional population.
[b]Hispanics may be of any race.
[c]For election years 1996 and 1992, the age breakdowns for age groups are 18–24, 25–44, 45–64, and 65 and older.

port. The turnout gap is greater during nonpresidential election years, which is usually the case for all voters. (See box 7.4 for discussion of the 2010 midterm elections.) Nevertheless, the challenge for Latinos is to demonstrate an updated electoral trajectory for all national elections. At the same time, if we take into account the high population growth rate among Latinos, even unchanged registration and turnout rates can have an impact. For example, Latinos in California have increased in population by 42.6 percent since 1990. Their growth rate is five times that of the non-Hispanic population. Even though their voter-registration and voter-turnout rates have not changed appreciably, their proportion of the electorate has increased by "natural growth." In 1990 Latinos constituted 2 percent of the state's electorate, and in 1996, 7 percent.

These kinds of gains can enhance the Latino electoral base but represent slow process toward greater electoral empowerment. Dramatic gains can be accomplished by adding more native-born Latinos who are not currently registered. These additions can enhance Latinos' gains with relatively constant or declining registration and turnout levels for most other voters. As a result, the percentage of Latinos both registered and voting should increase, since all other groups are voting and registering at lower levels.

Critical Factors Affecting Latinos' Electoral Participation

What factors affect the level of Latino electoral involvement? The possibilities can be discussed based on two different data sources: (1) the Current Population Reports for the Voting Rights Act provisions, and (2) the extant social science research literature on voting and elections. After the November 2008 elections, the Current Population Survey included a battery of items among voting-age respondents and asked their reasons for not voting in the election. Overall, nearly 15.2 million people reported they were registered but did not vote in 2008. Slightly less than one in five reported they could not take the time off from work or school or were too busy (see table 7.3). Another 13.4 million did not vote because they were not interested or did not care about elections and politics. This predisposition is often associated with political cynicism, apathy, and inefficacy (García 1998; DeSipio 1996). If you compare these responses with those of nonvoters in 1980, more than twice as many (7.6 percent in 1980 versus 17.5 percent in 2008) indicated they had no time or were too busy to vote. Finally, the other noteworthy reasons given by nonvoters in 2008 were being ill or disabled (14.9 percent), not preferring any of the candidates (12.9 percent), being out of town (8.8 percent), and forgetting to vote or having no way to get to the polls (5.3 percent each).

In a general sense, the factors affecting nonvoting seem to center on voter apathy, disinterest, and some degree of cynicism. If we look at Hispanic nonvoters, their responses do differ somewhat from those of other nonvoters. One-fourth were too busy or had no time off, while another seventh (14 percent) were not interested in the elections. Hispanics were about 50 percent (12.9 percent versus 7.6 percent) less likely to not vote because they disliked the candidates. About 16 percent more Latinos reported registration problems than the general electorate. Overall, Hispanic nonvoters' reasons seem to parallel those cited by all other nonvoters. Given the rising "hostile" climate toward immigrants and Latinos, monitoring the reasons for nonvoting in light of visible voter-mobilization campaigns becomes part of the Latino electoral strategy.

Socioeconomic Status, Resources, and Voting

The existing research literature offers other insights and findings to explain voting and nonvoting. In many cases, when research examines the electoral arena, the question of who votes is answered in terms of important sociodemographic characteristics, psychological orientations, and situational and **structural factors** associated with the individual. The socioeconomic model (Verba and Nie 1972; Wolfinger and Rosenstone 1980) identifies educational attainment, income, and occupational status as the key factors that differentiate voters from nonvoters. Persons with higher levels of educational attainment, income, and occupational status (professionals, entrepreneurs, etc.) are much more likely to vote than individuals with less **human capital**.[4] The concept of human capital, found in the economics and political science literature, holds that as individuals invest in their human resource "portfolio," gaining more education, training, experience, and motivation, they are advantaged with greater returns in the job market via earnings. The acquisition of greater human resources is advantageous economically. In a sense, the idea of human capital can be thought of as political capital, for individuals with greater skills, knowledge, and interest in the political process can be more effective in their actions (Putnam 2000).

Acquiring these resources will give a person the relevant political information and a better understanding of the political process. With higher levels of educational attainment, the person has not only pertinent knowledge but communication and organizational skills and social status, which serve as beneficial assets for electoral participation. Similarly, higher levels of income afford an individual the economic resources to get involved in electoral activities and contribute to campaigns. Possessing a high-status job and money does enhance a person's available time and ability to see the direct benefits of political involvement.

The other key demographic characteristics are age and gender. In the case of the former, researchers use the idea of a life cycle. As a person becomes more "settled" in her work and household, she has a more direct stake in what happens politically. An older person is likely to be a homeowner, to be situated in a higher tax bracket, to have children in school, and so on, which motivates her to be more aware of public policy and policy impacts. In table 7.3, the voting participation by age certainly reflects the life cycle position.

Prior to 2000, much attention and discussion focused on the idea of a gender gap. With women historically excluded from the political process, there were noticeable differences between women's and men's political participation. The relative absence of women as political and organizational leaders, active voters and campaign contributors, and partisan activists reinforced the idea of politics being a man's game. The gender gap was highlighted in the electoral arena as fewer women were registered than men, and they voted less. As tables 7.1 and 7.2 show, the gender gap has closed electorally, and the voting gap no longer exists. Our discussion of the effect of sociodemographic factors on voting has application to other forms of political involvement. Chapter 8 explores other aspects of political involvement, specifically organizational involvement and local community activities.

Other contributing factors that influence the voter include psychological orientations, situational factors, and structural factors. The political orientations of efficacy, trust, and interest generate greater awareness and motivation to get involved in the

TABLE 7.3. Reported Reasons for Not Voting among Those Who Reported Registering but Not Voting by Race, Gender, and Age: U.S. Presidential and Congressional Elections, 1992 to 2008

Reasons	Total (in Thousands)	White	African American	Hispanic	Less Than High School	BA Degree or Higher	25–44 Years	45–64 Years	65+ Years
Total nonvoters	15,167.0	11,172.0	1,242.0	1,862.0	2,556.0	2,169.0	5,819.0	4,201.0	2,581.0
No transportation	2.7	2.3	3.3	4.1	4.7	1.4	1.4	3.4	4.5
No time off/too busy	17.5	16.2	16.9	24.8	12.2	16.9	24.3	14.9	3.0
Ill/disabled	14.9	15.6	20.3	10.8	25.6	12.5	6.8	14.8	45.3
Not interested	13.4	14.1	8.5	14.0	13.8	10.8	14.2	15.2	9.9
Disliked the candidates	12.9	15.2	4.3	7.6	16.6	11.4	12.7	16.5	12.5
Registration problems	6.0	5.6	5.6	7.0	3.2	7.4	7.3	4.3	2.6
Out of town	8.8	9.1	6.4	7.8	4.0	15.3	8.4	8.3	5.1
Forgot	2.6	2.4	1.2	2.4	3.0	1.9	2.8	1.8	1.3
Don't know/refused to answer	7.0	5.6	5.6	7.0	3.3	7.4	2.8	1.8	1.3
Other reasons	13.2	13.4	17.2	15.8	14.6	15.7	14.8	11.0	11.1

Source: File and Crisey 2010.

political process and public policy making. The sense of political and personal efficacy empowers an individual to get involved and feel that he can make a difference. Researchers like Verba and Nie (1972) and Rosenstone and Hansen (1993) point to socialization experiences as major factors in the development of these participatory attitudes, with family and schools being the primary agents.

The structural factors have to do with the rules of the game and how political institutions function, especially focusing on access, an individual's or group's legal standing, rights and protections, and the formal requirements for participation. Such practices as the poll tax, the white primary, literacy tests, limited registration locations, and economic and physical intimidation (Grofman, Handley, and Niemi 1992) serve as examples of structural impediments for racial, ethnic, gender, and social classes in the United States. The Civil Rights Act of 1964 and the Voting Rights Act of 1965 were intended to eliminate many of these structural barriers. The situational factors revolve around salient issues, controversies, charismatic candidates, and the like, which stir interest in specific elections, office races, and propositions. Measures such as **Proposition 187** (limiting immigrants' access to social services and education) or **Proposition 227** (ending bilingual education) in California serve as situational factors to stimulate Latino voters' interest and involvement.

Statewide Propositions As Mobilizing Factors

At the end of the millennium, a set of statewide propositions in California, beginning with Proposition 187 (limiting immigrants' access to health and social welfare services), were couched in terms of the negative impacts of undocumented and legal immigrants. The issue framing this proposition targeted primarily Mexicans and other Latinos as the source of a range of economic and social problems in the state. These factors included designating all immigrants as a burden, characterizing the "culprits" as Latinos who negatively impact the economy, increase social service expenditures, and overcrowd health facilities. This kind of targeted rhetoric stirred heightened political involvement by Latinos and Latino-based organizations. Voter-registration campaigns, mass demonstrations, ad hoc organizations in opposition to Proposition 187, statements by the Mexican consul, and so on, were directly associated with the dynamics of Proposition 187.

Subsequently, in 1996 and 1998, other propositions introduced in California raised issues about rolling back affirmative action, eliminating bilingual education in the public schools, and requiring unions to receive prior approval from their membership before making campaign contributions. These initiatives also served as catalysts to increase Latino political involvement. It has been noted that when the political system has a direct impact on you, your interest and motivation are significantly enhanced. The activated electoral involvement of Latinos in California not only had a direct impact on these initiatives but also carried over into a number of state legislative and local races. That is, the number of Latinos in the state assembly and senate increased as Cruz Bustamante was elected lieutenant governor in 2000. In addition, there was a noticeable increase in the numbers of naturalizations and newly registered voters. Finally, the stimulus of policy initiatives, particularly those negatively directed toward Latinos, motivated Latino organizations and leaders to mobilize broader segments of their communities.

The U.S. Congress has become more active in drawing up legislation regarding undocumented immigration and border security. For instance, the Border Protection, Antiterrorism, and Illegal Immigration Control Act of 2005, known as the Sensenbrenner bill (HR 4337), came before the 109th U.S. Congress. It was passed by the U.S. House of Representatives on December 16, 2005, by a vote of 239 to 182 (with 92 percent of Republicans supporting, 82 percent of Democrats opposing), but it did not pass the Senate. Nevertheless, this legislation served to frame immigration as primarily a national security and law enforcement issue. Attempts have failed to broaden the public discourse beyond "controlling the border" to include immigrants' rights and protections, the long-standing economic interdependence between the United States and especially Mexico, family reunification, more limited legal immigration processing, and temporary work status.

In the spring of 2010, Arizona (a state that has enacted a series of initiatives and laws focusing on illegal immigration since 2002) passed **Senate Bill 1070** (Support Our Law Enforcement and Safe Neighborhoods Act), empowering state and local law enforcement agencies, in the "course of their law enforcement activities," to question individuals about their legal status. While an injunction was invoked prior to the bill's implementation in July, state and local laws and initiatives continue to multiply in the immigration policy area. We discuss these developments and political ramifications for the Latino community in chapters 9 and 10.

Latino Electoral Participation: Social Science Findings

The socioeconomic status model, which is at the heart of the electoral participation model, does not fit Latinos in exactly the same way it does other populations. Educational attainment makes a difference for Latinos (J. A. García 1996) in terms of making them more likely to be registered and to vote regularly. As greater numbers of Latinos achieve high school diplomas and higher education, gains in Latino registration and turnout will continue. On the other hand, the strength of higher income attainment and occupational status does not have the same positive effect for Latinos that it does for non-Latinos. That is, there is no strong, explicit association for Latinos in higher income levels to be significantly more electorally active than those at lower economic levels. Similarly, Latinos in higher-status occupations are not significantly more electorally active than Latinos in lower-status occupations. Part of the explanation might lie with the relative concentration of Latinos in lower occupational positions and lower income categories. The emerging Latino middle class is a recent phenomenon, and its impact electorally is more a matter of speculation. As more Latinos experience greater socioeconomic mobility, and as a greater percentage of the community reaches the age of eighteen, we may see stronger relationships between socioeconomic status and Latino voter registration and turnout.

Latinos tend to be less politically interested and less aware of political events and information (J. A. García 1995). Correspondingly, with lower levels of political awareness and interest, there is less electoral involvement. On the other hand, Latinos exhibit levels of political trust (i.e., basic confidence in the fairness and evenness of governmental actions and actors) comparable to those of other voting segments of the population. This political orientation should reinforce people's belief in the political system and motivate them to exercise their vote. For Latinos, this association is a weak one, and some studies find an inverse relationship (J. A. García 1995; García and Arce 1988; DeSipio 1996; Hero 1992).

This is somewhat ironic in that Latinos respond with a positive orientation toward the U.S. political system (indicating confidence in how it works), yet do not register or vote to a degree comparable with non-Latinos. There is clearly a linkage problem or inconsistency in that evidence of Latinos' political support for the American political system does not translate into their taking a more active role as a voting public. Some researchers (DeSipio 1996; F. C. García 1988) have used the concept of **political incorporation** to assess the extent of involvement persons have with the political system. Individuals are politically incorporated via a socialization process that instills the core values and beliefs of the American political system (de la Garza, Falcón, and García 1996), and they assume the various roles of a participatory "citizen." Moving beyond socioeconomic status can lead us to another series of explanations for the lower rates of political participation, especially electoral behavior.

Culture, National Origin, and Latinos

The concept of political incorporation, although it focuses on how persons learn and involve themselves with the American political system, is generally directed toward newcomers to the political system (either as young persons assuming adult status or as immigrants) and toward marginalized populations such as minority-group members. For our purposes, political incorporation is the process by which group interests are represented in the policy-making process (Browning, Marshall, and Tabb 1990). Obviously, a central focus of this book is the efforts of the Latino community to become a more active and effective interest group in the American political system. We have been examining indicators and factors affecting Latino electoral behavior. In addition to socioeconomic status, mobilization by Latino organizations and leaders and situational circumstances (anti-Latino backlash, Latino-targeted referenda, partisan outreach, etc.) contribute to the political incorporation of Latinos. The use of political incorporation has also centered on the systemic factors (discrimination, segregated institutions, exclusionary practices, etc.) that minimize or severely restrict the extent of incorporation as individuals and group members.

A critical element of the Latino community, in terms of political incorporation, is the immigrant segment. Latino immigrants are exposed to a different culture (culturally, politically, and civically) and require adjustment time to integrate into the American culture and mainstream. In his work on political adaptation of immigrants, J. A. García (1986b) outlines a three-step process involving political incorporation (integration). The first is the adaptive process, in which adjustments are made in terms of social relations, language, societal roles, and familiarity with institutions, norms, and values. After some degree of socialization has occurred, the second step deals with integration; the development of organizations serves as the vehicle for contact with social and political institutions, informational networks, and communication. This organizational development establishes the presence of the migrant community and its interests within the host society and pursues societal responses (Portes, Escobar, and Arana 2008). The last stage of incorporation is societal absorption, in which immigrants' political and economic participation is regularized (or falls within the conventional realm of political involvement), and they are recognized as an active group interest engaged in the American policy-making process. Thus, one of the challenges for the Latino communities is the integration of the Latino immigrant segment into all of the other dimensions that connect Latinos (national-origin subgroup, class, regional location, varying histories in the United States, etc.).

In the case of the immigrant Mexican-origin community and other Latino immigrant subgroups, there is considerable debate about how to view Latinos. Do they make up a series of major waves of incoming immigrants from different political cultures, or are they part of a stream of indigenous populations? Historians Rodolfo Acuña (1976, 1981, 1998) and Mario García (1989) and political scientist Mario Barrera (1979) have analyzed the experience of Mexican-origin people in the Southwest as a politically and economically subjugated indigenous population. Since the 1970s, the influx of Mexican migrants into the United States has served to augment the Mexican-origin community, which has entered the adaptation phase. As a result, this community can simultaneously represent both an indigenous and a migrant population. Analysis of other Latino immigrant subgroups (Dominicans, Puerto Ricans, Cubans, etc.) by Sassen-Koob (1988) and Morales and Bonilla (1993) focuses on the global economy and how Latino migration is "manipulated" so that there is movement from less developed countries to more industrialized ones. The perspective suggests that an individual's migration decision is not determined solely by his desires and motivations but also by structural conditions (especially economic opportunities or the lack of them in the country of origin). These factors serve as the backdrop for understanding the Latino political-incorporation process and the varied experiences that can either unite or divide the Latino communities. Our discussion of Latino political incorporation focuses on the adjustments and the congruence (or lack thereof) with American political culture.

Thus, the concept of political incorporation entails full and articulated political involvement and activity, as well as adjusting to core American values and political practices (de la Garza, Falcón, and García 1996). For Latinos, politics coalesces as a **community of interests** and a **community of common or similar cultures.** We have numerous accounts about the political incorporation of European immigrants such as the Irish, Italians, and Jews (Fuchs 1990). Part of that discussion lies in the analysis of how cultural values and practices (self-help associations, residential clustering, closed social networks, etc.) played a central role in the adjustment to living in America. Cultural factors such as language, values, the political culture of the country of origin, familialism, the extent of ties with the mother country, and the presence or absence of organizational life, for example, can be key determinants of the extent of political incorporation among Latinos (Almond and Verba 1963; Wilson 1977; Esman 1995).

A partial explanation of Latinos' "limited" political incorporation (DeSipio 1996) lies with the persistence of Spanish-language use and their coming from more autocratic, less democratic, and elitist political systems that produce a legacy of limited participatory experiences, a sense of fatalism, a lack of organizational experience, and cultural and linguistic isolation (Skerry 1993; DeSipio and de la Garza 1998). Latinos come from nonparticipatory political cultures, and ethnic group cultural maintenance is seen as a deterrent to active participation in the American political system. For example, a strong sense of familialism would tend to deter Latinos (Tirado 1970;

Márquez 1993) from joining secondary groups or formal organizations. As a result, primary social networks and knowledge gathering about the social and political system comes primarily from family and other Latino community members.

This discussion of political involvement shows that organizational affiliation and involvement are directly connected to heightened political participation (Verba, Scholzman, and Brady 1995; García and de la Garza 1985). Thus, being a Latino can be a liability in terms of political incorporation due to lesser organizational affiliation and involvement. Cultural values and traditions can serve as obstacles to integration into the American political system and group effectiveness. At the same time, maintaining Latino identification can serve as a basis for group mobilization around particular concerns or issues. These perspectives are not mutually exclusive but represent realities that exist within the Latino community and make up part of the challenges for Latino political participation.

Proponents of these explanations can take two different routes. The first suggests that unless assimilation (Gordon 1964) takes place (i.e., political, cultural, social, associational, identificational, and marital), Latinos will be located in a marginal position both in the society at large and as political participants. The assimilation process would involve departure from traditional cultural practices and values. It would involve becoming Americanized such that any distinctiveness as Latinos or as part of a specific Latino subgroup would be, at best, symbolic (Barrera 1988). The second route suggests that although assimilation is a necessary precondition for greater political involvement, the process of acculturation is a more realistic characterization of what happens in American society. That is, assimilation does take place; yet, it is not a one-way process that by necessity includes complete loss of group identity, affiliation, practices, and social networks. This latter perspective portrays the American political system in culturally and politically pluralistic terms.

Social Structures and Participatory Roles

Given the adjustments that have been discussed, are Latinos assured of comparable levels of participation with non-Latinos and of being effective at policy making? To construct a fuller picture of the variety of factors that can influence participatory roles, we need to introduce the role of social structures. This is the strand of participation explanations that involves structural conditions and institutional practices and customs (Barrera, Ornelas, and Muñoz 1972; Barrera 1979). Concepts such as equality, fairness, discrimination, institutional racism, ethnocentrism, and subordination are used to describe **power relations** between the dominant society and minority populations. This perspective examines factors other than merely individual characteristics, orientations, and behaviors that can lead to specific levels of participation. Laws that exclude persons from voting, registering, participating in political parties, and so on, serve as examples of social structures and institutional practices. As a result, Latinos are viewed as marginalized—economically, socially, and politically.

This line of analysis sees low rates of participation as purposive actions by the political system and its representatives to have minorities serve as subjects rather than active participants. In the electoral arena, restrictive policies such as poll taxes, literacy tests, limited registration places and times, hostile polling locations, physical intimidation, and so on (J. A. García 1986a), are structural examples that have negatively affected Latinos and other minority voters. The net effect ranges from the outright prohibition of participation to the active discouragement of Latino political involvement. Similarly, political institutions such as legislatures, city councils, and school boards can operate under election systems and rules (e.g., off-year, nonpartisan, or **at-large elections**) that can disadvantage Latino communities (Grofman and Davidson 1992) in terms of representation and productive participation. During the early 2000s, there were state initiatives to require prospective voters to show proof of citizenship (legal status) in addition to a voter-registration card. While the courts recently overturned an Arizona law (for conflicting with national voter legislation), the climate of voter intimidation can have a depressing effect.

The legacy of such structural conditions can be passivity, acquiescence, or withdrawal. To apply this perspective to Latinos, we will examine the provisions of the Voting Rights Act and its subsequent amendments, focusing on linguistic protections in the form of bilingual ballots, more facilitative registration systems, **preclearance** of election law changes prior to their implementation, and specified protective status for the purposes of Latinos' civil and voting rights.[5] These provisions identify some of the existing structural conditions and systematic responses that have been used to limit Latino electoral participation. The legal remedies listed represent policies to remove these obstacles.

Active civil rights leadership and organizations, in combination with a number of other social liberation movements, have applied both political and economic pressure for the removal of biased practices that inhibit political participation (Tarrow 1998; Piven and Cloward 1988, 2000). Continuous advocacy and monitoring are still required to ensure protection from structural barriers. As a result, organizations like the Mexican American Legal Defense and Education Fund (MALDEF), the Puerto Rican Legal Defense and Education Fund (PRLDEF), and the Southwest Voter Registration and Education Project (SVREP) serve as vigilant Latino interest groups to ensure a fair and equitable electoral system and process. Since the early 2000s, there have been more active and sustained political mobilizations by Latino organizations and labor unions. The anti-immigrant sentiments and actions, as well as the push from the 2000 general elections, have resulted in the devotion of greater human and economic resources to such efforts (Michelson 2003, 2006; Michelson, García-Bedolla, and McConnell 2009).

Chapter 10 on voting rights discusses the specific efforts by MALDEF and PRLDEF for voting rights protection. The primary target in this litigation was at-large elections (Brischetto and de la Garza 1983; J. A. García 1986a), which made electing minority candidates very difficult. As the result of many successful class-action suits and favorable interpretation of the Voting Rights Act and its amendments, the use of district or ward elections became more the norm. Subsequent **redistricting** efforts after the decennial censuses sought to create competitive and favorable districts in which Latino candidates had a higher probability of success. Work by Barreto et al. (2005) has now demonstrated that Latino candidates have a direct effect on higher turnout among Latino voters, as well as stronger levels of Latino candidates' support. That is, when Latino candidates are on the ballot, Latino voters are more likely to take an interest in the elections and vote at higher levels than usual.

The Aftermath of the 2000 Elections and Latino Empowerment

The closeness of the presidential election, growth of the Latino electorate, notable partisan attention directed to the Latino communities, and number of Latinos seeking elected office all provided evidence for the political gains that Latinos have brought into the new millennium. Both parties vigorously vied for control of both chambers of Congress; the latest round of redistricting opened more opportunities for Latino office competition; gains in naturalization and voter registration afforded another chance to exercise political clout; and both political parties continued their targeted efforts to expand their respective Latino support.

The National Arena and the Bush Administration

Following the 2000 elections, Latinos had high expectations for gains in presidential appointments at the cabinet and White House staff levels. Only one Latino (Secretary of Housing and Urban Development Mel Martínez) served in the cabinet, and Alberto Gonzáles served as special counsel to the president, although other Latinos had been appointed to various subcabinet positions, commissions, and judgeships. President George W. Bush initiated the first presidential radio broadcast in Spanish in 2002 as part of his (and the Republican Party's) efforts to establish closer links with the Latino community. In addition, the Republican Party initiated a weekly "news-oriented" broadcast on Spanish-language television. To some extent, the Democratic Party has sought to strengthen its support within the Latino community through policy proposals focusing on immigration reform, greater access by permanent resident aliens to social welfare programs, minority small business support, health-care coverage, and racial profiling.

In the 2000 election, Al Gore outdistanced George W. Bush by 20 percentage points, but current poll results indicated a near toss-up (46 percent versus 44 percent) if the election were held today. Explanations for closing this gap were attributed to a rising Latino middle class, policy responsiveness by the Bush administration (i.e., Bush reiterated continued support of the U.S. economic embargo of Cuba), and a "softening of the GOP's image." Part of the White House strategy was based on the 7 to 8 percent of the electorate that Latinos now assumed and building on the 35 percent Latino vote received in 2000. On the other hand, the CNN–All Politics polls found that the same Latinos indicated support for the Democratic congressional candidates (49 to 23 percent) over Republican candidates.

This raises a question of the expected trickle-down effect of President Bush's popularity to other GOP candidates and possible partisan shifts. Ronald Reagan enjoyed similar levels of popularity among Hispanic voters, receiving over 40 percent of the Latino vote in his reelection in 1984. At the same time, levels of Democratic support for all other offices remained solidly high among Latinos. It is not unusual for voters to distinguish between their choices for president and for congressional and other political offices. While presidential races are clearly couched in a partisan context, appeals to the political center often transcend partisan appeals, and crossover voting takes place, while more conventional partisan voting occurs for all other races.

BOX 7.2. Hispanics in the U.S. Congress, 1877 to 2010

Hispanic Representative	Years Served	State	Partisan Affiliation	Congressional District
U.S. House of Representatives				
Romualdo Pacheco	1877–1878	California	Republican	4th
Ladislas Lazaro	1913–1927	Louisiana	Democrat	7th
Benigno C. Hernandez	1915–1917, 1919–1921	New Mexico	Republican	At-large
Dennis Chavez	1931–1935	New Mexico	Democrat	1st
Joachim O. Fernandez	1931–1941	Louisiana	Democrat	1st
Antonio M. Fernandez	1943–1956	New Mexico	Democrat	1st
Joseph Montoya	1957–1964	New Mexico	Democrat	1st
Henry B. González	1961–1998	Texas	Democrat	20th
Edward Roybal	1963–1993	California	Democrat	33rd
Eligio de la Garza	1965–1997	Texas	Democrat	15th
Manuel Lujan Jr.	1969–1989	New Mexico	Republican	1st
Herman Baldillo	1971–1977	New York	Democrat	21st
Robert García	1978–1990	New York	Democrat	21st
Anthony L. Coelho	1979–1989	California	Democrat	15th
Matthew Martínez	1982–2001	California	Democrat	31st
Solomon Ortiz	1983–2011	Texas	Democrat	27th
William B. Richardson	1983–1997	New Mexico	Democrat	3rd
Esteban Torres	1983–1999	California	Democrat	34th
Albert G. Bustamante	1985–1993	Texas	Democrat	23rd
Ileana Ros-Lehtinen	1989–	Florida	Republican	18th
José E. Serrano	1990–	New York	Democrat	16th and 18th
Ed L. Pastor	1991–	Arizona	Democrat	2nd and 4th
Henry Bonilla	1993–2007	Texas	Republican	23rd
Lincoln Díaz-Balart	1993–2011	Florida	Republican	21st
Robert Menendez	1993–2006	New Jersey	Democrat	13th
Frank M. Tejada	1993–1997	Texas	Democrat	28th
Xavier Becerra	1993–	California	Democrat	30th and 31st
Luis Gutiérrez	1993–	Illinois	Democrat	4th
Lucille Roybal-Allard	1993–	California	Democrat	33rd and 34th
Nydia M. Velázquez	1993–	New York	Democrat	12th
Silvestre Reyes	1996–	Texas	Democrat	16th
Ciro D. Rodríguez	1997–2005, 2007–2011	Texas	Democrat	28th and 23rd
Rubén Hinojosa	1997–	Texas	Democrat	15th
Loretta Sanchez	1997–	California	Democrat	46th and 47th
Joe Baca	1999–	California	Democrat	42nd and 43rd
Charles A. González	1999–	Texas	Democrat	20th
Grace Napolitano	1999–	California	Democrat	34th and 38th
Hilda Solís	2001–2009	California	Democrat	31st
U.S. Senate				
Octaviano Larrazolo	1928–1929	New Mexico	Republican	
Dennis Chavez	1935–1962	New Mexico	Democrat	
Joseph M. Montoya	1964–1977	New Mexico	Democrat	
Robert Menendez	2006–	New Jersey	Democrat	

BOX 7.3. Hispanics Who Have Served As Cabinet Secretaries

Hispanic Cabinet Officer	Years Served	President in Office When Nominated	Cabinet Office Held
Hilda Solis	2009–present	Barack Obama	Department of Labor
Kenneth Salazar	2009–present	Barack Obama	Department of Interior
Mel Martínez	2001–2003	George W. Bush	Department of Housing and Urban Development
William Richardson	1998–2000	William Clinton	Department of Energy
Federico Peña	1997–2000	William Clinton	Department of Energy
Federico Peña	1993–1997	William Clinton	Department of Transportation
Henry Cisneros	1992–1997	William Clinton	Department of Housing and Urban Development
Martin Lujan	1989–1992	George H. W. Bush	Department of Interior
Lauro Cavazos	1988–1992	Ronald Reagan	Department of Education

The overall political equation would not be complete without examining the Latino community's actions and strategies. Even with specific strategies by the major political parties and their leadership, Latino organizations advance their own agendas and enhance their political empowerment. An assessment for Latinos to make is to distinguish between the rhetoric and actual results and behaviors of the political parties, such as identifying their primary political objectives for the short term (targeting more Latinos for state level and congressional offices, pursuing specific policy reforms and initiatives, and expanding the electoral base). It is the seizing of opportunities and pursuing of policies that will define the dynamics between Latinos and the American political system.

The State and Local Levels and Latinos

The post-2000 election period made a significant impact at the state and local levels as well. Although Latinos have in the past been absent at the gubernatorial level, they have targeted governor's mansions and state legislatures to increase their representational levels. In 2002, Latinos vied for the governorships of New Mexico and Texas. In the Texas case, the Democratic primary was a contest between two Latinos, Dan Morales and Tony Sanchez, with Sanchez winning out to face Republican governor Rick Perry. Despite record minority turnout and significant financial backing, Sanchez lost to Perry in a race characterized by negative campaigning, high-stakes spending, the incumbency factor, and eleventh-hour stumping by President Bush on behalf of his gubernatorial successor. In New Mexico, Bill Richardson faced a Republican Latino opponent who was closer to the electorate but less established politically. Richardson was elected governor of New Mexico in 2002 with a sizable margin of victory.

In 2010, gubernatorial gains among Latinos increased by two with the election of Republicans Brian Sandoval in Nevada and Susana Martinez in New Mexico. Gains in Congress saw the election of Florida Republican Marco Rubio in the Senate and five new Latino Republicans in the House: in Idaho's first district, Raúl Labrador; in Florida's twenty-fifth district, former Florida state representative David Rivera; in Texas's seventeenth district, businessman and political newcomer Bill Flores; in Texas's twenty-third district, businessman Francisco Canseco; and in Washington State's third district, Representative Jaime Herrera. Several of these candidates successfully ran in districts that did not have Latino majorities. The new members-elect join reelected representatives Ileana Ros-Lehtinen and Mario Díaz-Balart of Florida for a record total of eight Republican Latinos in both chambers. On the Democratic incumbent side, three Democratic Latino members of the U.S. House, Ciro Rodriguez and Solomon Ortiz of Texas and John Salazar of Colorado, were unsuccessful in their reelection bids. In the election of 2012, partisan support and intensity, salient community issues, candidate choices, and district composition should provide opportunities and challenges for Latinos to continue on the road toward greater political empowerment.

BOX 7.4. Latinos and the 2010 Midterm Elections

Following the historic 2008 presidential election of Barack Obama, the midterm elections, as is typical, resulted in modest partisan shifts, with the "out" party making some gains. The 2010 midterm elections had some noteworthy occurrences. That is, the Republican Party gained almost sixty seats in the House and captured majority party leadership. The Republicans also narrowed the Democrats' majority in the Senate with six newly elected Republicans. Marco Rubio succeeded in winning one of Florida's senatorial seats. In addition, Susana Martinez and Brian Sandoval were elected as the governors of New Mexico and Nevada, respectively. These new, nationally prominent Latino officials were all elected as Republicans. Some Latino congressional incumbents were defeated (e.g., Representatives Ciro D. Rodríguez and Solomon Ortiz), and a total of five new Latinos were elected to the House of Representatives (Flores in Texas, Herrera in Washington State, Canseco in Texas, Labrador in Idaho, and Rivera in Florida). Again, all of these new congresspersons ran as Republicans. An additional backdrop to these midterm elections was the rise of the Tea Party Movement, a grassroots effort to move a policy agenda emphasizing smaller government, fewer taxes, free market principles, and "core" American values. Our analysis of the 2008 elections focuses on the role and impact of Latinos in national elections. Thus, this brief discussion will examine the 2010 midterm elections in a similar manner.

With the demonstrated linkages between Latinos and the Democratic Party, one basic issue was the anticipated levels of partisan support by Latinos. The University of Washington Institute for the Study of Ethnicity and Race conducted Latino Decisions (LD) tracking polls throughout the midterm election cycle. Other issues that form part of Latino politics and the midterm elections include competitive levels of voter turnout, maintaining and expanding numbers of Latino elected officials, influencing policy discourse and agenda setting, and serving as an important voting segment. Now that the 2010 midterm elections are over, we can briefly discuss some of the major outcomes and directions for Latinos.

Latinos continued to identify with the Democratic Party by a ratio of more than 2.5:1 (60 to 22 percent). Latinos' vote choices for the midterms reflected this registration pattern. According to the LD polls, for the contested gubernatorial races in eight states (California, Colorado, Arizona, Nevada, Illinois, New Mexico, Florida, and Texas), the Democrat received between 71 and 85 percent of the Latino vote. The only departure was the 38 percent Republican Susana Martinez received in New Mexico's gubernatorial race. Similarly, in states that had senatorial campaigns, Latinos supported the Democratic candidate by over 75 percent. Using the LD exit poll results, we can determine that the range of percentages for Latino respondents to vote for Democratic candidates for the House was between 74 and 90 percent. In the case of the latter, 90 percent of Latinos supported Harry Reid for reelection to the U.S. Senate. A similarly high percentage (approximately 86 percent) supported Barbara Boxer's reelection.

In several instances, the Latino candidate was a Republican. In most of these cases, Latinos supported the Democratic nominee, with Latino Republican candidates receiving about 66 percent higher support than their non-Latino Republican counterparts. This introduces a cross-pressure situation in which the relevance of ethnicity interacts with a partisan preference or affiliation. That is, the 2010 election, like most previous elections, indicated a strong Democratic voting bloc among Latinos. For example, in Florida, Marco Rubio received 70 percent of the Cuban vote, while he received 40 percent support among non-Cuban Latinos. Cubans have supported the Republican Party much more than any other Latino subgroup such that voting for Senator Rubio was a consistent choice among Cuban voters, while the drop-off of non-Cuban support was mediated by a higher proportion of Democratic Party affiliates.

Some other aspects of the 2010 midterm elections include the continued focus by political parties and advocacy groups on influencing Latino vote choices. Again drawing from the LD surveys, over one-half of the Latino respondents in every state interviewed reported seeing political advertisements directed toward Latinos specifically. In addition, over one-third of the ads were presented in a bilingual format, and another one-fifth were in Spanish. Since 2004, the use of Spanish-language media has increased, as has advertising in Spanish. The use of Spanish-language media (both television and radio) has generated more research into effective media and how to segment the Latino community for effective communication. It has become almost the political campaigning norm to "court" the Latino vote via targeted media and groups. One could suggest that this development shows recognition of the salience of the Latino vote and the use of more diverse mechanisms to reach this community.

Two other important developments during this round of midterm elections relate to issue salience and partisan interest and support. In the case of the former, the top two issues in the Latino community were the economy (and all of its iterations) and immigration. While immigration ran a close second, the LD surveys indicated that at least one-third to two-fifths of Latino respondents indicated that voters' choice was influenced significantly by positions on immigration reform and characterization of immigrants. This carried over to Latinos' interest and enthusiasm for the Democratic Party and its candidates and is reflected by ratings given to President Barack Obama. His approval ratings have been declining for the past year or so, and Latino opinion reflected that pattern, although to a lesser degree than among the general public. A major basis for low enthusiasm is Latinos' disappointment with the absence of immigration policies. Given the rise of state and local government actions that tend to be restrictive and punitive toward immigrants (spilling over to all Latinos), there are real expectations that the Democrats and president should assume a more proactive leadership in this area. LDS projected that low Latino enthusiasm could possibly affect turnout negatively. Yet the exit polls indicate comparable turnout levels to previous elections and strong Democratic Party support.

Overall, the general results of the 2010 midterm election suggest some strong pressures for the Obama administration to change its directions and emphases. At the same time, Latinos' policy emphases and expectations of the Democratic Party leadership are clear. Issue salience and preferences are guiding Latinos' voting choices, and the challenge is one of options. That is, if they view the Democratic Party as unresponsive to Latino policy priorities, do Latinos have alternative political choices for directing their vote? Our brief discussion of the 2010 midterm elections points out some continuous themes of enhancing the Latino voter base and raising turnout levels. At the same time, more proactive mobilization by Latino organizations, political parties, and labor unions helps to build on an increasing level of awareness and interest in the body politic. The expanding role and influence of the Latino community have become more established.

Local Politics and Latinos

Latinos have been very active politically at the local levels. The greater concentration of Latinos in the major cities has also resulted in more contested mayoral elections. In 2001 and 2002, Latinos sought the mayoralty in Los Angeles, New York, Houston, San Antonio, and San Jose. They were successful in the latter two cities. Despite the unsuccessful efforts of Fernando Ferrer (New York City), Orlando Sanchez (Houston), and Antonio Villaraigosa (Los Angeles), their strong campaigns demonstrated more political experience, which could carry over to subsequent elections. They also highlight the competitive and cooperative relations that can occur between the African American and Latino communities. (See chapter 11 for more discussion of coalitions.) In Los Angeles, Mayor James Hahn received substantial support from the African American community over Antonio Villaraigosa, while in New York, Ferrer gathered significant support from African Americans over Michael Bloomberg. The greater likelihood of significant Latino and African American populations in our major cities will be an important ingredient in electoral politics. Finally, in the mayoral runoff between incumbent Lee Brown (African American) and Orlando Sanchez, voter polarization patterns reflected the respective racial/ethnic backgrounds of the candidates.

Increasing mayoral competition has not been limited to the largest American cities, as gains among Latino officeholders are increasing for communities of all sizes and for other local offices. In addition, the presence of Latino candidates from subgroups other than the Mexican-origin, Puerto Rican, and Cuban communities is becoming more evident. In the second decade of the new millennium, a larger pool of candidates will come from these Latino subgroups. For example, Ana Maria Sol Gutiérrez, former school board member in Prince George County, was the first Salvadoran to run for the Maryland state legislature in 2002. She was elected to the Maryland General Assembly in November 2002. The pool of Latino candidates holding local offices becomes the next wave of Latinos vying for state and federal offices. In some cases, there will be competition between Latinos of different subgroup status. For example, the Chicago congressional district held by Luis Gutiérrez (a Democrat of Puerto Rican heritage) is being challenged by a Mexican American candidate, and issue positions are more similar than not. In 2010, in Providence, Rhode Island, Democrat Angel Taveras, a forty-year-old Dominican American lawyer, became the state's first elected Latino mayor. In addition to the contest for more local offices, matters of service delivery, social service programs, education quality and funding, community relations, and profiling remain policy concerns for Latinos. With the fiscal crises at all levels of government, especially at the state and local levels, lack of resources has resulted in service reductions, hiring cutbacks or freezes, and fiscal austerity. A question of differential impact upon the Latino community when governmental resources are scarcer remains a central area of research into local politics.

Finally, there has been a 37 percent increase in the total number of Latinos holding elected office—from 3,743 in 1996 to 5,129 in 2007. At the highest levels of office, there has been an even greater increase, with the number of Latinos serving in federal and state legislatures growing by more than 50 percent. Between 1996 and 2007, the number of Latina elected officials grew faster than the number of male Latino officials: the number of Latinas increased by 74 percent, compared to 25 percent for male Latinos. As a result, the female share of all Latino elected officials grew from 24 percent in 1996 to 31 percent in 2007. There has been a significant increase (142.1 percent) in the number of Latinos representing jurisdictions outside of the traditional areas of Latino population concentration, with Latinos serving in forty-three states in 2007, up from thirty-four in 1996. There are now Latino elected officials serving in nine states—Alaska, Georgia, Kentucky, New Hampshire, Missouri, North Dakota, Oklahoma, South Carolina, and Virginia—whereas eleven years ago, there were none.

Latino Electoral Participation, Key Factors, and the Future

This chapter has provided basic information about the level of Latino electoral participation as voters and the various explanatory factors that contribute to Latino voting patterns. Historically, Latinos have had lower voter-registration and voter-turnout rates. Part of the difficulty lies with the significant foreign-born proportion of the Latino population. In addition, the youthfulness of Latinos overall (on the average, they are ten years younger than the general population) reduces potential voting strength. From these two starting points, we also see the effects of socioeconomic status, participatory orientation, structural factors (e.g., discrimination), and cultural factors (e.g., nativity, language, and homeland political culture). Finally, the effects of Latino voting behavior and choices are also affected by given situations and issues that arise, such as statewide propositions directly impacting Latinos.

With our focus on elections, voting behavior, and Latinos, I have tried to paint a contemporary portrait of Latino registration and turnout. Despite some periodic improvements, there has also been some backsliding, and the electoral gap is still evident. In terms of Latino voter-participation trends, gains have been made, assisted by Latino organizations and leaders, in stimulating more Latinos to become involved in the American electoral system. Part of that attention has been directed toward increasing the number of foreign-born Latinos who become citizens. In addition, more targeted and sophisticated voter-education and -registration drives have been more prominent since the late 1990s. The early part of this new millennium saw greater evidence that conversion of potential Latino voting clout is being realized more significantly. Gains have been made in the absolute number of Latinos registered and voting as well as in their percentage of the total electorate. Given the greater percentage of Latinos over the age of eighteen and gains in the number of legalized Latino immigrants, naturalized citizens should add to recent Latino electoral gains.

Conclusion

I conclude this chapter with recent indicators of significant changes among the Latino electorate that could carry over into the new millennium. Some very specific developments and activities since the mid-1990s could well indicate upsurges in the electoral liveliness of Latino communities. These developments appear to have long-term implications and will alter the existing definition of the electoral profile for Latinos for the future. In a real sense, both the 2008 and the 2010 elections provide additional confirming evidence, which is presented in boxes 7.1 and 7.5.

Recent electoral developments and activities can be viewed as positive indicators that Latino electoral participation is realizing more of its potential. Specific trends involved rising voter-registration rates among Latinos. Although many of the specific examples are set in California, there is evidence of increased voter registration throughout "Latino America." This increase is even more noteworthy in light of declining voter participation among other Americans. Two key segments within the Latino community that are becoming more involved in the electoral arena are those under thirty and the foreign-born. The youthfulness of the Latino community contributes to its overall growth; yet, a large proportion remains too young to vote. The eighteen-to-thirty age group will be the fastest-growing segment into the next decade, potentially bringing new voters. The data on increased naturalization petitions reflect a major shift that started in the 1990s and is projected to continue into the next decade. To some extent, the anti-immigrant climate and restrictive state and local policy initiatives following September 11, 2001, have served as catalysts for permanent resident aliens to pursue naturalization and more ardent Latino political engagement. In addition, Mexico recently joined the ranks of other Latin American nations that recognize dual citizenship, which has reduced the stress of maintaining Mexican citizenship at the expense of not pursuing American citizenship. Thus, the conversion of the continued development of Latino communities into a more significant electoral actor has become increasingly evident since the mid-1990s.

Latinos' increased electoral competition for political offices is seeing more success at local levels and enjoying a relatively stable level at the state level. There is some recent evidence of newly elected Latino officials in areas where Latinos are not the dominant demographic. The added dimensions of partisan affiliation (i.e., Latinos running as Republican candidates) and salient issue clusters (i.e., immigration reform, the economy) will affect Latinos' interest, enthusiasm, and candidate preferences in the 2012 election cycle. Part of the gain in representation is the result of an expanding and increasingly active Latino electorate; yet, more energetic and effective Latino organizations and leadership are expanding the Latino political realm. Finally, external factors such as a negative climate directed toward Latinos, public policies and initiatives that directly impact Latino communities, direct partisan appeals by both major parties, and broader public networks of information and connection among the diverse Latino communities are important sources of increased Latino electoral participation. The role of Latino organizations and leadership and their concomitant mobilization efforts are the subject of the following chapter. The intersection of Latinos with leaders and organizations soliciting, directing, and encouraging participation and involvement will convert political potential into concrete action.

Discussion Questions

1. In more recent elections, Latinos have been characterized as a critical force in national and state elections. What is the basis for making such a claim?
2. Even with gains in voter registrations and regular voting, there are noticeable variations among different Latino national-origin groups regarding electoral politics. What are possible explanations for Latino subgroup differences?
3. Even when an individual decides to become involved electorally, structural factors can affect the extent and nature of electoral engagement. In the second decade of the new millennium, what are these structural factors? Do they differ from those of the 1960s and 1970s?
4. There seems to have been an increase in propositions and referenda on most states' election ballots. How have Latinos experienced this aspect of electoral politics?
5. An expanding segment of the Latino electorate has consisted of immigrants who have become naturalized citizens. Discuss the motivations, requisites, and benefits of naturalization for Latinos and their communities.

CHAPTER 8

Latino Organizations and Leadership

La maquinaría de la edad moderna, estas estructuras sociales que pretenden representar nuestros sentimientos, nuestros puntos de vista pero realmente son personas de carne y hueso que dirigen estas máquinas sociales y estas son el vínculo con el pueblo.

The machinery of this modern age, these social structures that seek to represent our feelings, our points of view, are directed by real people—and they are the connections with our community.

OUR EXAMINATION OF VOTING AND ELECTIONS has centered upon the changing numbers of Latinos who register and vote in U.S. elections. I have outlined and discussed the major contributing factors that affect Latino electoral participation: socioeconomic status, participatory orientations, structural conditions and practices, and cultural dimensions. Progress has been made in terms of increasing Latino electoral and other modes of political involvement. In the past decade, Latinos have shown gains in educational attainment, household income, and higher rates of naturalization. At the same time, organizational **mobilization** and leadership can play positive roles in increasing Latino political involvement. This mobilization can take the form of continuous efforts to activate the Latino community, as well as responses to external movements like anti-immigration initiatives and proposals to eliminate bilingual education.

This chapter focuses on the role of organizations and leaders in Latino political life. We are seeing these elements as linkages or bridges between individual Latinos and American political processes and institutions. Our earlier discussions of political involvement and participation noted how increased individual political capital can position a person to join and be active in organizations, develop communication skills, and become part of social networks that reinforce becoming and staying active. Therefore, the political resources that a Latino can develop and obtain have payoffs for organizational involvement as well as leadership enhancement.

How do organizations serve the Latino political community? What role do leaders play in linking Latino community interests and experiences to focused activities in political arenas? Being asked to participate, especially by someone who plays an important role in whether and how a person may become politically active, serves as a key ingredient in activating Latino participants. Organizations are part of the mobilizing "force" that can subsidize political involvement (reduce the costs of participation) for individuals by providing information, access to decision makers, forums for discussion, and potential benefits (employment, services, tax benefits, etc.). Just as the Latino population has grown dramatically over the past three decades, the rise of newer organizations, as well as the expanded scope of long-standing Latino organizations, is quite evident. Let us begin by examining, in a general manner, the purposes and bases for the existence of several Latino-based organizations.

Latinos and Organizations: Historical Origins

One of the benefits of sustained and directed research about Latinos,[1] particularly since the late 1960s, is the extent of knowledge about Latino organizations, past and present. We know that organizations are an aggregation of individuals with common interests. For Latinos in the United States, the existence of Latino-based organizations served a number of purposes and/or objectives. We know much more about Mexican-origin organizations than any other Latino subgroup due to the extensive research literature. For the most part, Mexican American or Chicano organizations can be grouped by major purposes or goals (Tirado 1970): mutual aid societies/*mutualistas*, cultural/home-community clubs (largely immigrant-based groups), adaptation-/adjustment-focused organizations, civil rights and advocacy organizations, social service providers or facilitators, political organizations, professional (occupation-related) organizations, and community (or grassroots-based) organizations.

It is important to understand the different bases from which Latino organizations are formed. Each basis for organizational existence impacts the organizational base (grassroots membership, immigrants, local residents, elites or professionals, etc.) and the principal strategies employed. At the same time, there are other important dimensions to identify and understand in examining organizations and their links to Latino political involvement. In addition to their membership bases, organizational size and resources, goals and objectives, and modes of political action link Latino organizations with specific political arenas. Is the organization a mass-based group, or is it composed of elites? For example, the Mexican American Legal Defense and Education Fund (MALDEF) is composed primarily of attorneys and other professionals but acts on behalf of a broader Latino constituency. Is the organization primarily local or national in scope? For a Latino-based group, what is the role of culture, group identity, and national origin in attracting members and influencing the organization's agenda or mission? Does class or gender come into play regarding the group's mission, membership base, and major organizational issues? Has assimilation or cultural pluralism, cultural nationalism or political integration affected the formation of the Latino organization, its strategies, and its membership base?

Since the mid-1980s and beyond, the development of **pan-ethnicity** has broadened the organizational base to include more Latino subgroups. This places different organizational pressures and expectations on longer-standing Latino organizations and entails ample challenges for newer organizations. Latino organizations are trying to represent the wider spectrum of all Latinos in national arenas. For example, the

National Council of La Raza (NCLR) was originally the Southwest Council of La Raza with its primary constituency of Mexican Americans or Chicanos. While its goal of reducing poverty and discrimination, as well as improving opportunities for Mexican Americans, has not changed, its activities now target all Hispanics/Latinos. Similarly, the arena is more focused on Washington, DC, and national issues. It has extended its chapters into the Northeast, Midwest, and South. The research and advocacy unit of NCLR focuses much of its activities on national policies such as immigration reform, social welfare reform, and affirmative action policies. We explore these pan-ethnic efforts and developments in organizations that have adjusted their bases, strategies, and political arenas later in this chapter. Clearly, obtaining a full grasp of Latino organizations involves more than identifying the organizations and their primary objectives and missions.

In this chapter I try to weave the critical components of the origins and life cycles of Latino organizations through organizing principles that emerge from the questions raised above and through specific Latino organizations. Box 8.1 presents a general description of the central elements found in Latino organizations, as well as in most organizations in American political life.

The key components include the following: (1) membership base, (2) primary organizational objectives or goals, (3) geographic base and focus of operation, (4) organizational structure and leadership, (5) organizational strategies and approaches, (6) role of culture, class, and gender in organizational development, and (7) organizational resource base and adaptations to pan-ethnic developments.

The existence and activity of Latino-based organizations have been evident as long as Latinos have inhabited the land now called the United States. As mentioned earlier, there is significant documentation of Mexican-origin communities and their organizations. Organizations like Orden de los Hijos de America and La Alianza HispanoAmericano (Briegal 1970) operated in the nineteenth century largely to assist Mexicanos with

BOX 8.1. Latino Organizations

Organizational Dimensions	Organizational Aspects
Membership base	Mass or elite base (professionals), class based, gender based
Goals/objectives	Specific (material benefits, services, job placement, etc.) or general (assimilation, pluralism, equality, etc.), cultural maintenance, social, civil rights
Strategies	Electoral, voting, lobbying, direct actions/protests, coalitions, etc.
Organizational structure	Decentralized, local chapters, regional, centralized, permanent professional staff
Geographic base	Local or citywide, neighborhood base, national policy making, regional
Organizational resources	Membership dues, foundation grants, federal grants/funds, litigation judgments
Leadership	Autocratic, charismatic, popularly elected, bureaucratic, institutionalized, regularized

surviving in the United States (providing burial insurance, rotating credit associations, cultural maintenance, etc.). The Alianza established chapters throughout the Southwest and even into Mexico. Its adaptability over the years of its operation[2] involved social service delivery programs directed to the Mexican-origin community, especially its immigrant segment. These organizations reflected the segregated and marginalized position that Mexicanos held in American society. Day-to-day survival and adaptation were the focus of early Mexican American organizations.

The turn of the nineteenth century saw a major influx of Mexicanos into the Southwest, partially due to political turmoil and the Mexican Revolution. As a result, migration continued to the Southwest and industrial, manufacturing sites in the Midwest (J. R. García 1980, 1995). The steel, automobile, railroad, and tanning industries, among others, served as employment magnets for many Mexican workers. In the Southwest, Mexican American organizations formed around labor groups and unions, mutual aid societies, social clubs based on community of origin, and groups that promoted assimilation into mainstream American society.

League of United Latin American Citizens

A good example of the latter type of Latino organization is the League of United Latin American Citizens (LULAC). Formed in Texas in 1927, this group consisted of Mexican American citizens who sought to acquire the rights and privileges of American citizenship, as well as to honor the duties and responsibilities of being American. Membership was restricted to Mexican-origin citizens, and loyalty to the United States was a central aspect of the organization's creed. Nevertheless, LULAC (Márquez 1988) engaged in activities that dealt with Mexican culture and pride. Initially the group focused on promoting the use of English, educational achievement and opportunities, economic opportunities (jobs and job training), and **political participation** and access. Thus, the LULAC community did not include all Mexican-origin persons, although social service activities were not limited to citizens. For example, in the 1950s it founded the Little Schools of the 400, a preschool program to equip Mexican-origin children with a four-hundred-word core English vocabulary prior to entering public school.

Politically, this group saw itself as a nonpartisan policy advocacy organization. In the late 1940s and early 1950s, it sought to eliminate segregation of Mexican students (San Miguel 1987) in both California and Texas through litigation. Education has consistently been a central issue for LULAC, which, since the late 1990s, has concerned itself with access to higher education and school financing for Latinos, as well as continuing its efforts to generate greater scholarship awards. It located its central offices in Washington, DC, and gave its executive director considerable latitude, with appropriate staffing to engage in national lobbying on Latino issues. In the mid-1980s, LULAC joined organizational forces with the NCLR, MALDEF, and the Congressional Hispanic Caucus (CHC) to defeat and then significantly modify the **Immigration Reform and Control Act of 1986** (Sierra 1991), and it has been a continuous proponent of comprehensive immigration reform since 2004.

Over the course of its organizational development, the group has adapted its scope, broadened its membership base, and become more involved at the national level. The scope was widened to deal with issues of immigration, civil rights, affirmative action, and bilingualism (in areas other than school curricula, such as public documents, court proceedings, and the like). Its base was expanded to include noncitizens and all Latinos, not just Mexican Americans. LULAC chapters were formed in regions outside the Southwest and in Puerto Rico. While it had not excluded other Latinos, as a southwestern organization its core base was the Mexican-origin population. LULAC characterizes itself as a national organization, but it has been "fully entrenched" in Washington, DC, with federal policy makers since the 1970s. A national office with sufficient staffing, sustained lobbying efforts, and national media attention are the elements of LULAC. It maintains a decentralized organizational structure with local-ized chapters and officers and holds an annual national convention at which national officers and policy decisions are determined.

Civil Rights, Litigation, and Latino Organizations

While LULAC can be seen as a Latino organization that has evolved into a national advocacy organization, its strategies have been largely constructed around a large, "mass-based" membership that provides its leadership with a loud and sizable voice to exert pressure regarding issues important to the Latino community. Other Latino organizations have a different membership base and pursue different strategies for Latino sociopolitical advancement. Two such organizations are the Puerto Rican Legal Defense and Education Fund (PRLDEF) and MALDEF.

Civil rights and equal opportunities for Latinos have been the bailiwick of both of these groups. Founded in the early 1970s, their central objectives have been protection under law and civil rights for Puerto Ricans and Mexican-origin populations. Over time, the scope has been expanded to be more inclusive of all Latinos. Each group's membership base consists primarily of attorneys, and funding is derived from founda-tion grants, legal fees and judgments, and fund-raising (private and corporate gifts). For the most part, their areas of focus include educational equity, equal employment, voting rights, equal housing opportunity, and leadership development. MALDEF in-cludes the policy area of immigrant rights as part of its central mission.

These Latino litigation organizations identify specific practices, locations, and plaintiffs to pursue changes in current policies or seek the full implementation of the law. For example, in *Aspira v. New York Board of Education*, PRLDEF raised the area of language rights and access to bilingual education services and resources. MALDEF in *Tyler v. Phloe* challenged the area of free educational access by undocumented school-age children. The local school district required proof of legal status for school-age children to receive a "free" public education. As a result, the court ruled that access to education is a "basic right" accorded to all persons residing in a school district's jurisdiction. In the area of voting rights, PRLDEF and MALDEF have challenged the election structure of at-large districts since the 1970s (i.e., seeking district rather than **at-large elections**) and focused on **redistricting** plans in order to increase Latino rep-resentation (promoting the creation of **majority-minority districts**).

Both organizations have a board of directors and a general counsel to lead them. Representation comes primarily from the legal and corporate sectors, and they are less connected to a geographic or mass population base. The nature and policy arenas of PRLDEF and MALDEF render them unsuitable for being mass-based or grassroots-driven organizations. Even though their organizational bases are not directly linked to a mass-based Latino constituency, both organizations have ongoing ties with other

Latino organizations and leadership that enable them to be effective and strategic in determining which areas, issues, and plaintiffs to work with. These organizations have served as policy protectors and initiators of policy expansion for the Latino communities. Pursuing such issues as challenging existing election systems that are detrimental to Latino representation, contesting funding and program inequities in both K–12 and higher education in terms of educational quality, access, and opportunities, and fighting employment discrimination against Latinos due to phenotype, accent, or negative stereotypes all represent policy-expansion initiatives.

Exile Organizations: The Cuban Community?

In many respects, a number of Latino subgroups can be viewed as incorporating an exile orientation and organizational vehicles for influence and action. For Latinos from Nicaragua, El Salvador, Guatemala, Argentina, and Uruguay (to name a few), political factors affect their decision to come to the United States. Yet, political refugee immigration status is not automatically accorded to persons from any Latin American country but Cuba. For the most part, on a case-by-case basis, proof of imminent danger due to political beliefs and activities serves as the primary criterion for achieving political refugee status. As noted in chapter 4, the growing Cuban community in the United States has been characterized as an exile group (Pérez 1985, 1986). In this manner, much of the community's attention and energy has focused on U.S. foreign policy toward Cuba and the Castro regime. Goals have included trade embargoes, establishment of Radio-TV Martí, continued admission of Cuban émigrés as political refugees, democratization of Cuba via the growth of civil society, and the demise of Fidel Castro and his socialist state.

Thus, the major organizations in the Cuban community have the emphases of an exile community oriented toward Cuba. At the same time, Cuban organizations assist the adaptation and adjustment of Cubans in the economic and political arenas of the United States. An example of an exile-oriented organization is the Cuban American National Foundation (CANF), until recently[3] led by Jorge Mas Canosa and now headed by José Mas Santos. CANF actively promotes the self-determination of the Cuban people and the dismantling of the communist Castro regime. It stands against a centralized, government-controlled economy and a one-party state. Founded in 1981, CANF has lobbied in Washington, DC, for political refugee asylum for Cubans, trade embargoes and isolation of Castro's Cuba, aid for refugees, and media broadcasts (radio and television) as part of Radio-TV Martí. CANF has offices in Miami, Washington, DC, and Union City, New Jersey, as well as chapters in Texas, Georgia, Chicago, California, Spain, and Puerto Rico. Since 2003, CANF has placed greater emphasis on programs that promote expansion of an active civil society and democratic values, or what can be described as a "bottom-up" strategy.

This actively anti-Castro organization has been quite effective in influencing U.S. foreign policy toward Cuba. Programmatically, CANF supports the Cuban Exodus Relief Fund, informational and policy reports serving clearinghouse functions, Mission Martí, the Foundation for Human Rights in Cuba, the Endowment for Cuban American Studies, and the Commission for Economic Reconstruction of Cuba. In 1988, CANF was able to get legislation passed allowing fifteen hundred Cubans in other countries to come to the United States, with fifteen hundred more Cuban "exiles" admitted annually thereafter. By 1995, ten thousand Cubans had been brought to the United States under this program. Their primary focus on removing Fidel Castro and dismantling the communist system reinforces the image of Cuban organizations as exile oriented. Since 1994, the "wet foot, dry foot" policy has been in effect, which enables Cuban émigrés who try to enter the United States to receive asylum if they are able to physically reach American shores.

There is strong evidence of broad-based support within the Cuban community for CANF, as seven out of ten Cuban households have contributed to the foundation, and a Univision poll found that it was considered trustworthy and effective. Given its Cuba-centered focus, it has had strong ties to national Republican leadership, especially during the Reagan administration, and to Senator Jesse Helms (R-NC). This was evident with the passage of the Helms-Burton Act, the 1992 Cuban Democracy Act tightening the trade embargo on Cuba, and the 1996 Cuban Liberation and Democratic Solidarity Act. Policies by the William Jefferson Clinton and George W. Bush administrations have placed greater restrictions on remittances, travel, and humanitarian aid, to which CANF has raised objections.

CANF's pervasive character within the Cuban community may suggest to some both uniformity and singularity of vision among the Cuban population in the United States. Yet, other Cuban-based organizations take alternative positions regarding Cuba, and still others work on the domestic front. The Cuban American National Council (CANC) is active in the areas of education, housing, and economic-development services. As a nonprofit organization, it receives funding from numerous levels of government, private corporations, and foundations. This twenty-year-old organization has Latinos and other minorities as its primary "service" clientele. Its service projects include coordination and supportive services for thirty thousand Cubans and Haitians in Guantánamo, Cuba, building new housing units, providing direct job placements and at-risk-student intervention programs, and supporting over sixty policy publications and annual national conferences. CANC has dealt with interminority relations (especially between Cubans and African Americans), Cubanization effects in Miami, redistricting and bloc voting, and educational attainment and language. Overall, CANC directs its energies toward issues impacting Cubans and other Latinos once they reside in the United States.

Other organizations focusing on U.S.-Cuban policies are the Cuban Committee for Democracy and Cambio Cubano. Both are moderate in their orientation toward Castro's Cuba. Perhaps characterized as socially democratic ideologically, these organizations see a more involved role for government in providing jobs, housing, and bilingual education. The board members include several Cuban academics, and its policy directions lean toward reconciliation and dialogue with the Cuban regime and open travel to Cuba. The increasing proportion of Cubans born in the United States (Moreno and Warren 1992) is partially at play with a more diverse set of attitudes and policy preferences within the Cuban community. For example, in 2007, a Florida International University poll of Cubans surveyed public opinion about possible actions toward Cuba: 57.5 percent supported continuation of economic sanctions against Cuba, and 65 percent favored open dialogue with the Castro regime. Regarding the embargo more specifically, 71.7 percent supported the sale of medicine to the people, and 62 percent favored the sale of food. Finally, 55.2 percent supported unrestricted travel to Cuba, and 57.2 percent would support establishing diplomatic relations with Cuba. As

Cuban American organizational life develops in this new millennium, the continual focus upon exile-related issues (in addition to a wider range of policy responses toward Cuba) will evidence more variations among policy options. In addition, the focus on a broad range of domestic issues and similar minority-based concerns with other Latinos and minority groups has become more established.

Professional Organizations and Latinos

Any description of Latino organizations must include mention of the hundreds of groups focused on specific public policy issues and whose memberships largely consist of professionals. The range of policy interests includes bilingual education, mental health, small business development, immigration, job training, foreign trade policies, and access to and participation in most of the professional associations and societies. There are Latino groups in the health-care/medical, legal, academic, and business-related fields, the religious denominations, social welfare professions, unions, and education.

Most of these Latino-based organizations are organized around a specific policy arena, such as education, health care, social services, and so on. Their membership consists of Latinos active in these arenas as professionals, activists, and concerned citizens. For example, attorneys (HNBA), dentists (NAHD), engineers (SHPE), journalists (NAHJ), and bilingual educators (NABE) have access to Latino-related professional organizations. Within the public-office sector, the National Association of Latino Elected and Appointed Officials (NALEO) is an umbrella organization for appointed and elected Latino officials at all levels of government. Latinos also have caucuses or affiliated associations within the elected-official groups. Overall, these Latino organizations promote access, participation, opportunity, mobility, and nondiscriminatory treatment of Latinos and other minorities.

On the policy front, these organizations seek changes within their respective professional organizations; they also conduct research and advocate policy at all levels of government. For example, the **National Association of Bilingual Educators** (NABE) describes itself as both a professional and an advocacy association. Through its research, professional development, public education, and legislative advocacy, it strives to implement educational policies and practices to ensure equal educational opportunity for diverse students. As is consistent with its organizational objectives, NABE pursues its activities on behalf of language-minority students with an added dimension of multiculturalism. NABE pursues its goals through special interest groups (SIGs),[4] which enable its membership to pursue more salient interests in greater depth, as well as to benefit the organization with thoughtful ideas, policy positions, and analysis. The SIGs serve as working policy subgroups that enable members who specialize in subfields of bilingual education to focus their expertise on developing policy analysis and recommendations that will be presented to the general membership.

Another cluster of Latino organizations exists in the business and economic realms of public policy. These organizations emphasize the economic contributions of Latinos to economic growth and development, as well as to promoting greater participation by Latinos as entrepreneurs. Organizations such as the U.S. Hispanic Chamber of Commerce (USHCC) assist the economic development of Hispanic firms with the corporate sector and governmental initiatives and programs. Similar Latino organizations include the Hispanic Association for Corporate Responsibility (HACR), the National Hispanic Corporate Council (NHCC), and the U.S.-Mexican Chamber of Commerce. The USHCC defines its mission as "advocating, promoting, and facilitating the success of Hispanic businesses."[5] Its activities include strengthening national programs to assist Hispanic economic development, increasing business relationships and partnerships between the corporate sector and Hispanic-owned businesses, providing technical assistance to Hispanic business associations and entrepreneurs, and monitoring legislation, policies, and programs that affect the Hispanic business community.

While there exist business-oriented Latino organizations that focus on the employers' side of Latinos in the economy, others focus on the workers' side of economic issues. For example, the Labor Council for Latin American Advancement (LCLAA) is a trade union association that represents 1.4 million Latino workers in forty-three international unions. It serves as a Latino constituency group within the AFL-CIO and engages in advocacy and political work. Founded in 1973, the LCLAA states its mission as a "consciousness-raising organization to 'instill pride and unity among Latino workers and serve as a vehicle to advance issues that affect Latinos within their respective trade unions and communities.'"[6] It addresses issues such as low wages, employment-related discrimination, union recognition, and socioeconomic mobility. Another workers' organization is the United Farm Workers of America (affiliated with the AFL-CIO), founded by César Chávez, Dolores Huerta, and Larry Itlong in the early 1960s (Griswold del Castillo 1995). Focusing on agricultural workers, initially in the Southwest, it directed its efforts toward union recognition, wages, working conditions, health and safety issues, and employment-related benefits. Early struggles entailed organizing native-born and immigrant agricultural workers to seek collective bargaining status and legislation enabling federal and state coverage for these workers. Over the years, the United Farm Workers has had its share of victories and setbacks. Since the death of César Chávez in 1993, the union has been led by Arturo Rodríquez (president) and Dolores Huerta (secretary-treasurer).

Since 2000, the United Service Workers Union has been more aggressively involved in organizing the immigrant segment of the workforce. Strikes in Los Angeles and Chicago illustrated the organizational force of office service workers and the extensive involvement of Latino immigrants (both undocumented and permanent resident aliens). During the 1990s, labor reassessed its position on immigration reform and the undocumented segment of the labor force. In contrast, the AFL-CIO leadership stated it would press Congress to grant amnesty to the nation's 6 to 8 million undocumented immigrants (C. Rodríquez 2000). Also during the 1990s, labor looked around the country to identify unorganized workers and found them in agriculture, meatpacking, hotels, and restaurants. For Latino immigrants and other undocumented workers, an alliance with the labor movement represented an opportunity to press for legalization and improved wage levels and working conditions. Internal changes are also evident in the AFL-CIO with Latino gains as labor organizers and officials (e.g., the election of Linda Chavez-Thompson as executive vice-president of the AFL-CIO in 1995) within unions in the manufacturing, service, farming, and food-service sectors.

Another sector of organizations is more policy and research oriented. For instance, the Pew Hispanic Center began as a joint enterprise by the *Washington Post*, the Kaiser Family Foundation, and the Pew Research Centers to conduct a national survey of

Latinos in the United States. This program has been conducting surveys since 2001, covering a wide range of topics affecting the Latino community (i.e., immigration, political participation, education, immigration and immigrants). Since 2000, the Pew Hispanic Center has made available its survey data for further analysis by researchers, the media, and advocacy organizations. In addition, a number of Latino/Hispanic research centers at several colleges and universities (e.g., Washington Institute for Study of Ethnicity and Race at the University of Washington, Mexican American and Latino Research Center at Texas A&M, and Institute for Latino Studies at Notre Dame) are conducting major research projects that serve to affect a Latino policy agenda and public knowledge base for the Latino community and its organizations. These research centers and similarly oriented organizations also affect media coverage and content dealing with Latinos and the American sociopolitical system.

Latino Organizations within Political Institutions

The end of the second millennium brought a major shift for Latino organizations from a more regional and local scope to a greater national presence and involvement. Bridging the various Latino subcommunities to embrace a pan-ethnic focus has been a challenge and an opportunity to expand the Latino resource base and agenda. The Latino organizational leadership has become more institutionalized in the sense that organizational skills, networks, and institutional positioning have supplanted charismatic appeal. The creation of the CHC and its institute, the CHCI, in 1976 marked the creation of a legislative organization within the U.S. Congress. With only five Hispanic congresspersons at that time, the founders' goals were to work with other groups both inside and outside Congress to intensify federal commitment to Latinos, as well as to increase Latinos' awareness of the execution and purpose of the American political system.[7] By 1978, the CHCI had formed a 501(c)(3) nonprofit organization to add an educational component for leadership development and educational stipends and internships. Its board of directors has been expanded to include representatives from other Hispanic organizations and the corporate sector.

One of its primary functions is to unite its members around a collective legislative agenda for Latino interests, as well as to monitor executive and judicial policies that affect Hispanics. For example, for many years, the CHC had been advocating to fill Supreme Court vacancies from a pool of several Latino federal judges. In May 2009, President Barack Obama nominated Sonia Sotomayor for appointment to the U.S. Supreme Court to replace retired justice David Souter. The U.S. Senate confirmed her nomination in August 2009 by a vote of sixty-eight to thirty-one. Sotomayor was nominated to the U.S. District Court for the Southern District of New York by President George H. W. Bush in 1991, and her nomination was confirmed in 1992. In 1995, she issued a preliminary injunction against Major League Baseball, which ended the 1994 baseball strike. Sotomayor made a ruling allowing the *Wall Street Journal* to publish Deputy White House Counsel Vince Foster's final suicide note. In 1997, President Bill Clinton nominated her to the U.S. Court of Appeals for the Second Circuit. Her nomination was slowed by the Republican majority in the Senate, but she was eventually confirmed in 1998. On the Second Circuit, Sotomayor heard appeals in more than three thousand cases and wrote about 380 opinions. Sotomayor has taught at the New York University School of Law and Columbia Law School.

The CHC's task force structure focuses on a wide variety of policy areas in addition to the more readily identifiable ones: education, immigration, civil rights, and economic development. The "less traditional" policy areas include arts and entertainment, health, telecommunications, and social security. Although the number of Latino congresspersons has increased to twenty-seven, not all are members of CHC. Some of the eight Hispanic Republican representatives[8] (including those elected in the 2010 midterm elections) have been part of the CHC, but none are currently. To some degree, the partisan dominance in the CHC and foreign policy differences regarding Cuba have contributed to the nonaffiliation of Hispanic Republicans.

The other "insider" organization is NALEO, a nonprofit, nonpartisan organization founded in 1976 as a vehicle for political empowerment for the growing number of Latinos in public office. As of June 2010, there were 5,739 Latino elected officials, a 59 percent increase since 1984.[9] With its base, NALEO provides assistance and training to elected officials at all levels, as well as research reports and discussions of policy relevant matters. Its annual conference serves as a focal point for establishing policy priorities and cementing working networks among fellow public officials.

A major NALEO initiative begun in the late 1980s was a proactive effort to promote naturalization among Latino immigrants. Its analysis regarding further political empowerment revealed the significant percentage of the Latino community that was unable to participate electorally because of noncitizenship. In the American tradition, immigrants make the naturalization decision on an individual basis without active encouragement from "the government" or civic organizations. NALEO undertook a major campaign to inform Latino immigrants and encourage them to pursue naturalization. Part of the overall plan entailed research to understand the dynamics of that decision-making process, the level of information regarding the naturalization process, the myths or misinformation about naturalization, and improving the bureaucratic structures that deal with naturalization applications and approval. As a result, citizenship information lines and public relations programs were initiated. NALEO conducted a study of the Immigration and Naturalization Service (INS) regarding the processing of applications and the organization's accessibility to Latinos. This study, conducted by David North, documented extensive backlogs and wait periods of up to twenty-four months for a mandatory interview in some INS offices.

NALEO was involved in the Census 2000 planning. It supported the Census Bureau's plan to include sampling as part of the decennial enumeration process.[10] NALEO has also been active in promoting the full count of all Latinos with support for complete confidentiality, advertising targeted to Latinos, Spanish-language forms and information, and the hiring of bilingual and bicultural enumerators (citizens and permanent resident aliens). These actions are examples of strategies for Latino political empowerment. NALEO sees the connection between pursuing the expansion of the Latino political base (i.e., converting more Latino immigrants into citizens and making a full count of resident Latinos) and increasing the number of Latino elected and appointed officials. An active constituency and greater political representation serve the general purposes of NALEO.

Two more organizations focusing on the political process are the Southwest Voter Registration and Education Project (SVREP) and the Midwest Voter Registration and Education Project (MWVREP). Both organizations have conducted voter-registration campaigns and have linked voting with policy preferences and outcomes. Over the past twenty-five years, they have honed their planning and timing to produce better voter-registration results. For example, SVREP used to plan its voter-registration campaigns many months prior to a local election or in years when no elections were scheduled. Subsequent registration efforts in the same community would include reregistering several of the same persons who had been purged for nonvoting. Subsequent registration campaigns were timed closer to upcoming elections and involved one-on-one conversations about Latinos' views on politics, the government, public officials, and political participation.

This educational process connects Latinos' interests, elections, and representatives with higher rates of voting and more Latino candidates running for office. As a result, the voter-education dimension of these two organizations has enhanced the effectiveness of their voter-registration campaigns. Clearly, part of the political-empowerment goal for Latinos is to expand their electoral base to more closely approach the community's overall growth rate. While this book has focused on Latino organizations that are national in scope and tend to be pan-ethnic in representing Latino interests, a multitude of Latino organizations (often Latino subgroup only) exist throughout most communities in which Latinos live.

Latinos at the Grass Roots: Community-Based Groups

By their very nature, grassroots organizations are locally based and cover a wide range of electoral and nonelectoral political activities targeted to local institutions and issues. Many of their activities are nonelectoral and involve noncitizens as well. The history of Latino grassroots organizations in the United States is both long and dynamic. Latino organizations date back to the nineteenth century and are found in many communities where Latinos reside. By their very nature, grassroots groups are local in orientation, and their longevity depends on specific issues and situations. Since the post–World War II era, a distinctive brand of community organizations has had a major impact in many cities and subregions, especially in the Southwest.

The Industrial Areas Foundation (IAF), founded by Saul Alinsky (1971), developed an approach, structure, and general philosophy of organizing have-nots for purposes of securing political and economic power. Alinsky was active in African American neighborhoods, particularly in the Midwest and the East, that played a pivotal force in the local areas. Integral to any Alinsky-based organization were the components of a professional, full-time organizer, an umbrella organization to incorporate already existing groups in the neighborhood, direct action and confrontation tactics, multipurpose and concrete goals, and an active membership base. The Community Services Organization (CSO) in Southern California was the first Alinsky-style organization in which Latinos were involved as organizers and neighborhood activists. Latino leaders such as Edward Roybal, César Chávez, and Dolores Huerta were organizers trained by Fred Ross (the full-time Alinsky organizer assigned to the CSO). Issues such as voter registration, housing and landlord problems, and poor schools were the focus of CSO political actions.

In the late 1960s and 1970s, Community Organized for Public Services (COPS) surfaced in San Antonio, Texas, due to rising utility rates and inadequate drainage infrastructure on the heavily Mexican American west side of the city. COPS successfully involved previously less active westsiders with positive, tangible outcomes (Márquez

BOX 8.2. Latino Politics at the Grass Roots

In July 1998 the *Los Angeles Times* reported on an organization, Grupo Pro-mejoras (Pro-improvement Group) in Mayfield, California (a middle-class Latino community southeast of Los Angeles). The news story relayed the account of a neighborhood movement to address issues regarding the local water company (Maywood Mutual Water Company No. 2). The issues revolved around water rates, and residents were contesting rising water bills. The predominantly Mexican immigrant persons experienced a less than friendly response from company personnel and were often ridiculed for their poor English (Tobar 1998). As a result of trying to deal with the water company, neighbors began to meet weekly in a member's garage to discuss issues, concerns, and actions.

Over a three-year period, their membership base grew, and specific actions evolved (opposition to a road bond initiative, not identifying candidates for the water company board by name, etc.). As a result, Grupo Pro-mejoras "took over" the board with one of its members becoming president. Among newly involved persons, successes often reinforce continued involvement and an expanded range of activities and interests (e.g., exploring the school district or the chamber of commerce). This largely immigrant enclave (both long-term residents and more recent arrivals) has been activated and become involved in "small-town democracy" quite extensively. This brief example reflects how local neighborhood groups focus on local ad hoc issues and develop the skills, knowledge, and strategies to effect changes.

1993). Subsequently, COPS continued its local involvement and became a significant political force in San Antonio. Other COPS community organizations were formed in Houston, Corpus Christi, Fort Worth, and Austin, as well as in the Rio Grande Valley (Valley Interfaith), El Paso (El Paso Inter-Faith Service Organization), and Los Angeles (United Neighborhood Organizations).

The philosophy of the IAF and Saul Alinsky incorporates the key concepts of empowerment, motivating self-interest, direct action, targeting political and economic institutions, and negotiating concrete services and resources. Over time, the IAF expanded effectively into the Latino community. Ernesto Cortés Jr. (currently IAF southwest regional supervisor) was the community organizer for COPS and then for other IAF-based groups throughout the state of Texas (e.g., El Paso, Rio Grande Valley, Houston, Fort Worth). His influence has modified Alinsky's principles regarding institutional change. Cortés sees politics as engaging in public discourse and initiating collective action that is guided by that dialogue, which includes disagreements, arguments, confrontations, negotiations, and open conversations as part of the political process that makes it possible for people to act. As a result, most of the professional organizer's early organizing efforts involve conducting numerous individual meetings for the purpose of identifying potential leaders. Then successive one-on-one meetings serve to direct networks for agenda building and identifying specific areas and arenas for action.

The other significant component of the contemporary IAF approach is to work through religious congregations in a federation structure. Congregations of faith

BOX 8.3. Newer Latino Organizations Come Forward

The Dominican American National Roundtable (DANR) is a civic organization trying to bring together the voices of Dominicans residing in the United States. It focuses on issues pertinent to the Dominican community that cut across the existing organized sectors, such as grassroots groups, nonprofit organizations, and religious, social, and business entities. Since a significant segment of the Dominican community includes immigrants or first-generation residents. in the United States, there is an emphasis on recognizing and maintaining the "rich culture" of the Dominican Republic. The theme of the fall 2001 annual conference (held in Washington, DC) was "Empowerment through Education: The Way for Dominican Americans." The DANR provides a national forum for analysis, planning, and actions to advance the educational, economic, legal, social, cultural, and political interests of Dominicans. Over sixty organizations and supporters are affiliated with the DANR, and their locations extend beyond New York City to Rhode Island, Florida, New Jersey, and Washington, DC. Latino umbrella organizations will become more prevalent and inclusive of existing locally based Latino subgroups.

generally affirm meaningful goals in life and serve as institutions built on personal networks of family and neighborhood (Cortés 1996). This context reinforces congregations' struggles to understand and to act. The action component is central to the IAF philosophy. Delivering concrete goods to build and sustain communities has been a benchmark for Alinsky community organizations' longevity. More recently, the IAF strategy has been to use the federal government's Community Block Development Grant (CBDG) program as a process for eligible neighborhoods to meet and discuss potential projects with costs attached. As more projects and total costs exceed CBDG allocation, the IAF members must bargain, trim some projects, and delay others to acquire mutual support (Cortés 1996). This process of negotiating and facilitating the bargaining among neighborhoods is intended to produce a more collective culture.

Finally, the IAF orientation emphasizes leadership development by training its organizers to act as teachers, mentors, and agitators who cultivate leadership for the community organization. This process allows persons to develop a broadened vision of their own self-interest (a key concept that enables motivation and agenda setting) and makes possible the ability to recognize individuals' connections and responsibilities to others and communities. The IAF has adapted over the past forty years in both its strategies and community bases (which have become broader, more diverse, and less geographically defined to specific neighborhoods). Since the 1960s, the IAF has initiated community-based organizations, initially in the African American community and then in the Latino community.

This discussion of Alinsky and the IAF is meant to provide some insight into the IAF's significance, at the grassroots level, for a number of Latino communities, especially in the Southwest. While the membership of the organizations is overwhelmingly Latino, **ethnicity** and culture serve as the means of connecting with others and their experiences; nevertheless, the IAF approach does not want to define issues racially or ethnically. While the Alinsky philosophy focuses more on the self-interest of the community involved, and the IAF does not see itself as a minority-oriented organization, it seeks to empower the have-nots. There is a considerable overlap between the have-nots and communities of color. The character of IAF community organizations is also influenced by the background and experiences of their professional organizers. Many Alinsky organizations reflect the character and Latino-ness of their Latino-trained IAF organizers. At the same time, the existence of Latino grassroots groups extends beyond the long-standing presence of Alinsky-based organizations.

BOX 8.4. Social Movements, Latinos, Immigration, and Organizational Elements

The foreign-born segment had long been characterized as either apolitical or not equipped to be active participants in the American political system. Yet, in the spring of 2006, a significant number of American communities witnessed the mass protests of millions of immigrants, other Latinos, and proponents of comprehensive and more humanitarian immigration reform. More specifically, the House passage of HR 4437, or the Sensenbrenner bill, placed further emphasis of border "fortification" and enforcement as well as expanding the criminal "nature" of being an unauthorized immigrant in America. For example, on May 1, 2006, an estimated 1.2 to 2 million persons participated in organized rallies associated with an economic boycott in sixty-three cities (Cano 2008). This series of demonstrations over several months marked an unprecedented social protest largely by a segment that had been mostly faceless and voiceless. In this chapter, I have discussed organizations, mobilization, and contributing factors that influence some Latinos to be more politically and civically engaged.

Yet, the magnitude and coordination of this social movement also provides some other insight into the organizational and mobilization processes that warrant some attention. Established organizations, ad hoc groups, activists, and youthful segments of the Latino community created a synergy that resulted in an underlying organizational dynamic. That is, established organizations such as the Catholic Church, labor unions (e.g., the Service Employees International Union), immigration advocacy groups, and local activists initiated actions interdependently in response to HR 4437 and the restrictive and hostile narratives surrounding immigrants and immigration policies (Cano 2008). The next effect was an organic process in which galvanization in this policy domain served to expand mobilization efforts and approaches, as well as to develop greater organizational skills and reach through a series of events and actions. For example, Cardinal Roger Mahoney of the Los Angeles diocese wrote to President George W. Bush in opposition to HR 4437. Labor organizers, especially those with significant immigrant membership, began to organize members and their families to voice opposition to the legislation and provide a more human face and narrative about the lives and positive impacts of immigrants on American society.

A noteworthy aspect of this social movement is the use of traditional forms of political mobilization in addition to modern technology and ethnic media (Reyes 2006). In the case of the latter, three elements were critical to the success of this movement: Spanish-language media and especially radio personalities, the Internet, and text messaging. Spanish-language radio's clientele consists mostly of Spanish speakers and immigrant households. This medium provided information about the protest events as well as the "rules of engagement" and bases for the protests. For example, participants in the early protest marches displayed flags of their countries of origin, which raised questions about their affection for and ties to America. Subsequent marches included the carrying of the American flag. Popular DJ's would inform, motivate, and shape the nature of the pro-immigrant social movement, targeting a previously less politically engaged segment of the Latino community.

The use of the Internet as a tool to organize and promote civic engagement had been viewed as having a class bias (i.e., targeting middle and upper income segments); yet, evidence indicated that the Internet and text messaging were used to communicate and network for political purposes and represented a "low-cost" mechanism for Latino participants (Reyes 2006). There was a connection between the use of "newer" technologies and age segments in this social movement. That is, Latino youths took active roles in this movement as identifiable allied groups in addition being integrated into the overall social movement (Manzano et al. 2009). While the public display of political and civic engagement of these mass protests has subsided, both the contentiousness involved in immigration policy making and the debates about "appropriate" content of immigration and needed actions persist. More systematic attention has been directed toward the expanded range of mobilization strategies and techniques and toward previously underresearched segments of the Latino community (the foreign-born, undocumented, etc.). As a result, future discussions of Latino organizations and mobilization will have a broader scope and knowledge base.

In any community with a Latino population, there are some local organizations that focus on their concerns and lives. As mentioned at the beginning of this chapter, the organizational goals encompass important facets of daily living (work, religion, social networks, family, education, immigration, etc.). For example, Latinos United for Political Rights (LUPA) advocates for immigrant rights. ASPIRA, a long-standing, primarily Puerto Rican organization, focuses on educational issues, usually in the Northeast. Many local areas have social and mutual self-help groups that are largely organized around immigrants' hometown origins in the Caribbean, Mexico, and Central and South America. Historically, groups like the Alianza Hispano Americano and Orden de los Hijos de America served as mutual aid societies to assist immigrants economically (rotating credit loans, burial insurance, etc.) and as social and cultural support systems. In a contemporary sense, many local Latino organizations assist their lives in the United States. There is clearly a rise in grassroots organizations within the more recent Latino subgroups (Salvadorans, Dominicans, Colombians, etc.) as their communities grow in size and establish both presence and concerns.

Conclusion

Students of Latino organizational life in the United States need to keep in mind the various dimensions of organizations and follow up by looking at Latino activities in specific cities and metropolitan areas. The key aspects related to organizations include goals and their breadth or range; constituents and their characteristics; resources and sources of assets; strategies and methods; leadership styles, selection, and accountability; and arenas for action. This chapter has focused on the key aspects of Latino organizations and some of their activities without going into great detail regarding specific organizational and other types of leadership. Since leadership is primarily organizationally based, identifying and profiling specific Latino activists and leaders would require a much longer narrative.

Organizational life for Latinos is active and has become more evident at the national level. Many of these groups use a broader pan-ethnic configuration to increase their constituent and resource base, as well as to achieve greater legitimacy as national players in policy arenas. While I have not extensively profiled specific Latino leaders, the role of organizational leadership is central to effective Latino political involvement. This cadre of leaders, at both the national and local levels, contributes to the definition and clarification of group goals and issues, identification and planning of strategies, provision of motivating incentives and rationale for individual involvement, and negotiation of institutional responses on issues, demands, requests, and so on. The use of personal networks and a thorough understanding of cultural and personal experiences of Latinos in the United States enable Latino leaders to enlist Latinos' involvement, especially politically. Box 8.4 provides a brief organizational analysis of the social movement, primarily among Latino immigrants, in response to HR 4437 (the Sensenbrenner bill). Chapter 9 explores some of the key substantive policy areas and issues that are part of the Latino policy agenda. This will illustrate the role of organizations and leadership and explain why particular areas are salient for Latinos.

Discussion Questions

1. With greater national exposure and active Latino organizations, it has been suggested that a nationally recognized Latino leader would lead to greater political enhancement. Is this possible, desirable, and necessary for the Latino community to achieve greater political importance?

2. We have more Latino pan-ethnic organizations advocating on behalf of all Latinos at the national and state levels. What challenges do these organizations face in being effective for all Latinos?

3. Labor unions have been active in the political realm for a long time. With the rise of service unions such as the **Service Employees International Union** and the **Hotel and Restaurant Employees Union**, as well as of Latino union leaders and members, how have their efforts affected Latino politics?

4. The Congressional Hispanic Caucus has been a long-standing interest and advocacy group in Congress. For the most part, Democratic representatives have been the major players in the CHC. With the numbers of Latino Republicans newly elected to the House, how do you think the CHC will be affected?

CHAPTER 9

Immigration and Latino Immigrants

Ah, los pobres inmigrantes, los forasteros, los refugiados, los nativo americanos, con su larga historia en este país—formamos el mosaico de la comunidad hispana. Llevamos dentro muchas vivencias que han sido nuestro desafío para sobrevivir esta jornada a los Estados Unidos. Y a cado uno nos debe interesar oir todas las historias de cada persona en nuestras comunidades.

Ah, the poor immigrants, the foreigners, the refugees, the native-born sons and daughters with their long history in this country—we form a mosaic of the Latino community. We come with many different stories and challenges of survival from our journey to America, and we should listen to all of the stories of all our community members.

W**HAT GOVERNMENT CHOOSES TO DO** can be seen as the basis for public policy (Dye 1992). The range of actions that government takes can include regulating conflict, organizing society, distributing resources, and extracting money from individuals and corporations. We usually think in terms of building roads, establishing social services, providing educational funds for buildings and programs, maintaining national defense and security, collecting taxes, and expanding bureaucracies to manage and oversee governmental operations. The pervasiveness of public policy in people's lives is a daily occurrence.

This examination of public policy and Latinos aims, identifies, and analyzes the causes and consequences of governmental activities. What impacts do Latinos have on the content of public policies? What consequences do public policies have for Latinos and/or Latino subgroups? Are there institutional arrangements and political processes that limit access and effectiveness for Latino concerns and actions? Do Latinos pursue particular public policies and exhibit specific preferences?

Throughout this book, I have discussed the concept of community among the various national-origin groups identified as Latino. In addition, I have explored the nature of community among Latinos in which cultural practices and values can bridge the experiences of being Mexican or Salvadoran or Puerto Rican. Clearly, Spanish-language use and loyalty can contribute to public policies that both impact and concern Latinos.

Policy areas of education, especially bilingual education and **English-only initiatives**, reflect the extension of culture and public policy.

I have also discussed community as being established by Latinos experiencing common circumstances, conditions, and issues. For example, the poverty rate among Latinos increased substantially during the 1990s, so social welfare reforms associate that policy area with Latinos. These bases for community are important in our examination of Latino politics as they represent the content and direction for Latino **political participation** and influence. I will now direct previous discussions of organizations, issues, leadership, and participatory patterns and resources to three specific policy arenas—immigration, education, and voting rights—as issues that are central to most Latino subcommunities.

The area of policy studies includes the causes and consequences of governmental activities, as well as the development of a policy agenda from which governments move in certain directions and with explicit purposes. Latinos are not only responding to existing public policies but are trying to formulate new policies or reformulate current ones. J. A. García (1996) attempts to connect the Chicano movement with politics and public policy by looking at the elements or goals of the Chicano movement and how they translated into the policy arenas. In doing so, García uses the work of Milton Esman (1985), which sets out five conditions that are necessary and sufficient for the politicization of ethnic groups: (1) group identities based on objective social distinctions and feelings of solidarity that they generate; (2) grievances based on perceived social, economic, or cultural deprivation or discrimination; (3) rising expectations for improvement; (4) declining authority and effectiveness of the political center; and (5) effective political organization. These conditions formulate preconditions for Latinos and public policy. These combined elements of shared community, common issues, and interconnected organizations work to influence political institutions. The policy-making process deals with agenda setting and accessing decision makers.

What makes an issue, a concern, or a situation a Latino policy issue? Some general guidelines can place certain issues on a Latino agenda and designate particular public policy arenas. The first guideline is governmental actions having a different, and often negative, impact on Latinos. Are there situations or policies that affect Latinos in concrete and tangible ways? Given the cultural patterns of Spanish-language persistence and use, the educational attainment levels of many Latinos have lagged for decades. Thus, questions of language use, bilingualism, culture, and curriculum serve to influence Latino involvement in the educational arena. Concerns held by policy makers and the general public about too many immigrants coming to the United States and their perceived negative impact can target Latinos as the perpetuators of many societal ills.

The second key factor is an awareness and understanding among Latinos that an issue and current policies differentially affect many Latinos. It is not sufficient that some policies have an impact on Latinos; Latinos must identify and portray the issue or policy as targeting them specifically. When Congress considers immigration reforms and other related legislation, do Latinos see themselves as the catalyst for such changes, as well as the targets of such proposals? Clearly the first two factors are interrelated. Both the objective and subjective dimensions of policy impact Latino communities so that the experience and perception of public policies together magnify Latinos' interest and motivation in becoming involved in the political process. Our current focus on immigration is a very good illustration of how public and policy discourse places Latinos at the center of who immigrants are and what problems they create.

The third key factor is the involvement of Latino organizations and leaders in policy arenas. We are examining Latino politics as a collective or group action directed toward policy formation and implementation. It is through Latino organizations and activists that Latino issues and concerns get framed and directed toward specific policy arenas and policy makers. In some cases, Latino initiatives act to prevent the passage of proposed legislation, referenda, or initiatives. The long, involved immigration debate that resulted in the passage of the 1986 **Immigration Reform and Control Act (IRCA)** included extensive lobbying by Latino organizations to minimize the impact of or eliminate entirely the bill's proposed employee verification system (or national identification card). At the same time, lobbying by Latino organizations and efforts by members of the Congressional Hispanic Caucus (CHC) pushed to include a wide-reaching amnesty provision within IRCA, as well as civil rights protections.

Finally, since public policy involves what governments choose to do, the Latino focus on policy making centers on governmental institutions and all levels of government. The latter point reflects the federal system and decentralization of authority and decision making in American politics. There are many governments that affect Latinos and the arenas for contesting the policy-making process. A very recent example is the series of legislation and initiatives occurring in Arizona that target undocumented immigrants and foreign-born, thus consequently all, Latinos. It has been suggested that Latino politics mostly takes place at the local level with grassroots organizations and localized issues. Nevertheless, the policy-making process everywhere is similar, and regardless of policy-making arenas, the political processes that Latinos learn and strategically use are applicable in many arenas and over time. Latinos getting involved in the policy-making process find opportunities to translate concerns and issues into concrete proposals, influencing, and bargaining.

This chapter explores a policy area that has generated significant political activity, organizational involvement, and Latino protest. Immigration and the status of immigrants (legal, undocumented, and refugee), as well as the public policies that have come from the federal government, serve as the main focus of our discussion. Although immigration policy is the domain of the national government, state governments and municipalities have tried to enter this arena through referenda and other actions to define and limit immigrants' participation in governmental programs. For example, in April 2010 the Arizona State Legislature passed **Senate Bill (SB) 1070**—the Support Our Law Enforcement and Safe Neighborhoods Act—which requires police officers, "when practicable," to detain people they reasonably suspect are in the country without authorization and to verify their status with federal officials, unless doing so would hinder an investigation or emergency medical treatment. This resulted in major protest demonstrations, calls for economic boycotts, and legal challenges somewhat reminiscent of the 2006 protests in response to the Sensenbrenner bill.

Immigration Policies and Latino Communities

In 1998, a billboard in Blythe, California, read, "Welcome to California: The Illegal Immigrant State: Don't Let This Happen to Your State." Just two years earlier, Californians had voted on **Proposition 187**, which would have restricted undocumented persons' access to social services, public education, and health services. In the spring and summer of 2010, Arizona's SB 1070 sparked major responses from both sides of the immigration debate as Latinos were activated out of a sense of self-protection and a push to advance their political empowerment. Individuals, organizations, and immigrant advocacy groups rallied their collective forces and energies in response to what was viewed as an attack on their communities and an impugning of their connections to and affinity for the United States.

Persons who enter the United States and reside here without legal authorization are referred to as "illegal aliens," "wetbacks," undocumented workers, *sin papeles* (without papers), and so on. I will use the term *undocumented persons*. These two brief policy examples serve as an introduction to the area of immigration and Latinos. Interestingly, although the examples I cite discuss undocumented immigration and have received much national attention, they are not the sole basis on which to understand the relationship between immigration and Latinos. American immigration policies affect prospective entrants, family members, refugees and individuals seeking asylum, and possible investors, as well as border surveillance and enforcement, citizenship rights and protections, and access to federal and state entitlement programs.

U.S. Immigration Policies: A Historical Overview

This discussion of immigration policies and Latinos can only be grounded in the range and depth of issues and policies impacting U.S. immigration over time. Overall, U.S. immigration policy has undergone a number of changes since the founding of this nation. The period from 1790 to 1875 could be characterized as one of open immigration: few restrictions were placed on those who wished to enter the United States. Toward the latter part of this period, an organized anti-immigrant group, the Native American Party (a forerunner of the Know-Nothing Party), sought to extend the wait period for citizenship from five to twenty-one years. Another noteworthy change was the inclusion of the Fourteenth Amendment to the U.S. Constitution, making the "law of the soil" the basis for citizenship.

The years 1876 to 1924 saw U.S. immigration policy impose a series of qualitative controls on admittance into the United States; for example, prostitutes and convicts were banned from entering. Geographically and culturally, the exclusion of Chinese and Japanese immigrants resulted from formal treaty agreements. The American Protective Association was formed in 1887 as an anti-immigrant group advocating that persons should never vote for a Catholic candidate, never hire a Catholic worker over a Protestant one, and never join in a strike with Catholics. The anti-immigrant, antiforeigner, and non-Protestant policies are reoccurring elements in U.S. immigration history. Finally, Congress enacted a law declaring that any American woman marrying a foreign man would take on the citizenship of her husband and lose her U.S. citizenship.[1] Literacy tests were finally added in 1917, after several previous presidential vetoes. Fears of anarchists and seditionists also inspired restrictions.

The period from 1924 to the present can be characterized as one of both qualitative and quantitative restrictions for immigrants. The landmark **National Origins Act of 1924** set a ceiling on the number of immigrants admitted annually. A formula was based on 2 percent of the national-origin group registered in the 1890 census, which heavily favored natives of northern and western Europe. In this case, Japanese and citizens of the Asiatic zone were excluded. By 1938, the National Origins Act was fully operative, and 82 percent of those eligible to be admitted came from northern and western Europe, 16 percent from southern and eastern Europe, and 2 percent from the remainder of the world. Given these changes in immigration laws, countries from the Western Hemisphere (Mexico, Central and South America) were excluded from quotas. As a result, the U.S.-Mexican border became an "open border" with freer migration flows.

The key governmental agency involved with federal immigration policies is the Immigration and Naturalization Service (INS). An agency in the Department of Justice, the INS is responsible for enforcing laws regulating the admission of foreign-born persons to the United States as well as administering immigration benefits, including the naturalization of qualified applicants for U.S. citizenship. The INS works with other federal agencies in the admission and resettlement of refugees. In 1864 the INS was housed in the State Department with a commissioner of immigration. There was a problem of divided authority between the federal statutes being enforced at the state level and authorization at the federal level. As a result the Immigration Act of 1891 solidified federal control over immigration through a superintendent of immigration under the Treasury Department. INS was given authority over naturalization through the Naturalization Act of 1906.

The 1906 legislation shifted naturalization from the courts to the Bureau of Immigration and Naturalization to administer and enforce U.S. immigration laws and supervise the naturalization of aliens. These combined functions lasted for seven years as naturalization became a separate bureau in 1913, with the Departments of Commerce and Labor splitting the two functions. By executive order in 1933 the functions were consolidated again in the Labor Department. In 1940 the INS was transferred to the Department of Justice.

The **Border Patrol** was not established until 1924, and in 1933 the Bureaus of Immigration and Naturalization were merged with the Department of Labor. The primary mission of this agency has been to detect and prevent the smuggling and unlawful entry of undocumented aliens into the United States and to apprehend individuals in violation of U.S. immigration laws. Subsequently, the Border Patrol added drug interdiction along the land borders of the United States.

One of the more important activities of the Border Patrol is referred to as line watch. It involves the detection, prevention, and apprehension of undocumented migrants and their smugglers at or near the border by maintaining surveillance from covert positions. It follows up leads, responds to electronic sensor alarms, and uses infrared scopes during night operations, as well as low-light-level television systems, aircraft sightings, and the interpretation and following of tracks, marks, and other physical evidence. Examples of such activities include farm and ranch checks, traffic checks, traffic observation, city patrols, transportation checks, and administrative, intelligence, and antismuggling activities.

There have been times of heightened patrolling and surveillance. For example, stricter enforcement of Mexican immigrants was more evident during the Great Depression of the 1930s. Mexican nationals and native-born residents felt the backlash between 1930 and 1932 as 330,000 were repatriated (Hoffman 1979) to Mexico, with an estimated 500,000 Mexican people leaving under the "voluntary" program. The throes of the Depression, a negative view of foreigners, and a fear of too many immigrants on the welfare rolls were major factors contributing to this Mexican repatriation.

Another development during the 1930s was the American response to political upheavals and war. Refugees from the Spanish Civil War and Hitler's invasion of France, as well as Jews fleeing persecution in Germany and eastern Europe, were allowed to emigrate. This pattern held during World War II and subsequent military conflicts. During the 1960s and 1970s, immigrants from communist regimes were generally designated as political refugees. The next major immigration overhaul was the passage of the McCarran-Walter Act (also known as the Immigration and Nationality Act, or INA) of 1952. The quota system was made even more rigid with annual per-country caps. In 1965, amendments to the INA established an annual ceiling for Eastern and Western Hemisphere immigrants of 170,000 and 120,000, respectively.

A system of preference categories for close relatives and other family members was instituted for citizens and permanent resident aliens. Two categories of occupational preferences with specified skills, especially in the health professions, were also established. Finally, a seventh preference category was created for 10,200 refugees a year with particular attention to individuals fleeing communist regimes or the Middle East, fearing prosecution on account of race, religion, or political opinion, or people uprooted by catastrophic natural calamity. The per-country caps were applied to Western Hemisphere countries in 1976 (twenty thousand annually). Mexico's cap was originally expanded to forty thousand but eventually subjected to the same cap for all countries in the 1976 amendments to the act.

Overall, U.S. immigration policy can be characterized as trying to determine who is admitted, under what circumstances, how many will be allowed, and from what parts of the world. Historically, the borders of the United States have changed. The Southwest was once part of Mexico, both Cuba and Puerto Rico were formerly U.S. possessions, and the United States has been involved in Central and South America from the early 1800s (from the Monroe Doctrine and beyond); these circumstances have linked Latinos and U.S. immigration. Over the course of U.S. immigration policies, these courses of action have impacted Latinos directly, especially Mexicans. At the same time, immigration policies have received more attention since the 1970s. Much of the national discussion of immigration and policy initiatives has been directed toward Latinos. One significant contributor to this situation has been the dramatic global shift of source countries and the number of immigrants entering the United States.

During the 1990s, immigration-reform legislation allocated additional funding to the Border Patrol for added personnel and sophisticated equipment. The September 11, 2001, terrorist attacks in New York City and Washington, DC, added even greater concern for future terrorist attacks and other national security issues. As a result, already heightened border-control scrutiny increased even more. One effect has been to impact traditional flows of Latino immigrants along the border as well as the flow of undocumented immigration. Mexican president Vicente Fox initiated major policy initiatives to establish a bilateral agreement for Mexican guest workers in U.S. labor markets in 2000. Yet the terrorist attacks and the U.S. military response have intertwined immigration policy with a national security and antiterrorism enforcement emphasis.

Contemporary Immigration Patterns

Table 9.1 provides contemporary immigration information regarding the flow of legal immigrants and their areas of origin. A review of the years 2007 to 2009 demonstrates a steady but substantial flow of immigrants (over 1 million per year). While there are fixed hemispheric quotas, the family-reunification category of immediate family members fluctuates annually, mostly due to processing and clearance functions. The pattern of a majority of immigrants to the United States coming from Latin America and Asia remains the case. The immigration flows from Mexico and Central and South America are quite noteworthy. Almost half of the immigrants come from the Americas, and combined with Asian immigrants, they make up four-fifths of all immigrants for the 1990s and early 2000s.

The fixed caps per country, especially for Mexico, have created a backlog of applications for permanent residency, as well as the corresponding economic hardships of unemployment and low earnings. The economic interrelationship between the United States and Latin America, in terms of both its formal and informal economies, plays a direct role in the ebb and flow of international migration. Since the latest global economic recession, migration flows have tended to increase. This has been countered by heightened border fortification and more intense surveillance to "stem the tide" (see box 9.1 for an outline of recent immigration policies).

The categories for admission fall into either family reunification or occupational/ special skills. Persons having close family relationships with a U.S. citizen or legal permanent resident, those with needed job skills, and those who qualify as refugees account for most of the admissions. The other policy impact on the legal status of many Latino immigrants came from 2.6 million former "illegal aliens" from 1982 to 1992 who gained permanent resident status through the legalization provisions of the IRCA. For example, over 70 percent of the legalized IRCA immigrants were Mexican.

TABLE 9.1. Legal Permanent Resident Flow by State of Residence, Fiscal Years 2007 to 2009 (ranked by 2009 data)

State of Residence	2007		2008		2009	
	Number	Percentage	Number	Percentage	Number	Percentage
Total	1,052,415	100.0	1,107,126	100.0	1,130,818	100.0
California	228,941	21.8	238,444	21.5	227,876	20.2
New York	136,739	13.0	143,679	13.0	150,722	13.3
Florida	126,277	12.0	133,445	12.1	127,006	11.2
Texas	77,278	7.3	89,811	8.1	95,384	8.4
New Jersey	55,834	5.3	53,997	4.9	58,879	5.2
Illinois	41,971	4.0	42,723	3.9	41,889	3.7
Massachusetts	30,555	2.9	30,369	2.7	32,607	2.9
Virginia	29,682	2.8	30,257	2.7	29,825	2.6
Georgia	27,353	2.6	27,769	2.5	28,396	2.5
Maryland	22,657	2.2	23,170	2.1	27,562	2.4
Other	275,128	26.1	293,462	26.5	310,672	27.5

Source: U.S. Department of Homeland Security, Computer Linked Applicant Information Management System (CLAIMS), Legal Immigrant Data, Fiscal Years 2007 to 2009.

BOX 9.1. Immigration Policies and Developments from 2005 to the Present

Immigration-Police Collaboration Programs

Secure Communities: The Department of Homeland Security (DHS), Immigration and Customs Enforcement (ICE) implemented Secure Communities in 2008, allowing local police to send the fingerprints of persons arrested to DHS to match with immigration records to expedite deportations.[1]

287(g) Program: Named after a section of the 1996 immigration law, the 287(g) Program allows ICE to train and deputize law enforcement officers to assist with federal immigration policing to detect and deport persons with immigration-status violations.[2]

SB 1070: Arizona's Racial Profiling, Anti-Immigrant Law

SB 1070, passed by the Arizona state legislature and signed by the governor in April 2010, requires police to verify the status of suspected undocumented persons. Now no individual arrested in Arizona can be released until the police have verified his or her immigration status with ICE.[3]

U.S. Border Militarization

The United States spent over $800 million, or $15.1 million per mile, for fifty-three miles of "virtual fence" on the Arizona-Mexico border.[4] This includes cameras, heat and motion sensors, and other deterrents and detection mechanisms. Another $20.9 million has been spent on the U.S. border with Canada. By early 2010, the United States had built over six hundred miles of border wall along the southwest border, affecting natural habitat and wildlife migration, expropriating traditional indigenous lands,[5] and putting border communities under heightened scrutiny.[6]

Operation Streamline

Operation Streamline criminalizes status violations and unauthorized entry and denies, or "waives," the due process rights of migrants, significantly jeopardizing the constitutional criminal justice system.[7] Under Streamline, U.S. district courts along the border prosecute and convict persons of illegal entry prior to their formal deportation. In Tucson, Arizona, the U.S. district court processes an average of seventy migrants daily, prosecuting, convicting, and sentencing them en masse, Monday through Friday, all within less than two hours per session. The convicted migrant prisoners are then usually turned over to a Corrections Corporation of America private, for-profit prison to serve their sentences.

There seems to be public sentiment to continue and expand Operation Streamline.[8] Yet, in December 2009, the Ninth Circuit Court of Appeals found that the en masse plea hearings in Tucson violate federal law. As a result, the Obama administration and Congress had to restore due process rights everywhere, for all, and modify or end Operation Streamline.

Spillover onto Ethnic Studies Opposition: Repeal Arizona SB 2281

SB 2281, dubbed an "ethnic studies cleansing" law, was passed by the Arizona legislature and signed by the governor in the same year that SB 1070 was passed. SB 2281 attempts to eliminate ethnic studies programs, specifically targeting the Mexican American Studies (MAS) program in the Tucson Unified School District (TUSD). Tom Horne, the former superintendent of public instruction and recently elected state attorney general, was the prime operator for this legislation. Horne claimed that ethnic studies promoted divisions and hatred of the United States, despite evidence to the contrary. The Tucson community launched the organizing campaign Defend Ethic Studies to preserve the MAS program. The TUSD's MAS program has conducted programmatic assessments that show MAS has helped students increase their interest in education and achieve higher grades and improved AIMS test results. MAS is also credited with reducing dropout rates and producing a higher number of college entrants.

Denial of Birth Certificates and Public Education

The same Arizona legislature headed by SB 1070 proponent Arizona state senator Russell Pearce is working with Kris Kobach to draft legislation to prohibit granting birth certificates to children of undocumented parents. Kobach authored SB 1070 and is associated with the national group Federation for American Immigration Reform (FAIR) and other anti-immigrant organizations. This proposal challenges the U.S. Constitution's Fourteenth Amendment, which declares all person equal before the law and grants automatic citizenship to anyone born in the United States.

Provisions of Arizona's SB 1070

U.S. federal law requires aliens age fourteen or older who are in the country for longer than thirty days to register with the U.S. government and to have registration documents in their possession at all times. SB 1070 makes it a state misdemeanor for an alien to be in Arizona without carrying the required documents and mandates that police make an attempt, when practicable during a "lawful stop, detention or arrest," to determine a person's immigration status if there is reasonable suspicion that the person is not in the United States legally. Any person arrested cannot be released without confirmation of his or her legal immigration status by the federal government pursuant to §1373(c) of Title 8 of the United States Code. The first offense under SB 1070 requires a *minimum* fine of $500 for a first violation, and for a second violation, a minimum $1,000 fine and a maximum jail sentence of 6 months. A person is "presumed to not be an alien who is unlawfully present in the United States" if he or she presents any of the following four forms of identification: a valid Arizona driver license, a valid Arizona nonoperating identification license, a valid tribal enrollment card or other tribal identification, or any valid federal, state, or local government-issued identification.

The act also prohibits state, county, or local officials from limiting or restricting "the enforcement of federal immigration laws to less than the full extent permitted by federal law" and provides that any legal Arizona resident can sue such agencies or officials to compel such full enforcement. If the person who brings suit prevails, that person may be entitled to reimbursement of court costs and reasonable attorney fees.

The act also targets the practice of hiring day laborers who wait at street corners. It is a crime for any person, regardless of citizenship or immigration status, to hire persons congregating at street corners for the purpose of performing day labor. Hiring from a vehicle that "blocks or impedes the normal movement of traffic is unlawful." Vehicles used in such manner are subject to mandatory immobilization or impoundment. Moreover, for a person in violation of a criminal law, it is an additional offense to transport an alien "in furtherance" of the alien's illegal presence in the United States, to "conceal, harbor or shield" an alien, or to encourage or induce an alien to immigrate to the state, if the person "knows or recklessly disregards the fact" that the alien is in the United States illegally or that immigration would be illegal. Violation is a class 1 misdemeanor if fewer than ten "illegal aliens" are involved and a class 6 felony if ten or more are involved. The offender is subject to a fine of at least $1,000 for each "illegal alien" involved. The transportation provision includes exceptions for child protective services workers and ambulance attendants and emergency medical technicians.

Notes

1. See "Secure Communities: A Factsheet," Immigration Policy Center, www.immigrationpolicy.org/just-facts/secure-communities-fact-sheet; "Secure Communities," U.S. Immigration and Customs Enforcement, www.ice.gov/about/offices/enforcement-removal-operations/securecommunities/index.htm.

2. Eviatar 2009; also see DiBranco 2010; fact sheets on "Section 287(g) of the Immigration and Nationality Act," Gorena Blog, www.gorena.org/287g.htm.

3. Padilla 2010; also see text of the State of Arizona Senate, 49th Legislature, Second Regular Session, 2010, "SB 1070," at www.azleg.gov/legtext/49leg/2r/bills/sb1070s.pdf.

4. See Gamboa 2010.

5. See "Operation Streamline: Drowning Justice and Draining Dollars along the Rio Grande," Grassroots Leadership, http://grassrootsleadership.org/OperationStreamline/2010/07/19/operation-streamline-drowning-justice-and-draining-dollars-along-the-rio-grande.

6. See resource pages hosted by the School of Law, University of Texas, Austin, on affected communities, at www.utexas.edu/law/centers/humanrights/borderwall.

7. See "US-Mexico Border Fence/Great Wall of Mexico Secure Fence," GlobalSecurity.com, www.globalsecurity.org/security/systems/mexico-wall.htm.

8. Foley 2010; also see the Chief Justice Earl Warren Institute on Race, Ethnicity, and Diversity report: Lydgate 2010.

Another 10 to 14 percent came from other Latin American countries (González-Baker 1996). This adds significantly to the growing immigrant segments within the Latino community. Whereas the pipeline metaphor has been used for educational progression, the growing number of legal permanent resident aliens will enable more Latinos to pursue naturalization in the years to come (see table 9.1 for legal permanent resident flows from 2007 to 2009).

Recently, attention is being paid to employment-based preference categories. There are five categories for which persons can be admitted based on skills critical to the American labor market: (1) priority workers; (2) professionals with advanced degrees; (3) skilled workers, professionals without advanced degrees, and needed unskilled workers; (4) special immigrants; and (5) creative immigrants or investors. Policy discussions have assessed reducing the emphasis on family reunification as opposed to labor market skills.

George Borjas (2001) has argued for a more skill-oriented and economically driven immigration policy. This system would award points to prospective immigrants based on various characteristics and establish a passing grade to help the American government select among the applicants. Among other characteristics, the point system would take into account education, English-language proficiency, and age at time of entry (Borjas 2001, 194–99). Country of origin would be considered to ensure that no nation, culture, or language dominated the immigrant flow. Finally, point consideration would be given to persons seeking employment in immigrant-dependent industries.

While a full discussion of the merits and policy impact of such proposals is not the subject of this chapter, I have tried to illustrate some policy shifts within the immigration arena. The greater emphasis on an economic model for immigrant admission was reflected in the 1998 U.S. Commission on Immigration Reform, chaired by Shirley Hufstedler, who addressed the House of Representatives about the policy directions of the commission. She noted concerns about immigrants with poor English skills being confined to the lowest "rungs" of the American job market. "The national interest could be served by moderating entry of unskilled immigrants, except when other values prevail, notably nuclear family reunification, and by increasing the skills of those who have arrived" (Hufstedler 1999, 8–9). Continued reexamination of the quota limits based on family-reunification and employment-based preferences will affect immigration reform in the future.

Since 2004, many state and local governments have initiated legislation, ordinances, and initiatives that target undocumented persons' access to social services, housing, and employment; limit legal recourse coverage (i.e., civil suits for injury, eligibility for punitive damages, etc.); provide more stringent regulations against loitering, smuggling, and harboring illegal immigrants; and deny "birthright" citizenship to children born of undocumented parents. Strong anti-immigrant sentiments and dissatisfaction with the federal government's "ineffectiveness" have served as catalysts for a steady stream of state and local ordinances and laws targeting undocumented immigrants. A set of tracking polls conducted by Latino Decisions during the 2010 midterm election period has confirmed four major patterns: (1) a salient concern about restrictive and punitive immigration policies that cuts across virtually any sociodemographic distinction among Latinos; (2) a feeling that all Latinos are being targeted within the context of nativist, racist orientations; (3) a dissatisfaction with both major political parties, especially the Democratic Party, for not advocating or pursuing more humane, Latino-supported immigration reform; and (4) a heightened interest in elections and candidates' positions on key Latino issues. The externalities of divided public opinions, negative stereotyping of Latinos, and targeting have resulted in increased fervor for greater political engagement and empowerment. As already noted, immigration will remain a national priority, and Latinos will continue to be impacted and increase their efforts to affect policy making in directions consistent with this community's interests and the content of American immigration policies.

Immigration and Naturalization

One clear consequence of the increasing number of immigrants is the growing pool of those eligible for citizenship. For Latinos, the overall pattern has been a relatively low level of naturalization, especially for Mexican immigrants (J. A. García 1981c). The general naturalization requirements include being at least eighteen years of age; living as a legal permanent resident alien for five years in the United States; having good moral character; being able to read, write, speak, and understand commonly used words in the English language; and demonstrating a knowledge of U.S. history and government. In the 1990s there was a marked rise in the number of immigrants becoming U.S. citizens. Overall, slightly less than half of all permanent resident aliens have naturalized (INS 1997).

The proportion of immigrants naturalized varies substantially by country. For example, most of the immigrants admitted in 1977 became eligible to naturalize in 1982, and by 1995 about 46 percent had become citizens. Generally, the leading countries of origin are China, the former Soviet Union, and the Philippines, while immigrants from Mexico and Canada are the least likely to naturalize. The research literature on Latino naturalization has focused on Mexicans. For the most part, the key factors motivating Mexicanos to naturalize have been English-language proficiency, length of residence in the United States, higher levels of educational attainment, age of migration, and income (J. A. García 1981c; Pachón and DeSipio 1994; Smith and Edmondston 1998). While patriotism, allegiance, and cultural similarity with America have been seen as key determinants for naturalization, becoming a citizen tends to be a more pragmatic decision. Persons become citizens to ensure access to governmental program participation (Supplemental Security Income, food stamps, Medicaid, etc.), employment, educational financial aid and scholarships, and improved positioning for family-reunification preferences in immigration.

While naturalization rates for Latino immigrants have been lower than for immigrants from other regions of the world, they rose during the 1990s. With proximity to their mother country, especially Mexico, the Caribbean, and parts of Central America, a strong expectation to return served as a disincentive to pursue American citizenship. Mexicans would lose the right to own and inherit property in Mexico if they became U.S. citizens. The surge in naturalization in the 1990s was rooted in individual motivation, general circumstances, and sociopolitical developments. The INS Green Replacement Program, launched in 1993, the approval of Proposition 187, rising levels of immigration in the 1980s, the enactment of the Personal Responsibility and Work Responsibility Act, and Mexico's approval of dual citizenship have contributed to increased naturalization.[2] Table 9.2 takes the dramatic rise of immigrants in the 1990s and looks at naturalization from 2007 to 2009. Persons from Asia and North America (which includes Mexico) represent almost three-fourths of all naturalizations. Perhaps, offsetting some of the impetus for increased naturalizations has been the increase in fees ($680 per individual in 2011), a more extensive review process, and long wait periods between the filing and actual interview and approval notifications.

TABLE 9.2. Persons Naturalized by Region and Country of Birth, Fiscal Years 2007 to 2009 (countries ranked by 2009 data)

Region/Country of Birth	2007		2008		2009	
	Number	Percentage	Number	Percentage	Number	Percentage
Total Region	660,477	100.0	1,046,539	100.0	743,715	100.0
Africa	41,652	6.3	54,420	5.2	60,383	8.1
Asia[a]	243,783	36.9	330,361	31.6	276,375	37.2
Europe	81,756	12.4	108,618	10.4	90,149	12.1
North America	241,163	36.5	462,372	44.2	250,266	33.7
Caribbean	68,577	10.4	131,935	12.6	84,917	11.4
Central America	41,814	6.3	86,168	8.2	43,914	5.9
Other North America	130,772	19.8	244,269	23.3	121,435	16.3
Oceania	3,342	0.5	4,781	0.5	3,928	0.5
South America	48,133	7.3	84,853	8.1	61,674	8.3
Unknown Country	648	0.1	1,134	0.1	940	0.1
Mexico	122,258	18.5	231,815	22.2	111,630	15.0
India	46,871	7.1	65,971	6.3	52,889	7.1
Philippines	38,830	5.9	58,792	5.6	38,934	5.2
China, People's Republic	33,134	5.0	40,017	3.8	37,130	5.0
Vietnam	27,921	4.2	39,584	3.8	31,168	4.2
Cuba	15,394	2.3	39,871	3.8	24,891	3.3
Dominican Republic	20,645	3.1	35,251	3.4	20,778	2.8
El Salvador	17,157	2.6	35,796	3.4	18,927	2.5
Korea, South[b]	17,628	2.7	22,759	2.2	17,576	2.4
Colombia	12,089	1.8	22,926	2.2	16,593	2.2
Jamaica	12,314	1.9	21,324	2.0	15,098	2.0
Haiti	11,552	1.7	21,229	2.0	13,290	1.8
Pakistan	9,147	1.4	11,813	1.1	12,528	1.7
Iran	10,557	1.6	11,813	1.1	12,069	1.6
Poland	9,320	1.4	14,237	1.4	10,604	1.4
Peru	7,965	1.2	15,016	1.4	10,349	1.4
United Kingdom	7,752	1.2	12,095	1.2	10,060	1.4
Canada	8,473	1.3	12,387	1.2	9,753	1.3
Russia	7,660	1.2	10,778	1.0	9,490	1.3
Nigeria	6,582	1.0	8,597	0.8	9,298	1.3
All other countries	217,228	32.9	314,468	30.0	260,660	35.0

Source: U.S. Department of Homeland Security, N-400 naturalization data for persons aged eighteen and over, Fiscal Years 2007 to 2009.

[a]Beginning in Fiscal Year 2009, data for Asia in all fiscal years includes Armenia, Azerbaijan, Georgia, Kazakhstan, Kyrgyzstan, Tajikistan, Turkmenistan, and Uzbekistan.

[b]Data for South Korea prior to Fiscal Year 2009 includes a small number of cases from North Korea.

Four other pieces of immigration legislation passed in the 1990s contributed to rising naturalization rates. First, the 1986 IRCA included an amnesty provision in which 2.7 million undocumented residents were granted legal resident status. As a result, the first of these now legalized residents could apply for naturalization in 1994. This significantly increased the pool of potential Latino citizens as Latinos constituted over two-thirds of the eligibles.

Second, the **Illegal Immigration Reform and Immigrant Responsibility Act of 1996** (IIRIRA) included stipulations to bolster the monitoring of the U.S. border and set up measures to remove criminal and other deportable aliens. This law also provided increased protection for legal workers through work-site enforcement. As a result, the "negative" elements of the IIRIRA created incentives for immigrants to gain greater protections and rights through naturalization.

Third, the 1996 **Personal Responsibility and Work Opportunity Reconciliation Act** (PRWORA) severely limited immigrants' access to public benefits, especially social service programs. The Welfare Act restricted the eligibility of legal immigrants for means-tested public assistance, widened prohibitions against public benefits for undocumented immigrants, and mandated the INS to verify immigration status in order to determine which immigrants would receive public benefits. Part of the requirement for immigrant sponsorship included sponsors' assuming financial responsibility for immigrants if they were unable to sustain themselves. The PRWORA made the affidavit of support legally binding.

Fourth, the 1996 **Antiterrorism and Effective Death Penalty Act** (ATEDPA) greatly facilitated procedures for the removal of "alien terrorists," authorizing state and local law enforcement officials to arrest and detain certain undocumented persons and providing access to confidential INS files through court order. The overall effect of the 1996 legislation was to produce a more negative environment for immigrants, and naturalization became a protective and defensive response. The 9/11 terrorist attacks produced broader discretion regarding detainment and civil and legal rights for immigrants. While a comprehensive discussion of immigration policy goes beyond the available space in this book, some noteworthy developments since 9/11 have been the following: heightened border enforcement with dramatic increase in the numbers of Border Patrol personnel; use of National Guardsmen to intensify border monitoring; construction of over six hundred miles of fencing and other structural deterrents; continuation of **Immigration and Customs Enforcement** (ICE) workplace raids; formal deportation processing and hearings for apprehended undocumented persons; and governmental agreements with local law enforcement agencies to assist in identification and processing of undocumented persons. Overall, the tenor of immigration policy considerations is heavily laden with the stringent requirement of securing the border from the crossing of drugs, contraband, and people before any broader discussion of any other aspect of immigration policy reform.

The National Association of Latino Elected and Appointed Officials (NALEO) has pursued an educational and promotional program to encourage more Latino immigrants to pursue naturalization. Materials and informational hotlines were established to facilitate interested Latino immigrants' pursuit of citizenship. In addition, NALEO began working with the INS to streamline processing as long wait periods were developing in many offices. Finally, NALEO made use of public service announcements featuring well-known Latino personalities. The increased number of applicants produced bottlenecks within the INS organization. By 1998, the average processing time for applications was twenty-seven months (Singer and Gilbertson 2000). The backlog of unprocessed applications had risen to an all-time high of 2 million by March 1999. Even as more Latino resident aliens are applying for citizenship, long delays slow down the increased pool of prospective voters and may discourage other Latino immigrants from entering the naturalization process.

The Latino electorate is being boosted by the conversion of a growing Latino immigrant segment into citizens. A study by Bass and Casper (1999) examined the differences in registration and voting behavior between naturalized and native-born Americans. They found that naturalized citizens who were more likely to be registered and to vote tended to have more education and higher income levels, be employed, own a home, have lived for a longer period at their current residence, be female and older, have professional status, and be married. When researchers controlled for length of time in the United States and region of origin (i.e., Latin America), Latino naturalized citizens' voting and registration rates did not differ significantly from those of native-born Latinos.

Rising numbers of naturalization applications and eventual citizenship among Latinos will continue well into the twenty-first century. The Latino immigrant segment is not insulated from governmental policies, national movements, and Latino organizational activities. Local governments, media, community organizations, political leaders, and hostile policy initiatives have contributed to naturalization increases among Latinos, as well as created hesitancy to become citizens. For example, Jones-Correa's (1998) study of New York City Latino immigrants reinforces the important role that encouragement plays in their political involvement or lack of it. He found that immigrant participation was stymied by both the lack of support to participate and the requirement to renounce former citizenship, which raised the fear of never being able to return to the country of origin.

Proposition 187 and Undocumented Immigration

The 1994 elections, including congressional elections and state legislative and gubernatorial races, were particularly noteworthy in California. The California electorate passed the Save Our State proposition, or Proposition 187, banning undocumented immigrants from public education and other social services provided by the state. Proposition 187 was directed largely toward Latinos, specifically immigrants flowing in from Mexico (Armbruster, Geron, and Bonacich 1995). The initiative and subsequent campaign drive to pass Proposition 187 galvanized intergroup tensions and activated many native and foreign-born Latinos.

The impetus behind Proposition 187 was anti-immigrant fear and concern about a negative impact on the economy, jobs, social services, schools, crime, and the social-moral fabric of the state. California is the leading port of entry for immigrants, especially from Latin America and Asia. While illegal or undocumented immigration has been on the American policy agenda for some time, in 1994 initiatives at the state level were becoming more common, whether they pertained to Official English, billing the federal government for additional social service funds, or limiting undocumented immigrants' access to social services and education. When it came to state economic woes, crime, overcrowded schools, and crowded housing, the undocumented population was scapegoated for many of these problems.

The significance of Proposition 187 lies in the recurring themes of xenophobia and nativism that has existed throughout American history. In the 1970s, estimates of the undocumented population ranged from 1 to 12 million. Images were prevalent of hordes of people lining up daily on the Mexican side of the border and waiting for the cover of night to enter the United States. The debate regarding the undocumented resident population has included emotionalism as well as detailed analysis of cost/benefit assessments. These topics have been embedded in discussions of undocumented immigration for decades going back to the 1950s with varying degrees of emphasis and public discourse. Many economic sectors were vitalized by the influx of undocumented workers, and business income was being generated in local and regional economies and adding to tax revenues.

These patterns figured into the benefits of migration. On the other hand, job competition, depressed wage rates, overcrowded housing, bilingual education and other demands on the school system, and lost revenues through transfers and unreported tax returns were seen as the downside of undocumented migration.[3] In addition, there were negative perceptions of a group of people whose morals and values are not seen as compatible with the "American way of life." For example, Feagin and Feagin (1996) examined stereotypes of Mexican immigrants and found that many Americans saw them as lazy, unambitious, morally suspect, dirty, and a burden to society.

A 2008 report by the Pew Hispanic Center estimated that 11.9 million unauthorized immigrants were living in the United States; it concluded that the undocumented immigrant population grew rapidly from 1990 to 2006 but has since stabilized.[4] In this analysis, the center estimated that the rapid growth of unauthorized immigrant workers has been brought to a standstill. The survey found 8.3 million undocumented immigrants in the U.S. labor force in March 2008. California was the leading state of residence, with 2.7 million, or 22.7 percent, of the total undocumented population. The seven states with the largest estimated numbers of undocumented immigrants were California (2.7 million), Texas (1.45 million), New York (925,000), Florida (1.0 million), Georgia (475,000), New Jersey (550,000), and Arizona (500,000) (Passel and Cohn 2009). The vast majority of undocumented immigrants (four in five) come from Latin American countries. In March 2008, 9.6 million unauthorized immigrants from Latin America were living in the United States. Mexico is the leading country of origin, with Mexicans representing approximately two-fifths.

Proposition 187 passed with the support of almost 60 percent of California voters. Examination of voter support among different racial and ethnic categories reveals the following: whites or Anglos, 81 percent; Asian and African Americans, 54 percent; and Latinos, 23 percent. During the early part of the Proposition 187 campaign, polls indicated Latino support at 52 percent, but that changed dramatically during the campaign.

Latino and civil rights organizations and labor tried to mobilize their constituencies to turn out and vote against the proposition. The message sent out included appeals regarding infringement of basic human and civil rights, the need for the Latino community to come to its own defense, and the contribution made by immigrants. Yet the Save Our State initiative appealed so strongly to the racial anxieties of California voters that it seems unlikely that any different outcome could have resulted (Adams 1996). Nevertheless, Latinos and both established and ad hoc organizations actively mobilized against Proposition 187. Latino voter registration increased at a higher rate than for other segments of California voters (*Los Angeles Times* 1994b), and growing antagonism was directed toward the Republican Party and Governor Pete Wilson.

As a result, Latinos (including voters, eligible citizens, and noncitizens) demonstrated heightened political involvement and awareness. One of the legacies of the Proposition 187 experience was a backlash against and diminished support for Republicans among Latinos. Since the Reagan years, the Republican Party had focused more attention on promoting the party's ideology and policy positions as compatible with Latino values and traditions. Yet, the anti-immigrant **Propositions 227** (elimination of bilingual education) and **209** (anti–affirmative action), along with an initiative to require labor unions to obtain membership approval before using union funds for political contributions, found most Latinos in opposition with the Republican Party's policy stands and with its leadership. This pattern would have future ramifications in 2010 with Arizona's SB 1070.

Several lawsuits were filed challenging the constitutionality of Proposition 187. The day after the measure passed, a federal court in Los Angeles and a state court in San Francisco barred the enforcement of many of the provisions of Proposition 187 denying public education, social services, and nonemergency health care to undocumented immigrants. Two days later, a federal judge in Los Angeles dismissed significant aspects of the proposition, indicating that they conflicted with federal laws that supersede state laws. Judge Mariana Pfaelzer ruled that the state could not deny health care and social services to undocumented immigrants because they are entitled to those services under federal law. She also ruled that a 1982 Supreme Court decision gave undocumented children the right to attend public schools (K–12), although the judge did not overturn the provision that keeps undocumented people from attending public colleges and universities. Agents of social, health, and educational services were supposed to investigate, notify, and report alleged undocumented immigrants. Judge Pfaelzer ruled that this task belonged to the federal government, not state employees.

Basically, the court rulings found that Proposition 187 violated two provisions of the Constitution: the supremacy clause, by stepping on ground preempted by federal immigration law, and the Fourteenth Amendment. The court ruled that by effectively ordering the deportation of California residents without hearings or other due process and by denial of public education to undocumented children upheld by *Phyler v. Doe* (457 U.S. 202, 225 [1982]), this proposition violated federal policy and principles. The opinion was a five-to-four decision. Another consequence of Proposition 187 was the subsequent passage of federal legislation barring permanent resident aliens from participating in social welfare programs. Tighter provisions were put on sponsors of immigrants to provide financial support for admitted immigrants who were unable to support themselves.

There is some variation within the Latino community as to the "ideal" U.S. immigration policy. Many non-Latinos' negative attitudes toward the undocumented stem from perceived threats (economic, residential, and job competition), racism, negativity toward "legal" Mexican Americans, and conservative and authoritarian ideologies (Cowan, Martinez, and Mendiola 1997). A study of Latino attitudes toward greater liberalization of U.S. immigration policies found that levels of acculturation, perception of the undocumented as an economic threat, and residence with a significant undocumented population were associated with less support for liberalization (Hood and Morris 1997). Although the Latino community may have divided opinions about a more liberal immigration policy, it has concerns about fair and humane treatment, civil and human rights, social service benefits for permanent resident aliens, and the elimination of negative stereotypes about Latinos. An important factor for Latino attitudes and involvement in this policy area lies in the fact that immigrants and immigration impact (directly or indirectly) the overwhelming percentage of all Latinos.

The demise of Proposition 187 did not cancel out public concern about undocumented immigration. Even with a healthy economy and lower unemployment rates, a *Los Angeles Times* poll indicated that two-thirds of respondents saw immigration as a major problem (Kelly 1997). In addition, half of the respondents would deny undocumented people access to health care, welfare benefits, schools, and housing. Additional policy suggestions included denying citizenship status to children born in the United States to undocumented parents (54 percent), and half support the abolition of bilingual education.[5] In spring 2010, passage of Arizona's Senate Bill 1070 (Support Our Law Enforcement and Safe Neighborhoods Act) made it a state misdemeanor for immigrants not to have their registration documents with them at all times. It empowers state and local law enforcement to detain individuals to determine if they are in the United States legally and to crack down on those sheltering, hiring, and transporting undocumented persons.

Once the bill was signed on April 23, 2010, Latinos gave an even louder response, with Latino and immigration advocacy organizations challenging its constitutionality and compliance with civil rights law. Public opinion was bifurcated by race and **ethnicity**, as a majority of non-Latinos supported SB 1070, while Latinos overwhelmingly opposed the legislation as subjecting their community to racial profiling, harassment, racist treatment, and singling out for hostile treatment. Protests and mass demonstrations, legal challenges, and voter-registration drives were organized in Arizona and other American states. The Mexican government made human rights objections to Arizona and the federal government. Civil rights and Latino organizations initiated economic boycotts, while other state legislatures moved to pass legislation similar to SB 1070. Associated with these developments was the heightened politicization of the Latino community and elevation of immigration reform as the top issue for congressional action. The partisan aspect of SB 1070 was an even lower level of support for or affiliation with the Republican Party and frustration with the Democratic Party and President Barack Obama for not taking the lead on comprehensive immigration reform (e.g., creating more humanitarian, rights-oriented provisions, normalizing the status of the undocumented, and passing the **Development, Relief, and Education for Alien Minors, or DREAM,** Act) (Latino Decisions 2010). With the midterm elections occurring in the fall, Latinos became more politicized and showed greater interest in the elections; at the same time, they were less enthusiastic about the candidate choices. The midterm election results showed good turnout rates among Latinos and a high degree of support for Democratic candidates over Republicans. The longer-term implications lie with the continued growth and active political engagement accentuated in the 2010 elections and the carryover effects for 2012. It seems clear that policy positions will be a determining factor for Latino support.

The Political Nature and Involvement of Latino Immigrants

While research has been limited on political behavior and attitudes toward Latino immigrants, the general characterization is one of limited involvement and interest in the American political system. Jones-Correa's (1998) book on Latino immigrants in the New York metropolitan region portrays the Dominicans, Colombians, and other Latino immigrants as being in political limbo. They do not actively engage in the political process, for instance, by pursuing citizenship; nor are they involved in political parties or other political organizations. Part of the explanation lies with the "myth" of eventual return to their homeland and a lack of encouragement from political organizations and leaders to participate politically. Research conducted two decades earlier by García and de la Garza (1985) found a similar pattern of limited organizational involvement by Mexican-origin immigrants in their respective communities. If they belonged to any organization, it was likely to be a religiously based one. Nevertheless, these Mexican immigrants were less likely to be politically involved.

At the same time, Latino immigrants exhibit a very positive attachment to the United States in terms of loyalty, extolling the opportunities afforded by living in America, and support for political institutions (Pachón and DeSipio 1994; J. A. García 1997; de la Garza et al. 1993). They tend to exhibit participatory attitudes of political support and belief in core American values (de la Garza, Falcón, and García 1996) but do not follow through with concomitant political activities. Given the national origin of some Latino immigrants (those coming from repressive and nondemocratic regimes), it has been posited that these political cultures do not reinforce, or provide experiences that lead to, democratic participation. In 2001, Espenshade and Ramakrishnan found that coming from a repressive Latin American regime does not affect voting and registration, while anti-immigrant sentiment serves as a catalyst for participation.

Again we see immigration policies and public response to immigration being linked directly to the political world of Latino immigrants. During the latter part of the 1990s, naturalization rose significantly. In 1998 alone, over 1.2 million persons naturalized, which was more than twice the previous year's number. The Clinton administration initiated efforts in 1999 to reduce the backlog of naturalization applications (Pan 1999). Overall, wait periods were cut almost in half; in offices in San Francisco and Houston, the wait period was shortened from thirty-two to nineteen months. Similarly, the thirty-three-month wait period for a green card was reduced to twenty-four months. Ironically, there was a drop in naturalization applications the following year by almost half (McDonnell 2001).

Since the early 2000s, more systematic research has revisited the political world of foreign-born Latinos, beyond the act of naturalization. Works by Barreto and Muñoz (2003) and Barreto et al. (2009) demonstrate that this group's levels of political interest, awareness, civic engagement, and political involvement are not disparate from those of native-born Latinos. In addition, examining the Latino immigrant sector has brought the role of Spanish-language media, especially radio, into the politicization process. Finally, works by Portes, Escobar, and Radford (2007) and J. A. García (2011) have helped to link transnational activities and connections with civic and political engagement in the United States. Even though activities and connectedness with homeland issues are included in transnational networks, organized groups also become involved in local and domestic issues. Transnationalism among immigrant communities is not disjointed from interest and involvement in U.S.-based politics. For example, a salient interest in educational politics and policy is quite evident among Salvadorans and other Central Americans. O'Connor (1998) found that schools were seen as inadequate, and serious issues were raised about the quality and effectiveness of schooling children received. This finding was supported by the **Latino National Survey** (Fraga et al. 2006) regarding Latino involvement in school-related matters for both native- and foreign-born Latinos (Fraga et al. 2009). The second most frequently mentioned issue area was related to language difficulties and poverty. This interest in education was also reflected in Latino support for Proposition BB in California, which increased bond funding for schools. Latinos supported the proposition by 82 percent compared to 67 percent for Anglos and 76 percent for African Americans. Other concerns centered on immigrant human and civil rights and access to social services.

The 1990s witnessed concrete signs of Latino immigrant political involvement, especially at the local level, through their jobs and unionization. Labor has shown greater interest in and recognition of immigrant workers in traditional sectors—agriculture, manufacturing, construction—and, more importantly, in the service sectors. Immigrant workers in the restaurant and hotel industries, janitorial services, and child and elder care have been subject to unionizing activities and strikes. Janitorial worker strikes in Chicago and Los Angeles in 2000 marked significant involvement of immigrant workers (both documented and undocumented) in leadership roles as well as on the picket lines (Guarnizo 1994; Figueroa 1996; Milkman 2000). The labor issues, besides wages and benefits, focus on opportunities for legal entry into the United States; access to public services; increased regulation of labor, health, and safety standards; and limited voting rights for noncitizens in school board elections (Milkman 2000).

David Broder (2001) discusses the awakening of the Latino immigrant communities, which include the dishwashers, chambermaids, painters, and bellhops who help form the **Organization of Los Angeles Workers** (OLAW). This organization, which advocates for workers' rights, worked diligently for the mayoral campaign of Antonio Villaraigosa. The **Service Employees International Union** and the **Hotel and Restaurant Employees Union** were an integral part of OLAW and political-**mobilization** activities in the city. OLAW was able to recruit over six hundred canvassers and distribute over eighty thousand registration cards and forms. Similar organizational efforts were evident in Miami with the Hispanic Coalition. With over 130,000 immigrants naturalizing in Florida, the coalition helped register new citizens, and the partisan effect was a five-to-one Democratic advantage (Booth 1996). This was due to anxiety among immigrants and anti-immigrant sentiments associated with many Republican leaders and policy initiatives. The election of George W. Bush reoriented the Republican Party's stance on immigration and Latino immigrants. Future accounts of the political world of Latino immigrants will portray not only a wide range of political engagements but emphases on the socialization effects of immigrant youths on immigrant parents (García-Castañon 2010; V. Cruz 2010).

Conclusion

The awakening and greater political involvement of Latino immigrants will continue well into the twenty-first century. The saliency and impact of public policies on this subcommunity and the broader Latino community serve to maintain and build on the political capital of efforts in the late 1990s. Another example of the political engagement of foreign-born and naturalized Latinos is Salvador Espino, who is seeking political office as a city council member in Fort Worth, Texas. This thirty-three-year-old, Mexican-born, naturalized citizen sees his candidacy as an opportunity to show that the Latino community has a stake in what occurs in city hall (Tórrez and Jackson 2001). Other Latinos in this city are also seeking political opportunities at the city and county levels and transferring their work and business experiences into political organizing and mobilization. We have touched only lightly on the political world of Latino immigrants and the dynamics of activating this segment of the Latino community. Much research is being directed toward gaining a better understanding of the political integration of Latino immigrants. Clearly this is an important demographic and political segment of the Latino community. NALEO recognized this potential over twenty-five years ago, as it was the first Latino organization to target permanent resident aliens for naturalization drives and education. In 2011 more Latino organizations and leaders, as well as the American labor movement and religious institutions, are directing their attention to them. A recurring theme in this book involves the continual development of the dynamics of Latino politics.

Discussion Questions

1. Most recent polls on Latinos reveal comprehensive immigration reform as this community's most salient issue. What would a comprehensive immigration policy include from a Latino perspective?
2. Immigration and America's development have gone hand-in-hand since before the formation of the United States. Discuss the historical bases for U.S. immigration policies until the latter half of the twentieth century.
3. While immigration is the domain of the federal government, since the 1990s many states and some local governments have formulated laws and ordinances targeting the undocumented immigrant. What have been the contributing factors for such developments, the role of public opinion, and the responses of the Latino community?
4. Since 2005, the undocumented community has "come out of the shadows" and taken to the streets to protest restrictive and punitive immigration policies. How would you characterize the political activism of the undocumented Latino community and its effects on the larger Latino community?
5. The 1990s and early 2000s saw a rash of immigration laws as well as executive orders regarding immigration and border security. How would you depict the basic foci and objectives of these policies?

CHAPTER 10

Education and Voting Rights

Adquirir conocimiento, profundizar la sa-
biduría y proteger nuestros derechos huma-
nos comienzan con la formación académica
que sostiene nuestro afán por aprender. Lo
usamos para afirmar nuestro auto concepto
y vivir con dignidad.

Acquiring knowledge, deepening our wis-
dom, and protecting our human and
civil rights begins with an education that
sustains our desire to learn. We use that
knowledge to affirm our own self-esteem
and to live with dignity.

IN 2007, THE DEPARTMENT OF COMMERCE announced that the Hispanic population showed gains in its participation in higher education (Davis
and Bauman 2008). Hispanic students comprised 12 percent of full-time college
students (both undergraduate and graduate) in 2007, up from 10 percent in 2006 (Hispanics comprised 15 percent of the nation's total population). Women continued their
majority status, comprising 55 percent of undergraduates and 60 percent of graduate
students. Other highlights included the following: 53 percent of Hispanic four-year-
olds were enrolled in nursery school, up from 43 percent in 1997 and 21 percent in
1987; 27 percent of the population age three and older was enrolled in classes, from
nursery school to graduate studies. More than half (59 percent) of all four-year-olds
and 39 percent of three-year-olds were enrolled in nursery school. Students in grades
one through twelve made up 64 percent of people three and older enrolled in school.
Students thirty-five and older comprised 15 percent of people enrolled in college; they
made up 7 percent of full-time college students and 36 percent of those attending
part-time.

Although Latinos continue to demonstrate improvement in their educational
achievement, other groups in the nation are improving as well. African and Asian
Americans have made similar or even greater gains in educational attainment. For
example, while the percentage of Latinos who had completed high school in 2010
was 56 percent, the percentage of Asian Americans exceeded 85 percent. This chapter
examines two critical policy areas for Latinos: education or schooling and political representation. In the case of the latter, the origins and continued policy implementation
of the **Voting Rights Act** seek to align minority communities' candidate preferences

with election outcomes. That is, representation needs to reflect the community the elected official acts for.

Education: A Continual Latino Priority

Chapter 9 lays out the nature of the American public policy process and the resources and strategies Latinos need to pursue to secure policy outcomes and implementation that can make a difference. For over forty-five years, the Mexican American community and other Latino groups have focused their attention and activities on the educational system. Insufficient resources, segregation, exclusion from decision making, lack of representation in the teaching and administrative ranks, poor facilities, curricular needs, and the absence of bilingual programs represent a major portion of the educational issues facing Latino communities. In 1970, the U.S. Commission on Civil Rights published the six-volume *Mexican American Education Project.* This report outlined the major problems confronting Mexican American children and their parents. The thrust of the report (looking at the five southwestern states) documented the extensive problems Mexican Americans encountered in the educational system, which resulted in low educational achievement, high dropout rates, and thwarted aspirations.

Nearly thirty years later, a 1999 report, *Our Nation on the Fault Line,* by the **President's Advisory Commission on Educational Excellence for Hispanic Americans**, reported that the educational achievement gap between Latinos and non-Latinos persists and recurring problems have not changed. The magnitude of the crisis is unparalleled, according to the commission. An examination of conventional educational indicators reveals that Hispanic Americans are making progress at alarmingly slow rates from preschool through elementary, middle, and high school, on to higher education. The cumulative effect of such neglect is obviously detrimental not only to Hispanics but also to the nation (President's Advisory Commission 1999, 1).

The particulars of Latino educational well-being indicators identified by the commission include the following:

1. Less than 15 percent of all Latinos participate in preschool programs.
2. More than twice as many Latinos as non-Latinos are enrolled below grade level (are older than the age associated with the grade level).
3. Latinos drop out earlier and at unacceptably high rates.
4. The total proportion of bachelor's degrees for Latinos has risen only 1.4 percent from 1985 to 1993, even though Latino college enrollment has increased by 3.2 percent.
5. Illiteracy for Latino adults has remained high compared to other groups.
6. Latino students are segregated in schools that are resource poor (President's Advisory Commission 1999, 3–4).

To compound poor Latino educational achievement, inadequate school funding, treatment of bilingualism as a liability, and a lack of representation on educational policy-making boards are additional obstacles that need to be overcome in order to improve Latinos' educational experiences and outcomes. This long-standing pattern was reflected by a 1972 U.S. Commission on Civil Rights report that characterized the

Mexican American educational experience as one of neglect, isolation, discrimination, inadequate resources, and linguistic ostracization. So, while documentation of the substance and scope of Latinos and the educational system has produced repetitive and consistent findings, the range of recommendations has also carried prescriptions similar to those recommended by previous federal commissions. This President's Advisory Commission generated an extensive set of recommendations to try to alleviate the educational neglect of Latinos:

1. Model effective programs and intervention strategies in preschool education, dropout prevention, bilingual education, and student motivation.
2. End segregation of Latinos.
3. Oppose the prevention and termination of educational opportunities for immigrant children.
4. Train teachers to deal effectively with multicultural children.
5. Ensure adequate funding for bilingual education programs, Title VII of the Improving American Schools Act, and Goals 2000.
6. Increase four-year-college access for Latino high school graduates and community college transfer students, especially via financial support initiatives (President's Advisory Commission 1999, 4–6).

In 2010, President Obama signed a new executive order to establish the White House Initiative on Educational Excellence for Hispanics. Some of the focal areas for this new initiative include

1. promoting early-learning opportunities (i.e., preschool enrollment and experiences, a comprehensive zero-to-five plan, a Challenge Fund for states to establish model systems of early learning and to fund and implement pathways that will improve access to high-quality programs);
2. improving teaching (i.e., Race to the Top awards, where forty-six states plus the District of Columbia applied to compete for a Race to the Top award, including over thirty states that made significant changes in laws or policies to promote education reforms);
3. preparing Latino students for college and careers (i.e., by increasing college enrollments by improving access to rigorous standards that prepare students for college and a career; utilizing assessments that accurately measure student-learning growth; ensuring that all students, including our neediest, are taught by excellent teachers in schools led by effective leaders; ensuring better data and information to follow student learning and to inform teaching; and implementing strategies to transform and improve those schools that have been persistently low performing);
4. providing federal financial aid that puts students first by shifting the nation's student aid system to the Direct Loans Program and stabilizing funding for America's Pell Grant recipients;
5. providing more affordable student loans to ensure that Americans can better manage their student loan payments and have more choices as to how they will repay their loans;
6. improving college affordability and access;

7. building American skills through community colleges (i.e., innovations and reforms for the nation's community colleges to raise graduation rates, build industry partnerships, expand course offerings, and improve career and educational pathways);
8. strengthening Hispanic-serving institutions (the Health Care and Education Reconciliation Act of 2010 will invest over $2.55 billion in these institutions over the next decade, including $1 billion at America's HSIs).

Each presidential administration now has an established policy response to focus on the educational status of Latinos and produce recommendations with a partial list of solutions. Yet, our focus on public policy needs to extend beyond a listing of the problems and possible solutions. The educational system must extend beyond professional educators. Administrators and policy makers, like parents, communities, and Latino organizations, play a viable role in defining the policy agenda and impacting legislation. The Latino community has been trying to impact the educational system for decades and continues its struggle. One difficulty of this policy area lies in the multilayered nature of education (i.e., local school boards, state departments of education, federal agencies, etc.).

Structure of the Educational Political "System"

Historically and politically, the crux of educational decision making takes place at the local level. Local school boards and superintendents make policy decisions, and educational professionals are major participants in the decision-making process. At the same time, state governments play a major role in financing with their ability to raise tax revenues for local school districts. More recently, state government has also gotten involved in standardizing testing of student performance and exit exams for graduation. Finally, the federal government, with its significant revenues, provides intergovernmental aid, especially for desegregation programs, compensatory education programs, and bilingual education funding. Thus, the educational decision-making process involves several policy arenas, political jurisdictions, and key actors. The multiple points of access allow Latinos to develop many different strategies and pressure points to effect change.

A persistent theme resulting from social surveys during the past forty years is the importance of education among Latinos. Originally, surveys were conducted with Mexican Americans in the Southwest and nationally (Arce 1982) and later with Mexicans, Cubans, and Puerto Ricans (de la Garza et al. 1993), then with Latinos in the 2006 **Latino National Survey** (Fraga et al. 2006). In every case, when asked to identify key issues and concerns, Latinos consistently ranked education among the top three. At the same time, a popular notion about the reason for the poor educational track record among Latinos blames a lack of commitment and value placed on education by Latinos themselves. Again, the cultural dimension of being Latino comes into play as a possible explanation for poor educational attainment. The Latino response has centered on examining the structural dimensions and policy biases instead of blaming the deficiencies within the Latino community.

As is consistent with our theme of policy emanating from cultural and situational conditions, the policy area of education embroils both. The persistence of Spanish-language use has meant that many Latino children begin their school experience with limited or no English-language facility. With learning and understanding based on an English curriculum, the role of language impacts progress through the grades (K–12) and beyond. For many Latinos, grade repetition, placement in remedial classes, poor standardized test performance, lower participation in college-preparatory classes, and greater incidences of disciplinary actions are common (Duran 1983; Carter and Segura 1979; Meier and Stewart 1991).

Many Mexican Americans still attend **de facto segregated schools** (schools that, due to residential segregation and school-attendance zones, are highly segregated by race, **ethnicity**, and class). Until the midtwentieth century, de jure segregation (legally mandated segregation of students based on race and ethnic background) was evident in California and Texas. Two court cases, *Westminster v. Mendez* and *Bastrop I.S.D. v. Gonzalez*, challenged the segregation of Mexican American students. Part of the rationale for the segregation was based on educational or pedagogical needs. School administrators used Latinos' cultural "distinctiveness" as the basis for separating them from the rest of the other students in order to educate them properly, while taking nothing away from the educational progress of other students.

Another policy question affecting Latinos arose in the 1970s and 1980s regarding desegregation plans for many southern and southwestern communities. It was brought to a head in the cases of *Nichols v. Houston I.S.D.* and *Keyes v. Denver I.S.D.* In both situations, the school districts' original desegregation plans involved pairing or reassigning Latino children with African American students. In this manner, the school district would satisfy the racial mix targets without impacting many Anglo students. The courts ruled that for purposes of desegregation plans, Mexican Americans and other Latinos constituted a separate "ethnic group" and introduced a triethnic formula to determine how desegregation plans would be designed. Establishing Latinos as an official part of the desegregation mix opened the legal door to questions of educational quality and equity. Latinos were concerned about the educational curriculum, bilingual educational programs (or their absence), and overall quality of education, in addition to racial/ethnic isolation.

Even though these cases and others prohibited de jure segregation, the 1990s saw increasing numbers of Latinos being concentrated in ethnically segregated schools and school districts. The youthfulness of Latino populations, mentioned in previous chapters, is reflected in their growing numbers in school districts throughout the country. In many major school districts (e.g., Los Angeles, Houston, Tucson, New York, Denver), Latinos comprise the majority group, and their percentages will continue to increase in the future. Thus, a condition associated with rising numbers of Latino students is their location in resource-poor districts in terms of tax base, expenditure levels, facilities, teacher salaries, and so on.

In the 1970s and 1980s, these resource disparities were raised in *Serrano v. Priest* and *Rodriquez v. San Antonio I.S.D.* Relying on property taxes to underwrite most school funding disadvantages poorer communities. Much higher tax rates have to be instituted in order to generate revenues comparable to those collected in more affluent communities. Underlying the legal arguments for the plaintiffs was the matter of educational equity and access to a quality education as a fundamental right. Subsequently, state governments were brought into the policy area of school financing with court orders to equalize school financing statewide. Over time, greater significance has been given to the importance of educational achievement for all students in order to lead productive and economically rewarding lives. The association of successful completion and achievement in schooling with employability, earnings, overall quality of life, economic mobility, and improved social status emphasizes the centrality of educational success in a modern American society. While the courts did not completely embrace the fundamental-right arguments, states had to address the significant resource disparities across school districts and heavy reliance on property taxes. As a result, most state legislatures dealt with school equalization at the statewide level. State expenditures have increased in providing school financing. Yet, some forty years later, successful implementation of school equalization remains a problem.

Alexander Astin (1982, 1985) advanced the idea of an educational pipeline in which identifiable "leaks" illuminate problem areas for students. Normally, the example begins with a cohort of one hundred students entering kindergarten and counts the number who progress to high school graduation. In the case of Latinos, more than half (approximately fifty-five) of the original students do not make it to high school graduation. The list of explanations can range from lack of preschooling to English-language "deficiency," lack of bilingual or English-as-a-second-language programs, grade repetition, poor facilities and resources, segregation in poorer school districts, discriminatory disciplinary actions, tracking into vocational programs or into the general curriculum, inadequate support systems, underrepresentation on school boards and among administrators and teachers, and insensitive and culturally inappropriate standardized testing and assessment (Meier and Stewart 1991; Orfield 1991; Orfield and Ashkinaze 1991). A major point of "leakage" is the loss of many Latinos in the middle school years. For example, 40 percent of sixteen- to twenty-four-year-old Latino dropouts left school with less than a ninth-grade education, compared to 13 percent of non-Latino white dropouts and 11 percent of African American dropouts.

So far I have catalogued a long list of poor educational outcomes and the need for Latinos to interject themselves into the education policy process. With the primary assumption of successful educational progress being connected to better jobs and earnings potential and a better quality of life, why are there differential outcomes based on race, ethnicity, gender, and class? Are Latinos, as a group, less able, less motivated, less supportive of educational attainment, or culturally limited to succeed in education? Does the educational establishment operate in a way that creates obstacles, and is it designed so that Latinos will consistently do poorly? These questions, while polarizing in nature, can serve to sort through the policy perspectives and alternatives that come from Latinos and other interested parties.

The first perspective points to the primary source of the problem as emanating from Latinos themselves. Poor educational progress and performance can result from a lack of supportive educational values and efforts by families and the community. The cultural dimension for Latinos also comes into play, negatively affecting their educational progress. Persistent Spanish-language use and linguistic isolation reinforce many Latinos' lack of receptivity to an English-language curriculum. In addition, purported cultural values of traditionalism, superstition, machismo, and fatalism are attributed to Latinos (Carter and Segura 1979). Latinos' cultural values and beliefs are viewed as inappropriate to the American educational system. For example, people with a more traditional set of values and outlook assume that Latino students will have less interest in and ability to deal with science and mathematics. The segregation of Mexican Americans in their own schools or in separate classrooms is justified on pedagogical grounds. This policy to isolate Mexican American children aims to teach them separately in light of their cultural "drawbacks," as well as not to inhibit the learning of non-Latino children.

Language has been central in the analysis of the poor educational performance of Latino children. In the 1960s, advocates for bilingual education began to pursue federal legislation to support such a curriculum. It was felt that learning of both content and subject matter, as well as honing of English skills (not just verbal, but syntactic, writing, etc.), would be enhanced with the use of the student's home language. Given this broader view of English-language mastery, the bilingual curriculum would cover a number of grades or periods. In 1968, the Bilingual Education Act was passed with the congressional leadership of Texas senator Ralph Yarborough (Crawford 1992b).

At the same time, Latino educational activists and organizations like the **National Association of Bilingual Educators** lobbied diligently to get federal status and funding. By 1973, the federal government was spending $45 million a year to support bilingual education in twenty-six languages. The early expert witnesses, mostly Latinos, were linguists, psychologists, state legislators, curriculum specialists, school administrators and teachers, and labor and business leaders (Crawford 1992b). Part of the rationale for bilingual education has centered on the psychological effects of a monolingual English curriculum on non-English or limited-English-speaking children.

A. Bruce Gaarder, head of modern language programs for the U.S. Office of Education, stated in subcommittee testimony, "Language is the most important exteriorization or manifestation of the self, of the human personality. If the school, the all-powerful school, rejects the mother tongue of an entire group of children, it can be expected to affect seriously and adversely those children's concept of their parents, their homes, and . . . themselves" (Crawford 1992a, 78). Thus, the policy debates about bilingual education fold in many issues, concerns, values, and controversies, including

- the continuance of non-English languages and the extent of assimilation and integration into American life;
- the persistence of "foreign" cultural practices and norms;
- cultural and linguistic balkanization;
- the association of learning and intelligence with language use;
- the appropriateness of bi- or multilingualism in America;
- the state's involvement in promoting other cultures and languages;
- the meaning of "educational opportunities for all."

In the final analysis, bilingual education is about the growing political empowerment of Latinos in the United States. While bilingual education focuses on curricular methodologies and approaches for children with limited English proficiency, the long-standing problems those Latino children have encountered in school reflect a disempowered position in policy-making bodies. For Mexican Americans, school walkouts in the 1960s and 1970s raised awareness of bilingual education needs, as well as generated teacher and administrator recruitment, cultural studies courses, availability of ethnic foods in the cafeteria, review of disciplinary policies, access to extracurricular activities, and desegregation of schools. The underlying theme was recognition and direct involvement in the educational decision-making process. Similarly, school decentralization efforts in New York City (Gittell and Fantini 1970), especially in the Ocean Hill–Brownsville areas, reflected some major initiatives by Latinos and other minorities to have a greater impact on education.

The push for bilingual education is intermeshed with an overall move by Latinos for greater empowerment in all relevant realms pertaining to Latino educational needs and concerns. One lightning rod for bilingual education and the entire corollary of Latino concerns was **Proposition 227** in California, officially titled the English Language Education for Immigrant Children initiative, or the Unz initiative, which Californians voted on in June 1998. The goal of Proposition 227 was to teach English to children in public schools as rapidly as possible. Most instruction would be in English, and limited-English-proficiency students would be placed in English-immersion classes for a year, then "mainstreamed" into regular classes. Finally, the legislature would appropriate $50 million annually for ten years to subsidize English classes for adults who agreed to tutor English learners. Early polls indicated strong support for Proposition 227 across all racial and ethnic groups and partisans. The *Los Angeles Times* reported that almost two-thirds of Latino voters indicated support for Proposition 227. In addition, Official English initiatives at the state and congressional levels have been ongoing since the 1990s.

During the course of the campaign, political **mobilization** by both established Latino organizations (National Association of Bilingual Educators, Mexican American Political Association, League of United Latin American Citizens, etc.) and ad hoc groups pushed for Latinos to oppose Proposition 227. The bases for the opposition ranged from the misrepresentation of what bilingual education entails to the limited benefits of English immersion for non-English-speaking students, the proposition as a general attack on the Latino community in California, and the overall educational status of Latinos in the state. While the early preelection polls indicated strong support across all groups, on Election Day, Latinos voted 63 to 37 percent against Proposition 227. Overall, the proposition passed 60.9 percent (for) to 39.1 percent (against). Only two counties voted against the proposition (San Francisco and Alameda), and a majority of Anglos (67 percent), African Americans (57 percent), and Asian Americans (52 percent) voted for the Unz initiative.

Interestingly, some of the exploratory items in the *Los Angeles Times* exit poll revealed real differences between Latinos and non-Latinos. For instance, 12 percent of Latinos were first-time voters compared to 4 percent for all voters. Also, 39 percent of Latino voters indicated that they were motivated to vote because of Proposition 227 compared to 27 percent for all voters. Fully 49 percent of pro-Unz voters indicated that all persons should speak English (as a reason to vote for Proposition 227) in contrast to 24 percent of Latino voters (*Los Angeles Times* 1994a). On the other hand, 36 percent of Latinos versus 16 percent of non-Latinos indicated they were motivated to vote on Proposition 227 because they felt that it discriminated against non-English-speaking persons. As the campaign progressed, Latinos became more opposed to and invested in fighting the proposition.

It has been posited (Crawford 2000) that as individuals became more informed about the issues and many of the particulars of the bilingual education curriculum, they were less likely to support it. Part of the underlying issue was a continued activation within the Latino community in California in response to "negatively" targeted initiatives. Opponents of Proposition 227 connected the Unz initiative to several statewide referenda (discontinuing state affirmative action programs, denying immigrants social and educational services, and limiting union contributions to political campaigns) that placed undue burdens on Latinos. The activation of Californian Latinos, due in part to the rise of hostile propositions, stimulated not only greater participation in ballot propositions but also the election of more Latino legislators and local officials. There is a strong tendency among Latinos to maintain their culture, which includes the Spanish language, and to be bilingual. Thus, while Proposition 227 eliminated bilingual programs, the issue area was not just a pedagogical one. Bilingualism and the perpetuation of a bi- or multilingual American society were also at stake for Latinos.

A survey of Hispanics between 1999 and 2009 asked respondents to indicate the more pressing issues facing the Latino community. The policy area with the greatest concern and attention was education (Pew Hispanic Surveys 2001–2009; *Washington Post* 1999). Surveys in the 1960s and 1970s reflect the same prioritization in which the education policy area was the most salient. Although education continues to be a high priority among Latinos, some issues persist while others take on new forms. For example, the issue of bilingual education in the 1960s and 1970s addressed its implementation and funding. Once federal legislation was adopted, the focus turned to expanding the number of programs in place and generating broader inclusion of limited-English-speaking students. Only in the 1990s was an organized "backlash" directed toward the bilingual education curriculum. At the same time, matters of overcrowded schools, more racially and ethnically segregated schools and school districts, racially targeted disciplinary actions, social promotion, continued poor standardized test performance, and lack of political and administrative representation on school boards came to fill the Latino educational agenda.

The commitment to educational attainment and progress and their importance for social and economic mobility form a strong motivation for Latinos to invest in the educational policy arenas. In the span of this modest section on education and Latinos, I have tried to capture the underlying issues and policy directions that Latinos have pursued for decades. At the same time, more recent research has been directed toward the impact of immigrant parents and their children on the educational system. In addition, the upcoming reauthorization of federal No Child Left Behind legislation has raised many questions regarding attempts to standardize educational progress with state-mandated testing and provisions for improving poorly performing schools and their impact on Latino children. There is some division of perspectives about whether the **No Child Left Behind Act** has been beneficial (Rocha 2007; Sierra et al. 2006; L. Rodríquez 2006). Our continuing theme of forming and operating as a **community of common cultures** and/or interests is quite applicable in this policy area. While there is no absolute consensus on every policy dimension associated with education, Latinos exhibit more of an active, working community in this area.

Voting Rights, the Voting Rights Act, and Latinos

Besides education and the challenges that Latinos continue to face in achieving educational excellence and equity, another policy area of long-standing priority is representation and access to office holding. We have already seen the concerns for power and influence among Latinos, as well as the linkages between electoral participation, political influence, and policy outputs. Active electoral participation (voting, campaigning, contributing money, etc.) by Latinos has increased their political capital. During campaigns in 2008 and 2010, both major political parties devoted increasing attention to Latinos. In addition, more Latinos pursued elective offices at all levels throughout the country. The electoral gains made by Latinos in the 2000 elections can be attributed to such factors as a maturing or aging population, greater numbers of naturalizations, heightened political awareness, and more effective mobilizing by Latino organizations and leaders. This section explores another contributing dimension to the positive developments of electoral participation and representation by reviewing and analyzing the Voting Rights Act (VRA).

The Voting Rights Act of 1965 marked a major policy initiative to deal with long-standing practices that had excluded African Americans and other minorities from the electoral process. Such persistent problems had included annual registration systems, literacy tests, hostile election poll locations, economic and physical intimidation of minority-group members, and limited registration locations and hours. These practices had a direct bearing on the relative absence of minority elected officials and the resulting policy responsiveness by all levels of government. While the major impetus behind the VRA was the situation of African Americans in the South, subsequent amendments focused on Latinos and other linguistic minorities in other parts of the United States. Basically, the VRA extended federal authority over matters related to all aspects of elections. For the most part, elections were administered by the states. A major factor was the rise of the civil rights movement, which pressured Congress and the White House to deal with civil and voting rights, housing, public accommodations, and employment discrimination.

Even though the Fourteenth and Fifteenth amendments to the U.S. Constitution were designed specifically to guarantee African Americans the right to vote, implementation was far less than effective. For example, the Fifteenth Amendment forbids both states and the federal government from denying American citizens the right to vote on "account of race, color, creed, or previous condition of servitude." In addition, the **Enforcement Act of 1870** specifically prohibited denial of the right to vote in state and local elections. The **Force Act of 1871** gave federal-court-appointed supervisors the power to oversee registration and election processes upon the request of two citizens. Later in the 1800s, Congress repealed the Enforcement and Force acts, and protective voting rights legislation was virtually nonexistent until the 1950s. Then a series of legislative enactments (Civil Rights Acts of 1957, 1960, and 1964) attempted to provide protection, but the remedy was to enable individuals to sue in federal court for voting rights violations. This case-by-case character did not lend itself to any systematic or complete design (Cottrell 1986).

In the summer of 1965, all the inadequacies of previous federal attempts to address basic voting rights and protections were brought to a "policy head." The VRA passed the House by a vote of 328–74 and the Senate by 79–18. The involvement of many civil rights organizations and the civil rights movement played a major role in pressuring Congress to act. The major provisions of this historic piece of legislation included both nationwide applications and special provisions that applied only to certain states and political subdivisions or covered jurisdictions (the VRA applied to political jurisdictions in which registration and turnout were less than 50 percent of the potential electorate). For the most part, states in the South, including Texas and Arizona, were part of the covered jurisdictions. In addition, specific counties in states throughout the country[1] were also included in the VRA's coverage. The previous use of discriminatory tests, devices, and practices in the electoral process was a key determinant of which states, counties, and towns were brought under the VRA.

Essentially, the federal government took a more active role in monitoring state and local jurisdictional practices to ensure the availability of open and fair access to all residents. Section 2 of the VRA set out the bases in which voting requirements would be evaluated in terms of their effects on minority populations.[2] Section 5 of the VRA required covered jurisdictions to submit any election-related changes to the Department of Justice for **preclearance**. Preclearance involved the voting rights section of the Justice Department, which reviewed proposed election changes (different election dates, changed poll locations, election materials, annexations, etc.) in order to assess their impact on minority-group representation and possible voter dilution. The change could not result in minority-voter dilution or negatively impact the equal protection provisions for all citizens.

Additional examples of possible changes include changes in electoral boundaries resulting from reapportionment, changes in the method of election, changes in the composition of the electorate resulting from annexations, consolidations, or incorporations, provisions establishing voter-registration requirements and candidate qualifications, changes in the form of government, and provisions that set bilingual election procedures and assistance (Cottrell 1986). Amendments to the VRA in 1972 and 1977 expanded coverage to include more jurisdictions in the Southwest and were applicable to Native American and Latino populations.

For the most part, if groups could show that election changes or existing election provisions "harmed" the minority community electorally, then the Justice Department or the courts would deny the proposals or require placement of more neutral election procedures and practices. With the 1982 amendments to the VRA, the results test was included for litigation that challenged the discriminatory effects of election systems and other voting practices. An earlier Supreme Court decision in *Mobile v. Bolden*[3] had placed the burden on the plaintiffs to prove a purpose or intent to discriminate on the part of state or local officials, besides showing the effects of the disputed election practices. The 1982 VRA amendment revised the requirements of proof to center on the results of discrimination rather than intent. With that change, the plaintiffs did not face the highly difficult task of proving racial design or purpose. The VRA also made use of federal observers to oversee elections and ensure access to the electoral process for minority voters. Local organizations could request that federal examiners observe local elections.

The greater significance of the VRA for Latinos came with the 1975 amendments (section 203), which extended coverage to linguistic minorities and broadened coverage to fourteen states. The minority language groups included Asian Americans, Alaska Natives, various linguistic groups among the American Indians, and persons of Spanish heritage. As a result, these affected political jurisdictions had to provide all election materials in the language of the covered language minority group. This included registration materials, election notices, and the ballot. Until 1992, the linguistic minority had to comprise the equivalent of 5 percent of the covered jurisdiction's population to require production of bi- or multilingual materials. This was determined through the decennial census and the questions related to language use and abilities. For persons who spoke a language other than English, their responses as to their inability to understand English determined the threshold for VRA coverage. With the 1992 amendments, the minimum language threshold was set at ten thousand for each political jurisdiction.

The VRA and Latino Politics

Federal involvement in electoral systems at the state and local levels was designed to remove a legacy of exclusionary practices that impeded the participation of minority citizens. Our knowledge about levels of minority-voter participation also results from the VRA. The law stipulated that the U.S. Census Bureau biannually collect data on voter registration and turnout. In the bureau's 1972 survey, only 46 and 52.7 percent of Mexican Americans and Puerto Ricans, respectively, were registered to vote. Since then, there have been modest gains in the percentage of registered Latinos. Yet, as noted in the discussion of Latino electoral participation in chapter 7, these electoral levels have not changed dramatically.

In addition to opening the electoral process for Latino voters, the VRA provided the opportunity to elect more Latino officials. Increased numbers of Latino voters, the opening of the political process, and continued nonresponsiveness by existing officeholders are connected with greater efforts to elect more Latino officials. As Latinos got more involved electorally, **descriptive representation**[4]—referring to the population's racial and ethnic makeup and the characteristics of political representatives—became more realistic. In descriptive representation, the background characteristics of elected officials mirror the population percentages of racial and ethnic groups. According to records of Latino elected officials kept in the late 1960s and early 1970s (J. A. García 1986a), fewer than six hundred Latino elected officials held office at any level of government. Since the passage of the VRA, there has been a marked increase in Latino elected officials. In 1998 the number of Latino elected officials exceeded ten thousand. At the same time, the distribution of Latino elected officials is heavily concentrated at the local governmental level. More Latinos now serve on school boards, city councils, and county boards of supervisors than at the state or federal levels.

Studies by the U.S. Commission on Civil Rights and the Joint Center for Political Studies have documented significant gains among African American elected officials since the passage of the VRA. The rate of change for Latinos since 1970 has been much slower. A number of explanations have been offered for the pace of Latino representation. One factor is the existence of effective Latino organizations to capitalize on the VRA and convert Latino nonregistrants into registered voters. Organizations like the Southwest Voter Registration and Education Project (SVREP), the Mexican American Legal Defense and Education Fund (MALDEF), and the Puerto Rican Legal Defense and Education Fund have focused much of their energy on voter-registration drives and educating more Latinos about the electoral process. At times, these organizations encounter reluctance among Latinos to register, and the hesitancy includes distrust of the political system, lack of familiarity with American government and elections, fear of being called for jury duty, and disinterest.

Limited resources (education, income, and life cycle status) also come into play regarding Latinos' electoral participation. These types of factors suggest that Latinos have limited social capital and weaker participatory orientations to be as active electorally. The concept of social capital focuses on the connections that exist among members of civil and political society that serve as a glue connecting citizens to form a community. It is characterized as a set of horizontal associations between people such as social networks and common norms that affect productivity and collective endeavors for a recognized community. According to Putnam (2000), the accumulation of social capital is the "lubricant" for the working of a democratic society. Therefore, the short-term opportunities afforded through the VRA have had limited returns for registration and turnout levels. At the same time, it has been argued that the absence of any voting rights legislation would have made the situation worse.

A legacy of exclusion and informal practices has discouraged participation. Despite significant gains in the South for African Americans, economic intimidation and physical threats continued after the VRA. Similarly, in areas of the Southwest such as the Rio Grande Valley, powerlessness, economic intimidation, and very limited social capital made it difficult to improve the level of Latinos' representation in the 1970s. Yet, mobilization efforts, active political and social organizations, and leadership resulted in significant gains in the 1980s and beyond. One area of VRA coverage deals with the reapportionment process. Any plans for states under VRA jurisdiction must undergo preclearance. As a result, **redistricting**, since the 1980s, has helped produce legislative districts (congressional, state, and local) that are more conducive to attracting and electing Latinos to public office.

The structural and historical conditions of many communities with a Latino presence help provide a contextual basis to understand how Latinos have participated or not (Montejano 1987). Latino participation depends not solely on the individual and collective actions of Latinos but also on political and social institutions and legal provisions that can impede, prohibit, or facilitate political involvement. These legacies and continuing practices can mitigate individual initiatives and motivations to get involved politically. Also, hostile environments and biased "rules of the game" can make it quite difficult for Latino organizations to be effective politically. The VRA provisions recognized the role of social and political structures and historical legacies and attempted to remove these particular obstacles. It was hoped that underrepresented group members would be able to enter the electoral arenas more easily.

Political maturation and development have taken place within the Latino community. Since Latinos as a group have had lower levels of electoral involvement, it has been suggested that they have not understood the American political system well enough to be more competitive. With the passage of the VRA and its subsequent extensions and amendments, Latino organizations and their leadership had to design their strategies and actions more effectively regarding voter registration, educational campaigns, and developing a cadre of Latinos to run for elected office. For example, earlier efforts at voter registration were timed many months prior to an election, and newly registered voters did not follow through with using their vote. Door-to-door campaigns, more than just trying to convince Latinos to register and vote, also discussed concerns and issues. The timing of voter-registration campaigns was moved closer to election dates. Talking to potential Latino registrants about issues and concerns during the registration campaigns helped identify both important issues and community leaders who could be encouraged to seek elected office.

The gains in Latino elected officials over the past thirty years have been more noticeable at the local level, with increased representation on school boards and more Latina elected officials (S. García et al. 2008). At the same time, there have been some

Latino successes at the state and federal levels. In the 1980s, two Latinos were elected governor (Tony Anaya in New Mexico and Bob Martínez in Florida). Not until the 2000 elections did another Latino hold statewide office. Cruz Bustamante, currently the highest-ranking Latino elected state official, is lieutenant governor of California. Modest gains have been made in state legislatures, with California experiencing the most dramatic increases from the early 1990s. At the turn of the twentieth century, Latino candidates were seeking office in Kansas, Michigan, Missouri, Oregon, and Washington. There were five Latinos in Congress in 1970 but twenty-seven in 2010. The 1970 congressional cohort consisted entirely of Mexican Americans, while in 2011 Latino congresspersons included six Cubans and four Puerto Ricans. New Jersey's Robert Menendez was elected to the U.S. Senate in 2006. In 2010, two new Latinos were elected as governors: Susana Martinez (R-NM) and Brian Sandoval (R-NV). As a matter of fact, more members of the newly elected Latino congressional delegation were elected as Republicans (in Florida, Texas, and Idaho). The more visible and broader-based the elected office, the greater the resources and organization necessary for Latino candidates and the greater the difficulty of mounting a successful campaign.

Two major contributors to increases in the number of Latino elected representatives have been associated with the VRA (J. A. García 1986a): (1) the changeover of **at-large election systems** to **single-member districts**, and (2) reapportionment and redistricting. In the case of the former, litigation initiated by the MALDEF and the SVREP has challenged the discriminatory effects of the at-large election system. Under this system, candidates did not run and were not elected from any specific part of the community. The plaintiffs showed the exclusionary effects for Latinos under this system by demonstrating the following patterns: a history of exclusion in many facets of local life (schools, housing, representation, public access, etc.), unsuccessful attempts by Latino candidates to win elected office, evidence of voter polarization such that nonminority voters seldom voted for any Latino candidates, evidence of racially biased campaigns, and identifiable preference among Latino voters for Latino candidates. Once the litigants demonstrated these patterns, the defendants (municipalities, counties, school districts, etc.) had to show that they were not the result of discriminatory actions.

These successful litigation attempts resulted in the ordering of single-member districts, which improved opportunities for Latino candidates. In single-member districts, voters in a specific area of the city or county nominate and elect their representative. Thus, persons in other sections of the community elect representatives who live in their area. When the proposed districts were drawn up, specific attention was given to their racial and ethnic makeup. The preclearance process tied to the VRA approved districts with substantial and/or majority Latino constituencies, thereby opening up access to Latino representation. Subsequently, **alternative voting systems**, such as cumulative voting and **limited voting**, have been utilized to create structurally and procedurally better opportunities for minority candidates.

During the Reagan administration, the Department of Justice shifted the burden of proof to the plaintiffs, who must not only demonstrate patterns of exclusion but prove discriminatory intent on behalf of the political jurisdiction. When the VRA was extended in 1982, Congress "reinstated" the "results" so that plaintiffs needed to prove that the results of election systems, practices, and so on, diluted Latino voter participation and impact, but they no longer had to prove intent. Again, the political jurisdiction would then have to show that the results were not due to discriminatory practices. Over the next fifteen years, the federal courts in particular established the guiding principles used to determine if the voting rights of Latinos or other covered groups had been violated or not.

A critical court case that set the standard for creating **majority-minority districts** was *Thornburg v. Gingles* (106 S. Ct. 2752 [1986]). Majority-minority districts are political jurisdictions with primarily minority residents (over 50 percent of the population). The VRA has protected specifically against election measures and actions that result in minority-voter dilution. In *Gingles,* the courts upheld the constitutionality of creating majority-minority districts when their voting strength has been submerged in multimember districts with white majorities. The courts recognized a state's compelling interest to rectify a pattern of exclusion. The remedy of majority-minority districts is appropriate when racially polarized voting has minimized or canceled out the potential for minority voters to elect candidates of their choice from their own community (Grofman 1995). In addition, if it can be shown that the minority community is sufficiently large, politically cohesive, and geographically concentrated, and that the majority, when voting as a bloc, customarily defeats the minority community's preferred candidate, then a district can be drawn (Pinderhughes 1995). Thus, majority-minority districts became viable alternatives for Latinos and other minority communities to improve the chances that their political representatives will come from their community.

In the early 1990s, a number of lawsuits challenged the creation and existence of majority-minority districts. These suits originated in Texas (*Vera v. Richards*), Louisiana (*Hays v. Louisiana*), North Carolina (*Shaw v. Reno*), Georgia (*Miller v. Johnson*), New York, Illinois, and Florida. Congresspersons Luis Gutierrez (D-IL) and Nydia Velázquez (D-NY) were affected by litigation challenging their district boundaries. In each case, the plaintiffs challenged the predominance of race as the guiding force in the design of legislative or congressional districts, resulting in peculiarly shaped districts. The term *racial gerrymandering* was used to describe majority-minority districts. While the courts have supported such guidelines as compactness, contiguousness, and maintenance of **community of interests**, it is not the district shape per se that generated concerns among critics of voting rights redistricting (Grofman 1995). The plaintiffs objected to what they saw as racially motivated districting that takes the appearance of a system of proportional representation.

Shaw v. Reno brought majority-minority districts into question. The state of North Carolina submitted its redistricting plan to the Department of Justice preclearance division for review. One of its twelve congressional districts was a majority-minority district, but the Justice Department rejected the plan, stating that it had demonstrated neither the purpose nor the effect of preventing a dilution of minority-voting strength (Grofman 1995). At the same time, the Justice Department suggested that a second African American majority district could be drawn in the southeastern part of the state. The state legislature responded with a new plan, although the second majority-minority district was drawn elsewhere in the state. The resulting elongated and snake-like twelfth district was challenged, as its shape was deemed bizarre in the extreme.

Eventually the case went to the Supreme Court. The majority did not rule that the redistricting scheme violated white voter rights by unfairly diluting or canceling out their votes because white voters were not underrepresented. Ten of twelve districts had white majorities (Grofman 1995). The majority of the court asserted that equal protection could be betrayed if redistricting legislation "is so extremely irregular on its face that it rationally can be viewed only as an effort to segregate the races for purposes of voting, without regard for traditional districting principles and without sufficiently compelling state justification" (*Shaw v. Reno* 1993). Clearly this ruling brought the issue of the shape of legislative districts into question. Justice Sandra Day O'Connor pointed out those placing into one district African American voters "who are otherwise widely separated by geographic and political boundaries, and who have little in common with one another, but the color of their skin" (*Shaw v. Reno* 1993) raised the level of satisfying a compelling state interest.

Thus, the courts placed some real limitations on race-conscious decision making while, at the same time, not ruling that it was unconstitutional. There is still debate regarding the vagueness of the new equal protection test laid down in *Shaw v. Reno* (for future challenges).[5] At the same time, court decisions in 2000 and 2001 upheld majority-minority districts with "irregular shapes" due to the state's compelling interest to remedy past exclusionary practices. In addition, the courts have not indicated any violation of group rights as a basis for ruling against the North Carolina redistricting and subsequent cases. How can the equal protection clause have been violated when no group's rights have been violated? While this case does not hold race-conscious districting as prima facie unconstitutional, it does indicate the court has placed some parameters on a "race-conscious remedy." Finally, in *Georgia v. Ashcroft* (2003), the court argued that the state of Georgia did not retrogress and violate the VRA when minority voters were spread across several districts rather than being "packed" into a few urban districts. Although the Georgia plan reduced the number of African American voters in a district below a majority, there was support among African American leaders and organizations. This decision solidifies the notion of the influential district in which minority voters constitute a sizeable proportion (25 to 40 percent) and the courts' changing views about the necessity of majority-minority districts.

While the VRA provides monitoring and opportunities for legal challenges to election systems and procedures, the increased difficulty of race-conscious redistricting plans is particularly important for Latinos and increased representation. While the U.S. Constitution requires Congress to be reapportioned after each decennial census, Supreme Court cases such as *Baker v. Carr* and *Westberry v. Sanders* have similar effects for state legislatures and local governments. As a partial result, the more noticeable gains for Latino representation have come after reapportionment (J. A. García 1986a, 1992). Latino growth gains in districts or redrawn districts that concentrate more Latinos are closely associated with more Latino candidates and elected officials. For example, after the 1970 congressional reapportionment, Latinos in Congress went from five to nine. During the 1980s and 1990s, the number of Latinos in Congress increased to twenty-one. The reapportionment process is also potentially beneficial to Latinos in the future because of their geographical location in states such as California, Arizona, Texas, Florida, and Colorado, which will receive additional congressional seats due to population growth.

The release of 2010 population counts by states will have an important effect on 2011 reapportionment. The new U.S. population figure is 309,183,463 persons, representing a 9.6 percent increase. The regions of the South and West were the fastest-growing areas (14.3 and 13.8 percent, respectively). In addition, states with sizable

Latino populations that experienced higher than average growth were Nevada (35.1 percent), Arizona (24.6 percent), Texas (20.6 percent), Florida (17.6 percent), and New Mexico (13.2 percent). The following states are scheduled to add more congressional seats: Texas (+4), Florida (+2), Arizona (+1), Georgia (+1), and Utah (+1). In contrast, Illinois, Iowa, Massachusetts, Michigan, Missouri, New Jersey, and Pennsylvania will lose a seat. (Both New York and Ohio will lose two seats.) While Latinos contributed to the faster-growing states gaining seats in Congress and still represent sizable populations in states losing a seat, it is unclear how Latinos will benefit from this round of reapportionment. The noncitizen components, the partisanship plans of which party controls the legislature (especially the Republican Party), the courts' disposition to protect majority-minority districts, and Latino activism in the reapportionment process will determine whether Latinos receive gains in competitive congressional districts similar to their contribution to gains in the states' population growth. As suggested in other places in this book, population growth alone does not guarantee immediate representational gains for Latinos, but it does create many opportunities. Concentration in key states, regions, and urban areas is an asset, in combination with effective leadership and organization and an expanded voting base.

Safe Districts and Voter Participation

While the VRA, with its preclearance and coverage provisions, has contributed to gains in Latino registration and voting, there is concern about unintended consequences for Latino districts. Researchers such as de la Garza and DeSipio (1993, 1996) have raised some concerns about declining voter participation in Latino districts stemming from the creation of majority Latino districts, though this has also contributed to an increase in Latino elected officials. The issue in these districts is that with a Latino representative less in question, voter-turnout levels in the district decline, especially for Latino voters. De la Garza and DeSipio have argued that Latino voters should take more interest and participate in elections with Latino elected officials. These **safe districts** establish a Latino in a given elected office almost indefinitely (absent term limits). The idea of a safe district generally suggests that the incumbent and his or her party are firmly entrenched in the elected office. A safe district can be secure for a particular political party, member of a racial/ethnic group, or incumbent. Thus, the debate centers on the responsiveness of Latino elected officials to their constituencies and the voter-turnout level. If Latino turnout declines, that means Latino voters are less involved, and officials do not need to pay much attention to their constituencies (Wolfinger 1993; Cain and Kiewiet 1992).

The interplay of representation, participation, responsiveness, and accountability brings together a wide range of considerations and indicators. The criticism of Latino majority districts and declining voter turnout is characteristic of most safe districts, regardless of the racial/ethnic background of the representative and the constituency. Linking voter turnout and policy responsiveness is but one of several ways for constituents to influence their representatives and the policy agenda. Political scientists have examined the meaning of low turnout in terms of apathy, satisfaction, cynicism, disinterest, and representative-constituent issue congruence. To a significant degree, all of these dimensions operate in the constituent-representative relationship. Participation and representation are more inclusive than voter turnout. The networks between the Latino representative and local groups and leadership, issue and policy congruence, constituent evaluation of the representative, and the representative's voting record provide a more comprehensive picture of the relationship between Latinos and Latino elected officials.

It is estimated that in most congressional House elections, less than 10 percent of seats are competitive, and over 90 percent of incumbents are reelected (Tate 1993; Browning, Marshall, and Tabb 1984). While the number of Latino elected officials has been increasing steadily, work by Barreto (2007) indicates that there are real benefits for Latino constituents in Latino majority-minority districts. His research shows that Latinos have greater interest, higher levels of turnout, and more satisfaction with their representative in majority-minority districts. Latino support for coethnic candidates is a major factor in Latino voter choice. At the same time, there is a decline in turnout among non-Latinos in the district. In effect, Barreto's work substantiates the arguments for majority-minority districts, and the effect is multiplied if the majority-minority districts are congressional, state legislative, or even municipal. That is, living in political jurisdictions where they are the majority enhances Latinos' "political ownership" in American politics.

While the creation of new majority-minority districts may be likely, the creation of **impact or influence districts** and/or multiracial/multiethnic districts is even more likely. Impact or influence districts represent areas in which the Latino community (the principle can be applied to other minority groups or defined interests) constitutes a significant portion of the population and electorate. In this manner, the creation of districts with a sizable proportion of Latinos (30 to 40 percent) establishes a critical mass. Presumably, representatives will be more responsive, and Latinos can exert pressure more effectively. There also develops a closer proximity of Latino neighborhoods to other communities of color (i.e., African Americans and Asian Americans). Further, there is a greater mix of Latino subgroups (Salvadorans, Dominicans, Puerto Ricans, Mexican Americans, etc.) in urban areas such as Los Angeles, Miami, and New York City. This greater racial/ethnic mix of communities of color in political jurisdictions (i.e., congressional and legislative districts) affords an opportunity for inter-minority-group coalitions, such as those in Boston and Los Angeles (Jennings 1992; Sonenshein 1990) working to create cohesive and coordinated electoral redistricting strategies. The number of racially and ethnically diverse districts will be substantial after the next round of redistricting. The ways in which Latinos pursue coalitional partners in the redistricting process can produce increased Latino representation, in both the short and long term.

The VRA has also had a direct effect in the installation of alternative voting systems as a remedy for minority-voter dilution. Alternative voting systems are alternatives to the conventional plurality (i.e., winner-takes-all) or majority system, which is the common mode in American elections. They range from cumulative voting to limited voting, to single-transferable-vote and proportional voting schemes. In several small communities in Texas (and North Carolina) (García and Branton 2000), the result of voting rights litigation (initiated by the SVREP) has changed the at-large election system to a **cumulative voting system**, which enables voters to distribute their votes (the amount is equivalent to the number of positions available). If five city council seats are available, voters can give one candidate all five of their votes, or split their votes among two candidates, or divide them according to some other combination. Both this election system and limited voting allow cohesive interests (racial/ethnic groups, issue organizations, minority political parties, etc.) to direct their votes to their preferred candidate(s). In limited voting, each voter has fewer votes than the total number of seats or positions up for election. For a five-seat election, the voter has between one and four votes to cast. This method allows voters to target their support to a particular candidate or smaller subset of candidates. Studies by Engstrom (1994) and Engstrom, Taebel, and Cole (1997) in the South and Southwest have demonstrated noticeable gains among minority groups, especially for African Americans.

Engstrom, Taebel, and Cole (1997) and Brischetto and Engstrom (1997) indicate that more minority candidates run for office with cumulative or limited voting systems than under the prevailing system and enjoy greater success in winning office. There are some differences also. African Americans have been more active in fielding candidates and winning than Latinos. Recently Texas and North Carolina (García and Branton 2000) passed legislation that allows local governments the option to change to either cumulative (Texas) or limited (North Carolina) voting systems. In May 2000 the Amarillo, Texas, school district held its first cumulative election in which a Latina and an African American were elected to the school board. As voting rights litigation continues to be filed on behalf of Latinos, especially during the next 2011 round of redistricting, alternative voting systems will be more carefully evaluated and promoted.

While the VRA was enacted in 1965, it has undergone numerous extensions and amendments. The inclusion of linguistic minorities and bilingual-materials provisions served as major opportunities for Latinos to enhance their electoral participation. Over the subsequent extensions and congressional hearings associated with the VRA, efforts have been made to eliminate the bilingual-materials provisions, allow covered jurisdictions to be removed from preclearance review, and provide stricter tests for minority plaintiffs to prove minority-voter dilution and exclusionary practices. The VRA was extended for another twenty-five years in 2006. The role of Latino organizations, Latino leaders, and Latino members of Congress, as well as of other civil rights communities, was pivotal in both extending the VRA and determining whether its provisions took into account recent court rulings on redistricting.

Conclusion

This and the previous chapter have focused on three key policy areas that are salient for Latinos: education, immigration, and voting rights. Policy areas within the education area include the quality of education, bilingual education and curricula to meet the needs of Latino children, equitable funding for education, quality of school facilities, representation in decision-making bodies and among school personnel, disciplinary policies and enforcement, and greater local control and involvement. To a significant extent, the educational issues confronting Latino communities are much the same as those outlined and discussed by the U.S. Civil Rights Commission (1973) over two generations ago.

The ebb and flow of immigration to the United States and the state of the American economy are closely connected to public policy debates and legislation regarding more restrictive immigration. For the most part, issues surrounding immigration, especially undocumented immigration, have been directed largely toward Latino immigrants and Latino communities. As a result, Latino core concerns include matters of immigration admission policies and processing times, militarization of the U.S.-Mexican border, protection of civil and economic rights, participation in social service programs, more efficient naturalization processing, and political refugee status for Central Americans. A brief history of the Voting Rights Act and its impact on Latino representation and electoral participation shows that it assisted the political development of Latinos. The provisions of the VRA, especially preclearance and coverage status, enable Latino organizations, especially litigation-oriented ones, to challenge voting systems and practices. The introduction of bilingual materials was part of the amendment process that focused on linguistic minorities. Court decisions in the 1990s placed much tighter restrictions on the use of majority-minority districts as remedies for minority-voter dilution. The number of local Latino representatives has increased dramatically, with less dramatic gains at the statewide and federal levels.

What constitutes important policy areas for Latinos can extend beyond those discussed here. In many regards, issues and conditions that impact Latinos directly can fall under the Latino policy agenda. For example, if Latinos are concentrated residentially in certain parts of a city and lack basic urban amenities (paved streets, drainage, lighting, etc.), then basic services are a Latino policy issue. In a similar manner, crime, housing, the environment (Pardo 1998), and the like impact Latinos and motivate the community to engage politically. The effectiveness of such involvement can rest on Latinos working by themselves or in concert with other groups who share similar concerns or are impacted significantly. The latter approach, joining in cooperative ventures with other segments of the American political scene, serves as the focus of the next chapter.

Discussion Questions

1. The top issue for decades for Latinos has been education. Why does this salient issue continue to stay at the top of the Latino agenda? Have the subissues changed over time?
2. It seems that each of the past five or so presidential administrations has set up a commission to identify problems for Latinos in the educational system and make possible recommendations. Why make this kind of effort? What difference have such efforts made to Latinos' educational advancement?
3. While bilingual educational programs have been in existence for almost fifty years, how has the politics of bilingual education changed, if at all, over this period?
4. Both the U.S. Constitution (i.e., the mandate for reapportionment) and the Voting Rights Act will be integral to the 2011 round of legislative reapportionment. Discuss the political processes and institutions involved, the "interested parties," and the strategies that Latinos will pursue in this reapportionment round.
5. It has been a common practice for political parties to draw districts that enhance a partisan registration advantage. As a result we have safe districts in which the incumbent is in a secure position. How do safe districts for Latino elected officials affect Latino constituents in terms or representativeness, responsiveness, and access?

CHAPTER 11

Building Political Alliances

Nos damos cuenta que no dejamos de pre-guntarnos ¿cuál es el verdadero significado de "comunidad" y a quien consideramos nuestro pueblo? Reconocemos la relación que tenemos con nuestro propio pueblo o con otras personas cuya cultura y tradicio-nes son como las nuestras. O quizás hasta buscamos otras comunidades para explorar y con quien unirnos.

We realize we have not finished answer-ing the question, What is the real mean-ing of "community" and whom do we consider to be our people? We recognize the relationship that we have with our own people and with other people whose culture and traditions are similar to our own. Or perhaps more answers will come when we seek out other communities to understand and with whom to unite.

ONE OF THE THEMES IN THIS BOOK is the concept of community and how it is present, to varying degrees, in the Latino community. I have portrayed Latinos in terms of key and salient issues that are significant to most segments of the various Latino communities. In addition, I have identified and discussed the rise and adjustment of specific Latino organizations and leaders to ex-tend beyond group interests based only on national origin. Finally, we have explored the development of group identity and the rise of a **pan-ethnic** identity and conscious-ness. While there may be some debate as to the cohesiveness and viability of a Latino political community, we take the position that linkages and interactions have occurred already among Latinos.

Moreover, the recognition and cultivation of Latino-ness by the mass media, po-litical parties, and national leadership serve to establish even more community links. This chapter explores further the theme of community building and linkages and how they are evident among Latinos. The chapter title uses the word "alliances" to discuss both the coming together of individuals of different "Latino" national origin (or intracoalitional behavior) and intergroup associations between Latinos and other groups in American politics (i.e., African Americans, Asian Americans, whites, etc.). It is a mistake to assume that persons of Mexican origin (or any other Latino subgroup) automatically come together with other Latinos. Community is forged by interactions, commonalities, and mutual interests. This discussion of expanding community will include Latinos' working coalitions or alliances "within" and with other communities in American society.

I began this book by introducing the notion of communities based on commonalties of culture and interests. The common cultural base extends itself when individuals are connected closely together by their participation in a common system of meaning with accompanying patterns of customary interactions and behaviors that are grounded in a common tradition (Cornell 1985). Latinos' common culture can include language, religion and religious practices, familial networks, celebrations and holidays, folklore and customs, and the arts. On the other hand, a **community of interests** exists when Latinos are united by a common set of economic and political concerns due in part to their concentration in certain industries or occupational domains, residential segregation (Denton and Massey 1988; Bean and Tienda 1987), or political disenfranchisement (T. Smith 1990; Acuña 1996). Common conditions and interests should lead to the development of a shared sense of group identity, perceived common conditions and focus upon the contributing **structural factors** (discrimination, institutional racism, exclusionary practices, etc.), and a developing common policy agenda.

Latino Community Formation: Basis for Partnerships

I will try to augment the notion of shared Latino culture and interests by identifying concrete indicators forging a Latino community. The data vehicle for this exploration is the **Latino National Survey** (LNS) (Fraga et al. 2006). One benefit of the survey's results is the range of questions that can provide good indicators of commonalities. In addition, the LNS includes Latinos from all of the Latino national-origin groups with a sample of 8,634 respondents. The large numbers of Mexican-origin individuals, Puerto Ricans, and Cubans are well represented, as is the notable increase of Central and South Americans, allowing for the portrayal of a complete picture of the dynamic Latino community. The indicators that we use here are (1) Latino group identity, (2) interactions among Latinos, (3) perceptions of Latino group discrimination, (4) Latinos' affinity across groups and their home countries, and (5) perceived common cultural practices and political or economic interests.

Latino Group Identity

We begin with a series of questions regarding three social identities. The LNS asked each respondent if he or she identified with a national origin, with pan-ethnic terms (Latino, Hispanic), and as an American. The questions were asked separately; then a fourth question asked which of the three was more salient. The pattern exhibited was a high degree of identification with both a pan-ethnic identity (i.e., Hispanic, Latino, etc.) and with the respondent's own national-origin affiliation. Over four-fifths of the Latino respondents indicated a pan-ethnic identity (see table 11.1). In addition, a similar percentage indicated having a national-origin identity as well. These results differ dramatically from the **Latino National Political Survey** (LNPS) in which only about one-fifth of respondents indicated having a pan-ethnic identity and overwhelmingly preferred national-origin labels. The idea of multiple identities among Latinos is clearly demonstrated in table 11.1 as almost 80 percent of the Latinos identified both

TABLE 11.1. Distribution of Ethnic and Pan-ethnic Identities among Latino National Survey Respondents

Ethnic/Pan-ethnic Identities	Number and Percentage Saying Yes	Number and Percentage Saying No
National-origin identity	8,474 (84.7)	1,254 (12.5)
Latino identity	8,775 (87.7)	943 (9.4)
Latino as primary identity	3,829 (38.3)	5,850 (58.4)
Both national and pan-ethnic as salient identity	7,887 (78.8)	2,032 (20.3)

in pan-ethnic terms and with their own national-origin background. Our theme of an identifiable community is reflected by the widespread presence of Latino/Hispanic choices coexisting with the retention of a national origin as well.

Previous work by Jones-Correa and Leal (1996) uses the idea of primary or secondary identification, which places pan-ethnicity within a constellation of multiple identities. Latinos born in the United States, as well as those with families here for several generations, were more likely to select a pan-ethnic identification, particularly the Mexican-origin respondents. Jones-Correa and Leal (1996) suggest that pan-ethnicity has been socially constructed over time, contributing to increases in pan-ethnic identification among Latinos. It seems clear that members of Latino national-origin groups are recognized by the larger society as Latinos (more so than by specific Latino subgroup), and awareness is growing among Latinos to describe themselves consciously as a pan-ethnic group, as evident in table 11.2. In the book *Latino Lives in America: Making It Home* (Fraga et al. 2010), focus group participants freely identified themselves as Latinos or Hispanics, regardless of nativity or extent of time in the United States. With this pattern, how strong or salient is this identity, and what are the underlying bases for this sense of a broader pan-ethnic community?

Table 11.2 shows the results of how LNS respondents selected their primary identity among the three options, as well as some other items that tapped perceived commonalities among Latino subgroup members. When the LNS respondents were asked to indicate the most salient identity, the highest response was a pan-ethnic

TABLE 11.2. Pan-ethnic Identities among Respondents to the Latino National Survey

Pan-ethnic Identities	Number of Respondents	Percentage
Latino as a primary identity	3,829	38.3
Latino identity	8,774	87.6
Salient national-origin and Latino identity	7,887	78.8
Perceived socioeconomic commonalities with other Latinos	7,472	74.7
Perceived political commonalities with other Latinos	6,479	64.4
Perceived high level of linked fate with other Latinos	7,158	71.5
Perceived socioeconomic commonalities with other Latinos and national-origin groups	7,310	73.0
Perceived political commonalities with other Latinos and national-origin groups	6,274	62.7

(i.e., Latino or Hispanic) identity, with 38.3 percent of the respondents. It was followed by a national-origin choice, and American identity was third. While we have been discussing a sense of community among Latinos, the preference of particular labels does represent a shared sense of who you are and placement in the American social order. While much has been made of the extent of Latinos' attachment to and identification with American society, two observations are notable. The first is that the presence of multiple identities is not uncommon among most individuals. Second, for Latinos, incorporating a Latino identity comes as a form of American identity. That is, the idea of Latino and Hispanic has social meaning in the United States only and represents a recognition of being in America while maintaining a sense of culture and ancestry.

Other results from the LNS show the similarities between Latino native-born, foreign-born, and naturalized citizens. That is, there is little variation across these categories, as almost two-thirds of all Latinos, regardless of nativity or generational status, strongly identified with a pan-ethnic identity. This pattern is noteworthy among the first-generation, noncitizen Latinos. We have been suggesting that the development of a community among persons of Spanish origin is an American phenomenon, and it affects Latino immigrants residing in this country. While I cannot test this hypothesis directly, prospective Latino migrants might be aware of the notion of being Latino prior to coming to the United States due the communication networks both there and in the home country. Another important aspect of community building is the degree and composition of interpersonal networks that exist among Latinos.

The other important findings in table 11.2 are based on a battery of questions asking about perceived socioeconomic and political commonalities with other Latinos. In addition, the concept of "linked fate" (Dawson 1994) was measured. The questions of linked fate asked Latinos how much they felt their own well-being was affected by the overall well-being of other Latinos. A similarly worded question referenced the respondent's national origin group as doing well if other Latinos were doing well (i.e. "How much does [ethnic subgroup] 'doing well' depend on other Hispanics or Latinos also doing well? A lot, some, a little, or not at all?")

A review of table 11.2 reveals a high degree of perceived commonalities in both the socioeconomic and political domains (74.7 and 64.4 percent felt a lot or some degree of commonality in these domains, respectively). Similarly, these Latino respondents exhibited a high degree of linked fate as individuals and as members of a Latino subgroup. Our theme of community and sense of attachment is reinforced by these results from the LNS.

Another way to demonstrate the pervasiveness of pan-ethnicity among contemporary Latinos is to examine the strength of that identity. When Latinos in the LNS were asked if they identified with either the "Hispanic" or "Latino" pan-ethnic label, the possible responses ranged from "not at all" to "very strongly." Table 11.3 shows the similarities between Latino native-born, foreign-born, and naturalized citizens. Whether it was talking about their neighborhoods, or coworkers, or places and activities for social gatherings, there was a visible sense of group identification as Latinos, Hispanics, or "Hispanos" (Fraga et al. 2010) regardless of their nativity status. Our whole discussion about community and the manner in which persons relate to others with similar cultures and circumstances reemphasize a dynamic occurrence that

TABLE 11.3. Strength of Latino/Hispanic Identity by Generation and Citizenship

Response	Freq.	First Generation			Second+ Generation Citizens	Grand Total
		Noncitizens	Citizens	Total for the First Generation		
Not at all	Freq.	108	53	161	117	278
	Row%	67.08	32.92	57.91	42.09	100.00
	Col%	2.85	2.72	2.80	4.39	3.31
Not very strongly	Freq.	207	113	320	191	511
	Row%	64.69	35.31	62.62	37.38	100.00
	Col%	5.46	5.80	5.57	7.17	6.08
Somewhat strongly	Freq.	1,029	433	1,462	673	2,135
	Row%	70.38	29.62	68.48	31.52	100.00
	Col%	27.13	22.23	25.47	25.26	25.40
Very strongly	Freq.	2,449	1,349	3,798	1,683	5,481
	Row%	64.48	35.52	69.29	30.71	100.00
	Col%	64.57	69.25	66.16	63.18	65.21
Total	Freq.	3,793	1,948	5,741	2,664	8,405
	Row%	66.07	33.93	68.30	31.70	100.00
	Col%	100.00	100.00	100.00	100.00	100.00

Table Tests of Independence:
First and second+ generations: Chi-square (4 d.f.) 23.570 (P = 0.002).
Citizen/noncitizen (first generation only): Chi-square (4 d.f.) 24.620 (P = 0.006).

Note: Respondents born in Puerto Rico are coded as first generation.
Question wording: "In general, how strongly or not do you think of yourself as Hispanic or Latino?"

affects Latinos, regardless of their nativity, citizenship status, language use, and socioeconomic status.

Interactions among Latinos

How many interactions take place among Latinos both within and across the various Latino subgroups? The extent and nature of interactions can be analogous to a family setting, in which persons are linked to one another's lives, situations, and circumstances. Again drawing on the LNS, a series of questions explores whom the Latino respondent interacts with. The questions ask about the composition of respondents' friendship networks and workplace settings. The results, shown in tables 11.4 and 11.5, indicate that Latinos have a lot of contact with fellow Latinos as well as a relative mixture of non-Latinos and Latinos.

More specifically, table 11.4 lists the race/**ethnicity** of friendship networks for first-generation Latinos (i.e., naturalized citizens and foreign nationals) and members

TABLE 11.4. Race/Ethnicity of Friendship Network by Generation and Citizenship

Response	Freq.	First Generation			Second+ Generation Citizens	Total for All Respondents
		Noncitizens	Citizens	Total for First Generation		
Mix of all of	Freq.	841	674	1,515	907	2,422
the above	Row%	55.51	44.49	62.55	37.45	100.00
(do not	Col%	21.83	34.37	26.06	33.73	28.48
read)						
Mostly	Freq.	1,918	600	2,518	628	3,146
(Latino/	Row%	76.17	23.83	80.04	19.96	100.00
Hispanic)	Col%	49.78	30.60	43.31	23.35	37.00
Mostly white	Freq.	124	106	230	225	455
	Row%	53.91	46.09	50.55	49.45	100.00
	Col%	3.22	5.41	3.96	8.37	5.35
Mixed	Freq.	817	442	1,259	661	1,920
(Latino/	Row%	64.89	35.11	65.57	34.43	100.00
Hispanic)	Col%	21.20	22.54	21.65	24.58	22.58
and white						
Mostly black	Freq.	11	8	19	42	61
	Row%	57.89	42.11	31.15	68.85	100.00
	Col%	0.29	0.41	0.33	1.56	0.72
Mixed	Freq.	119	113	232	186	418
(Latino/	Row%	28.47	27.03	55.50	44.50	100.00
Hispanic)	Col%	3.09	5.76	3.99	6.92	4.92
and black						
Other	Freq.	23	18	41	40	81
	Row%	56.10	43.90	50.62	49.38	100.00
	Col%	0.60	0.92	0.71	1.49	0.95
Total	Freq.	3,853	1,961	5,814	2,689	8,503
	Row%	66.27	33.73	68.38	31.62	100.00
	Col%	100.00	100.00	100.00	100.00	100.00

Table Tests of Independence:
First and second+ generations: One-way (6 d.f.) 80.370 (P = 0.000).
Citizen/noncitizen (first generation only): One-way (6 d.f.) 37.310 (P = 0.000).

Notes: The categories for "mostly Asian" and "mixed Asian/Latino" have been eliminated from this table; they are only included for residents of California, Texas, New York, and Illinois. Island-born Puerto Ricans are coded as first generation.
Question wording: "How would you describe your friends? Are they (read response items)?"

TABLE 11.5. Race/Ethnicity of Coworkers by Generation and Citizenship

Response	Freq.	First Generation			Second+ Generation Citizens	Grand Total
		Noncitizens	Citizens	Total for First Generation		
Mix of all of the above (do not read)	Freq.	699	520	1,219	613	1,832
	Row%	57.34	42.66	66.54	33.46	100.00
	Col%	20.48	30.41	23.79	26.14	24.53
Mostly (Latino/ Hispanic)	Freq.	1,487	434	1,921	513	2,434
	Row%	77.41	22.59	78.92	21.08	100.00
	Col%	43.57	25.38	37.50	21.88	32.59
Mostly white	Freq.	288	262	550	516	1,066
	Row%	52.36	47.64	51.59	48.41	100.00
	Col%	8.44	15.32	10.74	22.00	14.27
Mixed (Latino/ Hispanic) and white	Freq.	755	345	1,100	467	1,567
	Row%	68.64	31.36	70.20	29.80	100.00
	Col%	22.12	20.18	21.47	19.91	20.98
Mostly black	Freq.	32	23	55	54	109
	Row%	58.18	41.82	50.46	49.54	100.00
	Col%	0.94	1.35	1.07	2.30	1.46
Mixed (Latino/ Hispanic) and black	Freq.	88	76	164	102	266
	Row%	33.08	28.57	61.65	38.35	100.00
	Col%	2.58	4.44	3.20	4.35	3.56
Other	Freq.	64	50	114	80	194
	Row%	56.14	43.86	58.76	41.24	100.00
	Col%	1.88	2.92	2.23	3.41	2.60
Total	Freq.	3,413	1,710	5,123	2,345	7,468
	Row%	66.62	33.38	68.60	31.40	100.00
	Col%	100.00	100.00	100.00	100.00	100.00

Table Tests of Independence:
First and second+ generations: One-way (6 d.f.) 62.590 (P = 0.000).
Citizen/noncitizen (first generation only): One-way (6 d.f.) 37.270 (P = 0.000).

Notes: The categories for "mostly Asian" and "mixed Asian/Latino" have been eliminated from this table; they are only included for residents of California, Texas, New York, and Illinois. Island-born Puerto Ricans are coded as first generation.
Question wording: "How would you describe your coworkers? Stop me when I get to your answer. Are they (read response items)?"

of the second generation and beyond. Almost half (49.78 percent) of the Latino immigrants had mostly other Latinos as part of their friendship network. In contrast,
30.6 percent of naturalized Latinos had mostly Latinos as friends, while the drop was
greater among members of the second generation and beyond (23.4 percent). The second-largest friendship type is a mix of friends of all different kinds of background (for
foreign-born, 26.1 percent; for native-born, 33.73 percent). Finally, the third-largest
category is a mix of Latinos and white persons. As the LNS asked only generally about
the racial/ethnic makeup of these networks, we cannot determine the specific proportions of any combinations. At the same time, *Latino Lives in America* (2010), written
by the LNS research team, yields some insight gleaned through the focus groups as to
this dynamic. That is, Latinos for the most part served as the anchor or core of Latino
networks (primarily other family members and neighbors), but residential location,
social activities, and intermarriage introduced non-Latino friends.

Does this pattern of visible Latino friendship networks in general social settings
duplicate itself in work settings? Both questions tap voluntary arrangements, but this
voluntary dimension will be less likely in a work situation. While some similarity exists
to the friendship pattern, there are greater shifts toward non-Latino coworkers. This
could represent the labor market sectors in which Latinos are located. That is, perhaps
the service and agricultural sectors are more immigrant dominated, whereas the construction and manufacturing sectors may be more mixed. In table 11.5, among the
first generation, or noncitizens, the modal category is mostly Latino coworkers (43.6
percent) followed by two other categories: a general mix of backgrounds (20.5 percent)
and a mix of Latinos and whites (22.1 percent). In contrast, the second generation
had 21.9 percent mostly Latino coworkers, with three other categories at comparable
levels: mix of all groups (26.1 percent), mostly white (22 percent), and mix of Latinos
and whites (19.9 percent). As indicated earlier, respondents should have less control
over the selection of workplace setting, but this item reflects the composition of the
Latinos' coworkers.

While the Latinos in the LNS are not totally "ethnically" immersed in dense Latino
social networks, there is clear indication that fellow Latinos are a substantial part of
their networks. At the same time, their friends and coworkers represent a more racially/
ethnically diverse world, indicating that they are not living in isolation. This has ramifications regarding knowledge and understanding of American society (especially for
the first generation), as diverse contacts can affect comparisons of Latinos' status and
circumstances in the United States relative to those of non-Latinos. This brief portrait
of Latinos' interaction patterns adds to our discussion of community building and
bases for such connections.

Perceptions of Latino Group Discrimination

A key criterion that characterizes minority-group status, besides a sense of group
identity, is differential treatment. Discriminatory practices directed toward Latinos can
serve to enhance group solidarity. While the direct experience of discrimination has
an important effect on individuals (de la Garza et al. 1993), individual perceptions of
discrimination are equally important in developing a sense of minority-group status.
Similar conditions, perceptions, and experiences can serve to establish the sense of
community under siege. Our discussion of **Proposition 187** in chapter 9 provided in-

sight into the external actions of a state initiative that clearly targeted Latinos for their purported negative impact on California.

Heightened group awareness and consciousness developed to combat that initiative and take on other political issues. In the United States, practices of discrimination based on race and ethnicity have been a prime motivation for group solidarity (Dawson 1994). In the LNS, each respondent was asked about his or her perceptions of the opportunity structure in the United States for Latinos. For the LNS's large segment of foreign-born respondents, a major reason for migration was to seek better opportunities in America. Respondents were asked to agree or disagree to varying degrees with the statement, "Latinos can get ahead in the United States if they work hard."

Overall, a vast majority of Latinos (92.8 percent) agreed strongly or somewhat agreed with the idea of the American dream—that hard work and persistence yield rewards. Although this belief declines somewhat across generations, there is still a strong belief in America as a land of opportunity. At the same time, what have been the actual experiences of Latinos regarding differential treatment or discriminatory behavior? The LNS was structured to ask respondents if they had been treated unfairly in a number of different settings: on the job, in obtaining housing, at restaurants, and by the police. The range of affirmative responses (treated unfairly) ranged from 5.9 percent (housing) to 16.4 percent in relation to a job or restaurant. These percentages are somewhat lower than the findings of Pew Hispanic surveys, where about 25 to 35 percent of Latinos indicated experiencing discriminatory behavior. In an earlier period, the LNPS found similar levels as the Pew surveys, with Mexican-origin respondents experiencing the greatest levels of discrimination. The LNPS also asked about the perception of discrimination directed toward Mexican-origin individuals, Puerto

BOX 11.1. The *Washington Post* Latino Survey

In 1999 the *Washington Post*, in conjunction with the Henry J. Kaiser Family Foundation and Harvard's John F. Kennedy School of Government, conducted a national survey of Latinos. A question was asked about the Latino respondents' perception of discrimination directed toward Latinos. In addition to people of Mexican-origin, Puerto Ricans, and Cubans, ample numbers of Central and South American respondents were queried. Overall, 82 percent of all the Latinos indicated that discrimination was a problem for Latinos in the United States, with a range of Latino subgroup responses from 77 percent (Puerto Ricans) to 90 percent (Central and South Americans). A follow-up question asked respondents if discrimination was a big problem for Latinos, how big of a problem was it. This question assessed the saliency of this perception in light of other concerns the Latinos respondents might have. For this item, among all Latinos, some 67 percent indicated that discrimination was a big problem. By Latino subgroup, the range was from 67 percent (Mexican-origin individuals) to 72 percent (Central and South Americans). These results illustrate the relatively high degree of agreement among Latinos regarding perception of discriminatory treatment directed toward group members. In addition, these perceptions are highest among the Central and South American respondents, who represent the fastest-growing segment of the Latino community.

Ricans, and Cubans. More than 30 percent of the Mexican-origin respondents and 35.8 percent of the Puerto Ricans felt that people belonging to Latino national-origin groups encountered a lot of discrimination. In contrast, Cubans responded at 22.1 percent for the upper level of discrimination. Overall, 54 to 75 percent of the Latino respondents from these three subgroups felt that Latino national-origin groups persons experienced a lot or some degree of discrimination.

LNS respondents who felt they had been discriminated against were asked about what they believed to be the reason for such unfair treatment. In table 11.6, the modal response (30.05 percent) across nativity and citizenship status was being Latino. The other top four answers were national origin (7.6 percent), language or accent (11.8 percent), immigrant status (7.6 percent), and skin color (14.0 percent). The interesting results lie with the explanation of being Latino as the most likely reason. In essence, the response level for this reason does not deviate by status as a foreign-born resident, a noncitizen, a naturalized citizen, or a member of the second generation and beyond. Again, the pan-ethnic connection suggests that being Latino forms a significant part of respondents' self-perception. Although the percentage is about half that for the Latino explanation, the national-origin explanation would also suggest self-perception both as a coethnic and as a member of a pan-ethnic community. Interestingly, darker skin color was cited highest among members of the second generation and beyond.

Clearly the recent research on both experiences with and perception of discrimination directed toward Latinos (Lavariega-Monforti and Sanchez 2010; Sanchez 2008) demonstrates its effects on sociomobility, identity, and political consciousness.

In the earlier LNPS, Cubans perceived lower levels of discrimination than their Puerto Rican and Mexican-origin counterparts directed toward Latino national-origin groups. Clearly, Mexican Americans and Puerto Ricans perceived higher levels of discrimination directed toward Cubans than the Cuban respondents themselves. There is evidence that discrimination aimed at Latinos cuts across the various Latino subgroups. This connection with discrimination, as an assessment of Latinos' status in the United States, binds people together through a sense of common circumstances. A sense of some degree of "out-group" status is not uncommon for many Latinos. Less clear is how these experiences are interpreted and internalized within and across the different Latino subcommunities.

Perceived Common Cultural Practices and Political/Economic Interests

A substantial portion of the survey items in the LNS battery of questions included ways to assess connections between Latinos regardless of national origin, nativity, language use, and the like. We have focused much of this book on the theme of community based on cultural and socioeconomic commonalities. We have seen already the growth and internalization of a pan-ethnic identity and use of the "Hispanic" and "Latino" labels. Our next step is to explore the extent of perceived commonality among Latinos (differentiated by nativity and citizenship status) and a sense of linked fate. Where there is general agreement about why Latinos are more alike, experience similar circumstances, and feel their futures are interrelated, then the opportunities for collective efforts are much better. We have also introduced the role of leadership and organizations directing this sense of community toward public polices and political engagement.

TABLE 11.6. Reason for Unfair Treatment by Generation and Citizenship

| Response | Freq. | First Generation | | | Second+ Generation Citizens | Grand Total |
		Noncitizens	Citizens	Total for First Generation		
For being Latino	Freq.	319	187	506	390	896
	Row%	63.04	36.96	56.47	43.53	100.00
	Col%	30.01	30.81	30.30	29.55	29.97
For being an immigrant	Freq.	172	42	214	12	226
	Row%	80.37	19.63	94.69	5.31	100.00
	Col%	16.18	6.92	12.81	0.91	7.56
For national origin	Freq.	64	52	116	110	226
	Row%	55.17	44.83	51.33	48.67	100.00
	Col%	6.02	8.57	6.95	8.33	7.56
For language or accent	Freq.	198	91	289	64	353
	Row%	68.51	31.49	81.87	18.13	100.00
	Col%	18.63	14.99	17.31	4.85	11.81
For skin color	Freq.	84	62	146	271	417
	Row%	57.53	42.47	35.01	64.99	100.00
	Col%	7.90	10.21	8.74	20.53	13.95
For gender	Freq.	12	14	26	40	66
	Row%	18.18	21.21	39.39	60.61	100.00
	Col%	1.13	2.31	1.56	3.03	2.21
For age	Freq.	19	26	45	86	131
	Row%	42.22	57.78	34.35	65.65	100.00
	Col%	1.79	4.28	2.69	6.52	4.38
For other reasons	Freq.	113	83	196	282	478
	Row%	57.65	42.35	41.00	59.00	100.00
	Col%	10.63	13.67	11.74	21.36	15.99
Don't know/NA	Freq.	82	50	132	65	197
	Row%	62.12	37.88	67.01	32.99	100.00
	Col%	7.71	8.24	7.90	4.92	6.59
Total	Freq.	1,063	607	1,670	1,320	2,990
	Row%	63.65	36.35	55.85	44.15	100.00
	Col%	100.00	100.00	100.00	100.00	100.00

Table Tests of Independence:
First and second+ generations: (2 d.f.) 33.190 (P = 0.000).
Citizen/noncitizen (first generation only): (2 d.f.) 13.770 (P = 0.000).

Notes: Island-born Puerto Ricans are coded as first generation. Variable label: whydisc.
Question wording: "There are lots of possible reasons why people might be treated unfairly. What do you think was the main reason for your experience(s)?"

TABLE 11.7. Levels of Commonality among Latino National Survey Respondents Regarding Socioeconomic and Political Domains

Areas of Commonality	Generation and Citizenship Status		
	Foreign-born Latinos	Naturalized Citizens (%)	U.S.-born Latinos (%)
Education, jobs, and income opportunities			
None	6.4	6.1	6.0
Little	18.3	15.1	16.7
Some	32.8	35.3	38.7
A lot	37.1	37.8	33.3
Government and politics			
None	7.6	6.6	5.9
Little	22.6	19.0	18.1
Some	32.0	33.2	37.1
A lot	28.8	33.1	31.0

The respondents were asked four questions about whether they perceived commonalities (from none to a lot) based upon socioeconomic circumstances and political or governmental activities. In addition, the frame of reference to assess commonalities was the respondent him- or herself or a member of his or her respective national-origin group in relation to all other Latinos. For example, the survey conductor might ask, "Now I'd like you to think about the political situation of Latinos in society. Thinking about things like government services and employment, political power and representation [or job opportunities, educational attainment, income, and the like], how much do you [or members of your national origin group, etc.] have in common with other Latinos?"

In table 11.7, almost seven-tenths of the LNS respondents indicated some or a lot of commonality with other Latinos regarding socioeconomic circumstances. Whether respondents were foreign-born residents, noncitizens, naturalized citizens, or U.S.-born Latinos, the pattern of their responses was almost identical. Similarly, about three-fifths (60.8 percent) indicated some or many common political circumstances. That is, on matters involving representation, political empowerment, and government services, most Latinos perceived a common basis for work in these areas (see table 11.7). Our underlying theme of a community of interests is reflected by the direction and extent of levels of perceptions that being Latino can provide.

Throughout this discussion of Latino politics, I have identified communities of interests and **communities of common cultures** as building blocks for a broad-based Latino community. If Latinos across the various national-origin subgroups interact based on perceptions of common cultural and structural conditions, then there will be greater motivation to engage in collective efforts. I have tried to identify salient issues and bridging organizations and leaders that promote an integrated Latino community.

Returning to the 2006 LNS results, table 11.8 provides more detailed distributions for the two linked-fate questions with specific reference to other Latinos. As noted in table 11.2, Latinos shared a high gradation of linked fate. Table 11.8 shows the strength of such a connection with other Latinos. Almost half of the Latino respondents evi-

TABLE 11.8. Measures of Linked-Fate Questions among Latino National Survey
Respondents

Linked-Fate Item	Number of Respondents	Percentage
How much does [national origin's] doing well depend on other Latinos also doing well?		
Not at all	692	8.0
A little	1,121	13.0
Some	2,161	25.0
A lot	3,988	46.2
Don't know/NA	672	7.8
How much does your doing well depend on other Latinos also doing well?		
Not at all	1,319	15.3
A little	1,274	14.8
Some	2,004	23.2
A lot	3,421	38.6
Don't know/NA	616	7.1
Totals	8,634	100.0

denced "a lot" of sentiments about their linked fate with other Latinos as members of
a Latino subgroup. The context of framing this question in terms of national origin
corroborates research on social identity. It is the individual who develops a sense of
group affiliation and attachment that can lead him or her to become more civically and
politically engaged on the behalf of the larger Latino community. Clearly, developing
a sense of community has many points of association, and group identity is but one of
those possibilities. An acknowledged sense of one's own well-being as associated with
that of other people (i.e., Latinos) has proven powerful in African American political
development. The nexus of connectors is present among Latinos, and a sense of linked
fate serves as another building block.

Again, comparing the LNS results with the earlier LNPS, the responses regarding
the commonalty of culture indicate that foreign-born respondents see more similarities
than their native-born counterparts. If we combine the responses of "very similar" and
"somewhat similar," from 70 to 73 percent of foreign-born respondents registered affirmatively. The native-born Mexican-origin respondents provided the only exception, as
78.6 percent indicated "very or somewhat similar culture" across the Latino subgroups.
These responses make it difficult to assess the impact of nativity. Overall, approximately
one-fourth of all Latino respondents expressed belief in little cultural similarity across
the Latino subgroups. This perception was higher among foreign-born Mexicanos (30.1
percent) and native-born Cubans (33.4 percent). Potentially, the experiences in each
subgroup, whether native or foreign-born, may be more self-defined than similar.

Using the LNPS results regarding political and economic similarities between
Mexican-origin individuals and Cubans, the difference between native- and foreign-
born respondents is significant. That is, native-born Latinos were more likely to
acknowledge a higher percentage of similarity than their foreign-born counterparts.
Again, the percentages for Cuban respondents were slightly lower, especially in the

"very similar" category. Similar response patterns were evident for the Puerto Rican–Mexican-origin pairing. In all three subgroups, native-born Latinos indicated a greater percentage of similarity than foreign-born Latinos. The response category most affected was "somewhat similar." Finally, the results of the political-and-economic-similarity item between Puerto Ricans and Cubans displayed a similar pattern as for the Mexican and Puerto Rican respondents, such that native-born individuals saw greater similarity of political concerns. At the same time, the Cuban foreign-born segment saw greater dissimilarity.

Again, a review of the LNS results concerning the absence of major deviations about perceived commonalities among the native- versus foreign-born segments does raise some interesting developments. There is research (García and Sanchez 2006) indicating that comparisons of status, progress, and opportunity do differ among native- and foreign-born Latinos. Native-born Latinos assess their status relative to other groups in American society. In this case, the idea of a minority group in the United States can have greater potential to mobilize persons for common action. In addition, perceptions of similarity (cultural and/or political) are influenced by the cultural, linguistic, and residential composition of individuals' networks. The foreign-born segment responds more favorably to cultural similarities, in part due to their closer proximity to Latino cultural practices than their native-born counterparts and because they compare their status with compatriots who remain in the countries of origin. Yet, it appears that seeing oneself as a Latino—perceiving commonalities along both socioeconomic and political dimensions regardless of nativity and citizenship status—can affect a sense of commonality, both regarding interactions with other Latinos and the experience of living in the United States, especially in terms of public opinion and policy debates. In an earlier chapter, we noted that the rise of immigration-related initiatives and legislation has had the effect of bringing Latinos together across nativity lines, socioeconomic classes, and cultural variations.

The concepts of Latino and Hispanic are U.S. based and have meaning in terms of a collection of communities from Latin America and the Iberian Peninsula. Thus, awareness of and orientation toward other Latinos may be more evident among the native-born. The additional factor of others (non-Latinos) seeing Latinos as a monolith (culturally, physically, socioeconomically, etc.) can affect how Latinos respond to one another. The work of Hayes-Bautista, Schenk, and Chapa (1988) explores the idea of disassimilation in which Latino medical students (who had been largely assimilated into the American culture) were admitted to a medical school program as part of affirmative action efforts. Being served by special programs that assisted their progress in medical school and being tagged as minorities and Hispanics had the effect of motivating these students to reexamine who they were. If other people or institutions see and treat one as different (whether or not particular individuals see themselves as such), then there is a tendency to examine why, being of Latino background, one does not exhibit the expected behaviors and attitudes. The Hayes-Bautista study chronicled the transformation or disassimilation of many of these Latino students in becoming more Latino and identifying as such (in this case developing a closer affinity with their Mexican or Chicano origins). Thus, the development of a broader-based Latino community results from not only how Latinos see each other but the effects of being defined by non-Latinos, public policies, mass media, and political leaders.

TABLE 11.9. Latinos and African Americans Doing Well by Generation and Citizenship

Response	Freq.	First Generation			Second+ Generation Citizens	Grand Total
		Noncitizens	Citizens	Total for First Generation		
A lot	Freq.	1,665	741	2,406	602	3,008
	Row%	69.20	30.80	79.99	20.01	100.00
	Col%	42.47	37.12	40.67	22.15	34.84
Some	Freq.	977	576	1,553	831	2,384
	Row%	62.91	37.09	65.14	34.86	100.00
	Col%	24.92	28.86	26.25	30.57	27.61
Little	Freq.	749	322	1,071	606	1,677
	Row%	69.93	30.07	63.86	36.14	100.00
	Col%	19.11	16.13	18.10	22.30	19.42
Nothing	Freq.	529	357	886	679	1,565
	Row%	59.71	40.29	56.61	43.39	100.00
	Col%	13.49	17.89	14.98	24.98	18.13
Total	Freq.	3,920.00	1,996.00	5,916.00	2,718.00	8,634.00
	Row%	66.26	33.74	68.52	31.48	100.00
	Col%	100.00	100.00	100.00	100.00	100.00

Table Tests of Independence:
First and second+ generations: (1 d.f.) 99.987 (P = 0.000)
Citizen/noncitizen (first generation only): (1 d.f.) 14.469 (P = 0.008)

Note: Island-born Puerto Ricans are coded as first generation.
Question wording: "How much does Latinos doing well depend on African Americans also doing well?"

We add to this discussion of linked fate by adding connection. That is, the LNS respondents were also asked, "How much does [national origin group's] 'doing well' depend on African Americans also doing well? A lot, some, a little, or not at all?" Table 11.9 shows the extent of linked fate that Latinos shared with African Americans. Interestingly, almost four-fifths of the first generation indicated a high degree of linked fate with African Americans. Later in this chapter, we discuss possible coalitions or alliances between Latinos and African Americans and other groups. There is a drop-off in linked fate with African Americans among Latinos of the second generation and beyond. Nevertheless, overall, more than three-fifths of all Latinos indicated some or a lot of linked fate with African Americans. Our later discussion of this aspect of Latino politics will delve more into the bases for such coalitions.

Our examination of a broader-based Latino community centers on a network of interactions, a common understanding of concerns and issues, and a sense of mutual respect. At the same time, the dynamic nature of any community does not require complete unanimity, consensus, or engagement in common activities at all times.

BOX 11.2. Another Look at the *Washington Post* Survey

Three questions on the *Washington Post* survey tap a sense of the attraction and utility of Latino subgroups politically. The first asked respondents to agree or disagree with the statement that Latinos share "few" political interests and goals. Overall, 44 percent of the Latino respondents disagreed. The range of Latino subgroup responses that disagreed with this statement ran between 37 percent (Central and South Americans) to 51 percent (Puerto Ricans). The next question asked if the respondent felt that "Latinos today are working together to achieve common goals or not." Overall, a majority (56 percent) of the Latino respondents felt that Latinos were working together. The range of working-together responses ranged from 59 percent (Mexican-origin individuals) to 52 percent (Puerto Ricans). Finally, the third item asked respondents if Latinos would be better off if Latino groups worked together politically, if they would be worse off, or if there would be no difference. Overwhelmingly, the Latino respondents answered affirmatively that they would be better off (84 percent) with virtually no variation among the subgroups (which ranged from 85 to 86 percent).

How do these additional pieces of information add to the previous results of the Latino National Political Survey? While it appears that Latino subgroups are "quicker" to recognize their cultural similarities, this is not as evident in assessments of their political and economic commonalities. At the same time, a significant segment of each subgroup makes those connections; this reinforces the fact that organizations and individuals are actively engaged in Latino political matters. These responses indicate strongly that greater Latino awareness and involvement would be aided by more visible and disseminated information and activities before broader segments of the Latino community.

We have only begun to examine and explore the community-building process across the various Latino communities in a systematic manner. At the same time, it can be useful to think of building community across Latino subgroups as a coalition-formation process. Latino subgroups come together for very specific purposes and at different times. Research on coalitions (Jackson and Preston 1991; Ture and Hamilton 1992) suggests that key elements need to be in place in order for groups to agree to combine resources in specific situations and on certain issues. I next extend this discussion of coalition formation by briefly looking at potential common political strands among Latinos and African Americans.

Coalitional Affinities: Discrimination and Social Distance

While there has been much emphasis on the growth of the Latino community, especially in the past decade, there has also been much discussion about the political influence achieved by the African American community (Walton 1997; Dawson 1994). Works by McClain and Karnig (1990) and McClain and Stewart (1999) have established the prospects and limitations of an interracial/interethnic coalition between Latinos and African Americans. Competitive forces have been the primary area of emphasis between these two groups. As a result, coalitions are made tenuous (due to competition for municipal employment positions, business contracts, elected positions, etc.), although they have served as the focal point of Latino–African American relations. At the same time, some recent research (J. A. García 2000; Jennings 1994; Jaynes 2000) has outlined possible inducements and/or situations for working together.

With this growing research literature on the causes and consequences of Latino–African American competition and the results of coalitional efforts, I here examine the nature of working coalitions between Latinos and African Americans. More realistically, the discussion tries to measure the receptivity among Latinos to connect with the African American community for collective endeavors. This discussion starts by asking why Latinos and African Americans would come together to work cooperatively. Then, it explores the nature of coalitions as purposeful, situation specific, and temporary. A discrimination model of coalition formation (Uhlaner 1991; J. A. García 2000), along with collective group orientations (sense of empowerment, efficacy, and consciousness) and socioeconomic status, can work concurrently to determine areas of cooperation and obtain resources to be effective. This type of model suggests that both Latinos and African Americans experience discriminatory practices in the United States, which creates a common link or bond.

This connection with discriminatory experiences can "produce" a sense of a group identity such as Latinos, African Americans, or some other minority-group members. This would motivate persons to get involved politically on behalf of common concerns. Having a group identity and consciousness already indicates a proclivity to participate on behalf of the group. For example, a pan-ethnic identification among Latinos serves as a predictor to engage in coalitional behavior with African Americans (Kaufman 2003). The expression of in-group identification and solidarity can serve as a marker of collectivist political orientations (Segura 2011) and seeing common issues across group boundaries.

Finally, socioeconomic status helps provide the political resources to be effective in political arenas. Works like Browning, Marshall, and Tabb (1990) have looked at local politics in the San Francisco Bay area to illustrate that minority coalition could include Anglo liberals for effective policy outcomes. In California, Jackson and Preston (1991) and Sonenshein (1994) examined electoral efforts that connected the Latino and African American communities, especially in Los Angeles.

The basis of the **discrimination-plus model** (J. A. García 2000) depends on common experiences, issue priorities, and values among minority-group members in order for them to be receptive to joint political activities and collective efforts. Even if individuals make these kinds of connections, minority organizations and leadership play a critical role in implementing strategies and plans to act on these common goals and issue concerns. Organizations and their leaders function to outline specific political strategies, activities, communication links to the community, and motivational cues to stimulate action. Carmichael and Hamilton (1967) identified necessary requisites for any coalition to form, which include (1) recognition of each party's self-interests, (2) recognition that each party's self-interest is benefited by alliances, (3) each party's having an independent base of support, and (4) the coalition's effort focusing on specific and identifiable goals. In essence, the continual political empowerment of Latinos strengthens their partnership contribution to any coalition effort. The link is the discrimination experienced perceived by Latinos and African Americans.

Uhlaner (1991) suggests that recognition of differential treatment can lead minority groups to feel sympathetic across groups, more disadvantaged than others, or inclined to protect their own group more. The discrimination connection also suggests that individuals who have experienced or perceived discrimination directed at their group are likely to possess a strong sense of racial and/or ethnic identity and support for specific issues or problems (Uhlaner 1991). The key for Latino–African American coalitions lies with each assessing its disadvantaged status and seeing the interconnectedness. Each group confronts similar problems and conditions and, perhaps, a common target. McClain and Karnig (1990) have demonstrated that in American cities with a critical mass of both Latinos and African Americans, political coalitions are viable if both minority groups see themselves as combating the "white power structure." When they share a common target in vying for elective office, Latino and African American officials make gains at the expense of current nonminority officeholders. At the same time, a minimal level of trust between the two groups is essential for any degree of success. Oliver and Johnson (1984) showed that a low level of trust between Latinos and African Americans exists in Los Angeles.

Again, the LNS afforded me the opportunity to examine the extent of perceived commonalities among Latinos with other groups in American society. We have already looked at the linked-fate items in terms of Latinos seeing their fate as tied to other Latinos and with African Americans. It is also clear that there have already been numerous situations in which Latino and African American communities have been engaged in cooperative and competitive interactions in cities around the United States. In addition, some of these collaborative efforts have also involved cooperation and competition with white and Asian American communities. The city of Los Angeles is a good example (Sonenshein 2006) of these inter-minority relations. The LNS asked Latino respondents the extent of commonality perceived along socioeconomic and political dimensions with African Americans and whites. The possible responses ranged from "nothing" to "a lot." Table 11.10 shows that more than a majority or a near majority of Latinos indicated perceived commonalities along socioeconomic lines with African Americans and to a lesser degree with whites. At the same time, there is a noticeable difference between native-born Latinos and the foreign-born segment. For both African Americans and whites, the native-born indicated greater commonalities by 11 to 22 percent.

More specifically, we differentiated the Latino respondents based on nativity and specific Latino national-origin subgroups. Native-born Latinos expressed perceived commonality with both African Americans (67.9 percent) and whites (56.1 percent), although noticeably more so with African Americans. Among the different Latino subgroups, Puerto Rican and Dominican respondents (65.5 and 53.7 percent, respectively) had the greatest percentages indicating perceived commonalities with African Americans. On the other hand, Cubans, Puerto Ricans, and Colombians had the highest percentage of perceived commonalities with whites. This brief snapshot supports the idea that forming coalitional partnerships with other groups is certainly a possibility. This appears to be slightly more the case between Latinos and other minority groups. One cautionary note: the prospect for collective efforts is dependent on many local circumstances and the prior history of intergroup relations, as well as the particulars of the political issue at hand.

BOX 11.3. Racial/Ethnic Coalitions in Los Angeles?

Recent works on Los Angeles (Waldinger and Bozorgmehr 1996; Yu and Chang 1995; Ong, Bonacich, and Cheng 1994) have introduced the added factor of the growing Asian American community and some corresponding political developments. The unsuccessful mayoral campaign of Michael Wu to succeed Tom Bradley included the strategy of forging a multiethnic/multiracial coalition. Interminority electoral coalitions elected Tom Bradley in Los Angeles, David Dinkins in New York, Federico Peña and Wellington Webb in Denver, and Harold Washington in Chicago. In essence, being a global city afforded Los Angeles, with its diverse ethnic/racial mix, greater opportunities and accumulated experience to build on working relationships. After Bradley decided not to run for mayor again, there were numerous discussions among African Americans, Latinos, Asian Americans, and white liberals (Sonenshein 1994) to reach an accord on a common candidate to support. Michael Wu, a longtime member of the city council and a close ally of the Bradley coalition, emerged as the coalition's bearer. The level of support and voting strength that Bradley had developed did not transfer to the Wu candidacy. While the strength of the rainbowlike Los Angeles coalition was not the sole factor in his defeat, it did play an important role.

Another dimension of interethnic relations in Los Angeles is the recent gains in political representation, especially among Asian Americans and Latinos. This development has altered political alignments and networks in Los Angeles local politics, in some ways challenging political positions and networks in the African American community, as well as between them and white liberal networks. In addition, gains among Latinos in the California State Assembly, particularly in leadership positions, were achieved by creating working coalitions. The combination of changing demographics, continued growth and political development (representation, organizational resources and skills, raised political capital, etc.) among minority groups, especially Latinos and Asian Americans, and broader networks across activists and organized groups make both cooperative and competitive activities take place more frequently.

Since each minority community had developed its own base of power and influence, they had created opportunities and challenges to interact with one another as potentially significant partners or adversaries in the Los Angeles political arena. As a result, members of different groups weigh overlapping interests and calculate the cost-benefit ratios of cooperation versus competition for enhancing their individual group's benefits (Henry and Muñoz 1991). By their very nature, these interracial coalitions tend to be short-lived and sustained by specific, identifiable goals and interpersonal connections and respect.

The second item regarding commonalities across groups asks about the extent of commonality between Latinos' political situation (i.e., representation, empowerment, government jobs, etc.) and those of African Americans and whites. In this context (see table 11.11), a similar pattern prevails. That is, three-fifths of native-born Latinos perceive political commonalities with African Americans; about half of native-born Latinos feel such commonality with whites. Across the different Latino subgroups, a

TABLE 11.10. Extent of Commonality among Latinos Regarding Jobs, Education, and Income Attainment with African Americans and Whites

Latinos in National Latino Survey	Commonality with African Americans	Commonality with Whites
Nativity	Some to a lot (%)	Some to a lot (%)
Native-born (2,408)[a]	67.9	56.1
Foreign-born[b] (5,704)	45.9	45.1
Latino subgroups		
Colombians (139)	46.8	53.2
Cubans (419)	51.3	55.4
Dominicans (335)	53.7	43.6
Salvadorans (406)	48.8	45.1
Guatemalans (149)	40.9	43.6
Mexicans (5,690)	51.0	47.2
Puerto Ricans (759)	65.5	54.2

[a]The numbers in parentheses represent the number of respondents in that category.
[b]The operational definition for foreign-born includes all persons born outside the United States, including in Puerto Rico.

greater percentage sees political commonalities with African Americans as opposed to whites. This proclivity could be due to greater geographical contact with African Americans (i.e., more so for Dominicans, Puerto Ricans, and Colombians) and a longer history of interaction (especially for Puerto Ricans). In contrast, over three-fifths of foreign-born Latinos indicated commonality with whites (almost fifty percent more than identified with African Americans). Table 11.11 also suggests that an ample proportion of Latinos see their lives as interwoven, to a noticeable degree, with those of African Americans. At the same time, there are connecting strands with whites. As our focus lies with politics and political activities, this perceived level of commonality with

TABLE 11.11. Extent of Commonality among Latinos Regarding Their Political Situation with African Americans and Whites

Latinos in National Latino Survey	Commonality with African Americans	Commonality with Whites
Nativity	Some to a lot (%)	Some to a lot (%)
Native-born (2,408)[a]	62.8	48.7
Foreign-born[b] (5,704)	43.4	64.1
Latino subgroups		
Colombians (139)	49.6	41.7
Cubans (419)	51.3	49.9
Dominicans (335)	52.8	43.3
Salvadorans (406)	45.3	40.9
Guatemalans (149)	40.9	39.6
Mexicans (5,690)	46.9	42.6
Puerto Ricans (759)	60.6	47.7

[a]The numbers in parentheses represent the number of respondents in that category.
[b]The operational definition for foreign-born includes all persons born outside the United States, including in Puerto Rico.

TABLE 11.12. Competition with African Americans in Getting Jobs by Generation and Citizenship

Response	Freq.	First Generation			Second+ Generation Citizens	Grand Total
		Noncitizens	Citizens	Total for First Generation		
Strong	Freq.	1,003	546	1,549	766	2,315
competition	Row%	64.75	35.25	66.91	33.09	100.00
	Col%	25.59	27.35	26.18	28.18	26.81
Weak	Freq.	678	436	1,114	809	1,923
competition	Row%	60.86	39.14	57.93	42.07	100.00
	Col%	17.30	21.84	18.83	29.76	22.27
No competition	Freq.	2,239	1014	3,253	1,143	4,396
at all	Row%	68.83	31.17	74.00	26.00	100.00
	Col%	57.12	50.80	54.99	42.05	50.91
Total	Freq.	3,920	1,996	5,916	2,718	8,634
	Row%	66.26	33.74	68.52	31.48	100.00
	Col%	100.00	100.00	100.00	100.00	100.00

Table Tests of Independence:
First and second+ generations: (1 d.f.) 29.754 (P = 0.000)
Citizen/noncitizen (first generation only): (1 d.f.) 18.048 (P = 0.002)

Note: Island-born Puerto Ricans are coded as first generation.
Question wording: "Some have suggested that Latinos or Hispanics are in competition with African Americans. After each of the next items, would you tell me if you believe there is strong competition, weak competition, or no competition at all with African Americans?"

other groups is intended to serve as the entry point for discussion and exploration of ways in which Latinos can work with other groups for common objectives.

We can also explore this possible working relationship by reversing the nature of the connection to one in which competition is seen as a strong component. In the LNS, the Latino respondents were asked, "Some have suggested that Latinos or Hispanics are in competition with African Americans. After each of the next items (jobs, education, government jobs, and elected offices) would you tell me if you believe there is strong competition, weak competition, or no competition with African Americans?" In table 11.12, the case of competition for jobs, there is a tendency to see little or no competition as opposed to strong competition (73.1 percent versus 26.8 percent, respectively) (see table 11.11). Similar patterns exist when the potential competitive arena is education and quality schools (71.6 percent versus 28.4 percent), governmental jobs (67.1 percent versus 32.9 percent), and holding elected office (64.15 versus 35.8 percent) (see tables 11.12 and 11.13). It would unrealistic, in any given area of the country, to expect no competition in these areas between Latinos and other groups in the community. At the same time, the modal responses would indicate that competition may not be a salient point of contention, or it may be one in which some resolution is more possible than not.

Use of the LNS and examination of the battery of items that tap perceived com-monalities among Latinos and other groups in the United States can provide us with a good informational base regarding coalitional efforts. Some literature suggests that rising Latino immigration in communities with other minority populations, especially African Americans, could accentuate competition in domains such as jobs, social services, and so forth (Rocha 2007; Meier et al. 2004; McClain et al. 2009). The com-petition for economic resources, attention from the major political parties, and educa-tional resources can pit the interests of each group against each other. At the same time, research by Rodrígues and Segura (2007) indicates that intergroup relations operate at both the elite and mass levels. They argue that one needs to observe and understand both sets of dynamics.

For example, evidence from mass attitudes can point to salient issues leading to-ward cooperation as well as perceived social distance. I have argued elsewhere in this book that elite leadership is a critical component in the initialization of contact and communication with other groups. In addition, the focus on the building blocks of community—common cultures and interests—is quite pertinent to the growing pres-ence and utility of a pan-ethnic identity. Kaufman (2003) found pan-ethnic identifica-tion to be positively associated with Latinos' positive perceptions of African Ameri-cans. Understanding the underlying bases of perceived linked fate and commonalities with other groups can serve as the fulcrum for collective endeavors.

A question regarding education provides a second look at the possible areas of competition between Latinos and African Americans. The question asks, "Some have suggested that [Latino national-origin groups] are in competition with African Ameri-cans. . . . Would you tell me if you believe there is strong competition, weak competi-tion, or no competition at all with African Americans . . . having access to education and quality schools?" Table 11.13 shows even higher percentages of Latinos indicating an absence of serious competition between the two groups. Overall, slightly more than 70 percent of all Latinos saw no or weak competition. The native- and foreign-born Latinos (41.5 and 48.6 percent, respectively) say there is weak competition in the educational arena with African Americans. For the most part, the levels of perceived competition in a variety of arenas seem minimal. These results would suggest greater positive "forces" for Latinos and African Americans to consider coalitional efforts.

This discussion of possible political alliances explores potential collective collabo-rators within the Latino community and between Latinos and non-Latinos. The "in-tracoalitional" possibilities among the various national-origin groups have become more established over the past fifteen to twenty years. Indicators would include the growing pervasiveness of pan-ethnic identification, inter-Latino group contacts, and organizations that advocate for and represent broader-based Latino interests. At the same time, national-origin-based organizations still exist and are active on behalf of their respective communities. Mexican-origin, Dominican, Cuban, Puerto Rican, Sal-vadoran, and other communities have organizations focusing on salient issues. At times, a given Latino national-origin group confronts more specific issues; on other occasions, there is overlap with other Latino communities, and collaborative or um-brella Latino organizations become engaged. In the first edition of this book, I sug-gested that the future of Latino politics would involve Latino national-origin groups concentrating on their own group's needs and issues, with occasional joint efforts with other Latino national-origin groups. A second scenario involved a more sustained pan-

TABLE 11.13. Competition with African Americans Having Access to Education and Quality Schools by Generation and Citizenship

Response	Freq.	First Generation			Second+ Generation Citizens	Grand Total
		Noncitizens	Citizens	Total for the First Generation		
Strong competition	Freq.	1,098	562	1,660	789	2,449
	Row%	66.14	33.86	67.78	32.22	100.00
	Col%	28.01	28.17	28.06	29.02	28.36
Weak competition	Freq.	860	518	1,378	803	2,181
	Row%	62.41	37.59	63.18	36.82	100.00
	Col%	21.94	25.96	23.30	29.53	25.26
No competition at all	Freq.	1,962	915	2,877	1,127	4,004
	Row%	68.20	31.80	71.85	28.15	100.00
	Col%	50.05	45.86	48.64	41.45	46.37
Total	Freq.	3,920.00	1,995.00	5,915.00	2,719.00	8,634.00
	Row%	66.27	33.73	68.51	31.49	100.00
	Col%	100.00	100.00	100.00	100.00	100.00

Table Tests of Independence:
First and second+ generations: (3 d.f.) 43.175 (P = 0.000).
Citizen/noncitizen (first generation only): (3 d.f.) 11.830 (P = 0.140).

Note: Island-born Puerto Ricans are coded as first generation.
Question wording: "Some have suggested that Latinos or Hispanics are in competition with African Americans. After each of the next items, would you tell me if you believe there is strong competition, weak competition, or no competition at all with African Americans?"

ethnic politics whereby national Latino pan-ethnic organizations would advance Latino interests. In reality, the two scenarios can operate in concert. Thus, this chapter's focus on alliances can treat Latinos of different national-origin backgrounds as coming together for collective purposes.

My additional examination of intergroup alliances with the African American community is driven by the commonality of negative differential treatment (discrimination), which can serve as a bridge to join together for cooperative ventures. In essence, I have outlined a common minority status model affecting cooperative efforts. Given this preliminary examination and the works of Uhlaner (1991) and J. A. García (2000), the preconditions for successful alliances or coalitions would include each group's having independent bases of leadership, resources, and well-defined goals. Agreeing on a common target and well-defined objectives increases the possibilities for cooperative efforts. At the same time, the LNS items allowed me to see the extent of Latinos' perceived commonality with whites. While there were some marked differences, this added information reinforces the role of common interests in enabling Latinos to coalesce not only with other minority groups but with nonminorities. Clearly policy concerns and priorities are a real bridge for collective action.

In light of research literature on **political participation** and **mobilization**, the additional dimensions of political interest, group identity, gains in socioeconomic status (educational attainment, income levels, higher-status occupations), and assertive organizational direction and involvement provide the needed political capital and motivation to work collectively. Clearly more opportunities and challenges will present themselves or will be initiated by Latino and African American leadership and organizations, as well as other groups. Physical proximity, at times sharing common residential and commercial areas, can also increase interactions. At the same time, undercurrents of greater competition for limited political and economic gains highlight the zero-sum calculation that working together may incur unequal costs and benefits to one's own group. The politics of alliances depends on a number of situational conditions and circumstances, as well as having the political resources to act. All of this represents a major growth area for research, and Latinos are enjoying more cooperative and competitive possibilities in many more communities than a decade ago.

BOX 11.4. Vieques and Coalitional Partners

A news story by *Orlando Sentinel* reporters Jeff Kunerth and Sherri Owens (2001) provides a good example of the swinging pendulum between cooperation and competition. The involvement of Jesse Jackson and Al Sharpton in protests over the navy's continued use of Vieques, Puerto Rico, for bombing tests can be interpreted as African American leaders extending protest concerns into the Latino policy arena. And the Osceola County chapter of the **National Association for the Advancement of Colored People** (NAACP) has selected a Hispanic as its vice president. These moves are welcomed by Latino leaders like Raul Yzaguirre of the National Council of La Raza, who feels that broadening the scope of civil rights beyond a black/white paradigm renders the issues and the participants more diverse and inclusive. The reporters also comment that both the NAACP and the National Urban League have increased their efforts to recruit Hispanic members by addressing important issues to that community. Hugh Price, national president of the National Urban League, is quoted as saying, "There are major issues that confront our communities— education, discrimination, employment. . . . We will move forward faster if we coalesce." An Orange County chapter president also states that "reaching out to Hispanics [makes sense] because we have some of the same issues. If we do not form some kind of unity, neither one of us will get anywhere." As further evidence of joint efforts in Osceola County, where Latinos grew 292 percent in the 1990s, whites and Latinos now compose one-third of NAACP membership.

At the same time, segments of the African American community have concerns regarding Latinos. One worry is that significant Latino growth could weaken the political influence that blacks have worked to build. Decreasing percentages become a numbers game in which blacks could lose access to opportunities earned through the struggles of the civil rights movement. In addition, some feel that Latinos do not face the same level of discrimination as African Americans. Since the number of Latinos is based on the Spanish-origin question asked by the census and other government agencies, a different question deals with race. As mentioned before, a Latino can be of any race. As a result some African Americans (e.g., Patterson 2001) suggest that many Latinos consider themselves racially white, and some may not consider themselves a minority. Thus, the NAACP, National Urban League, and other primarily African American organizations should keep their civil rights efforts focused on the needs of their own community. The exchange works on both sides as some Latino activists interpret Jackson and Sharpton at Vieques as motivated by a desire for high-profile visibility. They criticize Jackson and Sharpton for their silence on the violence and death along the Mexican border. Finally, distinctions are drawn between different policy emphases. Immigration and bilingual education are major issues for Latinos, whereas the African American community does not assign them a high priority and may see immigration as a threat to jobs held by African American workers. Another contested arena for these groups is redistricting, as mentioned in chapter 10. Thus, both factors and forces exist (i.e., movement in both cooperative and conflicting or competitive directions), and this will likely remain the case for the near future. Our discussion of current or possible future partnerships is meant to identify and analyze some bases for either of these directions. In reality, both options and directions are viable and necessary as each community continues to build on its resource and organizational bases.

Conclusion: A Pan-ethnic Community and Broader Partnerships

In light of the examination of community building based on the LNS, what is the extent of a working community among Latinos? Community building and working together, as presented in this chapter, are based on common status (cultural, political, and minority) and positive affinities toward one another. The data suggest major solidification of a pan-ethnic community with more promise and some limited optimism. There is clear evidence that the Latino communities are both aware of one another and connected in a variety of ways (geographic proximity, common issues, organizational activities and leadership, and pan-ethnic identification). The maintenance of a sense of national-origin identity does not impede the acquisition of and attachment to a pan-ethnic identification as well. As a matter of fact, within the LNS battery on key identities, it is quite possible for a respondent to identify him- or herself as a Peruvian, a Latino/a, and an American. External events, social movements, and treatment by interest groups, politicians, and parties serve to coalesce Latinos as an identifiable and working community. In addition, the density of Latino–African American networks has increased, and lines of communication and mutual awareness are more evident.

The activities directed toward Latinos in the 2008 elections increased the value of building a more active Latino community and attracted the attention of the major political parties, the media, and leadership in the economic sectors of America. In addition, there was strong support among Latino voters for Barack Obama's bid for the presidency. Chapter 12 presents four scenarios about the future of Latino communities and the political system. It is clear that the Latino community is a dynamic force both within its own subcommunities and in the larger aggregation of a national Latino community. Dynamism within the Latino community involves the process of defining itself further (its cultural and group boundaries, interests, and organizational landscape) and establishing itself as a political participant whose goals, interests, and impact will become more identifiable in the greater realm of political and economic life in the United States. This can manifest itself at times as a unified pan-ethnic effort and at other times as independent efforts within each Latino subgroup. The process of coalition formation remains more one of strategic maneuvering and pragmatic considerations. Yet, identifying someone you are willing to work with is enhanced by familiarity, trust, and commonality.

Discussion Questions

1. When we discuss alliances or coalitions, intergroup relations is the primary focus. At the same time, the Latino community comprises over twenty national-origin groups. How do the concepts of community of interests, community of common cultures, linked fate, discrimination, and pan-ethnic identity come into play in the formation of intracommunity alliances?

2. Focusing on intracommunity alliances, discuss the experiences and interactions between the Latino foreign- and native-born segments in terms of collective behaviors.

3. Shared minority status would suggest that issues of empowerment, representation, access, and policy responsiveness can serve as a bridge to unite different minority groups. Discuss the positives and obstacles for Latinos in forming coalitions with other minority communities, especially the African American community.

4. Coalition formation is usually based on common interests and policy agendas. If this is the case, are there any limitations for Latinos to form alliances with whites (Anglos) as well as with, or in addition to, other minority communities?

CHAPTER 12

The Latino Community: Beyond Recognition Politics

Hicimos nuestra peregrinación y nos preguntamos—¿Dónde esta nuestra comunidad y cuales son los elementos más importantes que sostienen nuestra comunidad? La verdad es que somos muchas diferentes comunidades que a la vez nos desarrollamos hasta alcanzar otro nivel como comunidad. Tenemos que insistir en preguntarnos ¿Dónde está nuestra comunidad?

We have made our pilgrimage, and we have asked ourselves, Where is our community, and which are the most important elements that sustain it? The truth is that we are many different communities simultaneously evolving toward a higher level of community. We have to persist in asking ourselves, Where is our community?

I BEGAN THIS BOOK BY EXPLORING the nature and extent of the community that exists within the various Latino subcommunities in the United States. Using the concepts of **community of common cultures** and **community of interests**, I constructed guidelines and analytical narratives to explore what kind of "political shape" the Latino community was in. I focused on political resource development among Latinos, their organizations, leadership, and the responses of the U.S. political system. In addition to their stunning population growth, particularly over the past thirty-five years, are Latinos increasing their political capital? Are they making significant gains in education, income, and occupational status, in increased numbers of naturalized citizens and elected officials at all levels, and in operating more cohesive and effective organizations?

I have suggested that community building among the twenty-plus Latino national-origin groups can provide greater resources, visibility, and political-economic leverage in the American political system. At the same time, the costs and energy required to establish the degree of community necessary for the inclusion of all Latino subgroups remain a significant challenge. This concluding chapter will develop some possible and quite probable scenarios to characterize the politics of the Latino community as we move through the early part of this new millennium.

Basic Community Facts:
Continued Latino Growth and Diversity

Before relating these scenarios, I will establish key advances and developments that have already occurred within Latino communities and in the American political system. The first "fact" lies with Latinos' projected population growth. While much has been made of the rapid and continuous growth of the "largest minority," this pattern will be reinforced in the future. U.S. Census Bureau (2002) population decennial counts and future projections into midcentury continue to show the Latino growth rate exceeding that of all other populations. It is estimated that by 2050, Latinos will make up one-fourth of the U.S. population (in 2011, they constitute one-seventh). The other major development in this continued population growth is their geographic dispersion throughout all regions of the United States. In 1990, approximately 90 percent of all Latinos lived in ten states. According the 2009 American Community Survey, 78.7 percent of all Latinos are located in these same ten states. That is, areas of traditional concentration continue to grow, but new areas, primarily in the South, Northwest, and Midwest, have experience dramatic growth.

The influx of Latinos into less "traditional" areas is becoming more evident. For example, during a Christmas season Protestant service in suburban Portland, Oregon, a call went out to congregational members to give clothing, books, and other practical gifts to needy individuals. The organizer said that the first twenty-eight of the seventy-five households on the list were Spanish speaking. There was another call for persons who could speak Spanish to help deliver the gifts. Other indicators in Portland include Spanish-language signs posted throughout the Oregon Museum of Science and Industry, as well as Spanish signs and voice recordings on the MAX (the light-rail system).

A Latino transformation has occurred in Dalton, Georgia (in the northwestern part of the state), where Latinos have been migrating, mostly from Mexico, to the "carpet capital of the world." In fall 2000, Latinos constituted a majority (51.4 percent) of the students in the public schools in this town of twenty-three thousand (Roedemeier 2000). Across northern Georgia, an influx of mostly Latino immigrants is arriving to work in the poultry-processing plants and carpet mills. This scenario can be recounted in many other communities throughout the South, the Rocky Mountain states, America's heartland, New England, and the suburban Northeast.

Finally, there is the burgeoning growth of Central and South Americans within the Latino community. While persons of Mexican origin continue to maintain high growth rates (in terms of both birthrates and immigration), Latinos from the Dominican Republic, Colombia, El Salvador, Guatemala, and the like are growing faster and becoming more geographically important. Latinos from Central and South America have settled, for the most part, in areas where people of Mexican origin, Cubans, and Puerto Ricans are located. While contributing to the overall Latino growth, this pattern also represents a broader mix of Latino interests and potential resource building.

For example, Dominicans in New York in 1980 numbered 125,380, which had grown to 332,713 by 1990 and reached 1.05 million by 2004. Such growth represents policy interests and demands on the New York educational system, housing, employment, and basic city services. The growing Dominican community has created its own organizations and seeks to enhance its political and economic influence in the city overall and in relation to Puerto Ricans and other Latino communities.

Similarly, at a recent **redistricting** conference in Los Angeles (sponsored by the Southwest Voter Registration and Education Project), activists from the Los Angeles Salvadoran community attended and involved themselves in providing their perspectives and interests in the strategy sessions and proposing boundaries for legislative and congressional districts. For the future, the continual significant growth of Central and South American–origin Latinos will help shape the nature of Latino politics in terms of issues, leadership, and challenges for collective efforts and cooperation.

The expansion of Latinos into metropolitan areas and regions of the country where they have been less evident serves a couple of political and social purposes. First, the continuing growth (but more geographically varied settlement patterns) provides Latinos with an even greater national presence. Even though the public and political-economic institutions are aware of the Latino communities, in some regions, especially the South, Northwest, and upper Midwest, public awareness of and experience with Latinos had been virtually nonexistent. At the same time, the expansion of Latinos into more locales can produce positive and negative consequences. The above-mentioned Latino movement to Dalton, Georgia, has helped meet the demand for jobs and workers. The other side of this rapid transformation is intergroup tensions and anti-immigrant sentiments among "native" Georgians.

For example, in 1989 there were 3,131 non-Latino white students, constituting almost 80 percent of the student body, enrolled in Dalton schools. In the fall of 2000, there were only 1,893 white students, many having transferred to private schools (Roedemeier 2000). Some parents complained that their English-speaking children were ignored as teachers paid more attention to children learning the English language. One store's plywood sign condemns "uncontrollable immigration" and declares, "Congress sold us for cheap labor" (Roedemeier 2000). On the other hand, Dalton's carpet industry clearly supports the Latino immigrants. Dalton produces 40 percent of the world's carpet, and in a community where the unemployment rate had been less than 3 percent, carpet mills are worried about maintaining a reliable workforce.

Obviously, part of the future of Latino politics is the process of community building within the Latino community, as well as joining with existing community interests and institutions in more recently settled areas. Continued growth exceeding the national average and movement into areas populated with fewer Latinos are some of the basic facts characteristics of about the future profile of Latinos in the United States. They represent both challenges and opportunities for Latinos to establish their roots in the community and develop the resource base and interest to influence local policy makers and employers.

Latino Pan-ethnicity and Its Viability

The second basic "fact" that bears relevance to the future of Latino politics is the existence of a **pan-ethnic** community. I have questioned the existence and form of community that may exist among the various Latino subgroups in the United States. Examination reveals that a high level of pan-ethnic community does exist among Latinos. Organizations continue to represent and advocate on behalf of Latinos, and numerous newer organizations have been formed. They have organized around issues of civil and political rights and salient policy areas (immigration, language policies, etc.), as well as work-related groups and culture- and neighborhood-based interests. Political and economic elites have established networks and, at times, cooperative activities that cut across specific Latino subgroups (Cubans, Dominicans, Salvadorans, etc.).

The dispersion of Latinos across different regions of the country has brought more Latinos into contact where previously only one group predominated. For example, the Latino mix in the Miami metropolitan area has changed, and a majority of Latinos are now non-Cubans. While inter-Latino group interactions may vary by group and may be more competitive than cooperative in nature (vying for scarce public and private resources, political resources, etc.), the changed Latino landscape has created pressures and incentives to come together as a broader community. These developments in conjunction with the media's attention have continued to reinforce the expansion and activities of Latinos throughout the country. These developments serve to influence Latino community building. I have suggested that community can come together as a result of both internal efforts by Latinos themselves and how the "larger" society, its institutions and key elites, perceive and act in recognition of their presence.

A central question for Latinos in the area of pan-ethnicity is, Who is defining Latinos and the Latino community, and for what purpose does it exist? The development and advancement of organizations and leadership address Latino interests, obtaining public recognition and definition(s) of the **social construct of race** for Hispanic/Latino ethnicity and enhancing more extensive interactions and contact among different Latino subgroups that help construct a Latino community. Thus, the question about the existence of a Latino community is answered in the affirmative. The next stage of this development is the functioning of an effective Latino community with an impact on political, economic, and social matters at the various levels of government and the economy.

The Latino Vessel Has Arrived

The mid-1990s firmly established the real political capital of Latinos in American politics. Sound-bites about "invisibility," "a sleeping giant," and Latinos "soon to have their place in the sun" have been used for decades, especially in reference to the Mexican-origin population. Since the mid-1990s, the mass media, political and economic leaders, and activists and organizational leaders from the different Latino communities have sounded similar themes of potentiality and the conversion of a significant, growing population into a major political, economic, and cultural force. Since the mid-1990s, there has been greater evidence that the "Latino vessel has arrived" on the American political and social shores.

An example of the more visible political front is the rise of Latino elected officials at the state and federal levels. California serves as one of the better cases, with Cruz Bustamante as lieutenant governor and Richard Polanco as California Senate majority leader. Significant gains in the California State Legislature have marked a major breakthrough for Latinos in that state. California had the greater number and percentage of Latinos, primarily of Mexican origin, for a number of decades; yet, electoral representation was not manifested in similar proportions. California Latinos now hold 762 elective offices statewide, in bodies from city councils to the U.S. Congress (Verdin 2000). Latinos account for 20 percent of the 120 state senators and assemblypersons. In twenty-nine of the fifty-two congressional districts, the Latino population is one hundred thousand or more. In spring 2002, two Latinos (Linda Sanchez and Dennis

Cardoza) secured the Democratic Party nomination in the primaries. In each case, the majority of registrants in the candidate's district were Democrats. The political developments in California augment the advances made by Latinos in Texas and Florida. It is estimated that there were over six thousand Latino elected and appointed officials in 2010 (NALEO 2011).

The combination of factors—such as more widespread and effective voter-registration campaigns, the California initiatives (**Propositions 187, 227, 229, etc.**),[1] anti-immigrant legislation and initiatives and Latino responses, increased numbers of Latino candidates (Barreto 2010), the opportunity to compete for elective offices due to term limits, greater Latino organizational effectiveness and cooperation, more visible and active local community efforts (labor movements, service-delivery issues, police matters, etc.), and higher rates of naturalization—all contributed to the "real" results of Latino politics.

Over half a million more Latinos voted in the 1998 congressional election than in 1994, increasing their presence at the polls from 3.5 million to 4.1 million (Day and Gaither 2000b). The number of Latinos of voting age increased from 10.4 million to 12.4 million in 1998. These changes occurred at a time when other groups (whites, especially) were evidencing a decline in voter registration. Projections for 2010 and beyond indicate that states with the largest number of voting-age Latinos will be California (7 million), Texas (4 million), New York (1.8 million), and Florida (1.8 million) (Day and Gaither 2000a; Barreto 2010). Finally, of the 2008 electorate, 3.5 million new voters were added to registration rolls: 2.75 million more African American voters; 1.5 million more Latinos; half a million more Asian Americans; and 1.2 million fewer white voters. Turnout in twenty-six states for the 2008 elections indicated that Latino voter turnout was higher than in the 2004 elections, especially in Georgia, Florida, and North Carolina. Finally, minorities as a proportion of the electorate increased so that Latinos constitute 8.5 percent; African Americans, 12 percent; Asian Americans, 3 percent; and non-Hispanic whites, 74 percent.

More specifically, the figures in table 12.1 demonstrate the significant gains in the number of Latino eligible voters, which increased by 15 percent over a span of seven years. The gains among both naturalized voters and second-generation Latino citizens increased by 21.1 percent each. The latter group represents sons and daughters of Latino immigrants who may or may not have become naturalized citizens. It should be noted that for any category of eligible voters, the increase is in the double digits for a relatively short period of time (i.e., seven years).

Socioeconomic developments among Latinos have contributed to a more concrete reality and impact for Latinos. That is, part of the growing population represents a greater percentage of younger Latinos reaching eighteen years of age. The continuing growing percentage of Latinos attaining voting age and/or becoming naturalized citizens has reached a critical mass so that gains in numbers of voter registrants will be steeper than during the previous fifteen years. This development is also reflected in the increasing numbers of Latinos who are registered and their proportion of the electorate (Jamieson, Shinn, and Day 2002). Similarly, there are continuing incremental gains in education attainment and income growth among Latinos. The year 1992 marked the first time that over 50 percent of Latino adults over the age of twenty-five had achieved a high school diploma. By 1998, that group had increased to 57.5 percent. At the same time, the gap between Latinos and others remains around 20 to 25 percent.

TABLE 12.1. Hispanic Eligible Voters by Nativity, 2000 to 2007

	November 2000	November 2004	November 2006	September 2007	Percentage	Increase 2004 to September 2007 (%)
Total	13,940,000	16,088,000	17,315,000	18,165,000	100	2,077,000 (14.9)
Naturalized citizens	3,358,000	4,026,000	4,392,000	4,734,000	26	708,000 (21.1)
Native-born citizens	10,581,000	12,062,000	12,923,000	13,431,000	74	1,369,000 (12.9)
Second-generation citizens	3,722,000	4,163,000	4,704,000	4,949,000	27	785,000 (21.1)

The proportion of Latino households earning above $30,000 has grown by 70 percent over the past two decades.

Economically, the growth of Latino-owned firms and their gross revenues have quadrupled over the past decade. These serve as indicators of economic and educational progress. The Latino population in Chicago increased by 18 percent from 1980 to 1990, and it was expected to grow to almost 1 million by 2000. Statistics from Chicago city planners Russell and Russell (1989) show that Latinos make up a majority of five of Chicago's seventy-seven communities, and marketing research revealed that Latinos constitute a $9 billion consumer market. Similarly, there were 2.6 million Latinos living in the twenty-eight counties in and around New York City, with an estimated $18.9 billion in buying power for 1989 (Schlossberg 1989). Nevertheless, a relative gap persists between Latinos and other groups, especially nonminority America.

Socioeconomic improvement among Latinos reinforces the social capital accumulating among Latinos individually and collectively as a viable community. The results of the 2000 census also showed a growing middle class among Latinos. Over 2.5 million Latino households earned between $40,000 and $140,000. From 1979 to 1999, the Latino middle class grew by 71.2 percent (Pimentel 2002). These households have a total purchasing power of $278 billion annually. If Latino households earning over $140,000 are added, then the figure rises to $333 billion. With an expanding middle class, as well as a larger percentage of the population over eighteen years, the political resource base for the Latino community will continue to provide opportunities for empowerment. Preliminary results from the 2010 census indicate a continued middle-class trajectory of expansion.

Similar developments are evident in other parts of the country. The Cuban community continues to expand its political presence in Florida, especially southern Florida. Mayors and city council members in most southern Florida cities (Miami, Hialeah, Coral Gables, etc.), as well as administrators and public employees, are well represented by members of the Cuban community. Likewise, Cubans, both from southern Florida and other parts of the state (Tampa-St. Petersburg, etc.), serve in the state legislature. With the political redistricting in 2001, Cubans continued to expand their political representation at the local, state, and federal levels. In 2010, Marco Rubio was elected to the U.S. Senate from Florida.

In 2000, Latino candidates appeared on the ballot in states not commonly associated with Latino candidates (e.g., Kansas, Massachusetts, Michigan, Wisconsin), and some were elected. George W. Bush also continued the trend of selecting Latinos for cabinet-level positions (i.e., Alberto Gonzáles, formerly a Texas Supreme Court justice, as chief White House counsel, and Mel Martínez, formerly housing administrator of Orange County, Florida, to head the Department of Housing and Urban Development). The greater sustained attention received by Latinos during the 2000 and 2002 elections, both at the presidential and other levels, reinforced rising Latino political capital and raised expectations among Latinos about the impact they can have in terms of public policy and partisan politics.

A record eight Latino Republicans were elected to Congress in 2010, bringing total Latino representation on Capitol Hill to a near-record twenty-seven, according to the National Association of Latino Elected and Appointed Officials (NALEO). Five new Latino GOP representatives, all of whom ousted Democratic incumbent opponents, will join Florida senator Marco Rubio in Washington. Rubio will be only the second

Latino in the Senate next to Democrat Robert Menendez. "This was the year of the Hispanic Republican candidate," said Arturo Vargas, NALEO executive director, praising the results. "We need to have strong roots in both political parties because not one political party will always be in control. We need to have access to people on both sides of the aisle, people who understand our community."

In addition, the governors of New Mexico (Susana Martinez) and Nevada (Brian Sandoval) are the first two Latinos to hold a governorship simultaneously. Other developments occurring in communities throughout the United States include Latino subgroups such as Salvadorans, Colombians, Dominicans, Nicaraguans, and other Central and South Americans gaining elective office. These communities have active organizations and leaders who are exerting influence and shaping local policy agendas. A more politically and economically visible Latino community at several levels of the American system is a fact of Latino life and American politics.

Latino Politics and the New Millennium: Some Possible Scenarios

Community constitutes ongoing links between leaders and general Latino publics as well as interactions on a variety of issues (housing, work, organizational life, and public policy). At the same time, community does not require complete consensus and uniformity of thought. This discussion of Latinos and politics characterizes community as an interconnected and interacting set of members who share basic goals and visions and work together regularly to advance these objectives. This type of community is pragmatic and goal oriented rather than ideologically "pure."

Do significant gains in **political participation** and representation represent a short-term pattern for Latinos, or do they indicate a more active political and economic future? Here I develop three possible scenarios for the future of Latino politics.

Scenario 1: Continual Latino Political Development

Some major contributing factors in the contemporary political development of Latinos include (1) activation of a greater part of the Latino community in various forms of political involvement (local community involvement, organizational affiliation, political awareness, campaigning, voting, etc.); (2) external actions and developments that serve as catalysts for political involvement (anti-immigrant and **English-only initiatives,** concerns about cultural balkanization, attention from national political parties and leaders, etc.); (3) an increase of individual social capital among Latinos (gains in educational attainment and income, expanding adult populations and citizens, occupational mobility, etc.); (4) expanding organizational networks across Latino subgroup lines and collaborative efforts; and (5) heightened local political activities in communities throughout the United States.

This scenario portrays the future of Latino politics as one of continued progress in political capital and effectiveness. In order for this progress to occur, the intersection of leadership, organizations, and the Latino publics must be expanded and made more integrative and cooperative. This necessary ingredient is building on the momentum established in the late 1990s. Maintaining political involvement and communication in both directions—on the part of leaders and general Latino publics—serves to delineate more clearly the Latino policy agenda and its priorities. In addition, enhanced political development occurs when pursued on a continual basis. Earlier accounts of Latinos' limited impact on the political system were tied to their low political capital, limited experiences with political processes, and lack of broad-based, active support. Latinos are now located in the formal political institutions and operate in established organizational vehicles of advocacy and influence, and they constitute an expanding electorate.

This scenario includes specific areas on which Latino political development could build. One is the accelerated conversion of Latinos as political actors (toward their becoming more politically engaged). Organizational and local community efforts continue to encourage eligible Latino permanent resident aliens to naturalize. Such activities not only educate Latino immigrants and activate them to file for citizenship, but they also ensure the efficient and receptive workings of the Immigration and Naturalization Service (INS). There are now policy initiatives to separate the border-enforcement and -monitoring functions from the naturalization function of the INS. The recent increases in Latino immigrant naturalization may slow down due to the rising fees for filing for citizenship and additional protocols for acquiring green cards.

Latino organizations and leaders are faced with designing immigration related reform policies that not only serve the Latino "immigrant" community but enhance further Latino political development. Latino organizations need to work with and/or pressure the INS to shorten the time between filing for naturalization and final swearing in, as well as to maintain civil rights protections (due process for deportation hearings, access to higher education for undocumented students, workplace protection, etc.). In the case of the latter, more systematic prosecutions of apprehended undocumented immigrants has resulted in family separations, formal deportation hearings and sentencing, incarcerations, and more restrictive legislation affecting immigrants. As a result, the primacy of immigration reform has risen across virtually all segments of the Latino community.

While there is a tendency to portray politics in national terms, attention to local issues and politics is a critical element for greater Latino political development. Local issues such as housing, jobs, crime and law enforcement, social services, gentrification, schools and educational services, and access to decision makers are primary concerns and conditions that many Latinos face on a daily basis. By focusing on the most pertinent and visible issues, Latinos continue to expand political skills and accumulate experiences from which to learn for future political involvement. I have presented evidence indicating that "politics is local"; getting persons involved in matters affecting them daily affords the opportunity to interact, use skills, gain greater political awareness and knowledge, and accumulate valuable civic experiences. A good example of these developments again falls into the area of immigration. Many state and local governments have initiated ordinances and laws affecting undocumented immigrants in a variety of settings (i.e., employment, housing, health services, court standing, etc.); one effect has been the activation of a broad spectrum of the Latino community.

A second area of attention is the greater density of interactions across the multitude of Latino subgroups. How do Latinos of many different national origins interact and come together in a variety of social and economic situations? The regional concentration of Latino subgroups is becoming less rigidly defined; there is greater residential and labor market overlap (living and working in the same areas), which affords Latinos greater opportunities to establish a broader sense of community. Yet, increased interactions do not guarantee harmonious and cooperative ventures. In this sense, the role of leadership and framing of common issues and visions become important elements in this equation.

Earlier discussions of Latinos and politics in the first edition this book revolved largely around the Mexican-origin community, as well as Cubans and Puerto Ricans. As a contemporary portrayal of the changing Latino community indicates, the inclusion and involvement of Central and South Americans, as well as Dominicans, together form an integral part of the Latino political-development scenario. These other Latino subgroups are becoming more actively engaged in issues particular to their respective communities. In many respects, issues about immigration status and adjustment, basic services, employment training and opportunities, educational quality, and language assistance are quite similar to the issues of importance to Mexican-origin people, Puerto Ricans, and Cubans. While the relative proportion of the Mexican-origin community remains at slightly over three-fifths of all Latinos, the growth of Central and South Americans and Dominicans has been dramatic. Early results of the 2010 census indicate that both Salvadorans and Dominicans have or will exceed the population of Cubans.

Each Latino subgroup must develop its own political capital (political resources, organizations, leadership base, political knowledge, and experience with its own political and economic institutions). As it does so, issues, interests, and the utility of collaborative efforts with other Latino subgroups become clearer. An emphasis on lines of communication and mutual discussions across Latino subgroups can further collective political empowerment and political-economic agendas. There is evidence that such linkages in the 1990s and continuation of these developments will enhance Latino political development.

Another concrete example of lines of communication is the Congressional Hispanic Caucus (CHC). The CHC has been in operation for almost thirty years, and its membership has grown from five to over twenty members. While the majority of Latino congresspersons are of Mexican origin and Democratic, the number of Puerto Rican and Cuban members has grown. The CHC has not always experienced unanimity, especially on matters of U.S. policy regarding Cuba and the Castro regime. Currently, the two Republican Cuban members of the House do not officially belong to the CHC. The 2011 CHC faces the influx of seven Latino Republican congresspersons, and it remains to be seen whether the CHC will become a more bipartisan organization. Again, our themes of communities of interests and a pan-ethnic policy agenda can facilitate open lines of communication and collective efforts.

There is a history of shared concerns about social welfare policies, immigration and refugee adjustments, language-focused legislation, expanding Latino political influence, and numerous other issues. It would be less than realistic to expect complete consensus across all members of any caucus all of the time. Even if the CHC does not include all Latino members of Congress, continuing dialogue and interaction among this core set of political representatives can serve the continued political development of this working community. The CHC is expected to grow even larger in 2012, with the next round of redistricting configurations and more Latino elected officials.

The third area of further Latino political development is an extension of the first area. I have already discussed mobilizing more Latinos to become politically involved in their communities, better informed politically, and more experienced in civic affairs. Converting the significant population base into a more powerful political force was the earlier point. The third area focuses on expanding economic resources from which Latino political endeavors would benefit. Studies like the **Latino National Political Survey** (de la Garza et al. 1993) indicate that the percentage of Latinos contributing to political campaigns and/or organizations is small. Increasing Latino political capital also includes receiving a greater economic commitment from community members for Latino efforts and organizations.

The economic resources come from individuals and the business sector. Recent gains in Latino political and economic advancement, the persistence of salient issues, and economic mobility and growth among Latino professionals and entrepreneurs serve as identifiable sources of economic resources for the Latino community. Obviously the linkage of more Latinos assessing their needs, interests, and affinities with the activities of Latino organizations and groups is a necessary condition. While many may see this type of focus directed toward more nationally visible Latino-based organizations, the act of directing money toward a variety of efforts (charities, neighborhood activities, specific projects, local organizations, etc.) both benefits particular recipients and establishes further the need for and impact of greater economic resources derived from Latinos to address common concerns and issues.

Scenario 2: A Symbolic Pan-ethnic Community and Independent Actions

Our second scenario reaffirms the existence of some level of a pan-ethnic community among the various Latino subgroups. Community connotes identifying and associating with perceived similar persons, as well as maintaining a level of awareness and public recognition of Latinos as a social category. This level of community is now quite evident. A dynamic community would include regular and positive interactions and collaborative activities. Thus, our second scenario suggests that the Latino umbrella takes on a symbolic, ceremonial connection for public display. The advent of Latinos is the result, in part, of governmental policies that combined, or "merged," the various Latino subgroups into the larger grouping. The mass media, choosing to characterize persons and nationalities of Spanish origin under the general category of Latinos or Hispanics, also reinforces general awareness of a symbolic community. This scenario posits a limited basis for the idea of a Latino community, which confines its practicality as to the status of a more strategic sociopolitical movement. Therefore, the similarities or cultural connections that may exist among the various Latino subgroups are not sufficient to form a working community setting. Within this scenario, a key consideration is who Latinos/Hispanics are defined to be and how. A pan-ethnic Latino community is more likely to be symbolic if defining and framing what constitutes it is the product of outside institutions and other non-Latino sources.

On the other hand, an active pan-ethnic community can depend on the breadth of issues salient across most Latino national-origin subgroups. For example, regarding Cuba, the communist Castro regime, trade embargoes, expanding refugee admissions, and the like are much more salient for the Cuban community than the rest of the

Latino subgroups. In addition, political perspectives and policy preferences toward Cuba may be quite different for other Latino communities and their leadership. Legalizing the immigration status of Central Americans or recognizing political refugee status may be more salient among Salvadorans, Guatemalans, and Nicaraguans than among Puerto Rican or Mexican-origin communities. The political status of Puerto Rico (statehood, independence, commonwealth) or immediate closing of the Vieques site for bomb testing may be of greater concern for the Puerto Rican community. Similarly, the foci and perspectives of each Latino subgroup are either limited to their respective communities or occupy a lower priority for other Latinos. This scenario would reinforce the decision of each Latino subgroup to pursue its own interests, consistent with its own salient issues, through its own organizations and activities.

As Latino subgroups pursue their respective agendas, they may use "Latino" as the context for their politics, but the reference is limited to their own group. For example, Dominicans in New York City may be seeking redress for poor educational quality (poor facilities, lack of curricular offerings, need for bilingual programs, etc.) in their neighborhood schools. In their public actions and public discourse, especially with the media, Dominican leaders may refer to these specific problems or concerns as Latino ones. Doing so can afford other Latino subgroups the opportunity to support their efforts as well as to piggyback in addressing their specific issues to the same political institutions.

The other factor that may influence the preference and reality of each Latino subgroup's going its own way is the assessment that each is in competition with the others. Again referring to the Dominican community in the New York City area, Dominican political and economic issues and concerns are viewed as vying for recognition and policy responsiveness with those of Puerto Ricans, Colombians, and other Latino subgroups. Advancement can be viewed as a potential zero-sum game in which the political system pits one group against the other for limited resources. Thus, Latino politics become a competition among various subgroups for political recognition, policies, and rewards. Specific Latino groups that have accumulated political resources and positions will try to maintain their power, while the other Latino subgroups will see them as obstacles to their own progress.

Another example is inter-Latino tension in southern Florida between the Cuban community, several Central American groups (Panamanians, Nicaraguans, etc.), and Puerto Ricans. This competition centers, in part, on access, influence, and power in southern Florida. Competition over economic policies that affect non-Cuban Latinos and concerns over political representation and access may be directed toward the Cuban political leadership and organizations.

The competitive nature of relations among Latino subgroups tends to accentuate intergroup differences rather than commonalties. As a result, maintaining any competitive advantage restricts cooperative and collaborative ventures. Within this scenario, a broader representation of Latino politics can be advanced, despite the competitive tensions, by each Latino subgroup portraying a more public depiction of cooperativeness and some unity, while dealing directly with differences in private forums. The analogy of keeping family matters and disparities *en la casa* and wearing a different public face outside the home describes this scenario of Latino politics. Thus, this scenario requires an adjustment by looking at Latino communities as a confederation of overlapping interests; under certain conditions, the communities may come together.

Scenario 3: A Latino Community with One or More Outliers

This third scenario represents a limited community membership in which some Latino subgroups engage in collaborative and cooperative activities or regular joint dealings. The latter form of Latino political community would mean broad-based organizations that are inclusive (in terms of constituencies, staffing, and agenda) of the various Latino subgroups. Thus, our theme of communities of common interests and cultures brings together most of the Latino subgroups to function as a political community, and it implies that Latino subgroups or coalitions may join forces outside the Latino communities.

The outlier component of this scenario suggests that one or more Latino subgroups will pursue its own agenda rather than negotiate or compromise with other Latino subgroups on its public policy agenda (be it in force or proposed) and identify its own issue priorities. In addition, each Latino subgroup sees its political resources, base, and previous effectiveness as sufficient to continue on its own path. Intragroup solidarity, established lines of political and economic communication and influence, clarity of political objectives, and relative unanimity among its leaders are factors that may encourage an outlier to operate in the American political system without active membership in the broader Latino community.

Based on earlier remarks about the different Latino subgroups and their organizations and political objectives, one example could be the Cuban community. For example, its long-standing, defined, and active involvement in shaping U.S. foreign policy regarding Castro's Cuba remains a central core of the Cuban policy agenda. Both the primacy of this issue and post-2005 different policy orientations (normalizing relations, removing the trade embargo, adjusting Cuban refugee admission) on the part of other Latino activists and politicians have contributed to Cubans' distancing themselves (policywise) from the larger Latino community. The extended political battle over Elian González[2] and the fervency and sustained effort within the Cuban community were not mirrored to the same degree among other Latino communities and leaders. The amount of expended political capital and mass media portrayal of the Cuban community served, in part, to accentuate policy divergence and tensions between Cubans and other Latinos. A possible mediating force within the Cuban community is the growing segment of native-born (second-generation) Cubans whose political preferences and foci could differ noticeably from those of their parents' generation.

Another item on the list of situations and patterns that may work with an outlier model for Cubans is their close ties, not shared by most other Latino subgroups, to the Republican Party. This relatively long-standing pattern heightens intergroup competitiveness as the Republican Party seeks to make greater inroads with other Latinos and to highlight differences in policy preferences. The regional concentration of Cubans (almost 90 percent live in Florida, especially southern Florida) makes them a political base with greater socioeconomic status and resources than other Latinos. Their strong group politicization operates as an independent basis of action and encourages them to follow their own path. Contributing strongly to the outlier strategy or position are the following: the political development of Cubans in the United States, the strength of their organizations, their relative success in penetrating political institutions, their economic resources and entrepreneurial activities, and their commitment to a clear agenda. More recently, the election of Marco Rubio to the U.S. Senate from Florida attracted the

Tea Party endorsement and support. Yet, given the Tea Party platform and policy positions, whether the relationship will be ongoing is unclear. Similar ties have been evident among Latino evangelicals and politically conservative action groups. In essence I am raising the possibility of other connections or working alliances among some Latinos with others outside the Latino community. Whether other Latino subgroups can pursue this scenario with similar results is not clear at this time.

A question that can arise from this scenario is, Does a Latino subgroup operate as an outlier for an indefinite period? Even if the outlier scenario continues, there are symbolic and public perceptions of linkages between Cubans and other Latino communities. In addition, this scenario does not preclude interaction, dialogue, and joint support between the outlier and the rest of the Latino community. For example, on matters of economic-development initiatives, sampling adjustments for Census 2000, affirmative action, benefits and services to immigrants, language policies, and voting rights (National Council of La Raza 1999), Cuban members of the U.S. House of Representatives voted in accord with the other Latino representatives. Therefore, this scenario lays out an independent direction and control of the agenda, strategies, and priorities within a specific Latino subgroup.

The Latino subgroup would not necessarily function in isolation. Other Latino subgroups might move in the same direction if good working relations do not exist within the broader Latino community or if their agendas and priorities do not receive adequate attention and support. An assessment of group resources and strengths may indicate that pursuing an independent path might be an effective approach. This last scenario shows how the concept of community can organize itself so that some semblance of community exists while functioning more meaningfully within the various subcommunities.

Conclusion: Latinos, Community, and Politics— a Dynamic Process

In this book the concept of community is developed as a series of interacting links among persons of Spanish origin and their experiences in the United States as a basis for the formation of a political community. The concepts of community of common cultures and community of interests have served as the organizing theme for the discussion of Latinos and their involvement in American politics. Given the diversity of national origins captured by the general description of Latinos or Hispanics, an immediate challenge lies in portraying and integrating important characteristics and experiences among twenty-plus national-origin groups. Demographic profiles, historical developments and experiences, and issue concerns provide some evidence of Latino community dynamics. Clearly the political development of Latino subgroups and Latinos as a broader community has evolved and will continue to so do.

Political actors, institutions, and parties, the mass media, public opinion, and the general social climate recognize that Latinos are not only altering the demographic landscape but also affecting political processes, agendas, and decision-making institutions. The theme of potentiality and promise, which has characterized discussions of Latinos for generations, has moved dramatically beyond speculation since the mid-1990s. I have tried to discuss those developments, as well as the issues and challenges that still confront greater Latino political effectiveness and more widespread political involvement.

Future analysis, interpretation, and discussion of Latinos and their politics and impact must be placed within a dynamic context. The internal forces of Latino activists, their ideas and perspectives, and their strategy assessments will affect the development and continued shaping of Latino politics and intergroup dialogues, along with the external climate and actions taken by political institutions, actors, and interest groups. Continued attention to improving intergroup communication and cooperation is part of future Latino political development. Further expansion of political resources (active participants, financial resources, positive participatory orientations, organizational infrastructures and resources) serves to enhance the growing political capital of Latinos and define their direction and purpose. Our examination of Latino politics has (1) a historical context, and (2) a dynamic nature. The second point deals with an evolving sense of community and how it can work in the American political system. In a very real sense, the ongoing discussion of these developments and important contributors precludes any formal ending to this book.

The whole area of intergroup relations outside the Latino community will play an even greater role as Latinos have reached partnership status to warrant other political communities' considering working collaborations more seriously. An additional evolving element is the role of partisanship and the major political parties. That is, both parties are seemingly more engaged in integrating Latinos into the core of their organizations and decision-making structures. For Democrats, maintaining their competitive advantage is a primary factor, while for Republicans, the potential of attracting a growing community works to diversity and expand their party's base. For Latino political aspirants, pathways to elected office may be greater given the political parties' climate and knowledge that a Latino base can be supportive of Latino candidates that address this community's interests, with party affiliation being less critical. The relevance and intrigue of Latino politics lie with its dynamic nature and the many paths toward greater empowerment and influence in the American political system.

Discussion Questions

1. I have suggested that Latinos' political capital and influence in American politics are still on an upward trajectory. Yet, promise and potential have been long-standing themes in Latino politics. What concrete indicators and developments would support this positive assessment of Latino political development?

2. While three scenarios have been presented to project the future of Latino politics, can other scenarios be developed and substantiated?

3. An ongoing issue for Latinos is how they will participate in partisan politics. Despite a long-standing preference for the Democratic Party, some have argued that the returns for such loyalty have been quite limited. What would you suggest as effective partisan strategies for Latinos?

4. Demographically, one could characterize the Latino community as more diverse (in terms of size and number of national-origin groups, especially Central and South Americans); the proportion that is of Mexican origin, however, continues to dominate the Latino landscape. How does the mix of Latino subgroups affect the political development of the overall Latino community?

Notes

Chapter 1

1. The concepts of race and ethnicity warrant additional clarification. The census recognizes five racial categories: white, black, American Indian/Alaska Native, Asian/Pacific Islander, and other. The last category, "other," represents persons who identify themselves racially in ways that differ from the other four categories. In the case of ethnicity, ancestry, or country forms the basis on which origin is categorized. Persons who identify themselves as of Spanish origin are asked a follow-up question seeking their particular ancestral group (i.e., Mexican, Cuban, Puerto Rican, Central/South American, or other [to be specified]). In essence, ethnicity in the census is limited to "Spanish origin."

2. By "mass interactions," I mean inter-Latino interactions at the grassroots level. What is the extent of contact between persons of specific Latino subgroup origin with other Latinos? These interactions could be social, familial, employment based, or related to any one of a variety of social interactions within the local community.

3. Pan-ethnicity refers to a sense of group affinity and identification that transcends one's own national-origin group. A pan-ethnic identity does not necessarily replace national-origin affinity, but it includes a broader configuration in defining the group. The labels "Latino" and "Hispanic" encompass several national origins.

4. The grandfather clause requires a potential registrant to show that his grandfather was a registered voter before he can register to vote. For African Americans, the grandfather clause hearkened back to the period of slavery, when blacks had no rights, much less voting rights.

Chapter 2

1. The terms *Hispanic* and *Latino* are used interchangeably to indicate persons from Mexico, Central America, South America, the Spanish Caribbean, and the Iberian Peninsula living in the United States. I prefer to use *Latino* as a pan-ethnic term, while recognizing the extensive use of *Hispanic* by the mass media, public officials, and the public.

2. The U.S. decennial census is an attempt to enumerate all persons living in the United States on April 1 in the first year of each decade. The short form includes basic information such as number of persons in the household, as well as their ages, races, genders, and relationships to each other. The short form is distributed to all households. The long form is sent randomly to one in six households and asks for much more detail (labor market, migration, ancestry, language use, etc.).

3. Racial categories in the census include the following: white, black, Asian/Pacific Islander, American Indian/Alaska Native, and other. For the 2000 census, race included the same categories but separated Asian populations from the Pacific Islanders, making five racial categories. Also, individuals were instructed to mark all applicable racial categories.

4. The creation of cross-national groups into a more singular ethnic group happened not only for Latinos but also for Asian Americans, Arab Americans, and American Indians. The basis for group aggregation is perceived cultural similarities, which are usually couched in cultural, linguistic, and religious terms.

5. The Latino National Survey (LNS) contains 8,634 completed interviews (unweighted) of self-identified Latino/Hispanic residents of the United States. Interviewing began on November 17, 2005, and continued through August 4, 2006. The survey instrument contained approximately 165 distinct items ranging from demographic descriptions to political attitudes and policy preferences, as well as a variety of social indicators and experiences. All interviewers were bilingual, speaking English and Spanish. Respondents were greeted in both languages and immediately offered the opportunity to interview in either language. Interviewers also provided a consent script that allowed respondents to opt out of the survey. Demographic variables include age, ancestry, birthplace, education level, ethnicity, marital status, military service, number of people in the household, number of children under the age of eighteen living in the household, political party affiliation, political ideology, religiosity, religious preference, race, and sex.

6. Only Latinos who indicated having a religious affiliation answered this question.

7. This example does not suggest that our hypothetical Guatemalan would see himself in only national-origin terms. An individual could incorporate gender roles, work roles, or familial identities as well.

Chapter 3

1. In terms of U.S. policy, "refugee" refers to political status and official designation—a person who is fleeing a totalitarian regime, experiencing political persecution and a threat to life. Seeking political asylum in the United States is a formal process. The State Department is primarily responsible for determining which regimes are totalitarian. This has been a particular point of contention, especially for Central Americans, whose countries have experienced significant political turmoil and violence.

2. In this context, the idea of critical mass would suggest that Latinos now comprise a major community of presence and possibly have the political and economic impact to influence their state's decision-making process.

3. The items from the census used to determine English-language proficiency are a self-reported three-item sequence. The first question asks the person if he or she speaks a language other than English. The person who answers affirmatively is then asked what that other language is. Finally, the respondent is asked how well (or not) he or she speaks English.

4. In 1997, the percentage of foreign-born persons in the U.S. population reached a record high since record levels in the early 1900s.

5. One of the requisites in petitioning to be admitted into the United States is having a sponsor. The two primary bases for admission are family reunification or needed job skills. In the case of family reunification, there are preferential categories among the different types of family members, and U.S. citizens have higher priority as sponsors than permanent resident aliens do.

6. It has been documented that the traditional American workforce is aging, and the newest and most expansive segments of the workforce are women and minorities. Given the youthfulness of Latinos, they should continue to increase their proportion of the workforce, as well as contribute significantly to the Social Security system.

7. The idea of educational isolation refers to students who attend racially and/or ethnically segregated schools, with lower-quality school facilities and less qualified instructional staff, as well as poorer educational outcomes (higher dropout rates, less high school completion, more disciplinary actions, lower standardized test scores, etc.).

8. This point illustrates the demand structure that can result with a critical mass of culturally similar persons, so that ethnic enterprises will cater to Latino customers and serve as potential employees. In addition, the mass media (print, radio, television), especially Spanish-language outlets, serve to highlight and inform the public about Latinos, as well as help to establish Latinos' economic impact as consumers.

Chapter 4

1. This latter point has been an area of some discussion and debate regarding the lower levels of Mexican American political participation. Close attachment to Mexico and the supportive system of political involvement in that country seem to suppress political involvement and interest in the American political system.

2. The term *pan-ethnic* refers to a socially constructed group identity that extends beyond traditional national-origin groupings like Irish, Mexican, Panamanian, and so on. The pan-ethnic movements represent an "umbrella" cluster of similar but distinctive group members. The labels "American Indian," "Asian American," and "Latino" serve as good examples of pan-ethnicity.

3. This legislation, also strongly pursued by Senator Jesse Helms, would allow lawsuits in U.S. courts against traffickers who seize property belonging to Cubans living in the United States.

4. Eighteen percent of Latinos live in the Los Angeles standard consolidated area alone.

5. I use the "youngest" descriptor to indicate the relatively recent Central and South American migration and residency in the United States. The majority of these Latinos arrived during the 1970s and later.

6. Joaquín Balaguer was president of the Dominican Republic on three different occasions: 1960 to 1962, 1966 to 1978, and 1986 to 1996. He held posts under the dictator Rafaél Trujillo, serving as vice president just prior to Trujillo's demise. He was ousted by the military in 1962 and returned in 1965 at the time of the U.S. military intervention. He won the presidency in 1966 and again in 1970 and 1974. His election in 1994 was so marred by fraud that opposition protests and international pressures forced Balaguer to agree to resign after an abbreviated two-year term.

7. A basic tenet of this book is that examination and discussion of Latinos consists of their own group interests and infrastructure providing the basis for connections with other Latino subgroups. This dynamic makes it quite possible to advance one's own specific group interest and/or the interests of the broader Latino community.

Chapter 5

1. Although I do not elaborate on gender consciousness and its ideological aspects related to pan-ethnicity here, chapter 3 on political community for Latinos discusses and analyzes its impact.

Chapter 6

1. The principle of "the rules of the game" entails the requisites for political involvement (by a citizen or permanent resident alien), including knowledge of the political system, regis-

tered status, knowledge of access points to the political system, information about procedures and decision making, and so on.

2. The specific nonpolitical job skills asked about in the Verba, Scholzman, and Brady (1995) study are as follows: writing a letter, attending a meeting and participating in making a decision, planning or chairing a meeting, and giving a presentation or speech.

3. The organizational skills items used in the Verba, Scholzman, and Brady (1995) survey include the following: serving as an officer of a club or organization, serving on a committee for a local organization, making a speech, and attending a public meeting on local or school affairs.

4. The components of the additive participation scale are as follows: voting in the 1988 national election; working as a volunteer for a candidate running for office; making a contribution to an individual candidate, party, or political action group; contacting governmental officials; taking part in a protest, march, or demonstration; working informally with others in the community to deal with some community issue or problem; serving in a voluntary capacity on any local governmental board or council; and being a member of, or giving money to, a political organization.

5. The Latino National Political Survey (LNPS) was designed as a national probability survey of persons of Mexican, Puerto Rican, and Cuban origin residing in the United States. These three groups represent the three largest Latino subgroups (approximately four-fifths of all Latinos). The sample design ensures a higher selection ratio for Cubans and Puerto Ricans to acquire greater numbers of respondents for intergroup comparisons and analysis. The LNPS was conducted in 1989 and 1990, and a total of 2,814 Latinos participated in face-to-face interviews.

6. Foreign-born persons living in the United States can be permanent resident aliens, can hold a temporary visa as a student or businessperson, or can be undocumented. The latter category includes individuals who come into this country illegally without formally petitioning the Immigration and Naturalization Service. Other terms are used to describe this segment of the population. Some wish to label the "undocumented" in more pejorative terms. For this reason, I place the term *illegal alien* in quotation marks.

7. The nine states with the most Latinos are California, Texas, New York, Florida, New Jersey, Arizona, New Mexico, Illinois, and Massachusetts (in descending order of population size).

8. The following propositions were state initiatives to enact policy in areas that directly impacted Latinos and made them the subject of targeted blame and/or perpetrators of the problem area. Proposition 187 would limit access to social services (medical, welfare) and public education to undocumented populations in California. Proposition 207 would remove state affirmative action provisions for employment and higher education in California. Finally, Proposition 209 would end bilingual programs as currently constituted in California and create transitional immersion programs for a one-year period.

Chapter 7

1. I use the term *arenas of participation* to identify electoral activities, in addition to organizational, protest, and individualized involvement at various levels of government and impacting the policy-making process.

2. By "absolute gain" I am referring to positive increases among Latino voters and registrants from the previous election period. By "relative gain" I am assessing the Latino gains in voting and registration relative to non-Latino populations. For example, if the Latino voter-turnout rate in 1996 was 45 percent and non-Latino rate was 60 percent, how much did it change in the subsequent election year? A concrete relative gain would exist if Latino turnout was 48 percent and non-Latino turnout was 59 percent. In this example, Latinos closed the gap from 15 percent to 11 percent over the two election periods.

3. States have primary responsibility for election laws and regulations within the protections of the U.S. Constitution. Some states, such as Georgia, Kentucky, Alaska, and Hawaii, gave

eighteen-, nineteen-, and twenty-year-olds the right to vote prior to the passage of the Twenty-fifth Amendment.

4. The concept of human capital is found in the economics literature. The idea is that as strongly motivated individuals invest in their human resource "portfolio" by obtaining more education, greater degrees of training, and more experience, they become poised to reap greater returns in the job market via earnings. The acquisition of greater human resources is advantageous for economic returns. Human capital also can be thought of as political capital in that those individuals with greater skills, knowledge, and interest in the political process can act more effectively.

5. The specification of which racial, national-origin, or linguistic groups are covered by the Civil Rights and Voting Rights acts constitutes a clarification and delineation of constitutionally protected rights for members of certain groups.

6. In this case, I am referring to the manner in which elected officials are selected within a political jurisdiction. District systems tend to be geographically drawn (ward), at-large, or a combination of the two. Thus, an at-large district configuration allows all voters within the jurisdiction to elect all of the representatives, whereas a ward system enables voters within the geographic district only to elect their own representative. In a mixed-mode system, some representatives are elected in a ward configuration whereas other officials in the same body are elected at-large.

7. Following the U.S. Constitution, after each decennial census, state representation in Congress has to be reapportioned according to population changes. This process has been further clarified in a cluster of court rulings regarding "one person, one vote," equal-sized districts, compactness, and contiguity. Once reapportioned, each state (usually its legislature) is responsible for drawing up districts (federal, state, and local) within constitutional guidelines. In this process, racial and ethnic "representativeness" has been a factor in the design of districts.

8. The concept of racial gerrymandering involves critical consideration of the racial and ethnic makeup of a political district in delineating geographical boundaries. In this context, more concentrated inclusion of racial/ethnic groups increases their proportion of the district's makeup.

9. This concept tries to take advantage of areas in which Latinos have experienced significant growth but do not constitute a majority. Thus, in a district that is 25 to 40 percent Latino, it becomes possible to create a "district of influence." Latinos are a sizable enough population in these kinds of districts that representatives would find it difficult to ignore them.

Chapter 8

1. I am referring to the expansion of Latino-oriented social science research since the mid-1960s that has examined prevailing notions about Latinos. Much of the earlier research focused on the Mexican-origin experience. One of the dominant notions was the absence of organizational history and experience among Chicanos. As a result, earlier research on Chicano organizations was directed toward demythologizing an absence of organizational experiences. Subsequently, additional research identified a wider range of Latino organizations, as well as their strategies, accomplishments and impact, organizational structure, leadership base and styles, and adaptability.

2. The Alianza Hispano Americano existed until the mid-1960s. Then issues of impropriety by its president and misuse of federal funds intended for employment-related programs resulted in its demise. The Chicano Research Collection at the Arizona State University Libraries holds many of the papers, newsletters, ledgers, and correspondence of the Alianza.

3. Jorge Mas Canosa founded the Cuban American National Foundation and served as its president beginning in 1981. When he died in late 1997, his son assumed leadership of the organization.

4. There are eighteen SIGs that focus on such topics as special education, early-childhood education, higher education, research and evaluation, and so on. All members can select any of the SIGs with another member of the National Association of Bilingual Educators serving as the chair.

5. See www.ushcc.com/index.cfm?fuseaction=Page.viewPage&pageId=477&parentID=472.

6. See www.lclaa.org/index.php/History/lclaa-history.html.

7. See www.chci.org/about.

8. The three Hispanic Republican congressional representatives are Henry Bonilla (TX), Ileana Ros-Lehtinen (FL), and Lincoln Diaz-Balart (FL).

9. "Who Is NALEO Inc.?" www.naleo.org/aboutnaleo.html.

10. The congressional oversight committee and the Republican congressional leadership felt that including a sampling component as part of Census 2000 would provide partisan advantage to the Democrats, as the previously undercounted minorities and lower-income groups would be larger with the adjusted totals. Eventually, the sampling component was challenged in two federal district courts and then reviewed by the U.S. Supreme Court. The Court held that, for purposes of reapportionment, results from a "full enumeration" would be the sole basis for this decennial census. At that time, the Court did not address directly the use of adjusted population totals (via integration of sampling results) for purposes of federal allocation of funds or redistricting.

Chapter 9

1. The U.S. Supreme Court reasoned that the principle of the identity of the husband and wife was a reasonable requirement in making foreign policy. The Cable Act of 1922 repealed automatic loss of female citizenship but did not include females who married alien men ineligible for citizenship. They continued to lose their citizenship upon marriage until 1931, when Congress repealed the 1907 law.

2. A green card is a form of identification administered by the Immigration and Naturalization Service that certifies an individual as a legal permanent resident alien (PRA) in the United States. Originally, the green card was the vehicle for identification, and bearers had to register annually to maintain their legal residence. PRAs can be required to produce their green cards at any time. Even though the identification is no longer a physical green card, it is still referred to as such.

3. "Transfer of payments" refers to immigrants sending part of their earnings back to family and relatives in their country of origin. It has been argued that such remittances represent an imbalance of money flow, as earnings derived in the United States are not "fed" back into the economy but are sent to fuel a foreign economy.

4. INS estimates are constructed by combining detailed statistics by year of entry for each component of change that contributes to the undocumented population residing in the United States. The undocumented usually enter the country through temporary visas and then stay beyond the specified period of admission. Approximately 40 percent of the undocumented are nonimmigrant overstays. The remainder crosses the border between ports of entry. Thus, there are five primary sets of data: (1) net entered before 1982; (2) net overstays from 1982 to present; (3) net entered without inspection; (4) mortality estimates of annual deaths among the resident undocumented population; and (5) emigration: number of undocumented immigrants who emigrated to the United States in the following four-year period.

5. In 1998, the Unz initiative, or Proposition 227, would eliminate bilingual education in California schools (K–12) within a year of its passage. Then, limited-proficiency or non-English-speaking students would be placed in a language-immersion program for a year. I discussed this proposition and its politics in the previous section of this chapter.

Chapter 10

1. Particular counties and towns are covered by special provisions in Connecticut, California, Colorado, Florida, Hawaii, Idaho, Massachusetts, Michigan, New Hampshire, New York, North Carolina, South Dakota, and Wyoming.

2. The language in section 2 included the following: "(a) no voting qualification or prerequisite for voting or standard, practice or procedure shall be imposed or applied by any State in a manner which results in a denial or abridgement of the right of any citizen . . . to vote on account of race or color, or in contravention of the guarantees set forth in section 1973b(f)(2) of this title, as provided in subsection (b) of this section; and (b) a violation of subsection (a) of this section is established if, based on the totality of circumstances, it is shown that the political processes are not equally open to participation by members of a class of citizens protected by subsection (a) . . . in that its members have less opportunity than other members of the electorate to participate in the political process and to elect representatives of their choice."

3. The plaintiffs challenged that the at-large election system in the city and county of Mobile, Alabama, served as a major obstacle for African American candidates and, subsequently, denied the local African American community opportunities to win elected office. Racial voter polarization, high campaign costs, and racialized campaigning were associated with this election system.

4. For example, the U.S. House of Representatives includes 435 congresspersons. If Latinos comprised about 11 percent of the population, then descriptive representation would constitute approximately forty-five representatives.

5. The test's lack of grounding lay in the absence of established criteria. For example, if two districts are drawn on similarly race-based principles, how does the court determine the injurious effect of either plan by virtue of its snakelike design? How does the court conclude any differential racial impact?

Chapter 11

1. The feeling thermometer is constructed so that the respondent is asked to indicate his or her feelings about a group or country based on a zero to one-hundred-degree thermometer. Thus, the one-hundred-degree marking represents the most positive feeling, and a zero-degree rating is the lowest.

Chapter 12

1. Propositions 187, 227, and 229 were referendums in California in the mid-1990s that proposed restricting immigrants' access to educational, medical, and social services, rescinding state affirmative action programs in education and employment, and replacing bilingual educational programs with one-year English-language-immersion programs.

2. Elian González was a six-year-old Cuban émigré whose mother and her significant other attempted to cross the Caribbean Sea in the spring of 2000. They took Elian with them. Both adults died at sea, and young Elian was rescued by the Coast Guard and taken to a hospital in Miami. Subsequently, an uncle in Miami sought to secure asylum for him, which began a major national debate and political incident, involving the Cuban government, Fidel Castro, the INS, the Department of Justice, the Cuban community and leadership, and eventually the Office of the President. Through a protracted legal battle, and despite rulings by the INS and the federal courts for the return of Elian González to his father in Cuba, the Cuban family, supported by the Cuban community, refused to surrender him to the authorities. Eventually an early morning INS "raid" secured Elian from the Miami relatives, and ultimately he was reunited with his father.

Glossary

287(g) program, one of ICE's top partnership initiatives, allows state and local law enforcement entities to enter into a partnership with ICE, under a joint memorandum of agreement. The state or local entity receives delegated authority for immigration enforcement within its jurisdiction.

Alternative voting systems are options that differ from the conventional plurality (winner-takes-all) or majority system used in American elections. They range from cumulative voting to limited voting, single transferable votes, and proportional voting schemes.

Antiterrorism and Effective Death Penalty Act of 1996 (ATEDPA) greatly facilitated procedures for the removal of "alien terrorists" and authorized state and local enforcement officials to arrest and detain certain undocumented persons and to provide access to confidential INS files through court order.

Arizona Senate Bill (SB) 1070, or the Support Our Law Enforcement and Safe Neighborhoods Act, is a broad and strict anti–illegal immigration measure adopted in Arizona. U.S. federal law requires certain aliens to register with the U.S. government and to keep registration documents in their possession at all times. SB 1070 makes it a state misdemeanor for an alien to be in Arizona without carrying the required documents, bars state and local officials and agencies from restricting enforcement of federal immigration laws, and penalizes those who shelter, hire, or transport "illegal aliens."

At-large election system is a process whereby candidates do not run or get elected from a specific part of the community but compete city- or countywide.

Border Patrol was not established until 1924, and in 1933 the Bureaus of Immigration and Naturalization were merged into the INS, whose primary mission is to detect and prevent the smuggling and unlawful entry of undocumented aliens into the United States and to apprehend individuals in violation of U.S. immigration laws.

Community of common or similar cultures exists when individuals are linked closely by their participation in a common system of meaning with concomitant patterns of customary interactions of culture (language, customs, art, etc.).

Community of interests refers to the conditions, statuses, and experiences that Latinos share with members of other Latino subgroups.

Cumulative voting systems enable voters to distribute their votes (they have one for each position available) in whatever manner they desire. For example, if three offices are to be decided, voters can cast their votes in any combination (all three votes to one candidate, two for one and one for another, etc.).

De facto segregated schools are those that, due to residential segregation and school-attendance zones, are highly segregated by race, ethnicity, and class.

Department of Homeland Security (DHS) oversees efforts to counter terrorism and enhance security, secure and manage our borders while facilitating trade and travel, enforce and administer our immigration laws, safeguard and secure cyber-space, build resilience to disasters, and provide essential support for national and economic security in coordination with federal, state, local, international, and private-sector partners.

Descriptive representation refers to the population's racial and ethnic makeup and the characteristics of political representatives. The population percentages of racial and ethnic groups mirror the background characteristics of their elected officials.

Development, Relief, and Education for Alien Minors Act (DREAM) is a legislative proposal introduced in the Senate on August 1, 2001, and reintroduced there and in the House on March 26, 2009. As yet unpassed, this bill provides conditional permanent residency to certain illegal and deportable alien students who are of good moral character, have graduated from U.S. high schools, arrived in the United States illegally as minors, and have been in the country continuously for at least five years prior to the bill's enactment. If they complete two years in the military or at a four-year institution of higher learning, they will obtain temporary residency for a six-year period. Within that period, a qualified student must have "acquired a degree from an institution of higher education in the United States or [have] completed at least 2 years, in good standing, in a program for a bachelor's degree or higher degree in the U.S." or have "served in the armed services for at least 2 years and, if discharged, [have] received an honorable discharge."

Discrimination-plus model characterizes coalition formation as influenced by minor-ity-group members' common experiences, issue priorities, and values, which make them receptive to joint political activities and collective efforts.

Enforcement Act of 1870 specifically prohibited denial of the right to vote in state and local elections.

English-only initiatives establish English as the official language of a state and require that all official business and activities be conducted only in English. Similar efforts have focused on the U.S. Congress for national legislation.

Ethnic identification is a cognitive process of seeing one's social identity defined in ethnic terms. The person undergoes a process by which she feels a sense of com-monality of association with other members of her ethnic group.

Ethnic identity is a set of self-ideas about one's ethnic group membership, which includes knowledge, feelings, and preferences about one's ethnicity. It includes a sense of self as a member of an ethnic group.

Ethnicity can be defined as a collectivity within the larger society having a real or puta-tive common ancestry, memories of a shared historical past, and a cultural focus on one or more symbolic elements defined as the epitome of peoplehood. Also, ethnicity is seen as a web of sentiments, beliefs, worldviews, and practices that individuals hold in common.

Force Act of 1871 gave federal-court-appointed supervisors the power to oversee registration and election processes when two citizens make that request. Later in the 1800s, Congress repealed the Enforcement and Force acts, and protective-voting-rights legislation was virtually nonexistent until the 1950s.

Hotel and Restaurant Employees Union (HERE) is a U.S. labor union, formed in 1891, representing workers in the hospitality industry. In 2004, HERE merged with the Union of Needletrades and Industrial and Textile Employees (UNITE) to form UNITE HERE. Major employers contracted with this union include several large casinos and hotel chains. UNITE HERE was affiliated with the AFL-CIO until September 2005, when UNITE HERE voted to leave the AFL-CIO and join the Change to Win coalition.

Human capital concept is found in the economics literature. As individuals motivated to obtain more education, greater degrees of training, and more experience invest in their human resource "portfolio," they are poised to reap greater returns in the job market via earnings. The idea is that acquiring greater human resources produces economic returns. Human capital can also be thought of as political capital: individuals with greater skills, knowledge, and interest in the political process can act more effectively.

Illegal Immigration Reform and Immigrant Responsibility Act of 1996 (IIRIRA) had stipulations to bolster the monitoring of the U.S. border and set up measures to remove criminal and other deportable aliens. In addition, this law provided increased protection for legal workers through work-site enforcement.

Immigration and Customs Enforcement (ICE) is the principal investigative arm of the U.S. Department of Homeland Security and the second-largest investigative agency in the federal government. Created in 2003 through a merger of the investigative and interior enforcement elements of the U.S. Customs Service and the Immigration and Naturalization Service, ICE now has more than twenty thousand employees in offices in all fifty states and forty-eight foreign countries.

Immigration Reform and Control Act of 1986 (IRCA) was a major reform bill that sought multiple policy goals. It attempted to restrict legal immigration by establishing more fixed annual admission ceilings; increasing border enforcement and staffing to interrupt the flow of undocumented migration; establishing criteria for an amnesty program for residing undocumented persons (agricultural workers and other workers/families); sanctioning employers and monitoring the hiring of undocumented workers; and requiring proof of legal status for employment.

Impact or influence districts represent areas in which the Latino community (the principle can be applied to other minority groups or defined interests) constitutes a significant portion of the population and electorate. Usually a population threshold of 30 percent is viewed as a sizable demographic presence to which officials are responsive.

Latino National Political Survey, conducted from 1989 to 1990, is the first national probability survey of adults of Mexican, Cuban, and Puerto Rican origin. It focuses on political attitudes and behavior, group identity, policy preferences, and other aspects of political life.

Latino National Survey is a probability survey conducted from 2005 to 2006 of 8,634 Latino adults in fifteen states and metropolitan Washington, DC. It covers subjects such as political and civic engagement, identity, transnationalism, public policy preferences, demographic characteristics, attitudes, partisanship, and voting.

Limited voting is a system in which the voter has fewer votes than the total number of positions up for election. For example, if three seats are to be decided, the voter has only one or two votes to cast. No uniform practice determines the number of votes allowed, other than there must be at least one fewer than the number of elected positions being contested.

Majority-minority districts are political jurisdictions in which residents are primarily minority (over 50 percent of the population).

Mobilization is the process by which political candidates, political parties, activists, and groups try to induce other people to participate and get involved. Participation involves three key ingredients: resources, psychological orientations, and recruitment.

National Association of Bilingual Educators (NABE) is a professional organization at the national level wholly devoted to representing both the interests of language-minority students and the bilingual education professionals who serve them.

National Association for the Advancement of Colored People (NAACP) strives to ensure the political, educational, social, and economic equality of rights of all persons and to eliminate race-based discrimination. The NAACP's vision is the creation of a society in which all individuals have equal rights without discrimination based on race.

National Origins Act of 1924 set a ceiling on the number of immigrants admitted annually. A formula was based on 2 percent of the national-origin group registered in the 1890 census. The implementation of the act heavily favored natives of northern and western Europe. Japanese persons and citizens of the Asiatic zone were excluded.

National Survey of Black Americans (NSBA) was a national probability study of 2,107 self-identified black Americans eighteen years of age and older interviewed in 1979 and 1980. These respondents were recontacted in eight-, nine- and twelve-year intervals, forming four waves of interviews. NSBA provided the basis on which social scientists could address social, political, and economic factors in African American life.

No Child Left Behind Act of 2001 (NCLB) is an act of Congress concerning the education of children in public schools. Passed during the administration of George W. Bush, it was guided through the Senate by Senator Ted Kennedy and received strong bipartisan support. President Bush signed it into law on January 8, 2002. NCLB includes standards-based education reform, setting high standards and establishing measurable goals that can improve individual outcomes in education. The act requires states hoping to receive federal funding for schools to develop assessments in basic skills to be given to all students in certain grades.

Organization of Los Angeles Workers (OLAW) promotes workers rights. It worked diligently for the mayoral campaign of Antonio Villaraigosa. The Service Employees International Union and the Hotel and Restaurant Employees Union were an integral part of OLAW and political-mobilization activities in the city. OLAW was able to recruit over six hundred canvassers and distribute over eighty thousand registration cards and forms.

Pan-ethnicity refers to a sense of group affinity and identification that transcends one's own national-origin group. Thus, a pan-ethnic identity does not necessarily replace one's national-origin affinity but encompasses a broader configuration to define the group: for instance, the terms *Latino* and *Hispanic* include several national origins. Pan-ethnicity can also apply to a sociopolitical collectivity made up of people of several different national origins.

Personal Responsibility and Work Opportunity Reconciliation Act of 1996 (PRWORA) restricted the eligibility of legal immigrants for means-tested public assistance, widened prohibitions on public benefits for undocumented immigrants, and mandated the INS to verify immigration status before immigrants could receive public benefits. Immigrant sponsorship required the sponsor to assume financial responsibility for an immigrant who was unable to sustain himself. The PRWORA made the affidavit of support legally binding.

Political incorporation focuses on how persons learn about and involve themselves with the American political system. It generally focuses on newcomers to the political system (young persons assuming adult status or immigrants) and "marginalized" populations such as minority-group members. For our purposes, political incorporation is the process by which group interests are represented in the policy-making process.

Political participation involves the process of influencing the distribution of social goods and values. The critical factors for involvement are resources, time, opportunities, beliefs, values, ideology, and participatory political attitudes. In addition, participation is affected by organizations, leaders, and political parties, which strategically choose to activate specific individuals and/or groups.

Power relations focus on political resources, agenda setting, organizational development, leadership and mobilization, authority, influence, and legitimacy. Power is distributed among individuals and groups in society, and power relationships deal with the use of power and interactions between groups and individuals.

Preclearance involves the voting rights section of the Justice Department, which reviews proposed election changes (affecting election dates, poll locations, election materials, annexations, etc.) in covered jurisdictions in order to assess their impact on minority-group representation and possible voter dilution. A change may not result in minority-voter dilution or negatively impact the equal protection provisions for all citizens. The voting rights division clears or rejects any proposed changes.

President's Advisory Commission on Educational Excellence for Hispanic Americans produced a report titled *Our Nation on the Fault Line*. President Bill Clinton created this presidential commission to examine the state of Hispanics and the educational system.

Proposition 187, or the Save Our State Proposition, was passed by the California electorate in 1994. This new law barred undocumented immigrants from public education as well as other social services provided by the state (welfare and health care).

Proposition 227, officially titled the English-Language Initiative for Immigrant Children (Unz initiative), was designed to eliminate bilingual education programs. Limited-English-proficiency children would take a one-year English-immersion program and then be mainstreamed into the regular English-language curriculum.

Redistricting is a decennial process by which political jurisdictions reconfigure their electoral districts to meet standards of equal size, compactness, and contiguity and to maintain communities of interest. The redistricting plan can be implemented by the state legislature, a local governmental body, the courts, or an independent redistricting commission.

Safe districts are generally those in which the incumbent and her party are firmly entrenched in an elected office. Thus, a safe district can be secure for a particular political party, member of a racial/ethnic group, and/or current incumbent.

Service Employees International Union (SEIU) is a labor union representing about 1.8 million workers in over one hundred occupations in the United States, Canada, and Puerto Rico. SEIU has focused on organizing workers in three sectors: health care (including hospital, home-care, and nursing home workers); public services (local and state government employees); and property services (including janitors, security officers, and food-service workers).

Single-member districts are specific areas of a city or county in which voters nominate and elect their representatives.

Social construct of race usually refers to a group of persons who define themselves as distinct due to perceived common physical characteristics. The sense or categorization of race is the result of self-identification, institutional definitions of racial categories, and organized segments that develop or construct ideas about and elements of racial membership.

Structural factors have to do with the rules of the game and how political institutions function, especially focusing on access, individual or group legal standing, rights and protections, and the formal requirements for participation.

Targeted mobilization involves the identification of persons who, when contacted, are more likely to respond to calls for involvement.

Thornburg v. Gingles (106 S. Ct. 2752 [1986]) is a Supreme Court ruling upholding the constitutionality of creating majority-minority districts when minority voting strength has been submerged in multimember districts with white majorities. The courts recognized a state's compelling interest in rectifying a pattern of exclusion. The remedy of majority-minority districts is appropriate when racially polarized voting has minimized or canceled out the potential for minority voters to elect candidates of their choice from their own community.

Voting Rights Act of 1965 (VRA) was a major policy initiative addressing long-standing practices that had served to exclude African Americans and other minorities from the electoral process, including annual registration systems, literacy tests, hostile election poll locations, economic and physical intimidation of minority-group members, and limited registration locations and hours. Consequently, suspension of literacy tests, use of federal monitors, review of election-related changes, the right for local persons or groups to mount legal challenges, and standards for voter dilution were key elements of the legislation.

White House Initiative on Education Excellence for Hispanics, originally launched by President George H. W. Bush, has been expanded by President Barack Obama to improve educational opportunities for Hispanic students at every level. The order includes an enhanced interagency working group and a thirty-member presidential advisory commission.

References

Acuña, Rodolfo. 1976. *Occupied America: A History of Chicanos.* 2nd ed. New York: Harper & Row.

———. 1981. *Occupied America: A History of Chicanos.* 3rd ed. New York: Harper & Row.

———. 1988. *Occupied America: A History of Chicanos.* 4th ed. New York: Harper & Row.

———. 1996. *Anything but Mexican: Chicanos in Contemporary Los Angeles.* New York: Verso.

———. 1998. *Sometimes There Is No Other Side: Chicanos and the Myth of Equality.* Notre Dame, IN: University of Notre Dame Press.

Adams, Greg D. 1996. "Legislative Effects of Single-Member vs. Multi-Member Districts." *American Journal of Political Science* 40 (February): 129–44.

Alinsky, Saul. 1971. *Rules for Radicals: A Practical Primer for Realistic Radicals.* New York: Vintage.

Allsup, Carl. 1982. *The American GI Forum: Origins and Evolution.* Austin: University of Texas Press.

Almond, Gabriel, and Sidney Verba. 1963. *The Civic Culture.* Princeton, NJ: Princeton University Press.

Alvarez-López, Luis, S. Baver, J. Weisman, R. Hernandez, and N. Lopez. 1997. *Dominican Studies: Resources and Research Questions.* New York: Dominican Research Monographs, City University of New York Dominican Studies Institute.

Arce, Carlos. 1982. "A Reconsideration of Chicano Culture and Identification." *Daedalus* 110, no. 2: 177–91.

Armbruster, Ralph, K. Geron, and Edna Bonacich. 1995. "The Assault on California Immigrants: The Politics of Proposition 187." *International Journal of Urban and Regional Research* 19 (December): 655–64.

Astin, Alexander. 1982. *Minorities in Higher Education.* San Francisco: Jossey-Bass.

———. 1985. *Achieving Academic Excellence.* San Francisco: Jossey-Bass.

Barrera, Mario. 1979. *Race and Class in the Southwest: A Theory of Race and Class Inequality.* Notre Dame, IN: University of Notre Dame Press.

———. 1988. *Beyond Aztlan: Ethnic Autonomy in Comparative Perspectives.* New York: Praeger.

Barrera, Mario, Charles Ornelas, and Carlos Muñoz. 1972. "The Barrio As an Internal Colony." In *People and Politics in Urban Society,* edited by H. Hahn, 465–98. Los Angeles: Sage.

Barreto, Matt. 2003. "National Origin (Mis)Identification among Latinos in the 2000 Census: The Growth of the 'Other Hispanic or Latino' Category." *Harvard Journal of Hispanic Policy* 15 (June): 39–63.

———. 2007. "Sí Se Puede! Latino Candidates and the Mobilization of Latino Voters." *American Political Science Review* 101 (August): 425–41.

———. 2010. *Ethnic Cues: The Role of Shared Ethnicity in Latino Political Participation.* Ann Arbor: University of Michigan Press.

Barreto, Matt, Sylvia Manzano, Ricardo Ramírez, and Kathy Rim. 2009. "Immigrant Social Movement Participation: Understanding Involvement in the 2006 Immigration Protest Rallies." *Urban Affairs Review* 44, no. 5: 736–64.

Barreto, Matt, and José Muñoz. 2003. "Reexamining the 'Politics of In-Between': Political Participation among Mexican Immigrants in the United States." *Hispanic Journal of Behavioral Sciences* 25 (November): 427–47.

Barreto, Matt, Gary M. Segura, and Nathan D. Woods. 2004. "The Mobilizing Effect of Majority Minority Districts on Latino Turnout." *American Political Science Review* 98:65–75.

Barreto, Matt A., Ricardo Ramírez, and Nathan D. Woods. 2005. "Are Naturalized Voters Driving the California Latino Electorate? Measuring the Effect of IRCA Citizens on Latino Voting." *Social Science Quarterly* 86, no. 4 (December): 792–811.

Barvosa, Edwina. 1999. "Multiple Identities and Coalition Building: How Identity Differences within Us Enable Radical Alliances among Us." *Contemporary Justice Review* 2, no. 2: 111–26.

———. 2008. *Wealth of Selves: Multiple Identities, Mestiza Consciousness, and the Subject of Politics.* College Station: Texas A&M University Press.

Bass, Loretta, and Lynne Casper. 1999. *Are There Differences in Registration and Voting Behavior between Naturalized and Native-Born Americans?* Population Division Working Paper 28. Washington, DC: U.S. Census Bureau.

Bean, Frank, and Marta Tienda. 1987. *The Hispanic Population of the United States.* New York: Russell Sage Foundation.

Benitez, Christina. 2007. *Latinization: How Latino Culture Is Transforming the United States.* Ithaca, NY: Paramount Market Publishing.

Bernal, Martha, and Phylis Martinelli, eds. 1993. *Mexican American Identity.* Encino, CA: Floricanto.

Bonilla, Frank, and Rebecca Morales. 1998. *Borderless Borders: Latinos, Latin Americans, and Paradox of Interdependence.* Philadelphia: Temple University Press.

Booth, William. 1996. "In a Rush: New Citizens Register Their Political Interest As Mexican Immigrants Become Naturalized." *Washington Post,* September 26.

Borjas, George. 2001. *Heaven's Door: Immigration Policy and the American Economy.* Princeton, NJ: Princeton University Press.

Boswell, Thomas. 1994. *A Demographic Profile of Cuban Americans.* Miami: Cuban American National Planning Council.

Boswell, Thomas, and J. R. Curtis. 1984. *The Cuban American Experience: Culture, Images, and Perspectives.* Totowa, NJ: Rowman & Allanheld.

Brady, Henry, Sidney Verba, and Kay Scholzman. 1995. "Beyond SES: A Resource Model of Political Participation." *American Political Science Review* 89 (June): 271–94.

Briegal, Kaye. 1970. "The Development of Mexican American Organizations." In *Mexican Americans: An Awakening Minority,* edited by Manuel Servin, 160–78. Beverly Hills, CA: Glencoe.

———. 1974. "Alianza Hispano Americano and Some Civil Rights Cases in the 1950s." In *Mexican Americans: An Awakening Minority,* edited by Manuel Servin, 174–87. 2nd ed. Beverly Hills, CA: Glencoe.

Brischetto, Robert, and R. de la Garza. 1983. *The Mexican American Electorate: Political Participation and Ideology.* Austin: Center for Mexican American Studies, University of Texas.

———. 1985. *The Mexican American Electorate: Political Opinions and Behavior across Cultures in San Antonio.* Austin: Center for Mexican American Studies, University of Texas.

Brischetto, Robert, and R. Engstrom. 1997. "Cumulative Voting and Latino Representation: Exit Surveys in Fifteen Texas Communities." *Social Science Quarterly* 78, no. 4: 973–1000.

Broder, David. 2001. "Awakening of the Latino Community Will Change the Political Map." *Washington Post*, May 23.

Browning, Rufus, D. Marshall, and D. Tabb. 1984. *Protest Is Not Enough: The Struggle of Blacks and Hispanics for Equality in Urban Politics.* Berkeley: University of California Press.

———. 1990. *Racial Politics in American Cities.* New York: Longman.

Cain, Bruce, and R. Kiewiet. 1992. *Minorities in California.* New York: Seaver Foundation.

Cano, Gustavo. 2008. "Political Mobilization of Latino Immigrants in American Cities and the U.S. Immigration Debate." Paper delivered at the 2008 Annual Meeting of the American Political Science Association, August 28–31.

Carmichael, Stokely, and Charles Hamilton. 1967. *Black Power: Politics of Liberation in America.* New York: Vintage.

Carter, Thomas, and Roberto Segura. 1979. *Mexican Americans in School: A Decade of Change.* New York: College Entrance Examination Board.

Casper, Lynne, and Loretta Bass. 1998. *Voting and Registration in the Election of 1996.* Current Population Reports P20-523RV. Washington, DC: U.S. Census Bureau.

Chapa, Jorge. 1995. "Mexican American Class Structure and Political Participation." *New England Journal of Public Policy* 11, no. 1 (Fall).

Cornell, Stephen. 1985. "The Variable Ties That Bind: Context and Governance in Ethnic Processes." *Ethnic and Racial Studies* 13:368–88.

———. 1988. *The Return of the Native.* New York: Oxford University Press.

Cornell, Stephen, and Douglas Hartman. 1998. *Ethnicity and Race: Making Identities in a Changing World.* Thousand Oaks, CA: Pine Forge.

Cortés, Ernesto. 1996. "What about Organizing?" *Boston Review* 21, no. 6.

Cottrell, Charles. 1986. "Introduction: Assessing the Effects of the U.S. Voting Rights Act." *Publius* 16, no. 4: 5–17.

Cowan, Gloria, Livier Martinez, and Stephanie Mendiola. 1997. "Predictors of Attitudes toward Illegal Immigrants." *Hispanic Journal of Behavioral Sciences* 19, no. 4: 403–17.

Crawford, James. 1992a. *Hold Your Tongue: Bilingualism and the Politics of "English Only."* Menlo Park, CA: Addison-Wesley.

———. 1992b. *Language Loyalties: A Sourcebook on the Official English Controversy.* Chicago: University of Chicago Press.

———. 2000. *At War with Diversity: U.S. Language Policy in an Age of Anxiety.* Buffalo, NY: Multilingual Matters.

Croucher, Sheila. 1997. *Imagining Miami: Ethnic Politics in a Postmodern World.* Charlottesville, VA: University of Virginia Press.

Cruz, Jose. 1998. *Identity and Power: Puerto Rican Politics and Challenges of Ethnicity.* Philadelphia: Temple University Press.

Cruz, Vanessa. 2010. "Tucking in the Sleeping Giant: Political Socialization As It Relates to the Incorporation and Family Dynamics of Latino Families." Paper presented at the annual meeting of the Midwest Political Science Association, Chicago, Illinois.

Cuello, José. 1996. *Latinos and Hispanics: A Primer on Terminology.* Detroit, MI: Wayne State University Press.

Davis, Jessica W., and Kurt J. Bauman. 2008. *School Enrollment in the United States: 2006* Current Population Reports P20-559. Washington, DC: U.S. Bureau of the Census.

Dawson, Michael. 1994. *Behind the Mule: Race and Class in African American Politics.* Princeton, NJ: Princeton University Press.

Dawson, Michael, Ronald Brown, and James S. Jackson. 1993. National Black Politics Study [computer file]. ICPSR02018-v2. Ann Arbor, MI: Inter-university Consortium for Political and Social Research [distributor], 2008-12-03. doi:10.3886/ICPSR02018.

Day, Jennifer. 1998. *Hispanic Population Shows Gains in Educational Attainment.* Census Bureau Reports CB98-107. Washington, DC: U.S. Census Bureau.

Day, Jennifer, and Avalaura Gaither. 2000a. "California, Texas, and Florida Will Show Biggest Increases in Voting Age Populations in November, 2000." Census Bureau Reports CB00-125. Washington, DC: U.S. Census Bureau.

———. 2000b. *Voting and Registration in the Election of November 1998.* Current Population Reports P20-523RV. Washington, DC: Department of Commerce.

De la Garza, Rodolfo, and L. DeSipio. 1992. *From Rhetoric to Reality: Latino Politics in the 1988 Elections.* Boulder, CO: Westview.

———. 1993. "Save the Baby, Change the Bath Water, Get a New Tub: Latino Electoral Participation after Seventeen Years of Voting Rights Coverage." *University of Texas Law Review* 71:1029–42.

———. 1996. *Ethnic Ironies: Latino Politics in the 1992 Elections.* Boulder, CO: Westview.

De la Garza, Rodolfo, L. DeSipio, F. C. García, J. A. García, and A. Falcón. 1993. *Latino Voices: Mexican, Puerto Rican, and Cuban Perspectives on American Politics.* Boulder, CO: Westview.

De la Garza, Rodolfo, A. Falcón, and F. Chris García. 1996. "Will the Real Americans Please Stand Up: A Comparison of Anglo and Mexican American Support for Core American Values." *American Journal of Political Science* 40, no. 2: 335–51.

De la Garza, Rodolfo, A. Falcón, F. C. García, and J. A. García. 1994. "Mexican Immigrants, Mexican Americans, and American Political Culture." In *Immigration and Ethnicity: The Integration of America's Newest Arrivals*, edited by B. Edmondston and J. Passel, 227–50. Washington, DC: Urban Institute Press.

De la Garza, Rodolfo Z., Anthony Kruszewski, and Tomas Arciniega, eds. 1973. *Chicanos and Native Americans: The Territorial Minorities.* Englewood Cliffs, NJ: Prentice Hall.

De la Garza, Rodolfo, M. Menchaca, and L. DeSipio. 1994. *Barrio Ballots: Latino Politics in the 1992 Elections.* Boulder, CO: Westview.

De la Garza, Rodolfo Z., and David Vaughn. 1984. "The Political Socialization of Chicano Elites: A Generational Approach." *Social Science Quarterly* 65:290–307.

Del Olmo, Frank. 1998. "Giant Is Awake and Is a Force in California: Latino Voters' Pivotal Role in the Elections Puts All Politicians on Notice." *Los Angeles Times,* June 7.

———. 2001. "Bush Is Reaching Out to Latinos beyond the Beltway." *Los Angeles Times,* April 22.

Denton, Nancy, and Douglas Massey. 1988. "Residential Segregation of Blacks, Hispanics, and Asian Americans by Socioeconomic Status and Generation." *Social Science Quarterly* 69: 797–817.

———. 1989. "Racial Identity among Caribbean Hispanics: The Effects of Double Minority Status on Residential Segregation." *American Sociological Review* 54, no. 5: 790–809.

DeSipio, Louis. 1996. *Counting the Latino Vote: Latinos As a New Electorate.* Charlottesville, VA: University of Virginia Press.

DeSipio, Louis, and Rodolfo de la Garza. 1998. *Making Americans and Remaking Americans: Immigration and Immigrant Policy.* Boulder, CO: Westview.

———. 2002. "Forever Seen As New: Latino Participation in American Elections." In *Latinos: Remaking America*, edited by Marcelo M. Suárez-Orozco and Mariela M. Páez, 398–409. Berkeley: University of California Press.

DeSipio, Louis, and Carole Jean Uhlaner. 2007. "Immigrant and Native: Mexican American 2004 Presidential Vote Choice across Immigrant Generations." *American Politics Research* 35, no. 2 (March): 176–201.

Díaz-Briquets, Sergio. 1990. "The Central American Demographic Situation: Trends and Implications." In *Mexican and Central American Population in U.S. Immigration Policy*, edited by Frank Bean, J. Schmandt, and S. Weintraub. Austin: University of Texas Press.

DiBranco, Alex. 2010. "DHS Analysis Finds That 287(g) Program Is a Big, Fat Flop." ImmigrationChange.org, April 7. http://immigration.change.org/blog/view/dhs_analysis_finds_that_287g_program_is_a_big_fat_flop.

Duran, Richard. 1983. *Hispanics' Education and Background: Predictors of College Achievement.* New York: College Entrance Examination Board.

Dye, Thomas R. 1992. *Understanding Public Policy.* 7th ed. Englewood Cliffs, NJ: Prentice Hall.

Elliston, Jon. 1995. "The Myth of the Miami Monolith." *NACLA Report on the Americas* 29, no. 2: 40–42.

Engstrom, Richard. 1992. "Modified Multi-seat Election Systems As Remedies for Minority Vote Dilution." *Stetson Law Review* 21:743–70.

———. 1994. "The Voting Rights Act: Disenfranchisement, Dilution, and Alternative Election Systems." *PS: Political Science and Politics* 27, no. 4: 685–88.

Engstrom, Richard, D. Taebel, and R. Cole. 1997. "Cumulative Voting As a Remedy for Minority Vote Dilution: The Case of Alamogordo, New Mexico." *Journal of Law and Politics* 5: 469–97.

Esman, Milton. 1985. "Two Dimensions of Ethnic Politics: A Defense of Homeland and Immigrant Rights." *Ethnic and Racial Studies* 8:438–50.

———. 1995. *Ethnic Politics.* Ithaca, NY: Cornell University Press.

Espenshade, Thomas, and S. Ramakrishnan. 2001. "Immigrant Incorporation and Political Participation." *International Migration Review* 35, no. 3.

Espiritu, Yen Lee. 1992. *Asian American Pan Ethnicity: Bonding Institutions and Identities.* Philadelphia: Temple University Press.

———. 1996. "Colonial Expression, Labour Importation, and Group Formation: Filipinos in the United States." *Ethnic and Racial Studies* 19:28–48.

———. 1997. *Asian American Women and Men: Labor, Laws, and Love.* Thousand Oaks, CA: Sage.

Eviatar, Daphne. 2009. "Immigration Program Expands, Despite Abuse Record." *Washington Independent,* July 23. http://washingtonindependent.com/52197/immigrationprogram-expands-despite-abuse-record.

Falcón, Angelo. 1988. "Black and Latino Politics in New York City." In *Latinos and the Political System,* edited by F. C. García. Notre Dame, IN: University of Notre Dame Press.

———. 1992. "Time to Rethink the Voting Rights Act." *Social Policy* (Fall–Winter): 17–23.

———. 1995. "Puerto Ricans and the Politics of Racial Identity." In *Racial and Ethnic Identity: Psychological Development and Creative Expression,* edited by Ezra Griffith, Howard Blue, and Herbert Harris, 193–207. New York: Routledge & Kegan Paul.

Falcón, Angelo, and J. Santiago, eds. 1993. *Race, Ethnicity, and Redistricting in New York City: The Garner Report and Its Critics.* IPR Policy Forums Proceedings. New York: Institute for Puerto Rican Policy.

Farley, Reynolds. 1996. *The New American Reality: Who We Are, How We Got There, Where We Are Going.* New York: Sage.

Feagin, Joseph, and Clarice Feagin. 1996. *Race and Ethnic Relations.* 5th ed. Englewood Cliffs, NJ: Prentice Hall.

Fernández, Edward. 1985. "Persons of Spanish Origin in the United States." March 1982, Series P-20, no. 396. Washington DC: U.S. Government Printing Office.

Fernández, Maria Elena. 1999. "Prop. 187 Backers Pushing New Initiatives." *Los Angeles Times,* December 3.

Figueroa, Hector. 1996. "The Growing Force of Latino Labor." *NACLA Report on the Americas* 30 (November–December): 19–24.

File, Tim, and Sarah Crisey. 2010. *Voting and Registration in the Election of 2008.* Current Population Reports P20-562. Washington DC: U.S. Census Bureau.

Fitzgerald, Joseph. 1971. *Puerto Rican Americans: The Meaning of Migration to the Mainland.* Englewood Cliffs, NJ: Prentice Hall.

Fitzpatrick, P., and L. T. Parker. 1981. "Hispanic Americans in the Eastern U.S." *Annals of the American Academy of Political and Social Sciences* 454:98–110.

Fix, Janet. 2001. "The Changing Face of Unions." *Detroit Free Press,* April 30.

Foley, Douglas. 1988. *From Peones to Politicos: Class and Ethnicity in a South Texas Town.* Austin: University of Texas Press.

Foley, Elise. 2010. "Kyl Pushes for Expansion of Operation Streamline." *Washington Independent,* July 23. http://washingtonindependent.com/92374/kyl-pushes-for-expansion-of-operation-streamline.

Fox, Geoffrey. 1997. *Hispanic Nation: Culture, Politics, and Construction of Identity.* Tucson: University of Arizona Press.

Fraga, Luis R., John A. García, Rodney Hero, Michael Jones-Correa, Valerie Martinez-Ebers, and Gary M. Segura. 2006a. Latino National Survey (LNS) [computer file]. ICPSR20862-v4. Ann Arbor, MI: Inter-university Consortium for Political and Social Research [distributor], 2010-05-26. doi:10.3886/ICPSR20862.

———. 2006b. "Su Casa Es Nuestra Casa: Latino Politics Research and the Development of American Political Science." *American Political Science Review* 100, no. 4 (November): 515–22.

———. 2009. "Education and Latinos: Civic Engagement in School Related Matters, Results from the Latino National Survey" Paper presented at the annual meeting of the Midwest Political Science Association, Chicago, IL, April.

———. 2010. *Latino Lives in America: Making It Home.* Philadelphia: Temple University Press.

Fraga, Luis R., Linda Lopez, Valerie Martinez-Ebers, and Ricardo Ramírez. 2006. "Gender and Ethnicity: Patterns of Electoral Success and Legislative Advocacy among Latina and Latino State Officials in Four States." *Journal of Women, Politics and Policy* 28, no. 3/4: 121–45.

Fraga, Luis R., and Gary Segura. 2006. "Culture Clash? Contesting Notions of American Identity and the Effects of Latin American Immigration." *PS: Political Science and Politics* 4, no. 2 (June): 279.

Fuchs, Lawrence. 1990. *The American Kaleidoscope: Race, Ethnicity, and the Civic Culture.* Middleton, CT: Wesleyan University Press.

Gamboa, Suzanne. 2010. "At Least $800M Spent for Boeing's 53-Mile Border Fence." *Seattle Times,* June 17. http://seattletimes.nwsource.com/html/politics/2012140924_apusbordersecurityvirtualfence.html.

García, F. Chris, ed. 1974. *La Causa Politica: A Chicano Politics Reader.* Notre Dame, IN: University of Notre Dame Press.

———. 1988. *Latinos and the Political System.* Notre Dame, IN: University of Notre Dame Press.

———. 1997. *Pursuing Power: Latino Politics.* Notre Dame, IN: University of Notre Dame Press.

García, John A. 1977. "Chicano Voting Patterns in School Board Elections: Bloc Voting and Internal Lines of Support for Chicano Candidates." *Atisbos* (Winter): 1–14.

———. 1981a. "The Political Integration of Mexican Immigrants: Explorations into the Naturalization Process." *International Migration Review* 15:608–25.

———. 1981b. "Yo Soy Chicano: Self-Identification and Sociodemographic Correlates." *Social Science Quarterly* 62:88–98.

———. 1981c. "Political Integration and Mexican Immigrants: A Preliminary Report." In *U.S. Immigration Policy and the National Interest,* edited by U.S. Commission on Immigration Reform. Washington, DC: U.S. Government Printing Office.

———. 1982. "Ethnic Identification, Consciousness, Identity: Explanations of Measurement and Inter-relationships." *Hispanic Journal of Behavioral Sciences* (September): 295–313.

———. 1986a. "The Voting Rights Act and Hispanic Political Representation." *Publius* 16:49–66.

———. 1986b. "Caribbean Migration to the Mainland: A Review of Adaptive Experiences." *Annals of the American Academy of Political and Social Science* 487 (September): 114–26.

———. 1987. "Political Orientations of Mexican Immigrants: Examining Some Political Orientations." *International Migration Review* 21:377–89.

———. 1989. "Chicano Electoral Behavior and Orientations." In *Curriculum Resources in Chicano Studies*, edited by Gary Keller, 174–82. New York: Bilingual Review Press.

———. 1992. "Hispanic Americans in the Mainstream of American Politics." *Public Perspective* 3, no. 5: 19–23.

———. 1995. "A Multi-cultural America: Living in a Sea of Diversity." In *Multi-culturalism at the Margins: Non-dominant Voices on Differences and Diversity*, edited by D. Harris, 29–38. Westport, CT: Bergen & Garvey.

———. 1996. "The Chicano Movement: Its Legacy for Politics and Policy." In *Chicana/os at the Crossroads: Social, Economic, and Political*, edited by David Maciel and Isidro Ortiz, 83–107. Tucson: University of Arizona Press.

———. 1997. "Hispanic Political Participation and Demographic Correlates." In *Pursuing Political Power: Latinos and the Political System*, edited by F. Chris García, 44–71. Notre Dame, IN: University of Notre Dame Press.

———. 2000. "The Latino and African American Communities: Bases for Coalition Formation and Political Action." In *Immigration and Race: New Challenges for American Democracy*, edited by Gerald Jaynes, 255–76. New Haven, CT: Yale University Press.

———. 2009. "Latino Public Opinion: Exploring Political Community and Policy Preferences." In *Understanding Public Opinion*, edited by Barbara Norrander and Clyde Wilcox, 25–42. 3rd ed. Washington, DC: Congressional Quarterly Press.

. 2011. "Latino Immigrants: Transnationalism and Patterns of Multiple Citizenship Patterns." In *Latinos, Transnationalism and Immigration,* edited by David Leal. South Bend, IN: University of Notre Dame Press.

García, John A., and Carlos Arce. 1988. "Political Orientations and Behavior of Chicanos." In *Latinos and the Political System*, edited by F. Chris García. Notre Dame, IN: University of Notre Dame Press.

García, John A., and Regina Branton. 2000. "Alternative Voting Systems: Explorations into Cumulative and Limited Voting and Minority Representation and Participation." Paper presented at the annual meeting of the American Political Science Association, Washington, DC, September.

García, John A., and R. de la Garza. 1985. "Mobilizing the Mexican Immigrant: The Role of Mexican American Organizations." *Western Political Quarterly* 38:551–64.

García, John A., R. de la Garza, F. C. García, and A. Falcón. 1994. "Ethnicity and National Origin Status: Patterns of Identities among Latinos in the U.S." Paper presented at the annual meeting of the American Political Science Association, Washington, DC, September.

García, John A., and Sylvia Pedraza-Bailey. 1990. "Hispanicity and the Phenomenon of Communities of Interest and Culture among Latinos." Paper presented at the annual meeting of the American Political Science Association, Washington, DC.

García, John A., and Gabriel Sanchez. 2004. "Electoral Politics." In *Latino Americans and Participation of Latinos*, edited by S. Navarro and Armando Mejia, 121–72. Santa Barbara, CA: ABC-CLIO.

García, Juan R. 1980. *Operation Wetback: The Mass Deportation of Mexican Undocumented Workers in 1954*. Westport, CT: Greenwood.

———. 1995. *Mexican American Women: Changing Images*. Tucson, AZ: Mexican American Studies and Research Center.

García, Mario. 1989. *Mexicans and Americans: Leadership, Ideology, and Identity*. New Haven, CT: Yale University Press.

García, Sonia R., Valerie Martinez-Ebers, Irasema Coronado, Sharon A. Navarro, and Patricia A. Jaramillo. 2008. *Políticas: Latina Public Officials in Texas*. Austin: University of Texas Press.

García-Castañon, Marcela. 2010. "Politica and Politics: The Role of Country of Origin Political Participation in the Political Socialization Process of Immigrants." Paper presented at the annual meeting of the Midwest Political Science Association, Chicago, Illinois.

Ginorio, Angela, and Michelle Huston. 2000. *Si, Se Puede! Yes We Can: Latinas in School*. Washington, DC: American Association of University Women.

Gittell, Marilyn, and Mario Fantini. 1970. *Community Control and the Urban School*. New York: Praeger.

Gómez, David. 1982. *Somos Chicanos: Strangers in Our Own Land*. 2nd ed. New York: Macmillan.

Gómez, Laura. 1992. "The Birth of the Hispanic Generation: Attitudes of Mexican American Political Elites toward the Hispanic Label." *Latin American Perspectives* 19, no. 4 (February): 45–59.

Gómez-Quiñones, Juan. 1990. *Chicano Politics: Realities and Promise*. Albuquerque: University of New Mexico Press.

———. 1994. *The Roots of Chicano Politics, 1640–1940*. Albuquerque: University of New Mexico Press.

González-Baker, Susan. 1996. "Su Voto Es Su Voz: Latino Political Empowerment and the Immigration Challenge." *PS: Political Science and Politics* 29, no. 3: 465–69.

Gordon, Milton. 1964. *Assimilation in American Life: The Role of Race, Religion, and National Origins*. New York: Oxford University Press.

Grassmuck, Sheri, and Patricia Pesser. 1996. "Dominicans in the United States: First and Second Generation Settlement." In *Origins and Destinies: Immigration, Race, and Ethnicity*, edited by Sylvia Pedraza and Ruben Rumbault, 280–92. Belmont, CA: Wadsworth.

Griswold del Castillo, Richard. 1995. *Cesar Chavez: A Triumph of Spirit*. Norman: University of Oklahoma Press.

Grofman, Bernard. 1995. "*Shaw v. Reno* and the Future of Voting Rights." *PS: Political Science and Politics* 28 (March): 25–26.

Grofman, Bernard, and Chandler Davidson, eds. 1992. *Controversies in Minority Voting: A 25-Year Perspective on the Voting Rights Act of 1965*. Washington, DC: Brookings Institution.

Grofman, Bernard, L. Handley, and R. Niemi. 1992. *Minority Representation and the Quest for Voting Equality*. New York: Cambridge University Press.

Grossman, Milton M. 1964. *Assimilation in American Life: The Role of Race, Religion, and National Origins*. New York: Oxford University Press.

Guarnizo, Luis. 1994. "Los Dominicanyorks: The Making of a Bi-national Society." *Annals of the American Academy of Political and Social Science* 533:70–86.

Guzman, Betsy. 2001. *The Hispanic Population: Census 2000 Brief*. May. C2KBR/01-3. Washington, DC: U.S. Census Bureau.

Hansen, Kristen, and Carol Faber. 1997. *The Foreign-Born Population, 1996*. Current Population Reports P-20-497. Washington, DC: U.S. Census Bureau.

Hardy-Fanta, Carol. 1993. *Latina Politics and Latino Politics: Gender, Culture, and Political Participation*. Philadelphia: Temple University Press.

———. 2000. "A Latino Gender Gap? Evidence from the 1996 Election." *Milenia* 2 (February).

Hardy-Fanta, Carol, and Carol Cardoza. 1997. "Beyond the Gender Gap: Women of Color in the 1996 Election." Paper presented at the annual meeting of the American Political Science Association, Washington, DC, August.

Hayes-Bautista, David. 1980. "Identifying Hispanic Populations: The Influence of Research Methodology on Public Policy." *American Journal of Public Health* 70:353–56.

Hayes-Bautista, David, and Jorge Chapa. 1987. "Latino Terminology: Conceptual Basis for Standardized Terminology." *American Journal of Public Health* 77:61–68.

Hayes-Bautista, David, Werner Schenk, and Jorge Chapa. 1988. *The Burden of Support: Young Latinos in an Aging Society.* Stanford, CA: Stanford University Press.

———. 1992. *No Longer a Minority: Latinos and Social Policy in California.* Los Angeles: UCLA Chicano Research Center.

Henry, Charles, and Carlos Muñoz. 1991. "Ideology and Interest Linkage to California's Rainbow Coalition." In *Race and Ethnic Politics in California,* edited by B. Jackson and M. Preston. Berkeley: Institute for Governmental Research, University of California.

Hernández, Jose, L. Estrada, and D. Alvirez. 1973. "Census Data and the Problem of Conceptually Defining the Mexican American Population." *Social Science Quarterly* 53, no. 4: 671–87.

Hernández, Ramona, and Francisco Rivera-Batiz. 1997. *Dominican New Yorkers: A Socioeconomic Profile, 1997.* New York: Dominican Research Monographs. City University of New York Dominican Studies Institute.

Hernández, Ramona, and S. Torres-Saillant. 1996. "Dominicans in New York: Men, Women, and Prospects." In *Latinos in New York: Latinos in Transition,* edited by G. Haslip-Viera and S. Baver, 30–56. Notre Dame, IN: University of Notre Dame Press.

Hero, Rodney. 1988. "The Election of Frederico Peña As Mayor of Denver." *Western Political Quarterly* 40:93–105.

———. 1992. *Latinos and the Political System.* Philadelphia: Temple University Press.

———. 1996. "Ethnic Ironies: Latino Politics in the 1992 Elections." In *Latinos and the 1992 Elections,* edited by R. de la Garza and L. DeSipio, 75–94. Boulder, CO: Westview.

Hero, Rodney, F. Chris García, John García, and Harry Pachon. 2000. "Latino Participation, Partisanship, and Office Holding." *PS: Political Science and Politics* 33, no. 3: 529–34.

Hill, Kevin, and Dario Moreno. 1996. "Second-Generation Cubans." *Hispanic Journal of Behavioral Sciences* 18, no. 2: 175–93.

———. 2001. "Language As a Variable: English, Spanish, Ethnicity, and Political Opinion Polling in South Florida." *Hispanic Journal of Behavioral Sciences* 23, no. 2: 208–28.

Hirsch, Herbert, and Armando Gutierrez. 1973. "The Militant Challenge to the American Ethos: Chicanos and Mexican Americans." *Social Science Quarterly* 53:830–45.

———. 1974. "Political Maturation and Political Awareness: The Case of Crystal City Chicanos." *Aztlán* 5:295–312.

Hoffman, Abraham. 1979. *Unwanted Mexican Americans in the Great Depression: Repatriation Pressures, 1929–1939.* Tucson: University of Arizona Press.

Hood, M. V., and Irwin Morris. 1997. "Amigo or Enemigo? Context, Attitudes, and Anglo Public Opinion toward Immigration." *Social Science Quarterly* 78, no. 32: 309–24.

Hood, M. V., Irwin Morris, and Kurt Shirkey. 1997. "Quedete or Vete: Unraveling the Determinants of Hispanic Public Opinion toward Immigration." *Political Research Quarterly* 50:627–47.

Hufstedler, Shirley. 1999. "The Final Report of the Commission on Immigration Reform." Statement before the U.S. House of Representatives Subcommittee on Immigration and Claims, Washington, DC.

Immigration and Naturalization Service. 1996. *1996 Statistical Yearbook of the Immigration and Naturalization Service.* Washington, DC: U.S. Government Printing Office.

———. 1997. *Annual Report on Legal Immigration: Fiscal Year 1997.* Washington, DC: U.S. Government Printing Office.

———. 2000. *1998 Statistical Yearbook of the INS.* Washington, DC: U.S. Government Printing Office.

Jackson, Bryon, E. Gerber, and B. Cain. 1994. "Coalitional Perspectives in a Multi-racial Society: African American Attitudes toward Others." *Political Research Quarterly* 47, no. 2: 277–94.

Jackson, Bryon, and Michael Preston, eds. 1991. *Racial and Ethnic Politics in California.* Berkeley: University of California Press.

Jackson, James S., Vincent L. Hutchings, Ronald Brown, and Cara Wong. 2004. National Politics Study, 2004 [Computer file]. ICPSR24483-v1. Ann Arbor, MI: Inter-university Consortium for Political and Social Research [distributor], 2009-03-23. doi:10.3886/ICPSR24483.

Jamieson, Amie, Hyon Shinn, and Jennifer Day. 2002. *Voting and Registration in the Election of November 2000.* Current Population Reports P20-542. Washington, DC: Department of Commerce.

Jaynes, Gerald, ed. 2000. *Immigration and Race: New Challenge for American Democracy.* New Haven, CT: Yale University Press.

Jennings, James. 1977. *Puerto Rican Politics in New York City.* Washington, DC: University Press of America.

———. 1992. *The Politics of Black Empowerment: Transformation of Black Activism in Urban America.* Detroit, MI: Wayne State University Press.

———. 1994. *Blacks, Latinos, and Asians in Urban America.* Westport, CT: Greenwood.

Jennings, James, and M. Rivera. 1984. *Puerto Rican Politics in Urban America.* Westport, CT: Greenwood.

Johnson, Hans, Belinda Reyes, Laura Mameesh, and Elisa Barber. 1999. *Taking the Oath: An Analysis of Naturalization in California and the United States.* San Francisco: Public Policy Institute of California.

Jones-Correa, Michael. 1998. *Between Two Nations: The Political Predicament of Latinos in New York City.* Ithaca, NY: Cornell University Press.

———. 2009. "Coming to America: Latinos and the Adoption of Identity." Paper presented at the annual meeting of the Midwest Political Science Association, Chicago, Illinois, April 12–15.

Jones-Correa, Michael, and David Leal. 1996. "Becoming Hispanic: Secondary Pan-ethnic Identity among Latin American Origin Population in the U.S." *Hispanic Journal of Behavioral Sciences* 18, no. 2 (May): 214–54.

Jordan, Barbara. 1994. *U.S. Immigration Policy: Restoring Credibility.* Washington, DC: U.S. Government Printing Office.

Jordan, Howard. 1995. "Immigrant Rights: A Puerto Rican Issue." *NACLA Report on the Americas* 29, no. 3: 35–39.

Kasarda, John D. 1985. "Urban Change and Minority Opportunities." In *The New Urban Reality*, edited by Paul Peterson, 33–68. Washington, DC: Brookings Institute.

———. 1989. "Urban Industrial Transformation and the Underclass." *Annals of the Academy of Political Science and Sociology* 501:26–47.

Kaufman, Karen. 2003. "Cracks in the Rainbow: Group Commonality As a Basis for Latino and African-American Coalitions." *Political Research Quarterly* 56 (June): 199–210.

Keefe, Susan, and Amado Padilla. 1989. *Chicano Ethnicity.* Albuquerque: University of New Mexico Press.

Kelly, Daryl. 1997. "Illegal Immigrants Remain a Concern Despite Economy." *Los Angeles Times*, November 2.

Krantz, Colleen. 2001. "Responses Are Mixed to Latino Immigrants." *Des Moines Register*, March 18.

Kunerth, Jeff, and Sherri Owens. 2001. "Hispanics Reshape Civil Rights Agenda." *Orlando Sentinel*, July 1.

Latino Decisions. 2010. "Latino Election Eve Poll Results: November 2, 2010." Latino Decisions. November 2, 2010. http://latinodecisions.wordpress.com/2010/11/02/latino-election-eve-poll-results-november-2-2010 (accessed May 4, 2011)

Lavariega-Monforti, Jessica, and Gabriel R. Sanchez. 2010. "The Politics of Perception: An Investigation of the Presence and Source of Perceived Discrimination toward and among Latinos." *Social Science Quarterly* 90, no. 1 (March): 245–65.

Leighley, Jan E. 2001. *Strength in Numbers: The Political Mobilization of Racial and Ethnic Minorities.* Princeton, NJ: Princeton University Press.

Leighley, Jan E., and A. Vedlitz. 1999. "Race, Ethnicity, and Political Participation: Competing Models and Contrasting Explanations." *Journal of Politics* 61:1092–114.

Lindholm, Kathryn, and Amado Padilla. 1981. "Socialization Communication: Language Interaction Patterns Used by Hispanic Mothers and Children in Mastery Skill Communication." In *Latino Language and Communicative Behavior*, edited by Richard Duran. New Jersey: ABLEX.

López, David, and Yen Espiritu. 1990. "Panethnicity in the United States: A Theoretical Framework." *Ethnic and Racial Studies* 13, no. 32: 198–223.

Los Angeles Times. 1994a. "Study No. 413 Exit Poll: California Primary Election." June 2.

———. 1994b. "The Post Election Study." June 7.

Lydgate, Joanna. 2010. *Assembly-Line Justice: A Review of Operation Streamline.* Berkeley: University of California, Berkeley Law School, January.

Manzano, Sylvia, Matt A. Barreto, Ricardo Ramirez, and Kathy Rim. 2009. "Mobilization, Participation, and Solidaridad: Latino Participation in the 2006 Immigration Protest Rallies." *Urban Affairs Review* 44:736–64.

Márquez, Benjamin. 1985. *Power and Politics in a Chicano Barrio: A Study of Mobilization Efforts and Community Power in El Paso.* Lanham, MD: University Press of America.

———. 1988. "The Politics of Racial Assimilation: League of United Latin American Citizens." *Western Political Quarterly* 42:355–77.

———. 1993. "The Industrial Areas Foundation and the Mexican American in Texas: The Politics of Mobilization." In *Minority Group Influence: Agenda Setting, Formation, and Public Policy*, edited by Paula McClain, 127–46. Westport, CT: Greenwood.

Martin, Philip, and E. Midgley. 1996. *Immigration to the United States.* Washington, DC: Population Reference Bureau Publications.

Martinez-Ebers, Valerie, Luis Ricardo Fraga, Linda Lopez, and Arturo Vargas. 2000. "Latino Interests in Education, Health, and Criminal Justice Policy." *PS: Political Science and Politics* 33, no. 3 (September): 547–54.

Masoukka, Natalie. 2006. "Together They Become One: Examining the Predictors of Panethnic Group Consciousness among Asian Americans and Latinos." *Social Science Quarterly* 87, no. 5 (December): 993–1011.

———. 2008. "Political Attitudes and Ideologies of Multiracial Americans: The Implications of Mixed Race in the United States." *Political Research Quarterly* 61:253–67.

Massey, Douglas. 1979. "Effects of Socioeconomic Status Factors on Residential Segregation of Blacks and Spanish Americans in United States Urbanized Areas." *American Sociological Review* 44:1015–22.

———. 1981. "Hispanic Residential Segregation: A Comparison of Mexicans, Cubans, and Puerto Ricans." *Sociology and Social Research* 65:311–22.

Massey, Douglas, and Nancy Denton. 1993. *American Apartheid: Segregation and the Making of an Underclass.* Cambridge, MA: Harvard University Press.

McClain, Paula. 2006. "Racial Intergroup Relations in a Set of Cities: A Twenty-Year Perspective" (presidential address). *Journal of Politics* 68, no. 4 (November): 757–70.

McClain, Paula, Niambi M. Carter, Victoria M. DeFrancesco Soto, Monique L. Lyle, Jeffrey D. Grynaviski, Shayla C. Nunnally, Thomas J. Scotto, J. Alan Kendrick, Gerald F. Lackey, and Kendra Davenport Cotton. 2006. "Racial Distancing in a Southern City: Latino Immigrants' Views of Black Americans." *Journal of Politics* 68, no. 3 (August): 571–84.

McClain, Paula, Jessica D. Johnson Carew, Eugene Walton Jr., and Candis S. Watts. 2009. "Group Membership, Group Identity, and Group Consciousness: Measures of Racial Identity in American Politics?" *Annual Review of Political Science* 12:471–85.

McClain, Paula, and Albert Karnig. 1990. "Black and Hispanic Socioeconomic Status and Political Competition." *American Political Science Review* 84:535–45.

McClain, Paula, and Joseph Stewart. 1999. *"Can We All Get Along?": Racial and Ethnic Minorities in American Politics.* Boulder, CO: Westview.

McDonnell, Patrick. 2001. "Citizenship Process Is Streamlined, but Applications Decline." *Los Angeles Times,* July 4.

Meier, Ken, and David L. Leal, eds. Forthcoming. *The Politics of Latino Education.* New York: Teachers College Press.

Meier, Ken, and J. Stewart. 1991. *The Politics of Hispanic Education.* Albany: State University of New York Press.

Meier, Kenneth J., Paula D McClain, Jerry L. Polinard, and Robert D. Wrinkle. 2004. "Divided or Together? Conflict and Cooperation between African-Americans and Latinos." *Political Research Quarterly* 57, no. 3: 399–410.

Meyer, David, and Sidney Tarrow, eds. 1997. *The Social Movement Society: Politics for a New Century.* Boulder, CO: Rowman & Littlefield.

Michelson, Melissa R. 2003. "The Corrosive Effect of Acculturation: How Mexican Americans Lose Political Trust." *Social Science Quarterly* 84:918–33.

———. 2005. "Does Ethnicity Trump Party? Competing Vote Cues and Latino Voting Behavior." *Journal of Political Marketing* 4:1–25.

———. 2006. "Mobilizing the Latino Youth Vote: Some Experimental Results." *Social Science Quarterly* 87, no. 1: 1188–206.

Michelson, Melissa R., Lisa García-Bedolla, and Margaret A. McConnell. 2009. "Heeding the Call: The Effect of Targeted Two-Round Phone Banks on Voter Turnout." *Journal of Politics* 71, no. 4 (October): 1549–63.

Michelson, Melissa R., and Amalia Pallares. 2001. "The Politicization of Chicago Mexican Americans: Naturalization, the Vote, and Perceptions of Discrimination." *Aztlán* 26, no. 2: 63–86.

Milbank, Dana. 2000. "The Year of the Latino Voter? Only in Campaign Rhetoric." *Washington Post,* May 21.

Milbrath, Lester, and M. L. Hoel. 1977. *Political Participation.* 2nd ed. Skokie, IL: Rand McNally.

Milkman, Ruth. 2000. *Organizing Immigrants: The Challenge for Unions in California.* Ithaca, NY: Cornell University Press.

Miller, Arthur, P. Gurin, Gerry Gurin, and Oksana Malanchuk. 1981. "Group Consciousness and Political Participation." *American Journal of Political Science* 25:494–511.

Monforti, Jessica, and Gabriel R. Sanchez. 2010. "The Politics of Perception: An Investigation of the Presence and Sources of Perceptions of Internal Discrimination among Latinos." *Social Science Quarterly* 91, no. 1 (March): 245–65.

Montejano, David. 1987. *Anglos and Mexicans in the Making of Texas, 1836–1986.* Austin: University of Texas Press.

Montoya, Lisa, Carol Hardy-Fanta, and Sonia García. 2000. "Latina Politics: Gender, Participation, and Leadership." *PS: Political Science and Politics* 33:555–61.

Moore, Joan, and Raquel Pinderhughes, eds. 1993. *In the Barrios: Latinos and the Underclass Debate.* New York: Russell Sage Foundation.

Morales, Rebecca, and Frank Bonilla, eds. 1993. *Latinos in a Changing U.S. Economy: Perspectives in Growing Inequality.* Newbury, CA: Russell Sage Foundation.

Moreno, Dario, and C. Warren. 1992. "The Conservative Enclave: Citizens in Florida." In *From Rhetoric to Reality: Latinos and the 1988 Elections,* edited by R. de la Garza and L. DeSipio. Boulder, CO: Westview.

Muñoz, Carlos. 1989. *Youth, Identity, and Power: The Chicano Movement.* London: Verso.

Nagel, Joanne. 1996. *American Indian Renewal: Red Power and Resurgence of Identity and Culture.* New York: Oxford University Press.

National Association of Latino Elected and Appointed Officials (NALEO) Educational Fund. 2011. *The Latino Vote.* Washington, DC: NALEO Publications.

National Council of La Raza (NCLR). 1999. *Legislative Update.* Washington, DC: NCLR.

National Hispanic Leadership Agenda (NHLA). 1998. *Congressional Scorecard, 105th Congress.* Washington, DC: NHLA.

———. 2000. *Congressional Scorecard, 106th Congress.* Washington, DC: NHLA.

Nelson, Candice, and Marta Tienda. 1985. "The Structuring of Hispanic Ethnicity: Historical and Contemporary Perspectives." *Ethnic and Racial Studies* 8:49–74.

Nelson, Dale C. 1979. "Ethnicity and Socioeconomic Status As Sources of Participation: The Case for Ethnic Political Culture." *American Political Science Review* 73, no. 4: 1024–38.

Nie, Norman, Jane Junn, and Kenneth Stehlik-Barry. 1996. *Education and Democratic Citizenship in America.* Chicago: University of Chicago Press.

O'Brien, Matt. 2011. "Salvadorans Now Fourth Largest Latino Group in U.S." *Contra Costa Times*, May 26.

O'Connor, Ann Marie. 1998. "School Is Top Issue for Two Immigrant Groups." *Los Angeles Times*, March 19.

Oliver, Melvin, and Charles Johnson. 1984. "Inter-ethnic Conflict in an Urban Ghetto: The Case of Blacks and Latinos in Los Angeles." *Social Movement, Conflict, and Change* 6:57–94.

Omni, Michael, and Howard Winant. 1994. *Racial Transformation in the U.S.: From the 1960s to 1980s.* New York: Routledge & Kegan Paul.

Ong, Paul, Edna Bonacich, and L. Cheng. 1994. *The New Asian Immigration in Los Angeles and Global Restructuring.* Philadelphia: Temple University Press.

Orfield, Gary. 1991. *Status of School Desegregation, 1968–1986: Segregation, Integration, and Public Policy—National, State and Metro Trends.* Alexandria, VA: National School Board Association.

Orfield, Gary, and Carole Ashkinaze. 1991. *The Closing Door: Conservative Policy and Black Opportunity.* Chicago: University of Chicago Press.

Pachón, Harry. 1987. "An Overview of Citizenship: Naturalization in the Hispanic Community." *International Migration Review* 21:199–210.

Pachón, Harry, and Louis DeSipio. 1990. "Future Research on Latino Immigrants and the Political Process." Paper presented at the Inter-University Program for Latino Research, Pomona, California.

———. 1994. *New Americans by Choice: Political Perspectives of Latino Immigrants.* Boulder, CO: Westview.

Padilla, Amado. 1974. "The Study of Bilingual Language Acquisition." Report to the National Science Foundation GY 411534. Spanish-Speaking Mental Health Center No. 1191. Los Angeles, CA: UCLA.

Padilla, Felix. 1986. *Latino Ethnic Consciousness: Case of Mexican Americans and Puerto Ricans.* Notre Dame, IN: University of Notre Dame Press.

Padilla, Steve. 2010. "Questions and Answers on SB 1070—a Guide to Arizona's New Immigration Law." *Los Angeles Times*, July 23. http://latimesblogs.latimes.com/washington/2010/07/arizona-immigration-law.html.

Pan, Phillip. 1999. "INS Says Citizenship Backlog Cut." *Washington Post*, October 29.

Pantoja, Adrian D. 2005. "Transnational Ties and Immigrant Political Incorporation: The Case of Dominicans in Washington Heights, New York." *International Migration* 43:123–44.

Pantoja, Adrian D., and Sarah Allen Gershon. 2006. "Political Orientations and Naturalization among Latino and Latina Immigrants." *Social Science Quarterly* 87, no. 1: 1171–87.

Pantoja, Adrian D., Ricardo Ramirez, and Gary M. Segura. 2001. "Citizens by Choice, Voters by Necessity: Patterns in Political Mobilization by Naturalized Latinos." *Political Research Quarterly* 54, no. 4: 729–50.

Pardo, Mary. 1998. *Mexican American Women Activists: Identity and Resistance in Two Los Angeles Communities.* Philadelphia: Temple University Press.

Passel, J., and D. Cohn. 2009. "A Portrait of Unauthorized Immigrants in the United States." Washington, DC: Pew Hispanic Center.

Patterson, Ernest. 1975. "Context and Choice in Ethnic Allegiance." In *Ethnicity, Theory, and Experience*, edited by Nathan Glazer and Daniel Moynihan. Cambridge, MA: Harvard University Press.

Patterson, Orlando. 2001. "Race by the Numbers." *New York Times*, May 8, A27.

Payne, Richard J. 1998. *Getting Beyond Race*. Boulder, CO: Westview.

Pedraza-Bailey, Sylvia. 1985. *Political and Economic Migrants in America: Cubans and Mexicans*. Austin: University of Texas Press.

Pedraza-Bailey, Sylvia, and Ruben Rumbault, eds. 1995. *Origin and Destinies: Immigration, Race, and Ethnicity*. Belmont, CA: Wadsworth.

Peña, Devon. 1998. *Chicano Culture, Ecology, and Politics: Subversive Kin*. Tucson: University of Arizona Press.

Pérez, Lisandro. 1985. "The Cuban Population of the United States: Results from the 1980 Census of Population." *Cuban Studies* 15, no. 2: 1–18.

———. 1986. "Immigrant Economic Adjustment and Family Organization: The Cuban Success Story Reexamined." *International Migration Review* 20:4–20.

Petersen, Mark. 1995. "Leading Cuban American Entrepreneurs: The Process of Developing Motives, Abilities, and Resources." *Human Relations* 48 (October): 1193–216.

Pew Hispanic Center. 2009. "Latinos and Education: Explaining the Attainment Gap." Washington, DC: Pew Hispanic Center. http://pewhispanic.org/data.

Phillips, Dan. 1999. "INS Said Citizen Backlog Cut." *Washington Post*, October 29.

Pimentel, O. Ricardo. 2002. "Hispanic Middle Class Growing Fast." *Tucson Citizen*, January 10.

Pinderhughes, Dianne. 1995. "The Voting Rights Act: Whither History." *PS: Political Science and Politics* 28, no. 2: 55–56.

Pitt, Leonard. 1966. *The Decline of the Californios: A Social and Political History of Spanish-Speaking California*. Berkeley: University of California Press.

Piven, Frances, and Richard Cloward. 1979. *Poor People's Movements: Why They Succeed, How They Fail*. New York: Random House.

———. 1988. *Why Americans Do Not Vote*. New York: Pantheon.

———. 1993. *Regulating the Poor: The Functions of Public Welfare*. New York: Vintage Books.

———. 2000. *Why Americans Still Don't Vote and Why Politicians Want It That Way*. Boston: Beacon.

Portes, Alejandro. 1998. "Morning in Miami: A New Era for Cuban-American Politics." *American Prospect* 9, no. 38 (May–June): 28–33.

Portes, Alejandro, Cristina Escobar, and Renelinda Arana. 2008. "Bridging the Gap: Transnational and Ethnic Organizations in the Political Incorporation of Immigrants in the United States." *Ethnic and Racial Studies* 31, no. 6: 1056–90.

Portes, Alejandro, Cristina Escobar, and Alexandria Walton Radford. 2007. "Immigrant Transnational Organizations and Development: A Comparative Study." *International Migration Review* 41, no. 1 (Spring): 242–81.

Portes, Alejandro, and R. Mozo. 1984. "The Rise of Ethnicity and Determinants of Ethnic Perspectives of U.S. Society among Cuban Exiles." *American Sociological Review* 49: 383–497.

———. 1985. "The Political Adaptation Process of Cubans and Other Ethnic Minorities in the United States: A Preliminary Analysis." *International Migration Review* 19:35–63.

Portes, Alejandro, and Rubén Rumbaut. 1990. *Immigrant America*. Berkeley: University of California Press.

Portes, Alejandro, and A. Stepnick. 1993. *City on the Edge: The Transformation of Miami*. Berkeley: University of California Press.

President's Advisory Commission on Educational Excellence for Hispanic Americans. 1999. *Our Nation on the Fault Line*. Washington, DC: U.S. Government Printing Office.

Pulído, Laura. 1996. *Environmental Racism and Economic Justice*. Tucson: University of Arizona Press.

Putnam, Robert. 2000. *Bowling Alone: The Collapse and Revival of American Democracy*. New York: Simon & Schuster.

Ramírez, Ricardo. 2007. "Segmented Mobilization: Latino Non-partisan Get Out the Vote Efforts in the 2000 General Election." *American Politics Research* 35, no. 2: 155–75.

Ramírez, Roberto. 1999. *The Hispanic Population in the United States: Population Characteristics*. Current Population Reports P20-527. Washington, DC: U.S. Census Bureau.

Reed, John. 1997. *The Hispanic Population in the United States: March 1995*. Current Population Reports P20-501. Washington, DC: U.S. Census Bureau.

———. 1998. *Hispanic Population Nears 30 Million*. Census Bureau Reports CB 98-137. Washington, DC: U.S. Census Bureau.

Reed, John, and Roberto Ramirez. 1998. *The Hispanic Population in the United States, March 1997*. Washington, DC: U.S. Census Bureau.

Renshon, Stanley A. 2009. *Non-Citizen Voting and American Democracy*. Denver, CO: Rowman & Littlefield.

Reyes, Corinna A. 2006. "Awakening the Sleeping Giant: 21st Century Latino Political Mobilization." Paper presented at the Midwest Political Science Association's Annual Conference, Chicago, Illinois, April 14.

Reza, H. G. 1998. "Group Stirs Outrage with Billboard Deploring Illegal Immigration." *Los Angeles Times*, May 6.

Rocha, Rene. 2007. "Black-Brown Coalitions in Local School Board Elections." *Political Research Quarterly* 60, no. 2: 315–27.

Rodrígues, Helena A., and Gary M. Segura. 2007. "A Place at the Lunch Counter: Latinos, African-Americans, and the Dynamics of American Race Politics." In *Latino Politics: Identity, Mobilization, and Representation*, edited by Kenneth Meier, Rodolfo Espino, and David Leal. Charlottesville: University of Virginia Press.

Rodríquez, Clara. 1998. *Puerto Ricans: Born in the USA*. Boston: Unwin Hyman.

———. 2000. *Changing Race: Latinos, the Census, and the History of Ethnicity in the U.S.* New York: New York University Press.

Rodríquez, Gregory. 1996. "The Browning of California: Proposition 187 Backfires." *New Republic*, September 18–28.

———. 1998. "Latino Voters Are Finally Awakening to Their Political Power: But Will Cultural Attitudes Reduce Their Effect?" *Los Angeles Times*, January 11.

Rodríquez, Lori. 2000. "Top Candidates Court Latino Vote in Key Primaries." *Houston Chronicle*, February 26.

———. 2001. "Latino Mix Becomes More Diverse." *Houston Chronicle*, May 23.

———. 2006. "Melting Pot: If No Child Is to Be Left Behind, Texas Must Do a Better Job of Classifying Its Students." *Houston Chronicle*, August 21.

Roedemeier, Chad. 2000. "Hispanic Transformation: Immigrants Stream into North Georgia for Jobs, Changing the Social Fabric of Town and Schools." Associated Press.

Rosenstone, Steve, and Mark Hansen. 1993. *Mobilization, Participation, and Democracy in the U.S.* New York: Macmillan.

Russell, Mark, and Martha Russell. 1989. "Chicago's Hispanics." *American Demographics* (September): 58–60.

Saito, Leonard. 1998. *Race and Politics: Asian Americans, Latinos, and Whites in a Los Angeles Suburb*. Urbana: University of Illinois Press.

San Jose Mercury News. 1998. "Vote Turnout Was a Record for Latinos." June 7.

San Miguel, Guadalupe. 1987. *Let Them All Take Heed: Mexican Americans and the Campaign for Educational Equality.* Albuquerque: University of New Mexico Press.

Sanchez, Gabriel. 2006. "The Role of Group Consciousness in Latino Public Opinion." *Political Research Quarterly* 59:433–46.

———. 2008. "Latino Group Consciousness and Perceptions of Commonality with African Americans." *Social Science Quarterly* 89, no. 2: 428–44.

Santillán, Richard. 1985. "The Latino Community and State and Congressional Redistricting, 1961–1985." *Journal of Hispanic Policy* 1:52–66.

Sassen-Koob, Saskia. 1979. "Formal and Informal Associations: Dominicans and Colombians in New York." *International Migration Review* 13, no. 2: 314–29.

———. 1985. "The Changing Composition and Labor Market Location of Hispanic Immigrants in New York City." In *Hispanics and the Economy*, edited by Marta Tienda and George Borjas. Orlando, FL: Academic.

———. 1988. *The Mobility of Labor and Capital: A Study in International Investment Flow.* New York: Cambridge University Press.

Schermerhorn, R. A. 1970. *Comparative Ethnic Relations: A Framework for Theory and Research.* New York: Random House.

Schlossberg, Jeremy. 1989. "Hispanic Hot Seat: Hispanics Who Live in New York City." *American Demographics* 10 (August): 49–52.

Segura, Gary M. 2007. "Transnational Linkages, Generational Change, and Latino Political Engagement." Paper presented at the annual meeting of the Midwest Political Science Association, Chicago, Illinois, May.

———. 2011. "In-Group Identification and Out-Group Attitudes: Latinidad and Relations with Whites and African Americans." Paper presented at the annual meeting of the Southern Political Science Association, New Orleans, Louisiana, January 6–8.

Segura, Gary, and A. Pantoja. 2003. "Fear and Loathing in California: Contextual Threat and Political Sophistication among Latino Voters." *Political Behavior* 25, no. 3: 265–86.

Segura, Gary, and Wayne Santoro. 2004. "Assimilation, Incorporation, and Ethnic Identity in Understanding Latino Electoral and Non-electoral Political Participation." Paper presented at the annual meeting of the Midwest Political Science Association, Chicago, Illinois, April 15–18.

Semana. 2001. "Colombians Are Fastest Growing Latino Group in the U.S." May 14.

Shaw v. Reno. 1993. 509 U.S. 630; 113 S. Ct. 2816.

Shockley, John S. 1974. *Chicano Revolt in a Texas Town.* Notre Dame, IN: University of Notre Dame Press.

Sierra, Christine. 1987. *Latinos and the New Immigration: Response for the Mexican American Community.* Renato Rosaldo Lecture Series Monograph 3. Tucson, AZ: Mexican American Studies and Research Center.

———. 1991. "Latino Organizational Strategies on Immigration Reform: Success and Limits of Public Policy-Making." In *Latinos and Political Empowerment for the 90s*, edited by R. Villareal and N. Hernandez. New York: Greenwood.

Sierra, Christine, Teresa Carrillo, Louis DeSipio, and Michael Jones-Correa. 2000. "Latino Immigration and Citizenship." *PS: Political Science and Politics* 33, no. 3: 535–40.

Sierra, Christine, Carol Hardy-Fanta, Pei-te Lien, and Dianne Pinderhughes. 2006. "Gender, Race and Descriptive Representation in the United States: Findings from the Gender and Multicultural Leadership Project." *Journal of Women, Politics and Policy* 28, no. 3/4: 7–41.

Singer, Audrey, and Greta Gilbertson. 1996. "Naturalization among Latin American Immigrants." Paper presented at the annual meeting of the American Sociological Association, New York, August.

———. 2000. *Naturalization in the Wake of Anti-immigrant Legislation: Dominicans in New York City.* Working Paper 10. Washington, DC: Carnegie Endowment for International Peace.

Skerry, Peter. 1993. *Mexican Americans: The Ambivalent Minority.* Boston: Free Press.

Smith, Anthony. 1981. *The Ethnic Renewal in the Modern World.* Cambridge: Cambridge University Press.

Smith, James P., and Barry Edmondston. 1998. *The Immigration Debate: Studies in the Economic, Demographic, and Fiscal Impacts of Immigration.* Washington, DC: National Academy Press.

Smith, Tom. 1990. *Ethnic Survey: The General Social Survey.* Technical Report 19. Chicago: National Opinion Research Center, University of Chicago.

Sonenshein, Raphael. 1990. "Bi-racial Coalitions Politics in Los Angeles." In *Racial Politics in American Cities,* edited by R. Browning, D. Marshall, and D. Tabb. New York: Longman.

———. 1994. *Politics in Black and White.* Princeton, NJ: Princeton University Press.

———. 2006. *The City at Stake: Secession, Reform, and the Battle for Los Angeles.* Princeton, NJ: Princeton University Press.

Sonenshein, Raphael, and Susan H. Pinkus. 2002. "The Dynamics of Latino Political Incorporation: The 2001 Los Angeles Mayoral Election As Seen in 'Los Angeles Times' Exit Polls." *PS: Political Science and Politics* 35, no. 1: 67–74.

Stavans, Ilan. 1996. *The Hispanic Condition: Reflections on Culture and Identity in America.* New York: Harper.

Stevens, Jeff. 2001. "Hispanics Next in Line for Power." *Odessa American,* May 17.

Tarrow, Sidney. 1998. *Power in Movement: Social Movements and Contentious Politics.* New York: Cambridge University Press.

Tate, Kathleen. 1993. *From Protest to Politics: The New Black Voters in American Elections.* Princeton, NJ: Princeton University Press.

Tilly, Charles. 1978. *From Mobilization to Revolution.* Reading, MA: Addison-Wesley.

Timberg, Craig, and R. H. Melton. 2001. "GOP Designs Mostly Latino N. VA. District." *Washington Post,* April 11.

Tirado, Miguel. 1970. "The Mexican American Minority's Participation in Voluntary Political Associations." PhD diss., Claremont Graduate School (the Claremont Colleges).

Tobar, Hector. 1998. "Water Bill Triggers off a Revolt from a Tiny Garage in Maywood, California." *Los Angeles Times,* July 24.

Torres-Saillant, Silvio. 1998. "The Tribulations in Blackness: States in Dominican Racial Identity." *Latin American Perspectives* 25 (May): 126–46.

Torres-Saillant, Silvio, and Ramona Hernández. 1998. *The Dominican Americans.* Westport, CT: Greenwood.

Tórrez, Adrianna, and Bechetta Jackson. 2001. "Hispanics Planning to Run for Council: Leaders Emerging, Latinos Say." *Ft. Worth Star Telegram,* April 22.

Ture, Kwame, and Charles Hamilton. 1992. *Black Power: The Politics of Liberation.* New York: Vintage.

Uhlaner, Carole. 1991. "Perceived Prejudiced and Coalitional Prospects among Blacks, Latinos, and Asian Americans." In *Ethnic and Racial Politics in California,* edited by Byron Jackson and Michael Preston, 339–71. Berkeley, CA: Institute for Governmental Studies.

Uhlaner, Carole, B. Cain, and R. Kiewiet. 1989. "Ethnic Minorities in the 1990s." *Political Behavior* 11:195–231.

Umana-Taylor, Adriana J., and Amy B. Guimond. 2010. "A Longitudinal Examination of Parenting Behaviors and Perceived Discrimination Predicting Latino Adolescents' Ethnic Identity." *Developmental Psychology* 46, no. 3: 636–50.

United States Census Bureau. 1993. *We the Americans . . . Hispanics.* Washington, DC: Department of Commerce.

————. 2002. *The Hispanic Population of the United States: Population Characteristics.* Current Population Reports P20-527. Washington, DC: Department of Commerce.

United States Civil Rights Commission. 1972. *The Unfinished Education: Outcomes of Minorities in Five Southwestern States.* Vol. 2 of *The Mexican American Education Project.* Washington, DC: U.S. Government Printing Office.

————. 1974. *Toward Quality Education for Mexican Americans.* Vol. 6 of *The Mexican American Education Project.* Washington, DC: U.S. Government Printing Office.

————. 2001. *Voting Irregularities in Florida during the 2000 Presidential Elections.* Washington, DC: U.S. Government Printing Office.

Verba, Sidney, and Jae-on Kim. 1978. *Participation and Political Equality.* New York: Cambridge University Press.

Verba, Sidney, and Norman Nie. 1972. *Participation in America: Political Democracy and Social Equality.* New York: Harper & Row.

Verba, Sidney, Kay Scholzman, and Henry Brady. 1995. *Voice and Equality: Civic Voluntarism in American Politics.* Cambridge, MA: Harvard University Press.

Verba, Sidney, Kay Scholzman, Henry Brady, and Norman Nie. 1992. "Race, Ethnicity, and the Resources for Political Participation: The Role of Religion." Paper presented at the annual meeting of the American Political Science Association, Chicago, Illinois, September 3–6.

Verdin, Tom. 2000. "Hispanic Influence Grows in California." Associated Press.

Waldinger, Roger. 1989. "Immigration and Urban Change." *Annual Review of Sociology* 15: 359–85.

Waldinger, Roger, and M. Bozorgmehr. 1996. *Ethnic Los Angeles.* New York: Sage.

Walton, Hanes. 1997. *African American Power and Politics: The Political Context Variable.* New York: Columbia University Press.

Warren, Mark. 1996. "Creating a Multi-racial Democratic Community: A Case Study of the Texas Industrial Areas Foundation." Paper presented at the Conference on Social Welfare and Urban Poverty, Russell Sage Foundation, New York.

Washington Post. 1999. "Survey Portrays Hispanic Poverty: In Alexandria, a Stark Picture of Growing Group." *Washington Post,* December 9, V1.

Welch, Susan, and John Hibbing. 1985. "Hispanic Representation in the U.S. Congress." *Social Science Quarterly* 65:328–35.

West, Cornel. 1994. *Race Matters.* New York: Vintage.

Wilson, Paul. 1977. *Immigration and Politics.* Amistral: Australian National University Press.

Wolfinger, Raymond. 1993. "Improving Voter Participation." In *What to Do: Improving the Electoral Process,* edited by P. Frank and W. Mayer. Boston: Northeastern University Press.

Wolfinger, Raymond, and Steven Rosenstone. 1980. *Who Votes.* New Haven, CT: Yale University Press.

Wong, Janelle. 2000. "The Effects of Age and Political Exposure on the Development of Party Identification among Asian Americans and Latino Immigrants in the United States." *Political Behavior* 22, no. 4 (December): 341–71.

————. 2006. *Democracy's Promise: Immigrants and American Civic Institutions.* Ann Arbor: University of Michigan Press.

Yu, Eu, and Edward Chang. 1995. "Minorities Talking Coalition Building in Los Angeles." A two-day symposium.

Index

Note: Page references followed by *b*, *n*, or *t* refer to boxed text, endnotes, and tables respectively.

absolute gain, 228*n*2
acculturation, *100b*
Acuña, Rodolfo, 65, 110, 184
Adams, Greg D., 156
additive participation scale, 228*n*4
AFL-CIO, 131
African Americans, 3; class bifurcation of,
    7; coalitions with, 118, 198–207, *202t*;
    economic competition with, 203–4,
    203t; educational competition with, 204,
    205t; linked fate with, 197, *197t*; political
    participation by, *88t*, 89; redistricting and,
    178; Voting Rights Act and, 172, 174
age: gender and, 38, *38f*; political
    participation and, 93; in Puerto Rican
    community, 51; Spanish language use and,
    19–20; voting and, 103, 105, *106t*, 120
AIPEUC (Association of Peruvian
    Institutions in the United States and
    Canada), 56
Alianza Hispano Americano, 125–26, 138,
    229*n*2
Alinsky, Saul, 134, 135–37
alliances. *See* coalitions
Allsup, Carl, 81
Almond, Gabriel, 110
alternative voting system, 176, 180–81
American dream, 191
American Protective Association, 144
Anaya, Tony, 176
ancestry, 3, 14, 64
Antiterrorism and Effective Death Penalty
    Act (ATEDPA, 1996), 154

Arce, Carlos, 166
arenas of participation, 228*n*1
Argentinean community, *36t*
Arizona, 30–31; Senate Bill 1070 of, 18, 31,
    73, 94, 108, 144, *148b–150b*, 158; Senate
    Bill 2281 of, *149b*
Armbruster, Ralph, 155
Asociación Communal de Dominicanos
    Progresistas, 60
Asociación Dominicanas, 60
Aspira v. New York Board of Education, 127
assimilation, 5, 52–53, 111
Association of Peruvian Institutions in the
    United States and Canada (AIPEUC), 56
Astin, Alexander, 168
at-large election, 112, 127, 176, 231*n*3
ATDEPA (Antiterrorism and Effective Death
    Penalty Act, 1996), 154

Baker v. Carr, 178
Balaguer, Joaquín, 227*n*6
Barrera, Mario, 110, 111
Barreto, Matt, 72, 74, 112, 180, 213
Barvosa, Edwina, 68, 70
Bass, Loretta, 155
Bastrop I.S.D. v. Gonzalez, 167
Batísta, Fulgencio, 53
Bean, Frank, 184
Benitez, Christina, 22
Bernal, Martha, 70
bilingual education, 5, 130, 169–70
Bilingual Education Act (1968), 169
bilingualism, 34

birth certificates, *149b*
bloc voting, 98
Bloomberg, Michael, 118
Bolivian community, *36t*
Bonilla, Frank, 5
Booth, William, 160
Border Patrol, 145–46
Border Protection, Antiterrorism, and Illegal
　Immigration Control Act (2005), 108,
　137b
Borjas, George, 151
Briegal, Kaye, 81
Brischetto, Robert, 112, 181
Broder, David, 160
Brown, Lee, 118
Brown Berets, 69
Browning, Rufus, 109, 180, 199
Bureau of Immigration and Naturalization,
　145
Bush, George H. W., *115b*, 132
Bush, George W., 31, 54, 113, *115b*, 129, 160,
　215
Bustamante, Cruz, 107, 176, 212

Cable Act (1922), 230*n*1
Cain, Bruce, 179
California, 30–31; elections in, 72, 101,
　104, 212; Latino political mobilization
　in, 72; Mexican-origin communities
　in (*see* Mexican-origin communities);
　Proposition 187 of, 73, 94, 107, 143–44,
　155–58, 190–91, 213, 228*n*8, 231*n*1;
　Proposition 207 of, 228*n*8; Proposition
　227 of, 107, 157, 170–71, 213, 230*n*5,
　231*n*1; Proposition 229 of, 213, 231*n*1
Cambio Cubano, 55, 129
CANC (Cuban American National Council),
　129
CANF (Cuban American National
　Foundation), 54, 128, 229*n*3
Canseco, Francisco, 116, *116b*
Cardoza, Dennis, 212–13
Carmichael, Stokely, 199–200
Carter, Thomas, 92, 167, 168
Castro, Fidel, 53, 54, 128–29
Catholicism, 20–21, 144
Cavazos, Lauro, *115b*
CBDG (Community Block Development
　Grant) program, 136
CCD (Committee for Cuban Democracy), 55
census. *See* United States census

Central American communities, 8, 14, 16,
　56–59, 210; definition of, 56; family in,
　41; nativity of, 34, *36t*, 58; naturalization
　in, 36–37; political mobilization in, 68;
　political participation in, 58–59, *87t*,
　88–89; political refugee status in, 58;
　population of, 29–30, *30t*
Centro Cívico Cultural Dominicano, 60
Chapa, Jorge, 81
Chávez, César, 131, 134
Chavez-Thompson, Linda, 131
CHC (Congressional Hispanic Caucus), 126,
　132–33, 218
Chicago, Illinois, 18, 22, 23, 49, 65, 215;
　Latino identity in, 68–70
Chicano, 65. *See also* Mexican-origin
　communities
Chilean community, *36t*
church attendance, 21
Cisneros, Henry, *115b*
citizenship, 35–37, 50. *See also* naturalization
Civil Rights Act (1964), 10, 107
class bifurcation, 7
Clinton, Bill, 54, 55, *115b*, 129, 132
Club de San Juan Pablo Duarte, 60
Coalition of Guatemalan Immigrants in the
　United States (CONGUATE), *51b*
coalitions, 183–208; discrimination model
　of, 199; discrimination-plus model of,
　199–200; group identity and, 184–87,
　185t, *187t*; Latino–African American,
　198–206, *202t*; perceived commonalities
　and, 192, 194–98, *194t*, *195t*, *197t*;
　perceived discrimination and, 190–92,
　193t; requirements for, 199–200; subgroup
　interactions and, 187–90, *188t*, *189t*
Colombian community, *36t*, 56, *57b*, 58–59,
　202, *202t*
Colorado, 30–31
Committee for Cuban Democracy (CCD), 55
community. *See* Latino community
Community Block Development Grant
　(CBDG) program, 136
community of common/similar cultures,
　8, 17–19, 110, 192, 194–95, *194t*, *195t*;
　language and, 31–34, *32t–33t*; nativity
　and, 34–37, *35f*, *36t*
community of interests, 8, 17–19, 37–41, 110,
　192, 194, *194t*
Community Organized for Public Services
　(COPS), 134–35

Community Services Organization (CSO), 134

competition: Congressional, 180; economic, 203–4, *203t*; educational, 204, *205t*; Latino subgroup, 58–69, 219–20

Congressional Hispanic Caucus (CHC), 126, 132–33, 218

CONGUATE (Coalition of Guatemalan Immigrants in the United States), *51b*

COPS (Community Organized for Public Services), 134–35

Cornell, Stephen, 3, 17, 18, 21, 64

Cortés, Ernesto, Jr., 135

Costa Rican community, *36t*

Cottrell, Charles, 172

Cowan, Gloria, 157

coworker networks, *189t*, 190

Crawford, James, 169, 170

Croucher, Sheila, 17

Cruz, Jose, 50, 53, 74

Cruz, Vanessa, 78, 160

CSO (Community Services Organization), 134

Cuban Adjustment Act (1966), 53

Cuban American National Council (CANC), 129

Cuban American National Foundation (CANF), 54, 128–29, 229*n*3

Cuban Committee for Democracy, 129

Cuban community, 13–14, 16, 53–56; African American/white commonalities with, 200–205, *202t*; education levels in, 20, 38; entrepreneurship in, 55; foreign-born in, 34; historical perspective on, 53; labor force participation in, 40; leadership in, 55–56; Mariel boatlifts and, 54; nativity of, *36t*; naturalization in, 36; organizations in, 128–30; political participation in, 54–56, *87t*, 88–89, 215, 221–22; population of, 29, *30t*; second-generation individuals in, 55; voting in, *117b*

Cuban Democracy Act (1992), 129

Cuban Liberty and Democratic Solidarity Act (1996), 55, 129

Cuello, José, 22

Cuevas, Daisy, 57

culture, 6–7

cumulative voting system, 176, 180–81

Dallas Morning News, 101

Dalton, Georgia, 210, 211

DANR (Dominican American National Roundtable), 60, *136b*

Dawson, Michael, 7, 186, 191, 198

de facto segregation, 167–68

de la Garza, Rodolfo, 74, 78, 109, 111, 159, 190, 219

Democratic Party, 77, *117b*

demographic profile. *See* sociodemographic profile

Denton, Nancy, 17, 52, 184

Department of Homeland Security, 100

descent, 3, 14, 64

descriptive representation, 174

DeSipio, Louis, 72, 93, 104, 109, 110, 152

Development, Relief, and Education for Alien Minors (DREAM) Act, 158

Díaz-Balart, Mario, 116

disassimilation, 196

discrimination, 17, 18, 190–92, *193t*, 199–200, 205

Dominican American National Roundtable (DANR), 60, *136b*

Dominican community, 59–61; African American/white commonalities with, 200–205, *202t*; historical perspective on, 59; nativity of, *36t*; occupation in, 60; political participation in, 60–61, *87t*, 88–89; population of, 29–30, *30t*, 59, 210

DREAM (Development, Relief, and Education for Alien Minors) Act, 158

Duran, Richard, 167

Dye, Thomas R., 141

Ecuadorian community, *36t*, 56, 58–59

education, 163, 164–71; bilingual, 5, 130, 169–70; competition and, 204, *205t*; cultural values and, 168–69; de facto segregation in, 167–68; decision-making process in, 166; desegregation of, 167–68; equal opportunity and, 10; gender and, 163; high school completion and, 164, 168, 213; Latino National Survey on, 20, 89–91, *89t*, 160, 166; levels of, 20, 37–38, *37f, 38f*, 213; MALDEF on, 127; in Mexican-origin communities, 20, 38, 126, 164–65, 167–68, 169; parental involvement in, 89–91, *89t*, 90; parent–school official interactions and, 90–91, *92t*; policy issue of, 142; political participation and, 71, 73–74, 78, 105; PRLDEF on, 127; PTA meeting attendance and, 90, *91t*; Spanish language use and, 166–67, 168, 169; surveys on, 166, 171; undocumented immigrants and, 157; White House Initiative on Educational Excellence for Hispanics for, 165–66

educational isolation, 168–69, 227*n7*

elections, 97–121; 2010, *116b–118b*; at-large, 112, 127, 176, 231*n3*; bloc voting in, 98; in California, 72, 101, 104, 212; critical swing vote in, 98–99; descriptive representation and, 174; impact/influence district, 180; at local level, 115–16, 118–19, 120–21, 174, 175–76, 212–13; participation in, 79–81, 84–86, *85t*, 97–98, 101–4, *102t*, *103t*, 108–9; presidential, 89–99, 99–104, *102t*, *103t*, 113, 115; redistricting and, 112, 127, 175, 178–79, 211, 229*n7*; safe district, 179–81; single-member district, 176. *See also* presidential elections; voter registration; voting

Elliston, Jon, 55

Enforcement Act (1870), 172

English Language Education for Immigrant Children. *See* Proposition 227 (California)

English-language proficiency, 31–34, *32t–33t*, 226*n3*

English-only initiatives, 7–8, 16, 31, 54

Engstrom, Richard, 181

Esman, Milton, 110, 142

Espenshade, Thomas, 159

Espiritu, Yen Lee, 8, 18, 21, 22, 63, 64

ethnicity/ethnic identity, 3–4, 9; culture and, 7; definition of, 3, 64; emotive component of, 64; legislative policy and, 4–5, 64; media projection of, 15; modern, 65, 68; vs. race, 3–4, 14–15; situational, 15–16; social construction of, 3, 4, 7, 9, 25–26. *See also* pan-ethnicity

Falcón, Angelo, 52, 60, 74, 81

familialism, 110–11

family, 40–41, 78

Feagin, Joseph, 156

Federation for American Immigration Reform, *149b*

feeling thermometer, 231*n1*

female-headed household, 41

Fernández, Edward, 64, 65

Ferrer, Fernando, 118

Fifteenth Amendment, 172

Figueroa, Hector, 56, 160

fingerprints, *148b*

Fitzgerald, Joseph, 52

Flores, Bill, 116

Florida, 30–31, 116. *See also* Cuban community

Foley, Douglas, 48

Force Act (1871), 172

foreign-born persons, 34–37, *35f*, *36t*, 58, 228*n6*; educational attainment and, 38; household income and, 20; perceived cultural commonality and, *194t*, 195–96; political participation by, *137b*, 159–60

foreign policy, 10, 128–29

Foster, Vince, 132

Fourteenth Amendment, 157, 172

Fox, Geoffrey, 13, 22

Fox, Vicente, 146

Fraga, Luis R., 19, 184

friendship networks, 187–89, *188t*

Fuchs, Laurence, 110

Gaarder, A. Bruce, 169

García, F. C., 2, 5

García, John A.: on alternative voting systems, 181; on coalitions, 199, 205; on community, 8, 17; on election restrictions, 111–12, 176; on ethnic labels, 65; on Latino identity, 22, *66b*, 69–70; on naturalization, 152; on perceived cultural commonalities, 196; on political incorporation, 109–10, 111; on political participation, 72, 74, 81–93, 108, 159–60, 178; on public policy, 142

García, Mario, 110

García, Sonia, 175

García-Castañon, Marcela, 78, 160

gender: age and, 38, *38f*; education and, 37–38, *37f*, 163; leadership and, 9–10; occupation and, 39–40, *39f*; parental educational involvement and, *89t*, 90; political participation and, 78, *88t*, 89; voting and, 102, *102t*, *103t*, 105

Georgia v. Ashcroft, 178

gerrymandering: racial, 177, 229*n8*

Gittell, Marilyn, 170

Gómez, Laura, 64–65

Gómez-Quiñones, Juan, 13, 65

Gonzáles, Alberto, 113, 215

González, Elian, 221, 231*n2*

González-Baker, Susan, 150

Gordon, Milton, 111

Gore, Al., 113
governorships, 115–16, *116b*, 176, 216
grandfather clause, 225*n*4
green card, 230*n*2
Griswold del Castillo, Richard, 131
Grofman, Bernard, 107, 112, 177
group consciousness, 21–22
group identity, 3, 21–23. *See also* pan-
    ethnicity
Grupo Pro-Mejoras, *135b*
Guarnizo, Luis, 60, 160
Guatemalan community, *36t*, *46b*, *51b*, 68,
    202t
Gutiérrez, Ana Maria Sol, 119
Gutiérrez, Luis, 119, 177

HACR (Hispanic Association for Corporate
    Responsibility), 131
Hansen, Kristen, 58
Hardy-Fanta, Carol, 74
Hayes-Bautista, David, 8, 18, 22, 196
Hays v. Louisiana, 177
Helms, Jesse, 129
Helms-Burton Act, 129
Henry, Charles, *201b*
Hernández, Jose, 26
Hero, Rodney, 109
Herrera, Jaime, 116, *116b*
Hill, Kevin, 55
Hispanic. See Latino/Hispanic label
Hispanic Association for Corporate
    Responsibility (HACR), 131
Hispanic Coalition, 160
HNCC (National Hispanic Corporate
    Council), 131
Hoffman, Abraham, 145–46
Honduran community, *36t*
Hood, M. V., 158
Horne, Tom, *149b*
Hotel and Restaurant Employees Union, 160
household income, 20, 40–41, *41f*, 215
Houston Chronicle, *46b*
Huerta, Dolores, 131, 134
Hufstedler, Shirley, 151
human capital, 105, 229*n*4

IAF (Industrial Areas Foundation), 134,
    135–37
identity (identities): culture and, 7; group, 3,
    21–23 (*see also* pan-ethnicity); multiple,
    65, 68, 184–85, *185t*; national-origin,

2, 25, 184–86, *185t*; politics and, 5–6;
    social, 21–22, 23. *See also* ethnicity/ethnic
    identity
Illegal Immigration Reform and Immigrant
    Responsibility Act (IIRIRA, 1996), 154
Illinois, 30–31
immigration, 141–61; border militarization
    and, *148b*; contemporary patterns of,
    147, *147t*, 150–58, *153t*; economic factors
    in, 110; economic model for, 151; in
    elections, *117b–118b*; local legislation
    on, 151; LULAC on, 126; marches
    about, *80b*, *137b*; Operation Streamline
    and, *148b*; political incorporation and,
    109–10; political participation and, 8,
    10, 108, 159–60, 217; polling on, 151–52;
    preference categories for, 146, 147, 151,
    226*n*5; 287(g) Program and, *148b*; state-
    specific, *147t*; undocumented, 72–73, 108,
    143–44, 151, 155–58, 228*n*6, 230*n*4; U.S.
    policies on, 108, *137b*, 144–46, *148b–150b*;
    war-related, 146. *See also* naturalization
Immigration and Naturalization Service
    (INS), 18, 133, 145
Immigration Reform and Control Act (IRCA,
    1986), 126, 143, 154
impact/influence district, 180
income, 20, 40–41, *41f*, 215
Industrial Areas Foundation (IAF), 134,
    135–37
Internet, *137b–138b*
IRCA (Immigration Reform and Control Act,
    1986), 126, 143
Itlong, Larry, 131

Jackson, Bryon, 198, 199
Jaynes, Gerald, 199
Jennings, James, 50, 53, 74, 180, 199
Jim Crow laws, 3
Jones Act (1917), 50
Jones-Correa, Michael, 94, 155, 159, 185
Jordan, Howard, 58

Kasarda, John D., 51
Kaufman, Karen, 199, 204
Keefe, Susan, 17
Kelly, Daryl, 158
Kennedy, John F., 99
Keyes v. Denver I.S.D., 167
Kobach, Kris, *149b*
Kunerth, Jeff, *206b–207b*

La Raza Unida, 48

Labor Council for Latin American Advancement (LCLAA), 131

labor force participation, 38–40, *39f*; African American competition and, 203–4, *203t*, *205t*; coworker networks and, *189t*, 190; in Cuban community, 55; in Dominican community, 60; equal opportunity and, 10; gender and, 39–40, *39f*; in Mexican-origin communities, 47; unionization and, 160

Labrador, Raúl, 116

Latin American Defense Organization (LADO), 69

Latino Coalition for Racial Justice, 58

Latino community, 2–3, 6–8, 17–23, 210–16; coherency and unity of, 67; common culture and, 17, 18, 19, 67, 192, 194–98 (*see also* community of common/similar cultures; community of interests); definition of, 14; demographics of (*see* sociodemographic profile); educational attainment and, 20; formation of, 184–98; group discrimination and, 190–92, *193t*; group identity and, 4–5, 21–23, 67–68, 184–87, *185t*, *187t*; income and, 20, 40–41, *41f*; leadership and, 66–68; political/economic interests and, 17–18, 19, *185t*, 186, 192, 194–98, *194t*, *195t*, *197t*; political mobilization and, 70–75 (*see also* political mobilization; political participation); population growth and, 26–27, *26f*, *27f*, *28f*; regional population distribution and, 27–28, *29f*; religion and, 20–21; Spanish language use and, 18, 19–20; subgroup interactions and, 187–90, *188t*, *189t*. *See also* Latino organizations; Latino population; Latino subgroups

Latino consciousness, 18–19

Latino Decisions, 77, *116b–118b*, 151–52

Latino family: income levels of, 40–41; political participation and, 78; size of, 41; type of, 41

Latino/Hispanic identity, 21–22, 184–87; historical development of, 64–65; policy making and, 4–5, 64; social construction of, 25–26. *See also Latino/Hispanic* label; pan-ethnicity

Latino/Hispanic label, 2–3, 225n1; focus group use of, *66b*, 69–70; historical

development of, 64–65; mass media use of, 15, 64; scope of, 65–66, 68; as self-descriptor, 23, 49, 186–87, *187t*; as umbrella term, 15–16. *See also* pan-ethnicity

Latino leadership, 9–10, 66–68; in Cuban community, 55–56; IAF training for, 136; in Mexican-origin communities, 49–50

Latino Lives in America: Making It Home (Fraga et al.), 185

Latino National Political Survey (LNPS), 19, 45, 49, 69–70, 219, 228n5

Latino National Survey (LNS), 19–21, 23, 45, 81, 184–98, 226n5; African American–related questions of, 197, *197t*; educational sector questions of, 20, 89–91, *89t*, 160, 166; focus groups in, 23, 49, *66b*, 69–70; group discrimination questions of, 190–92, *193t*; political participation questions of, *83t*, 84; racial/ethnic commonality questions of, 200–205; social identity questions of, 23, 184–87, *185t*; socioeconomic/political commonalities questions of, 192, 194–98, *194t*, *195t*; subgroup interaction questions of, 187–90, *188t*, *189t*

Latino organizations, 124–38; bases for, 124; community-based, 134–38, *135b*; components of, 125, *125b*; of Cuban community, 128–30; goals of, 124; of Mexican-origin communities, 124, 125–28, *135b*; pan-ethnicity and, 124–25; in political institutions, 132–38; professional, 130–32; public policy and, 130–31, 143; of Puerto Rican community, 127–28. *See also specific organizations*

Latino population: age and, 38, *38f*; growth in, 15–16, 26–27, *26f*, *27f*, *28f*, 31, 99, 178–79, 210; nativity of, 34–37, *35*, *36t*, 99; state distribution of, 27–28, *29f*, 30–31, 99, 210–11, 212, 228n7

Latino subgroups, 8, 45–62; competition among, 58–69, 219–20; English-language proficiency and, 34; family in, 40–41; foreign-born persons by, 34–35; independent actions by, 219–20; interactions among, 187–90, *188t*, *189t*, 217–18, 225n2; occupation and, 40; outlier, 221–22; political participation by, *83t*, 84, *87t*, 88–89; power relations among, 5–6; racial/ethnic commonality perceptions of, 200–205, *202t*. *See also* *specific subgroups*

Latinos United for Political Rights (LUPR), 138

Lavaríega-Monfarti, Jessica, 192

LCLAA (Labor Council for Latin American Advancement), 131

League of United Latin American Citizens (LULAC), 98–99, 126–27

Leighley, Jan, 72

limited voting, 176, 180–81

line watch, 145

linked fate, *185t*, 186, 194–95, *195t*, 197, *197t*

Little Schools of the 400, 126

LNPS. *See* Latino National Political Survey (LNPS)

LNS. *See* Latino National Survey (LNS)

Los Angeles, 22, 74, 118, 200, *201b*

Los Angeles Times, 72, 170

Lujan, Martin, *115b*

LULAC (League of United Latin American Citizens), 98–99, 126–27

LUPR (Latinos United for Political Rights), 138

Mahoney, Cardinal Roger, *137b*

majority-minority district, 127, 177, 178, 180

MALDEF (Mexican American Legal Defense and Education Fund), 112, 124, 127–28, 174

Manzano, Sylvia, *138b*

marches/rallies, *80b*, 84, *137b*

Mariel boatlifts, 54

Márquez, Benjamin, 81, 111, 126, 134

Martínez, Bob, 176

Martínez, Mel, 113, *115b*, 215

Martinez, Susana, 116, *116b*, *117b*, 176, 216

Mas Canosa, Jorge, 54, 229n3

Mas Santos, José, 128

mass media, 15, 64, 101. *See also* Spanish-language media

mayoral elections, 118–19, 176

McCarran-Walter Act (Immigration and Nationality Act, 1952), 146

McClain, Paula, 198, 200, 204

McDonnell, Patrick, 159

Meier, Ken, 38, 92, 167, 168, 204

Menendez, Robert, 176

Mexican American Education Project, 164

Mexican American Legal Defense and Education Fund (MALDEF), 112, 124, 127–28, 174

Mexican American Studies program (Tucson, Arizona), *149b*

Mexican-origin communities, 13, 16, 47–50; African American/white commonalities with, 200–205, *202t*; de facto educational segregation in, 167–68; education in, 20, 38, 126, 164–65, 167–68, 169; ethnic labels in, 64–65; family in, 41; historical perspective on, 47; leadership in, 49–50; League of United Latin American Citizens of, 126–27; migration into, 110, 126, 156; nativity of, *36t*; naturalization in, 36, 152; in New Mexico, 48; occupation in, 47; organizations in, 125–28, *135b*; pan-ethnicity in, 49, 64–65; political incorporation in, 110; political participation in, 48–49, *87t*, 88–89; population of, 29, *30t*; repatriation from, 145–46; in Texas, *46b*, 48

Miami, 22, 74

Michelson, Melissa R., 72, 74, 112

Midwest Voter Registration and Education Project (MWVREP), 133–34

migration patterns, 8, 15–16, 30–31

Milbrath, Lester, 78

Milkman, Ruth, 160

Miller, Arthur, 22

Miller v. Johnson, 177

minority groups, 17, 21–22

Miyares, Marcelino, 55

Mobile v. Bolden, 173

mobilization. *See* political mobilization

Montejano, David, 47, 48, 175

Moore, Joan, 52

Morales, Dan, 115

Morales, Rebecca, 40, 110

Moreno, Dario, 55, 81, 129

multiple identities, 65, 68, 184–85, *185t*

MWVREP (Midwest Voter Registration and Education Project), 133–34

NAACP (National Association for the Advancement of Colored People), *206b–207b*

NABE (National Association of Bilingual Educators), 130, 169

Nagel, Joanne, 21, 22, 64

NALEO (National Association of Latino Elected and Appointed Officials), 130, 133, 154–55, 215–16

National Association for the Advancement of Colored People (NAACP), *206b–207b*

National Association of Bilingual Educators (NABE), 130, 169

National Association of Latino Elected and Appointed Officials (NALEO), 130, 133, 154–55, 215–16

National Council of La Raza (NCLR), 49, 125

National Hispanic Corporate Council (HNCC), 131

national-origin identity, 2, 25, 184–86, *185t*. *See also* Latino subgroups

National Origins Act (1924), 144–45

National Political Ethnic Survey (NPES), 84–86, *85t*

National Urban League, *206b–207b*

nativity, 34–37, *35f*, *36t*, 58, 99; income and, 20; perceived cultural commonality and, *194t*, 195–96; political participation and, 93–94, 159–60

naturalization, 35–37, 120, 152–55; country-specific, *153t*; of Mexicans, 152; NALEO on, 154–55; rates of, 99, 100, 152; requirements for, 152; wait periods for, 155, 159

NCLR (National Council of La Raza), 49, 125

Nelson, Candice, 22, 52

New Jersey, 30–31, 56–57

New Mexico, 30–31, 48, 115

New York City, 16, 22, 30–31, 50, 60, 74, 215

Nicaraguan community, *36t*

Nichols v. Houston I.S.D., 167

Nie, Norma, 71

No Child Left Behind Act, 171

North, David, 133

NPES (National Political Ethnic Survey), 84–86, *85t*

Obama, Barack, 54–55, *115b*, *118b*, 132, 158, 165, 207

Obama, Michelle, 57

O'Brien, Matt, 30

occupation. *See* labor force participation

O'Connor, Ann Marie, 160

O'Connor, Sandra Day, 178

Office of Management and Budget (OMB), 1–2

OLAW (Organization of Los Angeles Workers), 160

Oliver, Melvin, 200

OMB (Office of Management and Budget), 1–2

Omni, Michael, 3

one-drop rule, 3, 14

Ong, Paul, *201b*

Operation Streamline, *148b*

Orden de los Hijos de America, 125–26, 138

Orfield, Gary, 168

Organization of Los Angeles Workers (OLAW), 160

organizations. *See* Latino organizations

Orlando Sentinel, *206b–207b*

Ortiz, Solomon, 116, *116b*

Our Nation on the Fault Line, 164

outliers, 221–22

Owens, Sherri, *206b–207b*

Pachón, Harry, 152, 159

Padilla, Amado, 18–19, 21, 22, 23, 65

Pan, Phillip, 159

pan-ethnicity, 2–3, 4–5, 8; coalitions and, 184–87, *185t*, *187t*, 199; community building and, 21–23, 67–68, 184–87, *185t*, *187t*; definition of, 21, 63–64, 225n3, 227n2; disassimilation and, 196; Latino organizations and, 124–25; in Mexican-origin communities, 49; vs. national-origin identity, 25–26, 184–85; political aspects of, 9, 16, 17, 18–19, 21–23; social construction of, 21–23, 26; symbolic aspects of, 219–20; viability of, 211–12

Panamanian community, *36t*

Pardo, Mary, 5, 74

Participation in America II study, 81

Patterson, Ernest, 65

Payne, Richard J., 3

Pearce, Russell, *149b*

Pedraza-Bailey, Sylvia, 20

Peña, Federico, *115b*

Pérez, Lisandro, 128

permanent resident alien, 5, 34, 35–37, 147–48, *147t*

Perry, Rick, 115

Personal Responsibility and Work Opportunity Reconciliation Act (PRWORA, 1996), 154

Peruvian community, *36t*, 56–57

Petersen, Mark, 55

Pew Hispanic Center, 81–83, *81t*, *82t*, 131–32, 156

Pfaelzer, Mariana, 157

Phyler v. Doe, 157

Pinderhughes, Dianne, 177

Pitt, Leonard, 48

Piven, Frances, 112

Polanco, Richard, 212

political alliances. *See* coalitions

political incorporation, 109–11

political leadership. *See* Latino leadership

political mobilization, 9, 70–75, 79; against Arizona Senate Bill 1070, 73; in California, 72, 73, 74, 107, 170–71; definition of, 70; at local level, 74; for marches, *80b*; pan-ethnicity and, 22–23, 65; personal connections and, 79; against Proposition 187, 73, 107, 170; against Proposition 227, 170–71; state Latino population size and, 30–31; statewide propositions and, 107–8; targeted, 73–74, 79; timing of, 74. *See also* Latino organizations

political participation, 9, 77–95; by African Americans, *88t*, 89; age and, 93; assimilation and, 111; barriers to, 72, 79, 93–94, 110–12, 119, 175; benefits of, 71; in Central American communities, 58–59, *87t*, 88–89; citizenship and, 72; comparative data on, 84–86, *85t*, *88t*, 89; contextual barriers to, 175; continual development of, 216–19; costs of, 71; in Cuban community, 54–56, *87t*, 88–89, 215, 221–22; decline in, 70–71; definition of, 77–78; direct contact, *81t*, 82, 86, *86t*, 88; disinterest in, 79, *87t*, 88–89, 108–9; in Dominican community, 60–61, *87t*, 88–89; education-related, 89–93, *89t*, *91t*, *92t*; educational attainment and, 71, 73–74, 78; in elections, 79–81, 84–86, *85t*, 89–90; forms of, 79–81, *81t*, 82; gender and, 78, *88t*, 89; generational, 86, *86t*, 88; historical perspective on, 70–71; individual basis of, 71, 72, 105, 107; interest in, *87t*, *88*, 88–89; at local level, 74, 84, 115–16, 118–19, 120–21, 212–13, 217; in Los Angeles, 74; in marches, *80b*, 84; meeting/demonstration attendance as, *81t*, 82; in Mexican-origin communities, 48–49, *87t*, 88–89; money contribution as, *81t*, 82; by national-origin category, *83t*, 84, *87t*, 88–89;

nativity and, 93–94, 159–60; participatory score in, *88t*, 89; population growth and, 31; problem-solving, *83t*, 84; in Puerto Rican community, 52–53, *87t*, 88–89; pull factors in, 71; rates of, 81, 82; resources for, 71, 78–79, 93, 94, 174–75, 219; rewards of, 71–72; safe districts and, 179–81; social structures and, 111–12; socialization for, 78; socioeconomic status and, 73–74; volunteer, 79, *81t*, 82–84, *82t*; Voting Rights Act and, 174–79. *See also* coalitions; elections; Latino organizations

political refugees, 14, 53–54, 58, 128, 146

politics: community in, 13–16 (*see also* community); contexts of, 5–6; identity and, 5–6; legislation and, 10; local level, 5–6, 10; pan-ethnicity and, 16, 18–19, 21–23; participation in, 9–10 (*see also* political participation; voting); power relations and, 5–6. *See also* political mobilization; political participation

Portes, Alejandro, 20, 55, 74, 94, 109, 159

Portland, Oregon, 210

poverty, 40–41

power relations, 4, 5–6, 111–12

presidential election(s): 1960, 98–99; 1996, 55, *103t*; 2000, *103t*, 113, 115; 2008, 55, 77, 98, 101, *103t*, 104; 2012, 31; nonvoting in, 104; state-specific population percentages and, 99; voter registration and, 99–100, 101, 102–3, *102t*; voter turnout for, 103–4, *103t*

President's Advisory Commission on Educational Excellence for Hispanic Americans, 165

PRLDEF (Puerto Rican Legal Defense and Education Fund), 52, 112, 127–28

professional Latino organizations, 130–32

Proposition 187 (California), 73, 94, 107, 143–44, 155–58, 190–91, 213, 228*n*8, 231*n*1

Proposition 207 (California), 157, 228*n*8

Proposition 227 (California), 107, 157, 170–71, 213, 230*n*5, 231*n*1

Proposition 229 (California), 213, 231*n*1

Protestantism, 21, 144

PRWORA (Personal Responsibility and Work Opportunity Reconciliation Act , 1996), 154

PTA meetings, 90, *91t*

Public Law 85-983, 2
public policy, 10, 16, 142–43; census
tabulation and, 2; class bifurcation and,
7; community awareness of, 142–43;
differential impacts of, 142; ethnicity and,
4–5, 64; governmental institutions in, 143;
organizational involvement in, 130–31,
143; power relations and, 5–6. *See also*
education; immigration; voter registration
Puerto Rican community, 13, 16, 50–53;
African American/white commonalities
with, 200–205, *202t*; age and, 51;
assimilation in, 52–53; culture in, 52, 53;
family in, 41; geographic distribution
of, 51; historical perspective on, 50;
household income in, 40; place of birth
in, 34–35, *36t*; political participation in,
52–53, *87t*, 88–89; political status issue in,
50; population of, 29, 30, *30t*; race in, 52
Puerto Rican Legal Defense and Education
Fund (PRLDEF), 52, 112, 127–28
Puerto Rico, 50, 52
Pulído, Laura, 5
Putnam, Robert, 71, 105, 175

race, 225n1; vs. ethnicity, 3–4, 14–15; in
Puerto Rican community, 52; redistricting
and, 178; social construct of, 3, 212; on
United States census, 1–2
racial gerrymandering, 177, 229n8
Radio-TV Martí, 54, 128
Reagan, Ronald, 113, *115b*
redistricting, 112, 127, 175, 177–79, 211,
229n7
refugees, 8, 14, 53–54, 58, 128, 146, 226n1
relative gain, 228n2
religiosity, 20–21
religious affiliation, 20–21
religious congregations: IAF work with,
135–36
Renshon, Stanley A., 94
Republican Party, 31, 113, 115–16, *116b*,
117b, 133, 157, 221–22
Reyes, Corinna, *138b*
Richardson, William, 115, *115b*
Rivera, David, 116, *116b*
Rocha, Rene, 171, 204
Rodrígues, Helena, 72, 204
Rodríguez, Ciro, 116, *116b*
Rodríguez, Nestor, *46b*
Rodríquez, Arturo, 131

Rodríquez, Clara, 52, 53, 131
Rodríquez, Lori, *46b*, 171
Rodriquez v. San Antonio I.S.D., 167
Roedemeier, Chad, 210, 211
Ros-Lehtinen, Ileana, 116
Rosenstone, Steve, 70, 71, 73, 78, 79, 107
Ross, Fred, 134
Roybal, Edward, 14, 64, 134
Rubio, Marco, 116, *116b*, *117b*, 215, 221–22

safe district, 179–81
Saito, Leonard, 74
Salazar, John, 116
Salazar, Kenneth, *115b*
Salvadoran community, 30, *30t*, 36, *36t*, *51b*,
68, *87t*, 88–89, *100b*, *202t*
San Miguel, Guadalupe, 38, 92, 126
Sanchez, Linda, 212–13
Sanchez, Orlando, 118
Sanchez, Tony, 115
Sanctuary for Salvadorans, 58
Sandoval, Brian, 116, *116b*, 176, 216
Sassen-Koob, Saskia, 60, 110
Schermerhorn, R. A., 3
schooling. *See* education
Segura, Gary M., 88, 94, 199
Senate Bill 1070 (Support Our Law
Enforcement and Safe Neighborhoods
Act, Arizona), 31, 73, 94, 108, 144,
148b–150b, 158
Senate Bill 2281 (Arizona), *149b*
Sensenbrenner bill (HR 4337), 108, *137b*
Serrano v. Priest, 167
Service Employees International Union, 160
Shaw v. Reno, 177–78
Shockley, John S., 48
Sierra, Christine, 5, 171
Singer, Audrey, 155
single-member district, 176
Skerry, Peter, 9, 110
Smith, James P., 152
Smith, Tom, 184
social capital, 174–75, 215
social construct, 3, 4, 7, 9, 21–23, 25–26, 212
socialization, 78, 107, 109
sociodemographic profile, 6, 8, 25–43;
education in, 37–38, *37f*, *38f*; family
structure in, 41; household income in, 40–
41, *41f*; language use in, 31–34, *32t–33t*;
national origin in, 29–30, *30t*; nativity in,
34–37, *35f*, *36t*; occupation in, 38–40, *39f*;

population growth in, 26–28, *26f, 27f, 28f,* 31; regional population distribution in, 28–29, *29f*

socioeconomic status, 6; coalitions and, 199; electoral participation and, 105, 108; middle-class, 215; political participation and, 73–74

Solis, Hilda, *115b*

Sonenshein, Raphael, 180, 199

Sotomayor, Sonia, 132

South American communities, 14, 16, 56–59; definition of, 56; family in, 41; nativity of, 34, *36t,* 58; naturalization in, 36–37; political interest/disinterest in, *87t,* 88–89; population of, 29–30, *30t*

South American community, 210

Southwest Voter Registration and Education Project (SVREP), 74, 112, 133–34, 174, 211

Spanish language, 18, 19–20, 31–34, *32t–33t*; age-related use of, 19–20; education and, 166–67, 168, 169

Spanish-language media, 20, 22, 34; in Cuba, 54; in elections, *117b*; political participation and, *80b*

Stavans, Ilan, 13

Supplementary Security Income (SSI), 5

supremacy clause, 157

SVREP (Southwest Voter Registration and Education Project), 74, 112, 133–34, 174, 211

Tarrow, Sidney, 112

Task Force for New Americans, 58

Tate, Kathleen, 180

Taveras, Angel, 119

Tea Party, 222

Texas, 30–31, *46b,* 48, 115, 116, 134–35

Thornburg v. Gingles, 177

Tilly, Charles, 70

Tirado, Miguel, 79, 110, 124

Tobar, Hector, 135

Torres-Saillant, Silvio, 52, 59, 60

transfer of payments, 230*n*3

Treaty of Guadalupe (1848), 47

Tucson Unified School District, *149b*

Ture, Kwame, 198

Tyler v. Phloe, 127

UFW (United Farm Workers of America), 131

Uhlaner, Carole, 199, 200, 205

Umana-Taylor, Andriane J., 78

undocumented persons, 72–73, 108, 144, *149b,* 151, 155–58, 156, 228*n*6, 230*n*4

unemployment, 38–39

unionization, 131, 160

United Farm Workers of America (UFW), 131

United Service Workers Union, 131

United States: borders of, 146; citizenship in, 35–37; immigration policy of, 144–46; population growth in, 26–27

United States census, 210, 225*n*2; categories of, 1–2, 226*n*3; English-language proficiency question of, 34, 226*n*3; NALEO participation in, 133; population tabulation from, 2; race question format of, 1–2, 4; sampling component of, 230*n*10; Spanish-origin question of, 1–2, 4, 14–15, 65, 67

United States Commission on Civil Rights (1972), 164–65

United States Commission on Immigration Reform, 151

United States Constitution, 157, 172

United States Hispanic Chamber of Commerce (HSHCC), 130, 131

United States House of Representatives: competitive/noncompetitive seats in, 180; Hispanic Caucus of, 126, 132–33, 218; Hispanics in, *114b,* 116, *116b,* 133, 176, 215–16; Sensenbrenner bill (IIR 4337) of, 108, *137b*

United States Senate: Hispanics in, *114b,* 215–16, 221–22

United States–Mexican Chamber of Commerce, 131

University of Washington Center for the Study of Race and Ethnicity, 77, *116b–118b*

Unz initiative. *See* Proposition 227 (California)

Uruguayan community, *36t*

Vargas, Arturo, 216

Velázquez, Nydia, 177

Venezuelan community, *36t*

Vera v. Richards, 177

Verba, Sidney, 6, 9, 22, 71, 72, 78, 89, 105, 107, 111

Verdin, Tom, 101, 212

Vieques, Puerto Rico, *206b–207b*
Villaraigosa, Antonio, 118, 160
voter registration, 101, 102–3, *102t*, 120, 213, *214t*; among young persons, 99–100; campaigns for, 175; naturalization and, 155; turnout and, 101–4; U.S. Census Bureau data on, 174
voting, 171–79; age and, 103, 105, *106t*, 120; barriers to, 104, *106t*, 111–12; bloc, 98; cumulative, 176, 180–81; gender and, *102t*, *103t*, 105; limited, 176, 180–81; patterns of, 101; psychological orientation and, 105, 107; in Puerto Rican community, 52–53; restrictive policies and, 111–12; safe district, 179–81; socioeconomic status and, 105, 108; Southwest Voter Registration and Education Project on, 74, 112, 133–34, 174, 211; structural factors in, 107; turnout for, 99, 101–4, *103t*, 213; voter registration and (*see* voter registration)
voting age population, 103
voting eligible population, 103, 213, *214t*

Voting Rights Act (1965), 4, 10, 71, 101, 107, 112, 163–64, 171–79, 231*n*2; alternative voting systems and, 180–81; amendments to, 173–74; political participation and, 174–79; preclearance provision of, 173, 175

Waldinger, Roger, *201b*
Wall Street Journal, 132
Walton, Hanes, 198
Washington, 30–31
Washington Post, 131–32, 171, *191b*, *198b*
West, Cornell, 7
Westberry v. Sanders, 178
Westminster v. Mendez, 167
White House Initiative on Educational Excellence for Hispanics, 165–66
Wilson, Paul, 22, 110
Wilson, Pete, 31, 157
Wolfinger, Raymond, 71, 179

Yarborough, Ralph, 169
Yu, Eu, *201b*
Yzaguirre, Raul, *206b*